Colonial Maryland Commissions, Appointments and Other Proceedings 1726-1776

Henry C. Peden, Jr., M.A.

Heritage Books
2026

HERITAGE BOOKS
AN IMPRINT OF HERITAGE BOOKS, INC.

Books, CDs, and more—Worldwide

For our listing of thousands of titles see our website
at
www.HeritageBooks.com

Published 2026 by
HERITAGE BOOKS, INC.
Publishing Division
5810 Ruatan Street
Berwyn Heights, MD 20740

Copyright © 2026 Henry C. Peden, Jr., M.A.

All rights reserved. No part of this book may be reproduced or transmitted in any form or by any means, electronic or mechanical, including photocopying, recording or by any information storage and retrieval system without written permission from the author, except for the inclusion of brief quotations in a review.

International Standard Book Number
Paperbound: 978-0-7884-4979-6

Introduction

The inspiration for this book, *Colonial Maryland Commissions, Appointments, and Other Proceedings, 1726-1776*, came from listings published in the *Maryland Historical Magazine* in 1931 and 1932. The information in those articles was gleaned from Maryland Commission Book No. 82, 1733-1773, being one of the records of the Council of Maryland. They contained primarily commissions for public service and appointments to various offices. There were also ship registrations with the name of the ship, its weight, when and where it was built, its master, its owner(s), and the date of registration. Inductions of clergyman and their licenses to preach, and convicted felons, their crimes, punishments and/or pardons, were included, mostly African Americans. There were also a number of naturalizations and denizations as well. Additional civil servants were subsequently found in selected county court minutes and proceedings for this book and any clarification of the information has been inserted in brackets herein and are comments of the author.

Another Maryland Commission Record book at the Maryland State Archives, titled "Governor and Council Commissioner Records, 1726-1794," and *Calendar of Maryland State Papers*, were reviewed and information was gleaned pertaining to commissioners of the peace, committee appointments, justices, sheriffs, constables, coroners, rangers, and convicted felons. More information was also gleaned from various volumes of the *Archives of Maryland*, and some other published sources, to fill in the unexplained gap between 1751 and 1761 in Maryland Commission Book No. 82. Researchers should certainly consult county court minutes and proceedings, and local history books, for more commissions, appointments and other proceedings that are not listed in my book.

Some of the men herein held a military rank. For more information about those who served in the colonial military, researchers should consult my books *Colonial Maryland Soldiers and Sailors, 1634-1734*, and *Marylanders and Delawareans in the French and Indian War, 1756-1763*, as well as my multi-volume series about Revolutionary War patriots in the counties of Maryland. They are available from Heritage Books, Inc. at www.heritagebooks.com on the Internet. Also, *A Biographical Dictionary of the Maryland Legislature, 1635-1789*, by Edward C. Papenfuse, et al., in two volumes, is an excellent source for government and military service.

All persons have been arranged alphabetically herein and names within the text have been cross-referenced, thus precluding the necessity for a separate index. In many cases their years of birth and death have been included. Information is documented with the reference cited after each entry. It is hoped that my book will be useful to family historians and those seeking a qualifying ancestor for membership in various colonial patriotic societies.

Henry C. Peden, Jr., M.A.
Bel Air, Maryland

About the Author

Henry C. Peden, Jr., M.A., is an award-winning author of over 200 historical and genealogical reference books and articles. He is a graduate of Towson University and a Vietnam War veteran. He is a past president and fellow of the Maryland Genealogical Society and the Historical Society of Harford County. He is also a past president of the Harford County Genealogical Society, the Hereditary Order of the Signers of the Bush Declaration, and the Maryland Self-Insurers & Employers Compensation Association. He has partnered with Jack L. Shagena, Jr. to create two dozen video shows titled *Harford's Heritage* for Harford Cable Television. In 2017, the Historical Society of Harford County named their library "The Henry C. Peden, Jr. Research Library" in his honor.

Mr. Peden is a member of the Veterans of Foreign Wars, The American Legion, and Disabled American Veterans. He served as Genealogist for the Maryland Society of the War of 1812 from 1990 to 2025 and is Genealogist General Emeritus for the General Society of the War of 1812. He is a member of the Sons of the American Revolution, Society of the Cincinnati, Society of Colonial Wars in Maryland, and Society of the Descendants of Washington's Army at Valley Forge.

His historical preservation efforts have been recognized by the Harford County Historical Preservation Commission, Harford County Government, Maryland General Assembly, Daughters of the American Revolution, and the Maryland & Pennsylvania Railroad Historical Society. Mr. Peden and wife Veronica reside in Bel Air, Maryland.

Colonial Maryland Commissions, Appointments, and Other Proceedings, 1726-1776

Abell, Samuel, Jr. (c1719-1777), of St. Mary's County, Deputy Sheriff, 1760. (*Calendar of Maryland State Papers, No. 1 The Black Books*, p. 160)

Adair, Robert (d. 1768), appointed a Commissioner of the Peace for Baltimore County, 8 Nov 1752. (Ref: Maryland State Archives, Governor and Council Commissioner Records, 1726-1794, p. 135); commissioned High Sheriff, 2 Oct 1764. (Ref: Maryland State Archives, Governor and Council Commissioner Records, 1726-1794, p. 208); commissioned one of the Coroners of Baltimore County, 12 Dec 1746; Court Justice, 1752-1767; Sheriff, Baltimore County, 1764-1766; Baltimore Commissioner, 1768; appointed commissioner to build Baltimore County courthouse, 1768. (Ref: Maryland Commission Book No. 82, p. 125; *Maryland Historical Magazine*, Vol. XXVI, p. 259; *A Biographical Dictionary of the Maryland Legislature, 1635-1789*, by Edward C. Papenfuse, et al., Vol. A-H, p. 97)

Adams, Alexander, reverend, induction into Durham Parish, Charles County, 19 Mar 1749/50; induction into St. James' Parish, Anne Arundel County, 4 Aug 1764. (Ref: Maryland Commission Book No. 82, pp. 143, 163; *Maryland Historical Magazine*, Vol. XXVI, pp. 345, 352); see Bennett Allen and John Scott.

Adams, James, see Negro Daniel.

Adams, John, appointed a Commissioner of the Peace for Somerset County, 20 Mar 1775. (Ref: Maryland State Archives, Governor and Council Commissioner Records, 1726-1794, p. 288)

Adams, Samuel, appointed a Commissioner of the Peace for Somerset County, 30 Jul 1754. (Ref: Maryland State Archives, Governor and Council Commissioner Records, 1726-1794, p. 156)

Adams, William (d. 1795), was appointed a Commissioner of the Peace for Somerset County, 8 Jun 1763. (Ref: Maryland State Archives, Governor and Council Commissioner Records, 1726-1794, p. 210); appointed a Commissioner of the Peace for Somerset County, 20 Mar 1775. (Ref: Maryland State Archives, Governor and Council Commissioner Records, 1726-1794, p. 288)

Addams, William, merchant, registered the sloop *William & Mary*, 28 tons, built in Dorchester County, 1747. William Addams and Richard Bennett, owners.

13 Jun 1747. (Ref: Maryland Commission Book No. 82, p. 130; *Maryland Historical Magazine*, Vol. XXVI, p. 261)

Addison, Henry (1717-1789), reverend, was inducted into King George's Parish, Prince George's County, 15 Oct 1742. (Ref: Maryland Commission Book No. 82, p. 97; *Maryland Historical Magazine*, Vol. XXVI, p. 247)

Addison, John (1713-1764), commissioned a Ranger for Prince George's County from Seneca Creek downward to the limits of the county, 23 Mar 1738/9. (Ref: Maryland Commission Book No. 82, p. 72; *Maryland Historical Magazine*, Vol. XXVI, p. 153); captain, of Prince George's County, appointed to Committee for Inspecting the Arms and Ammunition and Accounts Relating Thereto, 1755. (Ref: *Archives of Maryland*, Vol. LII, "Proceedings and Acts of the General Assembly of Maryland, 1755-1756," pp. 46, 156); commissioned High Sheriff of Prince George's County, 19 Oct 1768. (Ref: Maryland State Archives, Governor and Council Commissioner Records, 1726-1794, p. 227)

Addison, John, of Anne Arundel County, was commissioned Judge of Oyer, Terminer and Gaol [Jail] Delivery, 21 May 1736. (Ref: Maryland State Archives, Governor and Council Commissioner Records, 1726-1794, p. 52)

Addison, Thomas, Jr. (1715-1770), of Prince George's County, appointed a Commissioner of the Peace, 17 Nov 1764. (Ref: Maryland State Archives, Governor and Council Commissioner Records, 1726-1794, p. 220)

Aires, Jacob, see Levi Thompson.

Airy, Thomas, see Roger Peele.

Aisquith, Thomas (d. 1761), was appointed a Commissioner of the Peace for St. Mary's County, 2 Mar 1726/7. (Ref: Maryland State Archives, Governor and Council Commissioner Records, 1726-1794, p. 2)

Aisquith, William, appointed a Commissioner of the Peace for Baltimore County, 10 Nov 1762. (Ref: Maryland State Archives, Governor and Council Commissioner Records, 1726-1794, p. 207; commissioned a Coroner of Baltimore County, 5 Jan 1771. (Ref: Maryland Commission Book No. 82, p. 251; *Maryland Historical Magazine*, Vol. XXVII, p. 29)

Colonial Maryland Commissions, Appointments, and Other Proceedings, 1726-1776

Akin, John, convicted of destruction of tobacco and pardoned on 22 Nov 1735. (Ref: Maryland Commission Book No. 82, p. 40; *Maryland Historical Magazine*, Vol. XXVI, p. 146)

Alexander, Abraham, appointed Constable of Tonollowauy Hundred in Prince George's County, now Frederick County, 1746. (Ref: Prince George's County Court Records, 1736-1748, Extracts by Patricia Abelard Andersen, *Western Maryland Genealogy*, Vol. 18, No. 1, January 2002, p. 44)

Alexander, Amos (1729-1780), was appointed a Commissioner of the Peace for Cecil County, 2 Jun 1774. (Ref: Maryland State Archives, Governor and Council Commissioner Records, 1726-1794, p. 282)

Alexander, James, appointed a Commissioner of the Peace for Cecil County, 3 Mar 1726/7. (Ref: Maryland State Archives, Governor and Council Commissioner Records, 1726-1794, p. 2)

Alexander, Nathaniel, of Frederick County, appointed a Commissioner of the Peace, 17 Nov 1749. (Ref: Maryland State Archives, Governor and Council Commissioner Records, 1726-1794, p. 115); Court Justice, Frederick County, 1750. (Ref: *This Was The Life: Excerpts from the Judgment Records of Frederick County, Maryland, 1748-1765*, by Millard Milburn Rice, p. 47)

Alexander, Robert (1740-1805), was appointed to represent Baltimore County in the Provincial Convention, 1775. (Ref: *Calendar of Maryland State Papers, The Red Books*, No. 4, Part 1, p. 3)

Alexander, William, appointed a Commissioner of the Peace for Cecil County, 31 Oct 1741. (Ref: Maryland State Archives, Governor and Council Commissioner Records, 1726-1794, p. 72)

Alexander, William, registration of brigantine *The Batchelor's Club*, formerly the *Monokin*, 60 tons, built at Monokin River, Somerset County, 1725. Patrick Sympson, master. William Alexander, owner. 15 Mar 1733/4. (Ref: Maryland Commission Book No. 82, p. 8; *Maryland Historical Magazine*, Vol. XXVI, p. 140); registration of sloop *Crump*, 25 tons, built at Patapsco, 1735. Francis Kipps, master. William Alexander, owner. 20 Feb 1735/6. (Ref: Maryland Commission Book No. 82, p. 41; *Maryland Historical Magazine*, Vol. XXVI, p. 146)

Aley, Michael, planter, late of St. Luke's Parish, Queen Anne's County, under death sentence, pardoned 23 Dec 1734. (Ref: Maryland Commission Book No. 82, p. 24; *Maryland Historical Magazine*, Vol. XXVI, p. 142); however, it was later reported Michael Aley, of Queen Anne's County, convicted felon, was executed on 16 Jan 1734/5. (Ref: Maryland State Archives, Governor and Council Commissioner Records, 1726-1794, p. 45). Additional research will be necessary before drawing any conclusions.

Alfereno, Phineas, planter, of Talbot County, native of Florence, naturalized 30 Apr 1736. (Ref: Maryland Commission Book No. 82, p. 43; *Maryland Historical Magazine*, Vol. XXVI, p. 147)

Alkin, Thomas (d. 1773), reverend, licensed to preach in St. John's Parish, Queen Anne's County, 9 Oct 1766. (Ref: Maryland Commission Book No. 82, p. 181; *Maryland Historical Magazine*, Vol. XXVI, p. 354); induction into St. John's Parish, Queen Anne's County, 7 Jul 1769. (Ref: Maryland Commission Book No. 82, p. 225; *Maryland Historical Magazine*, Vol. XXVI, p. 359)

Allegood, William, appointed a Commissioner of the Peace for Worcester County, 7 Nov 1758. (Ref: Maryland State Archives, Governor and Council Commissioner Records, 1726-1794, p. 183)

Allein, William, appointed a Commissioner of the Peace for Calvert County, 26 Jul 1773. (Ref: Maryland State Archives, Governor and Council Commissioner Records, 1726-1794, p. 272)

Allen, Bennett (1737-1782), reverend, induction into St. Paul's Parish, Anne Arundel County, 1 Jan 1767. (Ref: Maryland Commission Book No. 82, p. 198; *Maryland Historical Magazine*, Vol. XXVI, p. 355); licensed to preach in St. James' Parish, Anne Arundel County, vacant by the death of Rev. Alexander Adams. 24 Oct 1767. (Ref: Maryland Commission Book No. 82, p. 204; *Maryland Historical Magazine*, Vol. XXVI, p. 356); induction into St. James' Parish, Anne Arundel County, 11 Feb 1768. (Ref: Maryland Commission Book No. 82, p. 207; *Maryland Historical Magazine*, Vol. XXVI, p. 357); induction into All Saint's Parish, Frederick County, 27 May 1768. (Ref: Maryland Com-ission Book No. 82, p. 213; *Maryland Historical Magazine*, Vol. XXVI, p. 357); commissioned Escheater and Receiver General, 26 Mar 1768, noting that. "This commission was superseded in consequence of a second commission that differed slightly from the first and contained a limitation of power." (Ref: Maryland Commission Book No. 82, p. 208; *Maryland Historical Magazine*, Vol. XXVI, p. 357)

Allen, Francis (d. 1745), of Somerset County, sheriff, 1726. (Ref: *Abstracts of the Testamentary Proceedings and Prerogative Court of Maryland, Vol. XVII, 1724-1727*, by Vernon L. Skinner, Jr., p. 119, citing original Liber 27, f. 314)

Allen, John, see Samuel Wilson.

Allen, William (d. 1792), commissioned High Sheriff of Somerset County, 21 Oct 1756. (Ref: Maryland State Archives, Governor and Council Commissioner Records, 1726-1794, p. 161); Court Justice, Worcester County, 1774. (*Calendar of Maryland State Papers, No. 1 The Black Books*, p. 214); appointed a Commissioner of the Peace for Somerset County, 5 Jan 1775. (Ref: Maryland State Archives, Governor and Council Commissioner Records, 1726-1794, p. 286)

Allnutt, William, appointed a Commissioner of the Peace for Calvert County, 11 Jun 1760. (Ref: Maryland State Archives, Governor and Council Commissioner Records, 1726-1794, p. 191)

Allyne, Samuel, merchant, of Boston, registration of schooner *Speedwell*, 15 tons, built in Annapolis, 1747. and called the *Cumberland*. Stephen Greenleaf, master. Samuel Allyne, owner. 27 Feb 1748/9. (Ref: Maryland Commission Book No. 82, p. 150; *Maryland Historical Magazine*, Vol. XXVI, p. 348); registration of ship *Loyd Frigate*, 140 tons, built in Cecil County, 1750. Samuel Allyne, master and owner. 17 Oct 1750. (Ref: Maryland Commission Book No. 82, p. 147; *Maryland Historical Magazine*, Vol. XXVI, p. 347)

Anderson, James, appointed a Commissioner of the Peace for Kent County, 16 Oct 1750. (Ref: Maryland State Archives, Governor and Council Commissioner Records, 1726-1794, p. 119)

Anderson, John, was appointed a Press Master in Dorchester County in 1745. (Ref: Dorchester County Judgment Records, 1743-1745, p. 476; *Judgment Records of Dorchester, Queen Anne's and Talbot Counties, Maryland*, by F. Edward Wright, 2001, p. 60); of Fishing Creek, appointed a Commissioner of the Peace, 5 Apr 1760. (Ref: Maryland State Archives, Governor and Council Commissioner Records, 1726-1794, p. 190); see William Edmonson.

Andrew, William, was commissioned one of the Corders of Wood in Baltimore Town, 13 Sep 1768. (Ref: Maryland Commission Book No. 82, p. 216; *Maryland Historical Magazine*, Vol. XXVI, p. 358)

Andrews, Ephraim, doctor, was appointed a Commissioner of the Peace for Baltimore County, 3 Nov 1757. (Ref: Maryland State Archives, Governor and Council Commissioner Records, 1726-1794, p. 178)

Andrews, John (1746-113), reverend, induction into St. John's Parish, Queen Anne's County, 8 May 1773. (Ref: Maryland Commission Book No. 82, p. 318; *Maryland Historical Magazine*, Vol. XXVII, p. 34)

Annan, Samuel, of Frederick County, convicted felon in 1763 for stealing a watch, was sent to the pillory for quarter of an hour, then received thirty-nine lashes on his bare back, and to pay 2,000 pounds of tobacco for the goods stolen. (Ref: *This Was The Life: Excerpts from the Judgment Records of Frederick County, Maryland, 1748-1765*, by Millard Milburn Rice, p. 248)

Ardnold, John George, of Prince George's County, native of Germany, naturalized 15 Jan 1739/40, and also his sons John, Daniel, Samuel and Andrew. (Ref: Maryland Commission Book No. 82, p. 78; *Maryland Historical Magazine*, Vol. XXVI, p. 155)

Armiger, William, planter, late of St. Paul's Parish, Talbot County, pardoned for felony, 27 May 1734. (Ref: Maryland Commission Book No. 82, p. 18; *Maryland Historical Magazine*, Vol. XXVI, p. 141)

Armstrong, Robert, commissioned a Coroner of St. Mary's County, 10 Dec 1773. (Ref: Maryland Commission Book No. 82, p. 332; *Maryland Historical Magazine*, Vol. XXVII, p. 36)

Arnold, David, appointed a Commissioner of the Peace for Calvert County, 11 Nov 1746. (Ref: Maryland State Archives, Governor and Council Commissioner Records, 1726-1794, p. 95)

Ashman, George (d. 1699/1700), appointed a Commissioner of the Peace for Baltimore County, 16 Dec 1751. (Ref: Maryland State Archives, Governor and Council Commissioner Records, 1726-1794, p. 131)

Askew, Thomas, see Patrick Creagh.

Askins, William, commissioned a Coroner of Dorchester County, 6 Oct 1766. (Ref: Maryland Commission Book No. 82, p. 181; *Maryland Historical Magazine*, Vol. XXVI, p. 354)

Atkinson, Milby, appointed a Commissioner of the Peace for Worcester County, 1 Oct 1768. (Ref: Maryland State Archives, Governor and Council Commissioner Records, 1726-1794, p. 238, spelled his first name Milbay); appointed a Commissioner of the Peace for Worcester County, 30 Apr 1770. (Ref: Maryland State Archives, Governor and Council Commissioner Records, 1726-1794, p. 250); appointed a Commissioner of the Peace for Worcester County, 26 Oct 1773. (Ref: Maryland State Archives, Governor and Council Commissioner Records, 1726-1794, p. 278)

Attaway, John, appointed a Commissioner of the Peace for St. Mary's County, 2 Mar 1726/7. (Ref: Maryland State Archives, Governor and Council Commissioner Records, 1726-1794, p. 2)

Austin, Henry, appointed a Commissioner of the Peace for Calvert County, 29 May 1734. (Ref: Maryland State Archives, Governor and Council Commissioner Records, 1726-1794, p. 42); appointed a Commissioner of the Peace for Calvert County, 22 Oct 1741. (Ref: Maryland State Archives, Governor and Council Commissioner Records, 1726-1794, p. 72)

Austin, William, planter, of St. Peter's Parish, Talbot County, pardoned for theft of tobacco from James Virgin, 9 Jun 1740. (Ref: Maryland Commission Book No. 82, p. 82; *Maryland Historical Magazine*, Vol. XXVI, p. 157)

Ayres, John, see Levin Gale.

Bacon, Anthony, registration of sloop *Rachel*, 40 tons, built in Baltimore County, 1748. John Coward, master. Anthony Bacon, Robert Morris and James Dickinson, owners. 4 Oct 1748. (Ref: Maryland Commission Book No. 82, p. 137; *Maryland Historical Magazine*, Vol. XXVI, p. 342); see Henry Lowes and John Williams.

Bacon, Thomas (c1700-1768), reverend, was inducted into St. Peter's Parish, Talbot County, 3 Mar 1745/6. (Ref: Maryland Commission Book No. 82, p. 119; *Maryland Historical Magazine*, Vol. XXVI, p. 256); minister of All Saints Parish, Frederick County, 1760. (Ref: *This Was The Life: Excerpts from the Judgment Records of Frederick County, Maryland, 1748-1765*, by Millard Milburn Rice, p. 215)

Bacon, William, appointed a Commissioner of the Peace for Somerset County, 5 Jan 1775. (Ref: Maryland State Archives, Governor and Council Commissioner Records, 1726-1794, p. 286)

Bailey, Clement, see Robert Jenckins Henry.

Bailey, Joseph, registration of sloop *Prudent Mary*, 15 tons, built in Dorchester County, 1746, and called the *Roe*. Joseph Bailey, master and co-owner. Levin Hodson, co-owner. 6 May 1749. (Ref: Maryland Commission Book No. 82, p. 151; *Maryland Historical Magazine*, Vol. XXVI, p. 349); registration of sloop *Vigilant*, 40 tons, built in Connecticut, 1746. Joseph Bailey, master and owner. 13 May 1748. (Ref: Maryland Commission Book No. 82, p. 134; *Maryland Historical Magazine*, Vol. XXVI, pp. 262-263)

Bainbridge, Peter, appointed a Commissioner of the Peace for Frederick County, 3 Nov 1757. (Ref: Maryland State Archives, Governor and Council Commissioner Records, 1726-1794, p. 178); Court Justice in Frederick County in 1758. (Ref: *This Was The Life: Excerpts from the Judgment Records of Frederick County, Maryland, 1748-1765*, by Millard Milburn Rice, p. 177)

Baird, Alexander, of Cecil Co., commissioned Receiver of His Lordship's Quit Rents in Cecil County. 17 Mar 1748/9. (Ref: Maryland Commission Book No. 82, p. 139; *Maryland Historical Magazine*, Vol. XXVI, p. 343)

Baird, William, of Frederick County, Court Judge, 1774. (*Calendar of Maryland State Papers, No. 1 The Black Books*, p. 217)

Baker, Charles, see John Christopher.

Baker, Henry (c1710-1768), was appointed a Commissioner of the Peace for Cecil County, 31 Oct 1741. (Ref: Maryland State Archives, Governor and Council Commissioner Records, 1726-1794, p. 72); see John Seegar.

Baker, John (d. 1730/31), of St. Mary's County, sheriff, 1726. (Ref: *Abstracts of the Testamentary Proceedings and Prerogative Court of Maryland, Vol. XVII, 1724-1727*, by Vernon L. Skinner, Jr., p. 119, citing original Liber 27, f. 313); renewed appointment as a Commissioner of the Peace on 4 Jun 1727. (Ref:

Maryland State Archives, Governor and Council Commissioner Records, 1726-1794, p. 4)

Baker, John, appointed Constable of Rock Creek Hundred in Frederick County, 1769. (Ref: "Frederick County Court Minutes, March 1769," by Patricia Abelard Andersen, *Western Maryland Genealogy*, Vol. 15, No. 2, April 1999, p. 62)

Baker, Nathan, appointed a Commissioner of the Peace for Cecil County, 31 Oct 1741. (Ref: Maryland State Archives, Governor and Council Commissioner Records, 1726-1794, p. 72)

Baker, Peter, native of Germany, denization, 16 Aug 1773. (Ref: Maryland Commission Book No. 82, p. 321; *Maryland Historical Magazine*, Vol. XXVII, p. 35)

Baldwin, John, was appointed a Commissioner of the Peace for Cecil County, 3 Mar 1726/7, and commissioned Sheriff of Cecil County, 5 Nov 1728. (Ref: Maryland State Archives, Governor and Council Commissioner Records, 1726-1794, pp. 2, 8)

Baldwin, John, gentleman, commissioned Sheriff of Charles County, 28 Oct 1729. (Ref: Maryland State Archives, Governor and Council Commissioner Records, 1726-1794, p. 13)

Ballard, Henry, appointed a Commissioner of the Peace for Somerset County, 9 May 1732. (Ref: Maryland State Archives, Governor and Council Commissioner Records, 1726-1794, p. 23); commissioned a Coroner for Somerset County, 6 May 1737. (Ref: Maryland Commission Book No. 82, p. 48; *Maryland Historical Magazine*, Vol. XXVI, p. 149); commissioned one of the Coroners of Somerset County, 30 Mar 1747. (Ref: Maryland Commission Book No. 82, p. 128; *Maryland Historical Magazine*, Vol. XXVI, p. 259); sheriff of Somerset County, 1753 and 1756. (Ref: *Calendar of Maryland State Papers, No. 1 The Black Books*, p. 112, and *Archives of Maryland*, Vol. LII, "Proceedings and Acts of the General Assembly of Maryland, 1755-1756," p. 232)

Ballard, John, commissioned High Sheriff of Somerset County, 3 Oct 1752. (Ref: Maryland State Archives, Governor and Council Commissioner Records, 1726-1794, p. 135)

Ballard, Levin, see Elizabeth Horner.

Banks, John, appointed Constable of the Lower Part of Andieatum [Antietam] Hundred in Frederick County in 1763. (Ref: *This Was The Life: Excerpts from the Judgment Records of Frederick County, Maryland, 1748-1765*, by Millard Milburn Rice, p. 249)

Banks, Samuel, appointed Constable of the Lower Part of Antietam Hundred in Frederick County, 1771. (Ref: "Frederick County Minute Book, March 1771, Extracts by Patricia Abelard Andersen," *Western Maryland Genealogy*, Vol. 18, No. 1, January 2002, p. 26)

Banning, Henry (c1736-1818), was appointed a Commissioner of the Peace for Talbot County, 2 Feb 1774. (Ref: Maryland State Archives, Governor and Council Commissioner Records, 1726-1794, p. 280); Court Justice, Talbot County, 1774. (*Calendar of Maryland State Papers, No. 1 The Black Books*, p. 211)

Banning, Sam, see Negro Sam Banning.

Barclay, John (b. 1732), reverend, licensed to preach in St. Luke's Parish, Queen Anne's County, vacant by death of Rev. Richard Harrison. 10 Mar 1763. (Ref: Maryland Commission Book No. 82, p. 165; *Maryland Historical Magazine*, Vol. XXVI, p. 353)

Barick, John, appointed Constable of the Lower Part of Potomac Hundred in Frederick County in 1751. (Ref: *This Was The Life: Excerpts from the Judgment Records of Frederick County, Maryland, 1748-1765*, by Millard Milburn Rice, p. 61)

Barker, John, Sr., was commissioned a Coroner of Charles County, 17 May 1739. (Ref: Maryland Commission Book No. 82, p. 72; *Maryland Historical Magazine*, Vol. XXVI, p. 153)

Barkley, Thomas, registration of boat *Buxome Jean*, 5 tons, built in Virginia, 1731. William Thomas, master. Thomas Barkley, owner. 26 Jul 1749. (Ref: Maryland Commission Book No. 82, p. 152; *Maryland Historical Magazine*, Vol. XXVI, p. 349)

Barnes, Abraham (d. c1778), was appointed a Commissioner of the Peace for St. Mary's County, 11 Jun 1739. (Ref: Maryland State Archives, Governor and Council Commissioner Records, 1726-1794, p. 63)

Barnes, John, appointed a Commissioner of the Peace for Charles County, 19 Oct 1770. (Ref: Maryland State Archives, Governor and Council Commissioner Records, 1726-1794, p. 252)

Barnes, John, registration of sloop *Unity*, – tons, built in Kent County, 1750. Nehemiah Covington, master. John Barnes, owner,(Ref: Maryland Commission Book No. 82, p. 147; *Maryland Historical Magazine*, Vol. XXVI, p. 347)

Barnes, Matthew, Jr., commissioned a Coroner for Charles County, 24 Mar 1735/6. (Ref: Maryland Commission Book No. 82, p. 42; *Maryland Historical Magazine*, Vol. XXVI, p. 146)

Barnes, Richard, appointed a Commissioner of the Peace for Charles County, 15 Oct 1774. (Ref: Maryland State Archives, Governor and Council Commissioner Records, 1726-1794, p. 284); commissioned a Coroner of Charles County, 17 Sep 1764. (Ref: Maryland Commission Book No. 82, p. 164; *Maryland Historical Magazine*, Vol. XXVI, p. 353); commissioned a Coroner of Charles County, 3 Jul 1773. (Ref: Maryland Commission Book No. 82, p. 318; *Maryland Historical Magazine*, Vol. XXVII, p. 34)

Barnes, William, registration of sloop *Valentine*, 12 tons, built in Somerset County, 1735. William Barnes, master and owner. 26 Dec 1738. (Ref: Maryland Commission Book No. 82, p. 65; *Maryland Historical Magazine*, Vol. XXVI, p. 152)

Barney, William, commissioned Weigher of Hay and one of the Corders of Wood in Baltimore Town. (Ref: Maryland Commission Book No. 82, p. 216; *Maryland Historical Magazine*, Vol. XXVI, p. 358)

Barnhouse, Richard, appointed a Commissioner of the Peace for St. Mary's County, 29 Feb 1743/4. (Ref: Maryland State Archives, Governor and Council Commissioner Records, 1726-1794, p. 84)

Barrett, Benjamin, labourer, of Calvert County, convicted felon "for breaking and entering the store house of a certain John Gray of the Clifts and taking thereout sundry goods and chattels," and to be executed on 14 May 1756, but was pardoned on 5 May 1756. (Ref: Maryland State Archives, Governor and Council Commissioner Records, 1726-1794, p. 153; *Archives of Maryland*, Vol. XXXI, "Proceedings of the Council of Maryland, 1753-1761," p. 119)

Barrett, John, of Baltimore County, convicted of murder, case recorded on 19 Nov 1753 and the "execution to be on Wednesday seven night and after he is dead his body to be hung in chains as near as conveniently may be to the place where the murder was committed." (Ref: Maryland State Archives, Governor and Council Commissioner Records, 1726-1794, p. 138)

Barriere, Anthony, native of France, denization, 26 Apr 1768. (Ref: Maryland Commission Book No. 82, p. 211; *Maryland Historical Magazine*, Vol. XXVI, p. 357)

Bartlett, John, registration of schooner *Hope-well*, 40 tons, built in Talbot County, 1736. John Coward, master. John Bartlett and Richard Bennett, owners. 8 Nov 1736. (Ref: Maryland Commission Book No. 82, p. 46; *Maryland Historical Magazine*, Vol. XXVI, p. 148)

Burton, John, appointed Constable of the Upper Part of Kittocton [Catoctin] Hundred in Frederick County, 1769. (Ref: "Frederick County Court Minutes, March 1769," by Patricia Abelard Andersen, *Western Maryland Genealogy*, Vol. 15, No. 2, April 1999, p. 63, mistakenly listed his name as John Barto; "Frederick County Court Minutes, June 1769," by Patricia Abelard Andersen, *Western Maryland Genealogy*, Vol. 15, No. 4, April 1999, p. 171)

Basnett, John, of Anne Arundel Co., convicted felon, was pardoned for uttering [putting into circulation] counterfeit money. 10 Dec 1743. (Ref: Maryland Commission Book No. 82, p. 106; *Maryland Historical Magazine*, Vol. XXVI, p. 250)

Bassett, Martha, of Baltimore County, convicted for murdering Sarah Clark, assisted by Mary Powell and John Berry, was executed on 10 Jan 1751/2. (Ref: Maryland State Archives, Governor and Council Commissioner Records, 1726-1794, p. 131)

Bates, Thomas, appointed a Commissioner of the Peace for Charles County, 3 Sep 1757. (Ref: Maryland State Archives, Governor and Council Commissioner Records, 1726-1794, p. 176)

Batter, John, of Cecil County, convicted felon and burglar, was executed on 20 Aug 1752. (Ref: Maryland State Archives, Governor and Council Commissioner Records, 1726-1794, p. 133)

Baxter, James, appointed a Commissioner of the Peace for Cecil County, 27 Oct 1747. (Ref: Maryland State Archives, Governor and Council Commissioner Records, 1726-1794, p. 101); commissioned High Sheriff of Cecil County, 8 Oct 1761. (Ref: Maryland State Archives, Governor and Council Commissioner

Records, 1726-1794, p. 191)

Baxter, William (d. 1773), of Cecil County, was appointed a Commissioner of the Peace, 21 Apr 1764. (Ref: Maryland State Archives, Governor and Council Commissioner Records, 1726-1794, p. 215); commissioned High Sheriff of Cecil County, 18 Oct 1762. (Ref: Maryland State Archives, Governor and Council Commissioner Records, 1726-1794, p. 196)

Bayard, James, see John Chandly, Peter Bayard andWilliam Deoran.

Bayard, Peter (1702-1766), was appointed a Commissioner of the Peace for Cecil County, 9 Feb 1743/4. (Ref: Maryland State Archives, Governor and Council Commissioner Records, 1726-1794, p. 84); merchant, registration of sloop *Bohemia*, 30 tons, built in Cecil County, 1746. Peter Bayard, master and co-owner. James Bayard, co-owner. 28 Jun 1746. (Ref: Maryland Commission Book No. 82, p. 120; *Maryland Historical Magazine*, Vol. XXVI, p. 257)

Bayard, Susannah, see William Deoran.

Bayley, Isme, was commissioned High Sheriff of Worcester County, 17 Sep 1765. (Ref: Maryland State Archives, Governor and Council Commissioner Records, 1726-1794, p. 212, and p. 222 spelled his surname Baley)

Baynes, John, appointed a Commissioner of the Peace for Prince George's County, 15 Mar 1769. (Ref: Maryland State Archives, Governor and Council Commissioner Records, 1726-1794, p. 241); appointed a Commissioner of the Peace for Prince George's County, 26 Jul 1773. (Ref: Maryland State Archives, Governor and Council Commissioner Records, 1726-1794, p. 272)

Beach, Peter, labourer, of Prince George's Co., convicted felon, was pardoned and then banished from the province, 26 Oct 1766. (Ref: Maryland Commission Book No. 82, p. 182; *Maryland Historical Magazine*, Vol. XXVI, p. 355)

Beal, George, see James Russell.

Beal, Thomas, appointed a Commissioner of the Peace for Prince George's County, 30 Nov 1741. (Ref: Maryland State Archives, Governor and Council Commissioner Records, 1726-1794, p. 72)

Beale, Elizabeth, see Negro Robin.

Beall, Alexander, appointed a Commissioner of the Peace for Frederick County, 1 Mar 1749/50. (Ref: Maryland State Archives, Governor and Council Commissioner Records, 1726-1794, p. 116)

Beall, Archibald, appointed Constable of the Lower Part of Newfoundland Hundred in Frederick County in 1753. (Ref: *This Was The Life: Excerpts from the Judgment Records of Frederick County, Maryland, 1748-1765*, by Millard Milburn Rice, p. 131)

Beall, Charles, appointed Constable of New Scotland Hundred in Prince George's County, now Frederick County, 1748. (Ref: Prince George's County Court Records, 1736-1738, Extracts by Patricia Abelard Andersen, *Western Maryland Genealogy*, Vol. 18, No. 1, January 2002, p. 46)

Beall, Elisha, appointed Constable of Linganore Hundred in Frederick County, 1771. (Ref: "Frederick County Minute Book, March 1771, Extracts by Patricia Abelard Andersen," *Western Maryland Genealogy*, Vol. 18, No. 1, January 2002, p. 25)

Beall, John, Jr., appointed a Commissioner of the Peace for Prince George's County, 29 Oct 1730. (Ref: Maryland State Archives, Governor and Council Commissioner Records, 1726-1794, p. 12)

Beall, John, Sr., appointed a Commissioner of the Peace for Prince George's County, 29 Oct 1730. (Ref: Maryland State Archives, Governor and Council Commissioner Records, 1726-1794, p. 12)

Beall, Joseph, appointed Constable of Eastern Branch Hundred in Prince George's County, now Frederick County, 1742. (Ref: Prince George's County Court Records, 1736-1748, Extracts by Patricia Abelard Andersen, *Western Maryland Genealogy*, Vol. 18, No. 1, January 2002, p. 38)

Beall, Joseph, of Ninian, appointed Constable of Linganore Hundred in 1751. (Ref: *This Was The Life: Excerpts from the Judgment Records of Frederick County, Maryland, 1748-1765*, by Millard Milburn Rice, p. 61)

Beall, Joshua, captain, commissioned High Sheriff of Calvert County, 27 Sep 1759. (Ref: Maryland State Archives, Governor and Council Commissioner Records, 1726-1794, p. 180)

Beall, Josiah (d. 1768), commissioned a Coroner for Frederick County on 13 Dec 1748. (Ref: Maryland Commission Book No. 82, p. 139; *Maryland Historical Magazine*, Vol. XXVI, p. 343); Court

Justice, Frederick County, 1750. (Ref: *This Was The Life: Excerpts from the Judgment Records of Frederick County, Maryland, 1748-1765*, by Millard Milburn Rice, p. 47); commissioned High Sheriff of Frederick County, 8 Dec 1752. (Ref: Maryland State Archives, Governor and Council Commissioner Records, 1726-1794, p. 137); appointed to a Committee to Inspect the Accounts and Proceedings of the Commissioners for Emitting Bills of Credit, 25 Feb 1755. (Ref: *Archives of Maryland*, Vol. LII, "Proceedings and Acts of the General Assembly of Maryland, 1755-1756," p. 5, spelled his name Bealle, pp. 46 and 51 both spelled it Beall)

Beall, Josias, appointed a Commissioner of the Peace for Frederick County, 1 Mar 1749/50. (Ref: Maryland State Archives, Governor and Council Commissioner Records, 1726-1794, p. 116); appointed a Commissioner of the Peace for Frederick County, 22 Nov 1752. (Ref: Maryland State Archives, Governor and Council Commissioner Records, 1726-1794, p. 135)

Beall, Mordecai, appointed Constable in the Upper Part of Monocacy Hundred in Frederick County in 1763. (Ref: *This Was The Life: Excerpts from the Judgment Records of Frederick County, Maryland, 1748-1765*, by Millard Milburn Rice, p. 249)

Beall, Nathaniel, Jr., Sheriff of Frederick County in 1755. (Ref: *This Was The Life: Excerpts from the Judgment Records of Frederick County, Maryland, 1748-1765*, by Millard Milburn Rice, p. 155)

Beall, Ninian, Jr., appointed Constable of New Scotland Hundred in Prince George's County, now Frederick County, 1736. (Ref: Prince George's County Court Records, 1736-1748, Extracts by Patricia Abelard Andersen, *Western Maryland Genealogy*, Vol. 18, No. 1, January 2002, p. 34)

Beall, Peter, of Kent County, convicted felon, executed on 29 Dec 1752. (Ref: Maryland State Archives, Governor and Council Commissioner Records, 1726-1794, p. 136)

Beall, Samuel (c1713-c1778), colonel, appointed a Commissioner of the Peace for Frederick County, 12 Mar 1763 and 15 Aug 1774. (Ref: Maryland State Archives, Governor and Council Commissioner Records, 1726-1794, pp. 209, 284)

Beall, Samuel, Jr., commissioned Sheriff of Frederick County, 1 Dec 1753. (Ref: Maryland State Archives, Governor and Council Commissioner Records, 1726-1794, p. 142; *Archives of Maryland*, Vol. LII, "Proceedings and Acts of the General Assembly of Maryland, 1755-1756," p. 57)

Beall, Thomas, Jr., appointed a Commissioner of the Peace for Frederick County, 22 Nov 1752. (Ref: Maryland State Archives, Governor and Council Commissioner Records, 1726-1794, p. 135)

Beall, William, Constable in the Middle Part of Monocacy Hundred in Frederick County, 1758. (Ref: *This Was The Life: Excerpts from the Judgment Records of Frederick County, Maryland, 1748-1765*, by Millard Milburn Rice, p. 185)

Bean, John, appointed Constable of Rock Creek Hundred in Frederick County in 1749 and the Middle Part of Rock Creek Hundred in 1748 and 1751. (Ref: *This Was The Life: Excerpts from the Judgment Records of Frederick County, Maryland, 1748-1765*, by Millard Milburn Rice, pp. 6, 61; Prince George's County Court Records, 1736-1738, Extracts by Patricia Abelard Andersen, *Western Maryland Genealogy*, Vol. 18, No. 1, January 2002, p. 46)

Beanes, Colmore, was commissioned Sheriff of Prince George's County, 7 Nov 1756. (Ref: Maryland State Archives, Governor and Council Commissioner Records, 1726-1794, p. 162)

Beanes, William, appointed a Commissioner of the Peace for Prince George's County, 26 Jul 1773. (Ref: Maryland State Archives, Governor and Council Commissioner Records, 1726-1794, p. 272)

Bear, John George, of Prince George's County, native of Germany, naturalized 3 May 1740, and also his son John. (Ref: Maryland Commission Book No. 82, p. 81; *Maryland Historical Magazine*, Vol. XXVI, p. 156)

Beard, Alexander, commissioned a Coroner of Kent County, April 1770. (Ref: Maryland Commission Book No. 82, p. 240; *Maryland Historical Magazine*, Vol. XXVI, p. 361); commissioned a Coroner of Kent County, 21 Sep 1773. (Ref: Maryland Commission Book No. 82, p. 323; *Maryland Historical Magazine*, Vol. XXVII, p. 35)

Beard, William, appointed Constable of Manor Hundred in Frederick County in 1760. (Ref: *This Was The Life: Excerpts from the Judgment Records of Frederick County, Maryland, 1748-1765*, by Millard

Milburn Rice, p. 216); appointed Constable of Salisbury Hundred in Frederick County, 1769. (Ref: "Frederick County Court Minutes, March 1769," by Patricia Abelard Andersen, *Western Maryland Genealogy*, Vol. 15, No. 2, April 1999, p. 63); appointed a Commissioner of the Peace for Frederick County, 20 Aug 1772 and 15 Aug 1774. (Ref: Maryland State Archives, Governor and Council Commissioner Records, 1726-1794, pp. 261, 284)

Beatty, Henry, appointed Constable of part of Monocacy Hundred in Prince George's County, now Frederick County, 1738. (Ref: Prince George's County Court Records, 1736-1748, Extracts by Patricia Abelard Andersen, *Western Maryland Genealogy*, Vol. 18, No. 1, January 2002, p. 35)

Beatty, John (d. 1811), appointed Constable of Manor Hundred in Frederick County, 1769. (Ref: "Frederick County Court Minutes, March 1769," by Patricia Abelard Andersen, *Western Maryland Genealogy*, Vol. 15, No. 2, April 1999, p. 63)

Beatty, Thomas (b. 1768), of Prince George's County, later of Frederick County, appointed a Commissioner of the Peace for Prince George's County, 15 Jun 1739. (Ref: Maryland State Archives, Governor and Council Commissioner Records, 1726-1794, p. 64); Court Justice in Frederick County, 1748, and Constable of Manor Hundred, 1760. (Ref: *This Was The Life: Excerpts from the Judgment Records of Frederick County, Maryland, 1748-1765*, by Millard Milburn Rice, pp. 1, 216, and p. 222 stated he was age 58 in 1761); appointed a Commissioner of the Peace for Frederick County, 13 Mar 1773. (Ref: Maryland State Archives, Governor and Council Commissioner Records, 1726-1794, p. 265; appointed a Commissioner of the Peace for Frederick County, 15 Aug 1774. (Ref: Maryland State Archives, Governor and Council Commissioner Records, 1726-1794, p. 284)

Beatty, William, appointed Constable of Manor Hundred in Frederick County in 1763. (Ref: *This Was The Life: Excerpts from the Judgment Records of Frederick County, Maryland, 1748-1765*, by Millard Milburn Rice, p. 249); Court Judge, 1774. (*Calendar of Maryland State Papers, No. 1 The Black Books*, p. 217)

Beaven, Thomas, of Anne Arundel County, convicted felon and burglar, for "breaking and entering the house of Charles Cole with an intent to deprive him of his life and rob him of his goods," executed 1 Nov 1751. (Ref: Maryland State Archives, Governor and Council Commissioner Records, 1726-1794, p. 129)

Beaver, John, native of Germany, denization, 12 Feb 1773. (Ref: Maryland Commission Book No. 82, p. 294; *Maryland Historical Magazine*, Vol. XXVII, p. 32)

Beaver, Sarah, of Cecil County, pardon granted, 15 Apr 1751. (Ref: Maryland Commission Book No. 82, p. 148; *Maryland Historical Magazine*, Vol. XXVI, p. 348)

Beck, Anthony, see Daniel Cheston and Patrick Creagh.

Beck, William, see Negro George.

Beckett, John, appointed a Commissioner of the Peace for Calvert County, 14 Mar 1761. (Ref: Maryland State Archives, Governor and Council Commissioner Records, 1726-1794, p. 195)

Beckingham, William, appointed a proctor by the Prerogative Court of Maryland, 10 May 1726. (Ref: *Abstracts of the Testamentary Proceedings and Prerogative Court of Maryland, Vol. XVII, 1724-1727*, by Vernon L. Skinner, Jr., p. 97, citing original Liber 27, f. 269); commissioned a Coroner of Dorchester County, 10 Apr 1735. (Ref: Maryland Commission Book No. 82, p. 28; *Maryland Historical Magazine*, Vol. XXVI, p. 143)

Beckwith, Basil, commissioned a Coroner for Prince George's County, 22 Oct 1735. (Ref: Maryland Commission Book No. 82, p. 34; *Maryland Historical Magazine*, Vol. XXVI, p. 145)

Becraft, Abraham, of George, of Frederick County, convicted for stealing hogs from Conrad Dutterer in March 1768 and was later pardoned. (Ref: Maryland Commission Book No. 82, p. 214; *Maryland Historical Magazine*, Vol. XXVI, p. 357, spelled his name Beacraft; *Archives of Maryland*, Vol. XXXII, "Proceedings of the Council of Maryland, 1761-1770," p. 233)

Becraft, George, late of Frederick County, convicted felon, was pardoned and banished for killing Thomas Buckingham. 8 Jul 1772. (Ref: Maryland Commission Book No. 82, p. 282; *Maryland Historical Magazine*, Vol. XXVII, p. 31); however, it later stated George Becraft, of Frederick County, convicted of murder, was executed on 24 Jul 1772. (Ref: Maryland State Archives, Governor and Council Commissioner Records, 1726-1794, p. 250). Additional research will be needed before drawing any conclusions.

Beech, Peter, labourer, of Prince George's County, convicted felon, sentenced to death in August 1766. (Ref: *Archives of Maryland*, Vol. XXXII, "Proceedings of the Council of Maryland, 1761-1770," p. 159)

Bell, George, see Thomas Ringold.

Bell, Hamilton (d. 1783), reverend, induction into Christ Church Parish on Kent Island. 26 Mar 1748. (Ref: Maryland Commission Book No. 82, p. 133; *Maryland Historical Magazine*, Vol. XXVI, p. 262); resignation from Christ Church Parish, 24 Aug 1748. On same day, induction into Somerset Parish, Somerset County. (Ref: Maryland Commission Book No. 82, p. 135; *Maryland Historical Magazine*, Vol. XXVI, p. 263)

Bell, John, Jr., appointed a Commissioner of the Peace for Prince George's County, 1 Nov 1729. (Ref: Maryland State Archives, Governor and Council Commissioner Records, 1726-1794, p. 12)

Bell, John, of Prince George's County, convicted felon, executed on 7 Jun 1738. (Ref: Maryland State Archives, Governor and Council Commissioner Records, 1726-1794, p. 60)

Bell, Jonathan, was appointed a Commissioner of the Peace for Worcester County, 26 Oct 1773. (Ref: Maryland State Archives, Governor and Council Commissioner Records, 1726-1794, p. 278); Court Justice, Worcester County, 1774. (*Calendar of Maryland State Papers, No. 1 The Black Books*, p. 214)

Belt, Benjamin, Jr., appointed Constable of Eastern Branch Hundred in Prince George's Co., Shannandore Mtns [Shenandoah Mountains] upwards, now Frederick County, 1736. (Ref: Prince George's County Court Records, 1736-1748, Extracts by Patricia Abelard Andersen, *Western Maryland Genealogy*, Vol. 18, No. 1, January 2002, p. 34)

Belt, Jeremiah, appointed a Commissioner of the Peace for Prince George's County, 3 Mar 1726/7. (Ref: Maryland State Archives, Governor and Council Commissioner Records, 1726-1794, p. 3); appointed a Commissioner of the Peace for Prince George's County, 1 Nov 1729. (Ref: Maryland State Archives, Governor and Council Commissioner Records, 1726-1794, p. 12)

Belt, John, late sheriff of Prince George's County, had ordinary license accounts still unpaid in 1756. (Ref: *Archives of Maryland*, Vol. LII, "Proceedings and Acts of the General Assembly of Maryland, 1755-1756," p. 568)

Belt, Joseph (c1680-1761), was appointed a Commissioner of the Peace for Prince George's County, 3 Mar 1726/7. (Ref: Maryland State Archives, Governor and Council Commissioner Records, 1726-1794, p. 3)

Belt, Joseph, Jr. (1717-1761), commissioned Sheriff of Prince George's County, 29 May 1746. (Ref: Maryland State Archives, Governor and Council Commissioner Records, 1726-1794, p. 92); see Osborn Sprigg.

Belt, Joseph 3rd, appointed Constable of Patuxent Hundred in Prince George's County, now Frederick County, 1738. (Ref: Prince George's County Court Records, 1736-1748, Extracts by Patricia Abelard Andersen, *Western Maryland Genealogy*, Vol. 18, No. 1, January 2002, p. 35)

Bennett, James, mariner, of Liverpool, registered the snow *Oxford*, 90 tons, built in Talbot County. 1750. James Bennett, master and co-owner. Foster Cunliffe and Ellis Cunliffe, co-owners. 23 Oct 1750. (Ref: Maryland Commission Book No. 82, p. 147; *Maryland Historical Magazine*, Vol. XXVI, p. 347)

Bennett, John, was appointed a Commissioner of the Peace for Dorchester County, 8 Apr 1770. (Ref: Maryland State Archives, Governor and Council Commissioner Records, 1726-1794, p. 250)

Bennett, John, of Prince George's County, convicted felon, was executed on 14 Nov 1733. (Ref: Maryland State Archives, Governor and Council Commissioner Records, 1726-1794, p. 39)

Bennett, Richard, registration of brigantine *Rebecca*, 60 tons, built at Choptank River, 1735. Andrew Price, master. Caleb Clarke and Richard Bennett, owners. 31 Mar 1736. (Ref: Maryland Commission Book No. 82, p. 42; *Maryland Historical Magazine*, Vol. XXVI, p. 146); registration of schooner *Hopewell*, 40 tons, built in Maryland and was taken by the Spaniards and retaken by the man of war *Rose*. Samuel Martyn, master. Richard Bennett, owner. 21 Oct 1742. (Ref:

Maryland Commission Book No. 82, p. 97; *Maryland Historical Magazine*, Vol. XXVI, p. 247); see Ashbury Sutton, George Steuart, Samuel Chew, Jr. and William Addams.

Bennett, Robert, appointed Constable of Linton Hundred in Frederick County, 1769. (Ref: "Frederick County Court Minutes November 1769 by Patricia Abelard Andersen," *Western Maryland Genealogy*, Vol. 16, No. 1, January 2000, p. 33)

Benson, Fleetwood, labourer, late of Frederick County, pardoned for horse stealing, 12 Sep 1765. (Ref: Maryland Commission Book No. 82, p. 172; *Maryland Historical Magazine*, Vol. XXVI, p. 353); convicted felon, was executed on 18 Sep 1765. (Ref: Maryland State Archives, Governor and Council Commissioner Records, 1726-1794, p. 207), Additional research will be necessary before drawing any conclusions.

Benson, Perry (1694-1751), of Talbot County, was appointed a Commissioner of the Peace, 2 Mar 1731/2. (Ref: Maryland State Archives, Governor and Council Commissioner Records, 1726-1794, p. 22); commissioned one of the Coroners of Talbot County, 21 Oct 1743. (Ref: Maryland Commission Book No. 82, p. 104; *Maryland Historical Magazine*, Vol. XXVI, p. 249)

Bentley, Richard, see William Roberts.

Bernard, Luke, served as constable in Frederick County, 1754-1755. (Ref: *Archives of Maryland*, Vol. LII, "Proceedings and Acts of the General Assembly of Maryland, 1755-1756," p. 57)

Berry, Andrew, appointed a Commissioner of the Peace for Cecil County, 30 Nov 1732. (Ref: Maryland State Archives, Governor and Council Commissioner Records, 1726-1794, p. 30)

Berry, John, of Baltimore County, convicted for assisting Martha Bassett and Mary Powell in the murder of Sarah Clark, executed on and hung in chains near the place of the murder, 10 Jan 1751/2. (Ref: Maryland State Archives, Governor and Council Commissioner Records, 1726-1794, p. 131)

Biggs, Samuel, appointed Constable of Sugar Land Hundred in Frederick County, 1769, 1771. (Ref: "Frederick County Court Minutes November 1769 by Patricia Abelard Andersen," *Western Maryland Genealogy*, Vol. 16, No. 1, January 2000, p. 32; "Frederick County Minute Book, March 1771, Extracts by Patricia Abelard Andersen," *Western Maryland Genealogy*, Vol. 18, No. 1, January 2002, p. 25)

Biglands, Henry, see Levin Gale.

Billings, James, registration of ship *Rider*, 80 tons, built at Nanticoke River, 1738. James Billings, master and owner. 20 Oct 1738. (Ref: Maryland Commission Book No. 82, p. 63; *Maryland Historical Magazine*, Vol. XXVI, p. 152); appointed a Commissioner of the Peace for Dorchester County, 1 Jun 1743. (Ref: Maryland State Archives, Governor and Council Commissioner Records, 1726-1794, p. 78)

Binney, Paul, merchant, of New England, registration of ship *Lyon*, of Boston, 380 tons, built in Boston, 1747. Richard Courtney, master. Paul Binney, owner. 19 Sep 1748. (Ref: Maryland Commission Book No. 82, p. 136; *Maryland Historical Magazine*, Vol. XXVI, p. 342)

Birstall, John, see Samuel Massey.

Biscoe, Bennett, appointed a Commissioner of the Peace for Somerset County, 26 Jul 1773. (Ref: Maryland State Archives, Governor and Council Commissioner Records, 1726-1794, p. 272)

Biscoe, John, appointed a Commissioner of the Peace for Charles County, 30 Oct 1732. (Ref: Maryland State Archives, Governor and Council Commissioner Records, 1726-1794, p. 27)

Black, John, appointed a Commissioner of the Peace for St. Mary's County, 15 Feb 1760. (Ref: Maryland State Archives, Governor and Council Commissioner Records, 1726-1794, p. 190)

Blackston (Blackiston), Ebenezer (c1684-1746), appointed a Commissioner of the Peace for Kent County, 30 Nov 1732. (Ref: Maryland State Archives, Governor and Council Commissioner Records, 1726-1794, p. 33); commissioned a Coroner for Kent County, 16 Jul 1737. (Ref: Maryland Commission Book No. 82, p. 49; *Maryland Historical Magazine*, Vol. XXVI, p. 149)

Blair, John, appointed Constable of Conogo-cheague [Conococheague] Hundred in Frederick County, 1771. (Ref: "Frederick County Minute Book, March 1771, Extracts by Patricia Abelard Andersen," *Western Maryland Genealogy*, Vol. 18, No. 1, January 2002, p. 26)

Blair, William, of Frederick County, Court Justice, 1763. (Ref: *This Was The Life: Excerpts from the Judgment Records of Frederick County, Maryland, 1748-1765*, by Millard Milburn Rice, p. 242); appointed a Commissioner of the Peace on 12 Mar 1763, 2 Apr 1770 and 15 Aug 1774. (Ref: Maryland State Archives, Governor and Council Commissioner Records, 1726-1794, pp. 209, 250, 284)

Blake, Thomas, see Negro Miall.

Blakistone, Richard, see Christopher Gist.

Blewer, John, registration of sloop *Ann*, 40 tons, built in Somerset County, 1737. Isaac Handy, master. James Blewer and Isaac Handy, owners. 8 Apr 1738. (Ref: Maryland Commission Book No. 82, p. 52; *Maryland Historical Magazine*, Vol. XXVI, p. 150)

Blyth, Joseph, see Sluyter Bouchell.

Boardman, James, of Prince George's County, convicted felon, executed on 25 Nov 1730. (Ref: Maryland State Archives, Governor and Council Commissioner Records, 1726-1794, p. 13)

Bodeker, Diederick William, planter, of Baltimore County, native of Germany, naturalized 18 Aug 1739. (Ref: Maryland Commission Book No. 82, p. 76; *Maryland Historical Magazine*, Vol. XXVI, p. 154)

Bolding, Thomas, appointed a Commissioner of the Peace for Cecil County, 20 Feb 1774. (Ref: Maryland State Archives, Governor and Council Commissioner Records, 1726-1794, p. 281)

Bolton, John, commissioned a Coroner of Kent County, August 1770 and 16 Aug 1773. (Ref: Maryland Commission Book No. 82, pp. 248, 323; *Maryland Historical Magazine*, Vol. XXVI, p. 361 and Vol. XXVII, p. 35)

Bond, George, Jr., appointed Constable of the Upper Part of Antietam Hundred in Frederick County, 1771. (Ref: "Frederick County Minute Book, March 1771, Extracts by Patricia Abelard Andersen," *Western Maryland Genealogy*, Vol. 18, No. 1, January 2002, p. 26)

Bond, John, appointed a Commissioner of the Peace for St. Mary's County, 1 Apr 1736. (Ref: Maryland State Archives, Governor and Council Commissioner Records, 1726-1794, p. 51)

Bond, John, doctor, appointed a Commissioner of the Peace for Calvert County, 26 Feb 1765. (Ref: Maryland State Archives, Governor and Council Commissioner Records, 1726-1794, p. 222)

Bond, John, of Fell's Point, was appointed a Commissioner of the Peace for Baltimore County, 20 Nov 1769. (Ref: Maryland State Archives, Governor and Council Commissioner Records, 1726-1794, p. 248)

Bond, Thomas, was appointed a Commissioner of the Peace for Baltimore County, 31 Oct 1768. (Ref: Maryland State Archives, Governor and Council Commissioner Records, 1726-1794, p. 238)

Bond, Thomas (d. c1797), appointed a Commissioner of the Peace for St. Mary's County, 26 Apr 1764. (Ref: Maryland State Archives, Governor and Council Commissioner Records, 1726-1794, p. 215); see Negro Abraham.

Bond, Thomas, of Thomas (c1730-1800), was appointed a Commissioner of the Peace for Harford County, 20 Feb 1774. (Ref: Maryland State Archives, Governor and Council Commissioner Records, 1726-1794, p. 281)

Bond, William, appointed a Commissioner of the Peace for Baltimore County, 5 Dec 1739. (Ref: Maryland State Archives, Governor and Council Commissioner Records, 1726-1794, p. 66)

Bond, William, Jr., appointed a Commissioner of the Peace for Baltimore County, 9 Apr 1773. (Ref: Maryland State Archives, Governor and Council Commissioner Records, 1726-1794, p. 266)

Bond, Zachariah (d. c1776), appointed a Commissioner of the Peace for St. Mary's County, 1 Aug 1746 and 28 Oct 1747. (Ref: Maryland State Archives, Governor and Council Commissioner Records, 1726-1794, pp. 93, 102)

Bonell, William, appointed Constable, Andietum [Antietam] Hundred in Frederick County, 1751. (Ref: *This Was The Life: Excerpts from the Judgment Records of Frederick County, Maryland, 1748-1765*, by Millard Milburn Rice, p. 61)

Boone, Charles, of Anne Arundel County, appointed Constable of Broad Neck Hundred in 1774. (Ref: Anne Arundel County Court Minutes, 1725-1757, 1774)

Boone, Humphrey, appointed a Commissioner of the Peace for Anne Arundel County, 8 Aug 1746. (Ref: Maryland State Archives, Governor and Council

Commissioner Records, 1726-1794, p. 93); Court Justice, 1754. (Ref: Anne Arundel County Court Minutes, 1725-1757)

Booth, Bartholomew, appointed a Commissioner of the Peace for Frederick County, 17 Feb 1775. (Ref: Maryland State Archives, Governor and Council Commissioner Records, 1726-1794, p. 287)

Booth, John, see Negro Peter.

Bordley, James, appointed a Commissioner of the Peace for Queen Anne's County, 13 Mar 1773. (Ref: Maryland State Archives, Governor and Council Commissioner Records, 1726-1794, p. 265)

Bordley, John Beale (1726-1804), was appointed a member of his Lordship's Honorable Council, 4 May 1768. (*Archives of Maryland*, Vol. XXXII, "Proceedings of the Council of Maryland, 1761-1770," p. 232)

Bordley, Stephen (c1710-1764), of Annapolis, Anne Arundel County, served on the Committee of Laws, 1755. (Ref: *Archives of Maryland*, Vol. LII, "Proceedings and Acts of the General Assembly of Maryland, 1755-1756," pp. 46, 61)

Bordley, Thomas, appointed a Commissioner of the Peace for Kent County, 20 Oct 1746. (Ref: Maryland State Archives, Governor and Council Commissioner Records, 1726-1794, p. 94)

Bordley, William, appointed a Commissioner of the Peace for Cecil County, 23 Aug 1756 and 2 Jun 1774. (Ref: Maryland State Archives, Governor and Council Commissioner Records, 1726-1794, pp. 168, 283)

Boreing, Joshua, Constable of North Hundred in Baltimore County, 1773. (Ref: *Inhabitants of Baltimore County, 1763-1774*, by Henry C. Peden, Jr., 1989, p. 65, citing a 1773 List of Taxables)

Borwell, John, of Anne Arundel Co., convicted burglar, was executed on 12 Oct 1770. (Ref: Maryland State Archives, Governor and Council Commissioner Records, 1726-1794, p. 240)

Bosley, James, see Negro Cesar.

Boteler, Alexander, appointed Constable of the Lower Part of Kittocton [Catoctin] Hundred in Frederick County, 1769. (Ref: "Frederick County Court Minutes, March 1769," by Patricia Abelard Andersen, *Western Maryland Genealogy*, Vol. 15, No. 2, April 1999, p. 63)

Boteler, Henry, appointed Constable of the Lower Part of Andiatum [Antietam] Hundred in Frederick County in 1760. (Ref: *This Was The Life: Excerpts from the Judgment Records of Frederick County, Maryland, 1748-1765*, by Millard Milburn Rice, p. 216)

Bouchell, Sluyter, registration of sloop *Bohemia*, 30 tons, built in Cecil County, 1749. Joseph Blyth, master. Sluyter Bouchell, owner. 17 Mar 1749/50. (Ref: Maryland Commission Book No. 82, p. 155; *Maryland Historical Magazine*, Vol. XXVI, p. 351)

Boucher, Jonathan (d. 1804), reverend, was inducted into St. Anne's Parish, Anne Arundel County, 10 May 1770. (Ref: Maryland Commission Book No. 82, p. 241; *Maryland Historical Magazine*, Vol. XXVI, p. 361); induction into Queen Anne's Parish, Prince George's County, 11 Nov 1771. (Ref: Maryland Commission Book No. 82, p. 273; *Maryland Historical Magazine*, Vol. XXVII, p. 31)

Boulte, Kenelm, was commissioned a Coroner of St. Mary's County, 13 Apr 1744. (Ref: Maryland Commission Book No. 82, p. 109; *Maryland Historical Magazine*, Vol. XXVI, p. 251)

Bourdillon, Benedict (d. 1745), reverend, was inducted into Somerset Parish, Somerset County, 3 Jan 1737/8. (Ref: Maryland Commission Book No. 82, p. 51; *Maryland Historical Magazine*, Vol. XXVI, p. 150); resignation from the Parish of Somerset in Somerset County. 16 May 1739. On same day, induction into St. John's Parish, Baltimore County. (Ref: Maryland Commission Book No. 82, p. 72; *Maryland Historical Magazine*, Vol. XXVI, p. 153); native of Geneva, resignation from St. John's Parish, Baltimore County. 24 Jul 1739. On same day, induction into St. Paul's Parish, Baltimore County and patent of naturalization to him, his wife Johanna Gertruijj and his son Andrew Theodore. (Ref: Maryland Commission Book No. 82, p. 76; *Maryland Historical Magazine*, Vol. XXVI, p. 154)

Bowers, Boardley, see Negro Lem.

Bowie, Allen, appointed a Commissioner of the Peace for Prince George's County, 22 Nov 1752. (Ref: Maryland State Archives, Governor and Council Commissioner Records, 1726-1794, p. 135, spelled his name Allan); appointed Constable of Newfoundland Hundred in Frederick County in 1763. (Ref: *This Was The Life: Excerpts from the Judgment Records of*

Frederick County, Maryland, 1748-1765, by Millard Milburn Rice, p. 249, spelled his name Allan)

Bowie, John (1747-1802), reverend, induction into Worcester Parish, Worcester County, 12 Jun 1773. (Ref: Maryland Commission Book No. 82, p. 318; *Maryland Historical Magazine*, Vol. XXVII, p. 34)

Bowie, Walter, see Negro Ben.

Bowie, William (1721-1791, was appointed a Commissioner of the Peace for Prince George's County, 25 Jul 1759. (Ref: Maryland State Archives, Governor and Council Commissioner Records, 1726-1794, p. 185)

Bowles, George, appointed a Commissioner of the Peace for St. Mary's County, 9 Jun 1732. (Ref: Maryland State Archives, Governor and Council Commissioner Records, 1726-1794, p. 24); commissioned Ranger for St. Mary's County, 17 Aug 1737. (Ref: Maryland Commission Book No. 82, p. 50; *Maryland Historical Magazine*, Vol. XXVI, p. 149); commissioned Ranger of St. Mary's County, 12 Mar 1747/8. (Ref: Maryland Commission Book No. 82, p. 133; *Maryland Historical Magazine*, Vol. XXVI, p. 262)

Bowles, Thomas, magistrate of Frederick County, 1766; appointed a Commissioner of the Peace for Frederick County, 2 Mar 1775. (Ref: *Archives of Maryland*, Vol. XXXII, "Proceedings of the Council of Maryland, 1761-1770," p. 166; Maryland State Archives, Governor and Council Commissioner Records, 1726-1794, p. 288)

Boyce, Roger, appointed a Commissioner of the Peace for Calvert County, 29 May 1734 and 22 Oct 1741. (Ref: Maryland State Archives, Governor and Council Commissioner Records, 1726-1794, pp. 42, 72)

Boyce, Roger [Jr.], was commissioned Sheriff of Baltimore County, 4 Nov 1748. (Ref: Maryland State Archives, Governor and Council Commissioner Records, 1726-1794, p. 108); appointed a Commissioner of the Peace for Baltimore County, 8 Nov 1752. (Ref: Maryland State Archives, Governor and Council Commissioner Records, 1726-1794, p. 135); see Negro Jacob.

Boyd, Archibald, appointed a Commissioner of the Peace for Frederick County, 17 Feb 1775. (Ref: Maryland State Archives, Governor and Council Commissioner Records, 1726-1794, p. 287)

Boyd, Benjamin, was appointed Constable of Patuxent Hundred in Prince George's County, now Frederick County, 1742. (Ref: Prince George's County Court Records, 1736-1748, Extracts by Patricia Abelard Andersen, *Western Maryland Genealogy*, Vol. 18, No. 1, January 2002, p. 38, spelled his name Boyde)

Boyd, George, registration of sloop *William*, 25 tons, built at Patowmeck [Potomac] River, 1735. Samuel Cannon, master. George Boyd, owner. March, 1735/6. (Ref: Maryland Commission Book No. 82, p. 42; *Maryland Historical Magazine*, Vol. XXVI, p. 146)

Boyd, George, Jr., appointed Constable of the Upper Part of Andietam [Antietam] Hundred in Frederick County, 1769. (Ref: "Frederick County Court Minutes November 1769 by Patricia Abelard Andersen," *Western Maryland Genealogy*, Vol. 16, No. 1, January 2000, p. 33)

Boyd, John, see Francis Mercier and Richard Floud.

Boyle, James, see Terrence Conner.

Bozman, John, commissioned High Sheriff of Talbot County, 19 Oct 1764. (Ref: Maryland State Archives, Governor and Council Commissioner Records, 1726-1794, p. 208)

Bozman, Risdon, appointed a Commissioner of the Peace for Talbot County, 29 Oct 1730. (Ref: Maryland State Archives, Governor and Council Commissioner Records, 1726-1794, p. 17); commissioned Deputy Surveyor of Talbot County, 18 Nov 1743. (Ref: Maryland Commission Book No. 82, p. 106; *Maryland Historical Magazine*, Vol. XXVI, p. 250)

Bozman, Thomas (c1693-1752), was a Commissioner of the Peace for Talbot County by 1726 and was commissioned again on 30 Jun 1727, 29 Oct 1730, 20 Feb 1731/2 and 22 Oct 1751; sheriff at various times between 1720 and 1733; justice of the Court of Oyer and Terminer and Gaol [Jail] Delivery, 1741. (Ref: Maryland State Archives, Governor and Council Commissioner Records, 1726-1794, pp. 6, 17, 22, 129; *A Biographical Dictionary of the Maryland Legislature, 1635-1789*, by Edward C. Papenfuse, et al., Vol. A-H, p. 157)

Bracco, John (c1725-1794), was appointed a Commissioner of the Peace for Queen Anne's County, 8 Mar 1754. (Ref: Maryland State Archives, Governor

Colonial Maryland Commissions, Appointments, and Other Proceedings, 1726-1776

and Council Commissioner Records, 1726-1794, p. 144); appointed to a Committee to Inspect the Accounts and Proceedings of the Commissioners for Emitting Bills of Credit, 25 Feb 1755. (Ref: *Archives of Maryland*, Vol. LII, "Proceedings and Acts of the General Assembly of Maryland, 1755-1756," p. 57; appointed to the Committee for Enquiring into the Accounts and Vouchers Relating to the Disposal of the Sum of £6000 Granted by Act of Assembly for His Majesty's Service, 14 Mar 1755. (Ref: *Archives of Maryland*, Vol. LII, "Proceedings and Acts of the General Assembly of Maryland, 1755-1756," p. 81); Court Justice, Talbot County, 1774. (*Calendar of Maryland State Papers, No. 1 The Black Books*, p. 211)

Bradford, Benjamin, commissioned High Sheriff of Cecil County, 18 Oct 1739 to at least 1756. (Ref: Maryland State Archives, Governor and Council Commissioner Records, 1726-1794, p. 65); *Archives of Maryland*, Vol. LII, "Proceedings and Acts of the General Assembly of Maryland, 1755-1756," p. 232)

Bradford, John, reverend, induction into Christ Church Parish in Queen Anne's County, 11 Jan 1741/2. (Ref: Maryland Commission Book No. 82, p. 89; *Maryland Historical Magazine*, Vol. XXVI, p. 245); resignation from Christ Church Parish, Queen Anne's County, 20 Nov 1744. On same day, induction into St. Mary Anne's Parish in Cecil County. (Ref: Maryland Commission Book No. 82, p. 111; *Maryland Historical Magazine*, Vol. XXVI, p. 253)

Bradford, William, was commissioned one of the Coroners of Baltimore County, 23 Mar 1742/3. (Ref: Maryland Commission Book No. 82, p. 101; *Maryland Historical Magazine*, Vol. XXVI, p. 249)

Bradlee, John, registration of schooner *Mary and John*, 4 tons, built in Somerset County, 1734. John Bradlee, master and owner. 6 Jan 1737/8. (Ref: Maryland Commission Book No. 82, p. 51; *Maryland Historical Magazine*, Vol. XXVI, p. 150)

Bradley, Robert, appointed a Commissioner of the Peace for Prince George's County, 18 Feb 1731/2. (Ref: Maryland State Archives, Governor and Council Commissioner Records, 1726-1794, p. 21)

Bramley, John, see William Dames.

Branner, Henry, of Prince George's County, native of Germany, naturalized 3 May 1740, and also his son John. (Ref: Maryland Commission Book No. 82, p. 81; *Maryland Historical Magazine*, Vol. XXVI, p. 156)

Branner, Jacob, of Prince George's County, native of Germany, naturalized 3 May 1740, and also his children Peter, Michael, John, Jacob, Mary and Elizabeth. (Ref: Maryland Commission Book No. 82, p. 81; *Maryland Historical Magazine*, Vol. XXVI, p. 156)

Branner, John, of Prince George's County, native of Germany, naturalized 3 May 1740, and also his children John, Jacob, Catherine, Barbara and Mary. (Ref: Maryland Commission Book No. 82, p. 80; *Maryland Historical Magazine*, Vol. XXVI, p. 156)

Branner, Joseph, of Prince George's County, native of Germany, naturalized 3 May 1740, and also his son Elias. (Ref: Maryland Commission Book No. 82, p. 80; *Maryland Historical Magazine*, Vol. XXVI, p. 156)

Brashears, William, Jr., appointed Constable of Linganore Hundred in Frederick County, 1769. (Ref: "Frederick County Court Minutes, March 1769," by Patricia Abelard Andersen, *Western Maryland Genealogy*, Vol. 15, No. 2, April 1999, p. 63)

Brealy, Nicholas, of Kent County, convicted felon and burglary, executed on 5 Mar 1740/41. (Ref: Maryland State Archives, Governor and Council Commissioner Records, 1726-1794, p. 69)

Brent (Brendt), George (d. 1782), appointed a Commissioner of the Peace for Frederick County, 2 Nov 1773 and 15 Aug 1774. (Ref: Maryland State Archives, Governor and Council Commissioner Records, 1726-1794, pp. 278, 284)

Brent, Henry, see Negro George.

Brerewood, Thomas, appointed a Commissioner of the Peace for Baltimore County, 4 Oct 1737. (Ref: Maryland State Archives, Governor and Council Commissioner Records, 1726-1794, p. 57)

Brerewood, Thomas, appointed a Commissioner of the Peace for Baltimore County, 9 Apr 1773. (Ref: Maryland State Archives, Governor and Council Commissioner Records, 1726-1794, p. 266)

Brett, John, see George Rock.

Brewer, John, of Prince George's County, convicted felon, was executed on 10 Nov 1736. (Ref: Maryland State Archives, Governor and Council Commissioner

Records, 1726-1794, p. 54)

Brice, John, appointed a Commissioner of the Peace for Anne Arundel County, 30 May 1731. (Ref: Maryland State Archives, Governor and Council Commissioner Records, 1726-1794, p. 19)

Briscoe, Hanson, appointed a Commissioner of the Peace for Somerset County, 26 Jul 1773. (Ref: Maryland State Archives, Governor and Council Commissioner Records, 1726-1794, p. 272)

Briscoe, James, of St. Mary's County, pardon for manslaughter, 18 Sep 1745. (Ref: Maryland Commission Book No. 82, p. 117; *Maryland Historical Magazine*, Vol. XXVI, p. 255)

Briscoe, John, appointed a Commissioner of the Peace for Charles County, 2 Mar 1726/7 and 31 Mar 1736. (Ref: Maryland State Archives, Governor and Council Commissioner Records, 1726-1794, pp. 2, 51)

Briscoe, John, appointed a Commissioner of the Peace for St. Mary's County, 11 May 1769. (Ref: Maryland State Archives, Governor and Council Commissioner Records, 1726-1794, p. 241)

Briscoe, Philip, appointed a Commissioner of the Peace for Charles County, 2 Oct 1771. (Ref: Maryland State Archives, Governor and Council Commissioner Records, 1726-1794, p. 258)

Briscoe, Samuel, appointed a Commissioner of the Peace for Charles County, 2 Oct 1771. (Ref: Maryland State Archives, Governor and Council Commissioner Records, 1726-1794, p. 258)

Britt, Robert, of Baltimore County, Ranger, 9 Aug 1775. (Ref: *Calendar of Maryland State Papers, The Red Books*, No. 4, Part 1, p. 5)

Brogden, William (d. 1770), reverend, induction into Dorchester Parish, Dorchester County, 20 Feb 1735/6; resignation from Dorchester Parish, Dorchester County, 22 Oct 1737; induction into All Hallows Parish, Anne Arundel County, 18 Jul 1739. (Ref: Maryland Commission Book No. 82, pp. 41, 51, 76; *Maryland Historical Magazine*, Vol. XXVI, pp. 146, 150, 154); see Edward Gant and John Forbes.

Brogden, William (1742/43-1824), appointed a Commissioner of the Peace for Anne Arundel County, 26 Jul 1773. (Ref: Maryland State Archives, Governor and Council Commissioner Records, 1726-1794, p. 272)

Brome (Broome), John, Jr. (1703-1748), was appointed a Commissioner of the Peace for Calvert County, 9 Dec 1731. (Ref: Maryland State Archives, Governor and Council Commissioner Records, 1726-1794, p. 20)

Brook, Leonard, see Patrick Creagh.

Brooke, Benjamin, see Negro Wapping.

Brooke, Isaac, commissioned Deputy Surveyor of Prince George's County, 29 Apr 1747. (Ref: Maryland Commission Book No. 82, p. 129; *Maryland Historical Magazine*, Vol. XXVI, p. 260); commissioned Deputy Surveyor of Frederick County, 12 Nov 1748. (Ref: Maryland Commission Book No. 82, p. 138; *Maryland Historical Magazine*, Vol. XXVI, p. 343)

Brooke, Joseph, see Patrick Creagh.

Brooke, Richard (1716-1783), commissioned Deputy Surveyor of Prince George's County, 12 Nov 1748. (Ref: Maryland Commission Book No. 82, p. 138; *Maryland Historical Magazine*, Vol. XXVI, p. 343)

Brooke, Thomas (1683-1744), commissioned Sheriff of Prince George's County, 19 Aug 1730. (Ref: Maryland State Archives, Governor and Council Commissioner Records, 1726-1794, p. 20)

Brooke, Thomas, Jr. (1706-1749), appointed a Commissioner of the Peace for Prince George's County, 18 Nov 1746. (Ref: Maryland State Archives, Governor and Council Commissioner Records, 1726-1794, p. 95)

Brooks, James, of Annapolis, commissioned Clerk of the Court and Keeper of the Records of the High Court of Appeals and Errors. 15 Dec 1767. (Ref: Maryland Commission Book No. 82, pp. 206, 305; *Maryland Historical Magazine*, Vol. XXVI, pp. 356-357, and Vol. XXVII, p. 33)

Broome, Henry, commissioned a Coroner of Calvert County, 19 Dec 1769. (Ref: Maryland Commission Book No. 82, p. 233; *Maryland Historical Magazine*, Vol. XXVI, p. 360)

Brown, Charles, appointed a Commissioner of the Peace for Queen Anne's County, 18 May 1758. (Ref: Maryland State Archives, Governor and Council Commissioner Records, 1726-1794, p. 180)

Brown, Charles, registration of sloop *The Whim* (formerly called the *Sarah*), 30 tons, built at Free

Town, Massachusetts, 1729. William Husband, master. Michael Coulter and Charles Brown, owners. 1 Aug 1735. (Ref: Maryland Commission Book No. 82, p. 33; *Maryland Historical Magazine*, Vol. XXVI, p. 144)

Brown, Gustavus, appointed a Commissioner of the Peace for Charles County, 2 Mar 1726/7. (Ref: Maryland State Archives, Governor and Council Commissioner Records, 1726-1794, p. 2)

Brown, Gustavus, appointed a Commissioner of the Peace for Charles County, 2 Oct 1771. (Ref: Maryland State Archives, Governor and Council Commissioner Records, 1726-1794, p. 258)

Brown, James (d. 1770), appointed a Commissioner of the Peace for Dorchester County, 22 Oct 1736. (Ref: Maryland State Archives, Governor and Council Commissioner Records, 1726-1794, p. 53)

Brown, James, appointed a Commissioner of the Peace for Queen Anne's County, 6 Jun 1739 and 28 Feb 1742/3. (Ref: Maryland State Archives, Governor and Council Commissioner Records, 1726-1794, pp. 63, 76)

Brown, John (c1725-1793), was appointed a Commissioner of the Peace for Queen Anne's County, 18 May 1758. (Ref: Maryland State Archives, Governor and Council Commissioner Records, 1726-1794, p. 180); Court Justice, 1774. (*Calendar of Maryland State Papers, No. 1 The Black Books*, p. 215); see Daniel Cheston, George Steuart and John Pagan.

Brown, Jonas, appointed Constable of Burnt House Woods Hundred in Frederick County, 1769. (Ref: "Frederick County Court Minutes, March 1769," by Patricia Abelard Andersen, *Western Maryland Genealogy*, Vol. 15, No. 2, April 1999, p. 63)

Brown, Joshua, appointed Constable of Pipe Creek Hundred in Frederick County, 1771. (Ref: "Frederick County Minute Book, March 1771, Extracts by Patricia Abelard Andersen," *Western Maryland Genealogy*, Vol. 18, No. 1, January 2002, p. 25)

Brown, Margaret, see Negro Charles.

Brown, Richard (1724-1789), reverend, was inducted into King and Queen Parish, St. Mary's County, 21 Jan 1750/1. (Ref: Maryland Commission Book No. 82, p. 148; *Maryland Historical Magazine*, Vol. XXVI, p. 347)

Brown, Richard, appointed Constable of Pipe Creek Hundred in Frederick County in 1763. (Ref: *This Was The Life: Excerpts from the Judgment Records of Frederick County, Maryland, 1748-1765*, by Millard Milburn Rice, p. 249)

Brown, Robert, appointed a Commissioner of the Peace for Baltimore County, 6 Mar 1775. (Ref: Maryland State Archives, Governor and Council Commissioner Records, 1726-1794, p. 288)

Brown, Thomas, of Frederick County, indicted for stealing a bell and collar off the neck of a horse belonging to the late Henry Crampton in 1749. (Ref: *This Was The Life: Excerpts from the Judgment Records of Frederick County, Maryland, 1748-1765*, by Millard Milburn Rice, p. 15)

Brown, Thomas, reverend, inducted into Dorchester Parish, Dorchester County, 30 May 1772. (Ref: Maryland Commission Book No. 82, p. 280; *Maryland Historical Magazine*, Vol. XXVII, p. 31)

Bruce, Normand (d. 1811), commissioned High Sheriff of St. Mary's County, 8 Oct 1761. (Ref: Maryland State Archives, Governor and Council Commissioner Records, 1726-1794, p. 191); appointed a Commissioner of the Peace for Frederick County, 1 Aug 1768, 2 Nov 1773 and 15 Aug 1774. (Ref: Maryland State Archives, Governor and Council Commissioner Records, 1726-1794, pp. 235, 278, 284)

Bruff, ----, of Talbot County, commissioned a Coroner of Talbot County, 19 Mar 1749/50. (Ref: Maryland Commission Book No. 82, p. 143; *Maryland Historical Magazine*, Vol. XXVI, p. 345, did not give his first name, but it was probably Richard Bruff who died in Talbot County in 1760 as noted in the biographical sketch of his son William Bruff in *A Biographical Dictionary of the Maryland Legislature, 1635-1789*, by Edward C. Papenfuse, et al., Vol. A-H, p. 177)

Bruff, Richard, see James Dickinson.

Bruff, Thomas, appointed a Commissioner of the Peace for Somerset County, 19 May 1774. (Ref: Maryland State Archives, Governor and Council Commissioner Records, 1726-1794, p. 282)

Bryan, Eleanor, see Negro Abraham.

Buchanan, Andrew (c1733-1786), was appointed a Commissioner of the Peace for Baltimore County, 20

Nov 1769. (Ref: Maryland State Archives, Governor and Council Commissioner Records, 1726-1794, p. 248); appointed a Justice in Baltimore County, 22 Feb 1773. (Ref: *Inhabitants of Baltimore County, 1763-1774*, by Henry C. Peden, Jr., 1989, p. 49, citing *Calendar of Maryland State Papers, No. 1 The Black Books*, p. 208)

Buchanan, George, appointed a Commissioner of the Peace for Prince George's County, 14 Mar 1736/7. (Ref: Maryland State Archives, Governor and Council Commissioner Records, 1726-1794, p. 53)

Buchanan, George (c1697-1750), doctor, was appointed a Commissioner of the Peace for Baltimore County, 13 Oct 1732. (Ref: Maryland State Archives, Governor and Council Commissioner Records, 1726-1794, p. 26)

Buchanan, John, see James Russell.

Buchanan, Lloyd (1729-c1762), of Baltimore County, attorney, Court Prosecutor and Clerk of Indictments, 1755. (Ref: *Archives of Maryland*, Vol. LII, "Proceedings and Acts of the General Assembly of Maryland, 1755-1756," p. 149; *A Biographical Dictionary of the Maryland Legislature, 1635-1789*, by Edward C. Papenfuse, et al., Vol. A-H, p. 180)

Buchanan, William, Sr. (1732-1804), appointed a Commissioner of the Peace for Baltimore County, 30 May 1774. (Ref: Maryland State Archives, Governor and Council Commissioner Records, 1726-1794, p. 283); appointed to represent Baltimore County in the Provincial Convention, 1775. (Ref: *Calendar of Maryland State Papers, The Red Books*, No. 4, Part 1, p. 3)

Buckner, William, appointed a Commissioner of the Peace for Baltimore County, 1 Nov 1729. (Ref: Maryland State Archives, Governor and Council Commissioner Records, 1726-1794, p. 12)

Buckner, William, appointed a Commissioner of the Peace for Baltimore County, 22 Oct 1728. (Ref: Maryland State Archives, Governor and Council Commissioner Records, 1726-1794, p. 8)

Bullard, Henry, commissioned a Coroner of Somerset County, 30 Nov 1742. (Ref: Maryland Commission Book No. 82, p. 99; *Maryland Historical Magazine*, Vol. XXVI, p. 248)

Bullen, John, appointed a Commissioner of the Peace for Anne Arundel County, 14 Nov 1741. (Ref: Maryland State Archives, Governor and Council Commissioner Records, 1726-1794, p. 72); Court Justice, Anne Arundel County, 1754. (Ref: Anne Arundel County Court Minutes, 1725-1757)

Bullen, Thomas, appointed a Commissioner of the Peace for Talbot County, 12 Jun 1739. (Ref: Maryland State Archives, Governor and Council Commissioner Records, 1726-1794, p. 64)

Bullingnee, Anne, spinster, late of Anne Arundel County, pardoned for theft, 11 Apr 1740. (Ref: Maryland Commission Book No. 82, p. 80; *Maryland Historical Magazine*, Vol. XXVI, p. 155)

Buncle, Alexander, registration of sloop *Royal Oak*, 30 tons, built in Somerset County, 1739. Samuel Wise, master. Alexander Buncle, owner. 1 Nov 1739. (Ref: Maryland Commission Book No. 82, p. 78; *Maryland Historical Magazine*, Vol. XXVI, p. 155); registration of sloop *Restoration*, 15 tons, built in Somerset County, 1742. Samuel Wise, master. Alexander Buncle, owner. 23 Jul 1742. (Ref: Maryland Commission Book No. 82, p. 93; *Maryland Historical Magazine*, Vol. XXVI, p. 246)

Bundrick, Nicholas, see Mary Macknaul.

Burch, Leonard, see Negro Pompey.

Burdus, Richard, was commissioned one of the Coroners of Anne Arundel County, 10 Nov 1743 and 10 Apr 1747. (Ref: Maryland Commission Book No. 82, pp. 105, 128; *Maryland Historical Magazine*, Vol. XXVI, pp. 250, 260)

Burgess, Basil, appointed a Commissioner of the Peace for Anne Arundel County, 16 Dec 1769. (Ref: Maryland State Archives, Governor and Council Commissioner Records, 1726-1794, p. 249); commissioned Deputy Surveyor of Anne Arundel County, 23 Oct 1771, 29 Apr 1773 and 26 Jul 1773. (Ref: Maryland Commission Book No. 82, pp. 272, 311; *Maryland Historical Magazine*, Vol. XXVII, pp. 31, 33; Maryland State Archives, Governor and Council Commissioner Records, 1726-1794, pp. 249, 272); Court Justice, 1774. (Ref: Anne Arundel County Court Minutes, 1725-1757, 1774)

Burgess, Charles, Jr., appointed Constable of Western Branch Hundred in Prince George's County, now Frederick County, 1738. (Ref: Prince George's County Court Records, 1736-1748, Extracts by Patricia Abelard Andersen, *Western Maryland*

Genealogy, Vol. 18, No. 1, January 2002, p. 35)

Burgess, Edward (c1733-1809), appointed a Commissioner of the Peace for Frederick County, 13 Mar 1773 and 15 Aug 1774. (Ref: Maryland State Archives, Governor and Council Commissioner Records, 1726-1794, pp. 265, 284); Court Judge, 1774. (*Calendar of Maryland State Papers, No. 1 The Black Books*, p. 217)

Burgess, John, appointed a Commissioner of the Peace for Anne Arundel County, 11 Jun 1762. (Ref: Maryland State Archives, Governor and Council Commissioner Records, 1726-1794, p. 203); appointed Constable in the Lower Part of Road [Rhode] River Hundred in 1774. (Ref: Anne Arundel County Court Minutes, 1725-1757, 1774)

Burgoon, Jacob, native of Germany, denization, 30 Sep 1771. (Ref: Maryland Commission Book No. 82, p. 270; *Maryland Historical Magazine*, Vol. XXVII, p. 30)

Burk, Jeremiah, see Robert Harvey.

Burke, Thomas, of Charles County, convicted felon, was executed on 28 Jan 1731/2. (Ref: Maryland State Archives, Governor and Council Commissioner Records, 1726-1794, p. 21)

Burley, John, appointed a Commissioner of the Peace for Anne Arundel County, 12 Jun 1739. (Ref: Maryland State Archives, Governor and Council Commissioner Records, 1726-1794, p. 63)

Burn, Sweetnam, see John Seegar.

Burton, John, appointed Constable of the Upper Part of Kittocton [Catoctin] Hundred in Frederick County, 1769. (Ref: "Frederick County Court Minutes, March 1769," by Patricia Abelard Andersen, *Western Maryland Genealogy*, Vol. 15, No. 2, April 1999, p. 63, mistakenly listed his name as John Barto; "Frederick County Court Minutes, June 1769," by Patricia Abelard Andersen, *Western Maryland Genealogy*, Vol. 15, No. 4, April 1999, p. 171, listed it as John Burton)

Burton, Thomas, appointed Constable of the Upper Part of Kittocton [Catoctin] Hundred in Frederick County, 1769, 1771. (Ref: "Frederick County Court Minutes November 1769 by Patricia Abelard Andersen," *Western Maryland Genealogy*, Vol. 16, No. 1, January 2000, p. 33; "Frederick County Minute Book, March 1771, Extracts by Patricia Abelard Andersen," *Western Maryland Genealogy*, Vol. 18, No. 1, January 2002, p. 26)

Burton, William, appointed a Commissioner of the Peace for Worcester County, 11 Dec 1742. (Ref: Maryland State Archives, Governor and Council Commissioner Records, 1726-1794, p. 75)

Bussey, George, Jr., appointed Constable of Seneca Hundred in Prince George's County, now Frederick County, 1742. (Ref: Prince George's County Court Records, 1736-1748, Extracts by Patricia Abelard Andersen, *Western Maryland Genealogy*, Vol. 18, No. 1, January 2002, p. 38)

Butler, Edward, of Charles County, convicted felon for robbing Trinity Parish Church, pardoned 13 May 1754. (Ref: *Archives of Maryland*, Vol. XXXI, "Proceedings of the Council of Maryland, 1753-1761," p. 32)

Butler, Edward, of Frederick County, Constable in Kittocton [Catoctin] Hundred, 1758. (Ref: *This Was The Life: Excerpts from the Judgment Records of Frederick County, Maryland, 1748-1765*, by Millard Milburn Rice, p. 185)

Butler, Gamaliel, carpenter, registration of schooner *Cumberland*, 15 tons, built at Annapolis, 1747. Martin Johnson, master. Gamaliel Butler and John Tullap, owners. 10 Aug 1747. (Ref: Maryland Commission Book No. 82, p. 131; *Maryland Historical Magazine*, Vol. XXVI, p. 261)

Butler, Peter, was Under Sheriff of Frederick County in 1752. (Ref: *This Was The Life: Excerpts from the Judgment Records of Frederick County, Maryland, 1748-1765*, by Millard Milburn Rice, p. 110)

Butler, Ralph, see George Rock.

Butler, Young Charles, see Negro Charles.

Button, Richard, appointed a Commissioner of the Peace for Baltimore County, 6 Mar 1775. (Ref: Maryland State Archives, Governor and Council Commissioner Records, 1726-1794, p. 288)

Byard, Adam, planter, of Baltimore County, native of Germany, naturalized 1 May 1736. (Ref: Maryland Commission Book No. 82, p. 43; *Maryland Historical Magazine*, Vol. XXVI, p. 147)

Byer, Philip, appointed Constable of Burnt House Woods Hundred in Frederick County, 1769. (Ref: "Frederick County Court Minutes November 1769 by

Patricia Abelard Andersen," *Western Maryland Genealogy*, Vol. 16, No. 1, January 2000, p. 32)

Byrne, Patrick, see John Howard.

Caile, John, Clerk of Dorchester County, 1756. (Ref: *Archives of Maryland*, Vol. LII, "Proceedings and Acts of the General Assembly of Maryland, 1755-1756," p. 232)

Caille, Hall, was commissioned High Sheriff of Dorchester County, 27 Oct 1758. (Ref: Maryland State Archives, Governor and Council Commissioner Records, 1726-1794, p. 173)

Calder, Alexander, commissioned High Sheriff of Kent County, 19 Oct 1768. (Ref: Maryland State Archives, Governor and Council Commissioner Records, 1726-1794, p. 226)

Calder, James, commissioned Deputy Surveyor of Baltimore County, 16 Oct 1771. (Ref: Maryland Commission Book No. 82, p. 271; *Maryland Historical Magazine*, Vol. XXVII, p. 30); captain, appointed a Commissioner of the Peace for Baltimore County, 30 May 1774. (Ref: Maryland State Archives, Governor and Council Commissioner Records, 1726-1794, p. 283)

Calder, James, commissioned Deputy Surveyor of that part of Frederick County which lies westward of the Main Branch or River of the Great Conogocheague [Conococheague], 20 Oct 1768. (Ref: Maryland Commission Book No. 82, p. 220; *Maryland Historical Magazine*, Vol. XXVI, p. 358)

Calder, James, see George Steuart, John Wallace, Negro Ben and Negro Charles.

Caldwell, John (d. 1747), was appointed a Commissioner of the Peace for Somerset County, 29 Oct 1730. (Ref: Maryland State Archives, Governor and Council Commissioner Records, 1726-1794, p. 17); merchant, registration of sloop *Mary*, 30 tons, built in Somerset County, 1734, and called the *Martha*. Joshua Calder, master. John Caldwell, owner. 28 Sep 1744. (Ref: Maryland Commission Book No. 82, p. 111; *Maryland Historical Magazine*, Vol. XXVI, p. 253); appointed a Commissioner of the Peace for Worcester County, 1 Jun 1743. (Ref: Maryland State Archives, Governor and Council Commissioner Records, 1726-1794, p. 78; see Henry Lowes.

Caldwell, Joshua, was commissioned Sheriff of Somerset County, 29 Jul 1730. (Ref: Maryland State Archives, Governor and Council Commissioner Records, 1726-1794, p. 20); appointed a Commissioner of the Peace for Somerset County, 20 Oct 1746. (Ref: Maryland State Archives, Governor and Council Commissioner Records, 1726-1794, p. 94); Court Justice, 1753. (*Calendar of Maryland State Papers, No. 1 The Black Books*, p. 112); see John Caldwell.

Calhoun, James, appointed a Commissioner of the Peace for Baltimore County, 30 May 1774. (Ref: Maryland State Archives, Governor and Council Commissioner Records, 1726-1794, p. 283)

Callister, Henry, appointed a Commissioner of the Peace for Kent County, 21 Mar 1760. (Ref: Maryland State Archives, Governor and Council Commissioner Records, 1726-1794, p. 190)

Callo, George, appointed a Commissioner of the Peace for Cecil County, 19 Dec 1751. (Ref: Maryland State Archives, Governor and Council Commissioner Records, 1726-1794, p. 131)

Calvert, Benedict (c1724-1788), esquire, was appointed a Privy Council on 10 May 1753. (Ref: *Archives of Maryland*, Vol. XXXI, "Proceedings of the Council of Maryland, 1753-1761," pp. 8, 14); commissioned Collector of the Port at Patuxent, 9 Jun 1761. Qualified 11 Sep 1761. (Ref: Maryland Commission Book No. 82, p. 158; *Maryland Historical Magazine*, Vol. XXVI, p. 352); commissioned one of the Judges and Registers of the Land Office, 29 Apr 1773. (Ref: Maryland Commission Book No. 82, p. 301; *Maryland Historical Magazine*, Vol. XXVII, p. 32)

Calvert, Charles, appointed a Commissioner of the Peace for Cecil County, Baltimore County, Kent County, Prince George's County, Anne Arundel County, Calvert County, Charles County, St. Mary's County, Queen Anne's County, and Talbot County, 4 Aug 1732 and 10 Aug 1732 and 20 Aug 1733. (Ref: Maryland State Archives, Governor and Council Commissioner Records, 1726-1794, pp. 32-37)

Campbell, Aeneas, of Frederick County, Court Justice, 1769. (Ref: "Frederick County Court Minutes, March 1769," by Patricia Abelard Andersen, *Western Maryland Genealogy*, Vol. 15, No. 2, April 1999, p. 62, spelled his name Eneas); appointed a Commissioner of the Peace, 2 Apr 1770. (Ref: Maryland State Archives, Governor and Council

Commissioner Records, 1726-1794, p. 250); see Enos Campbell.

Campbell, Daniel, merchant, registration of sloop *Batchelor*, 20 tons, built in Somerset County, 1744. Septimus Noell, master. Daniel Campbell and David Ross, owners. 10 Aug 1745. (Ref: Maryland Commission Book No. 82, p. 115; *Maryland Historical Magazine*, Vol. XXVI, p. 255); see James Dick.

Campbell, Ebenezer, appointed a Commissioner of the Peace for Worcester County, 1 Oct 1768, 30 Apr 1770 and 26 Oct 1773. (Ref: Maryland State Archives, Governor and Council Commissioner Records, 1726-1794, pp. 238, 250, 278)

Campbell, Enos, appointed a Commissioner of the Peace for Frederick County, 1 Aug 1768. (Ref: Maryland State Archives, Governor and Council Commissioner Records, 1726-1794, p. 235)

Campbell, Hugh, merchant, registration of schooner *Argyle*, 20 tons, built in Virginia, 1740. James Macarthen, master. 9 Mar 1741/2. (Ref: Maryland Commission Book No. 82, p. 91; *Maryland Historical Magazine*, Vol. XXVI, p. 246)

Campbell, Isaac (1724-1784), reverend, was inducted into Trinity Parish, Charles County, 12 Jun 1751. (Ref: Maryland Commission Book No. 82, p. 149; *Maryland Historical Magazine*, Vol. XXVI, p. 348, listed his name as "Rev. [ ] Campbel;" *Directory of Ministers and the Maryland Churches They Served, 1634-1900*, by Edna Agatha Kanely, Vol. I, A-K, p. 100, listed his name correctly as Isaac Campbell)

Campbell, James, see Negro Charles

Campbell, John, commissioned High Sheriff of Queen Anne's County, 8 Nov 1766. (Ref: Maryland State Archives, Governor and Council Commissioner Records, 1726-1794, p. 219)

Campbell, John, commissioned Sheriff of Cecil County, 1 Nov 1730. (Ref: Maryland State Archives, Governor and Council Commissioner Records, 1726-1794, p. 20)

Campbell, Walter (1665-1738), was appointed a Commissioner of the Peace for Dorchester County, 1 Aug 1729 and 29 Oct 1730. (Ref: Maryland State Archives, Governor and Council Commissioner Records, 1726-1794, pp. 11, 17)

Campble, John, appointed a Commissioner of the Peace for Dorchester County, 22 Oct 1756. (Ref: Maryland State Archives, Governor and Council Commissioner Records, 1726-1794, p. 171)

Cannon, Samuel, see George Boyd.

Carle, James, see Richard Gresham.

Carlisle, Hugh, reverend, induction into St. George's Parish, Baltimore County, 31 Mar 1744. (Ref: Maryland Commission Book No. 82, p. 108; *Maryland Historical Magazine*, Vol. XXVI, p. 251)

Carlisle, John, see John Handy.

Carlyle, John, merchant, of Virginia, registration of snow *Lawson*, 50 tons, built in Great Britain. Hugh Mackdowel, master. John Carlyle, owner. 10 Sep 1746. (Ref: Maryland Commission Book No. 82, p. 122; *Maryland Historical Magazine*, Vol. XXVI, p. 258)

Carmack, John, appointed Constable of Pipe Creek Hundred in Prince George's County, now Frederick County, 1748. (Ref: Prince George's County Court Records, 1736-1738, Extracts by Patricia Abelard Andersen, *Western Maryland Genealogy*, Vol. 18, No. 1, January 2002, p. 46); appointed Deputy Ranger in Frederick County in 1750. (Ref: *This Was The Life: Excerpts from the Judgment Records of Frederick County, Maryland, 1748-1765*, by Millard Milburn Rice, p. 34)

Carmack, William, was appointed Constable of Manor Hundred in Frederick County in 1753. (Ref: *This Was The Life: Excerpts from the Judgment Records of Frederick County, Maryland, 1748-1765*, by Millard Milburn Rice, p. 131)

Carmichael, James, was appointed a Coroner of Queen Anne's County, 17 May 1776. (Ref: Maryland State Archives, Governor and Council Commissioner Records, 1726-1794, p. 402)

Carmichael, Walter, appointed a Commissioner of the Peace for Queen Anne's County, 9 May 1732. (Ref: Maryland State Archives, Governor and Council Commissioner Records, 1726-1794, p. 23)

Carmichael, William, appointed a Commissioner of the Peace for Queen Anne's County, 24 May 1737, 18 May 1758 and 16 Jun 1773. (Ref: Maryland State Archives, Governor and Council Commissioner Records, 1726-1794, pp. 180, 366, 560)

Carr, Charles, see Patrick Creagh.

Carr, John, appointed Constable of the Upper Part of Monocacy Hundred in Frederick County, 1760. (Ref: *This Was The Life: Excerpts from the Judgment Records of Frederick County, Maryland, 1748-1765*, by Millard Milburn Rice, p. 216)

Carr, Moses, labourer, late of Frederick County, pardoned for horse stealing, April 1770. (Ref: Maryland Commission Book No. 82, p. 240; *Maryland Historical Magazine*, Vol. XXVI, p. 361)

Carr, Paul, labourer, late of Frederick County, pardoned for horse stealing, 18 Apr 1772. (Ref: Maryland Commission Book No. 82, p. 276; *Maryland Historical Magazine*, Vol. XXVII, p. 31)

Carroll, Charles (1691-1755), doctor, of Anne Arundel, appointed to a Committee for Enquiring into Ways and Means to Raise a Sum Sufficient for Payment of Eighty Rangers to Defend and Protect the Frontiers, 28 Jun 1755. (Ref: Maryland State Archives, Governor and Council Commissioner Records, 1726-1794, pp. 46, 151); registration of schooner *Baltimore*, 60 tons, built at Annapolis, 1734. Nathaniel Triggs, master. Benjamin Tasker, Daniel Dulany, Charles Carroll, chyrurgeon, Charles Carroll, Jr., and said Charles Carroll, owners. 8 Oct 1735. (Ref: Maryland Commission Book No. 82, p. 38; *Maryland Historical Magazine*, Vol. XXVI, p. 145); see Thomas Dicke.

Carroll, Charles, Jr., see Charles Carroll.

Carter, John, appointed a Commissioner of the Peace for Queen Anne's County, 3 Mar 1726/7. (Ref: Maryland State Archives, Governor and Council Commissioner Records, 1726-1794, p. 2)

Carter, Joseph, commissioned one of the Coroners of Worcester County, 16 Sep 1745. (Ref: Maryland Commission Book No. 82, p. 116; *Maryland Historical Magazine*, Vol. XXVI, p. 255)

Cartledge, Edmund, appointed a Commissioner of the Peace for Prince George's County, 15 Jun 1739. (Ref: Maryland State Archives, Governor and Council Commissioner Records, 1726-1794, p. 64)

Cartwright, John, appointed a Commissioner of the Peace for St. Mary's County, 1749. (Ref: Maryland State Archives, Governor and Council Commissioner Records, 1726-1794, p. 113)

Cartwright, John, commissioned High Sheriff of Charles County, 17 Apr 1738. (Ref: Maryland State Archives, Governor and Council Commissioner Records, 1726-1794, p. 59)

Carty, Enos, of Cecil County, convicted felon, was executed in March 1749/50. (Ref: Maryland State Archives, Governor and Council Commissioner Records, 1726-1794, p. 116)

Cary, John, of Frederick County, magistrate, 1766. (Ref: *Archives of Maryland*, Vol. XXXII, "Proceedings of the Council of Maryland, 1761-1770," p. 166)

Casler, John, appointed Constable of the Upper Part of Kittocton [Catoctin] Hundred in Frederick County, 1771. (Ref: "Frederick County Minute Book, March 1771, Extracts by Patricia Abelard Andersen," *Western Maryland Genealogy*, Vol. 18, No. 1, January 2002, p. 26)

Casson, Henry (d. c1788), appointed a Commissioner of the Peace for Queen Anne's County, 28 Feb 1742/3. (Ref: Maryland State Archives, Governor and Council Commissioner Records, 1726-1794, p. 76); appointed to Committee for Enquiring into Accounts and Vouchers Relating to the Disposal of the Sum of £6000 Granted by Act of Assembly for His Majesty's Service, 14 Mar 1755. (Ref: *Archives of Maryland*, Vol. LII, "Proceedings and Acts of the General Assembly of Maryland, 1755-1756," p. 81)

Caswell, Richard (1685-1755), was appointed a Commissioner of the Peace for Baltimore County, 21 Feb 1735/6. (Ref: Maryland State Archives, Governor and Council Commissioner Records, 1726-1794, p. 51); commissioned a Coroner of Baltimore County, 1 Apr 1736. (Ref: Maryland Commission Book No. 82, p. 42; *Maryland Historical Magazine*, Vol. XXVI, p. 146, spelled his name Caswall)

Cathel, Jonathan, appointed a Commissioner of the Peace for Worcester County, 30 Apr 1770. (Ref: Maryland State Archives, Governor and Council Commissioner Records, 1726-1794, p. 250)

Caton, Thomas, of Frederick County, was a Justice of the Peace in 1757. (Ref: *Archives of Maryland*, Vol. XXXI, "Proceedings of the Council of Maryland, 1753-1761," p. 249)

Catto (Cato), George, of Cecil County, appointed a Commissioner of the Peace, 8 Mar 1754 and 26 May 1756. (Ref: Maryland State Archives, Governor and Council Commissioner Records, 1726-1794, p. 143 spelled his name Cato, and p. 167, spelled it Catto)

Cawley, Cornelius, of Baltimore Co., convicted felon,

was executed on 29 Jun 1743. (Ref: Maryland State Archives, Governor and Council Commissioner Records, 1726-1794, p. 79)

Chaille, Moses, registration of the sloop *Mary*, 20 tons, built in Somerset County, 1746. Moses Chaille, master and owner. 24 Jun 1746. (Ref: Maryland Commission Book No. 82, p. 121; *Maryland Historical Magazine*, Vol. XXVI, p. 257)

Chalmers, Walter, reverend, induction into St. Margaret's Westminster Parish, Anne Arundel County, 26 Oct 1748. (Ref: Maryland Commission Book No. 82, p. 137; *Maryland Historical Magazine*, Vol. XXVI, p. 342); see William West.

Chamberlaine, James Lloyd (1732-1783), commissioned High Sheriff of Talbot County, 31 Oct 1758. (Ref: Maryland State Archives, Governor and Council Commissioner Records, 1726-1794, p. 173); see Negro Eve.

Chamberlaine, Samuel (1698-1773), esquire, of Talbot County, commissioned Naval Officer of the Port of Pocomoke, 18 Oct 1740 and 14 Oct 1742. (Ref: Maryland Commission Book No. 82, pp. 84, 96; *Maryland Historical Magazine*, Vol. XXVI, pp. 158, 247); appointed a Privy Council on 10 May 1753. (Ref: *Archives of Maryland*, Vol. XXXI, "Proceedings of the Council of Maryland, 1753-1761," pp. 8, 14); appointed to a Committee to Inspect the Accounts and Proceedings of the Commissioners of the Paper Currency Office, 25 Feb 1755. (Ref: *Archives of Maryland*, Vol. LII, "Proceedings and Acts of the General Assembly of Maryland, 1755-1756," p. 146)

Chamberlaine, Samuel, Jr. (1742-1811), of Talbot County, commissioned Naval Officer of Oxford on 18 Oct 1768, 28 Aug 1769 and 29 Apr 1773. (Ref: Maryland Commission Book No. 82, pp. 218, 227, 309; *Maryland Historical Magazine*, Vol. XXVI, pp. 359, 359, and Vol. XXVII, p. 33, mistakenly stated Patuxent, but it was actually Oxford, and did not style him as Jr. which was the case; *A Biographical Dictionary of the Maryland Legislature, 1635-1789*, by Edward C. Papenfuse, et al., Vol. A-H, pp. 208-209)

Chambers, Edward, see Levin Gale.

Chambers, Richard, see Joseph Huse.

Chambers, Samuel, appointed a Commissioner of the Peace for Anne Arundel County, 3 Mar 1726/7. (Ref: Maryland State Archives, Governor and Council Commissioner Records, 1726-1794, p. 3)

Chamier, Daniel, commissioned High Sheriff of Baltimore County, 31 Oct 1767. (Ref: Maryland State Archives, Governor and Council Commissioner Records, 1726-1794, p. 223)

Chance, Francis, of Anne Arundel County, convicted felon and burglar, was executed on 12 Oct 1770. (Ref: Maryland State Archives, Governor and Council Commissioner Records, 1726-1794, p. 240)

Chandly, John, registration of the sloop *Two Brothers*, 15 tons, built in Maryland, 1750. John Chandly, master and co-owner. James Bayard, co-owner. 1 Dec 1750. (Ref: Maryland Commission Book No. 82, p. 148; *Maryland Historical Magazine*, Vol. XXVI, p. 347)

Chaney, Charles, was appointed Constable of Antietam Hundred in Prince George's County, now Frederick County, 1745. (Ref: Prince George's County Court Records, 1736-1748, Extracts by Patricia Abelard Andersen, *Western Maryland Genealogy*, Vol. 18, No. 1, January 2002, p. 43)

Chaney, Ezekiel, appointed Constable of Marsh Hundred in Frederick County in 1760. (Ref: *This Was The Life: Excerpts from the Judgment Records of Frederick County, Maryland, 1748-1765*, by Millard Milburn Rice, p. 216)

Chaple, John, appointed a Commissioner of the Peace for Kent County, 11 Nov 1763. (Ref: Maryland State Archives, Governor and Council Commissioner Records, 1726-1794, p. 212)

Chaplin, Ruhamah, see Daniel Dunn.

Chapline, Joseph (1707-c1769), was appointed a Commissioner of the Peace for Prince George's County, 15 Jun 1739 and 21 Aug 1749. (Ref: Maryland State Archives, Governor and Council Commissioner Records, 1726-1794, pp. 64, 68, spelled his name Chaplin); Court Justice in Frederick County, 1748. (Ref: *This Was The Life: Excerpts from the Judgment Records of Frederick County, Maryland, 1748-1765*, by Millard Milburn Rice, p. 1); appointed Constable of the Lower Part of Antietam Hundred in Frederick County, 1769. (Ref: "Frederick County Court Minutes, March 1769," by Patricia Abelard Andersen, *Western Maryland Genealogy*, Vol. 15, No. 2, April 1999, p. 63); see Daniel Dunn.

Chapline, Moses, appointed Constable of Antietam Hundred in Frederick County in 1749. (Ref: *This Was The Life: Excerpts from the Judgment Records of Frederick County, Maryland, 1748-1765*, by Millard Milburn Rice, p. 7); appointed a Commissioner of the Peace for Frederick County, 16 Mar 1758. (Ref: Maryland State Archives, Governor and Council Commissioner Records, 1726-1794, p. 180)

Chapman, Constant, see Negro Jack.

Chapman, Nathaniel, appointed a Commissioner of the Peace for Charles County, 4 Nov 1758. (Ref: Maryland State Archives, Governor and Council Commissioner Records, 1726-1794, p. 182)

Chapman, Thomas, was appointed Constable of Armitage Hundred in Dorchester County, 1745. (Ref: Dorchester County Judgment Records, 1743-1745, p. 476; *Judgment Records of Dorchester, Queen Anne's and Talbot Counties, Maryland*, by F. Edward Wright, 2001, p. 60)

Chapman, William, Court Justice, Anne Arundel County, 1754. (Ref: Anne Arundel County Court Minutes, 1725-1757)

Chapman, William, Jr., appointed a Commissioner of the Peace for Anne Arundel County, 21 Nov 1743. (Ref: Maryland State Archives, Governor and Council Commissioner Records, 1726-1794, p. 83)

Charleton, Arthur, commissioned Ranger of that part of Prince George's County lying to the westward of Katochton [Catoctin] Creek. 13 Apr 1744; Arthur Charlton, of Frederick County, magistrate, 1766. (Ref: *Archives of Maryland*, Vol. XXXII, "Proceedings of the Council of Maryland, 1761-1770," p. 166; Maryland Commission Book No. 82, p. 109; *Maryland Historical Magazine*, Vol. XXVI, p. 252; *Archives of Maryland*, Vol. XXXII, "Proceedings of the Council of Maryland, 1761-1770," p. 166)

Charlton, Henry, was commissioned as Ranger of Codorus Hundred, Baltimore County, 2 Aug 1737. (Ref: Maryland Commission Book No. 82, p. 50; *Maryland Historical Magazine*, Vol. XXVI, p. 149, did not list his first name; *Baltimore County Families, 1659-1759*, by Robert Barnes, 1989, p. 105, mentioned Henry Charleton resided in Baltimore County before 1750)

Chase, Jeremiah, see Negro Jenny and Negro Anthony.

Chase, Jeremiah Townley (1748-1828), appointed to represent Baltimore County in the Provincial Convention, 1775. (Ref: *Calendar of Maryland State Papers, The Red Books*, No. 4, Part 1, p. 3)

Chase, Richard, reverend, was appointed Domestic Chaplain to Charles, Lord Baltimore, 25 Mar 1734. (Ref: Maryland Commission Book No. 82, p. 21; *Maryland Historical Magazine*, Vol. XXVI, p. 142); Chaplain to the Lord Proprietary, induction as Minister of Westminster Parish, Anne Arundel County, 23 Jul 1734. (Ref: Maryland Commission Book No. 82, p. 19; *Maryland Historical Magazine*, Vol. XXVI, p. 141); induction into All Hallow's Parish, Anne Arundel County, 4 Jan 1734/5. (Ref: Maryland Commission Book No. 82, p. 24; *Maryland Historical Magazine*, Vol. XXVI, p. 142); resignation as Rector of All Hallows Parish, Anne Arundel County, 28 May 1737, and on the same day induction into Christ Church, Calvert County. (Ref: Maryland Commission Book No. 82, p. 49; *Maryland Historical Magazine*, Vol. XXVI, p. 149); Rector of Christ Church Parish, Calvert County. Permission granted to go to Great Britain for one year without loss of revenue. 15 Aug 1738. (Ref: Maryland Commission Book No. 82, p. 60; *Maryland Historical Magazine*, Vol. XXVI, p. 151); resignation from Christ Church Parish, Calvert County, 1 Mar 1741/2. On same day, induction into Portobacco Parish in Charles County. (Ref: Maryland Commission Book No. 82, p. 91; *Maryland Historical Magazine*, Vol. XXVI, p. 245)

Chase, Samuel, see Thomas Dicke.

Chase, Thomas (d. 1779), reverend, induction into Somerset Parish in Somerset County, 17 May 1739. (Ref: Maryland Commission Book No. 82, p. 75; *Maryland Historical Magazine*, Vol. XXVI, p. 154); resignation from Somerset Parish, Somerset County, 5 Feb 1744/5. On same day, induction into St. John's Parish, Baltimore County. (Ref: Maryland Commission Book No. 82, p. 112; *Maryland Historical Magazine*, Vol. XXVI, p. 253)

Cheney, Charles, appointed Constable of Antietam Hundred in 1735 and Constable of part of Eastern Branch Hundred in Prince George's County, now Frederick County in 1746. (Ref: Prince George's County Court Records, 1736-1748, Extracts by Patricia Abelard Andersen, *Western Maryland Genealogy*, Vol. 18, No. 1, January 2002, pp. 35, 44)

Cherry, Thomas, appointed Constable of Tonnolloway Hundred in Prince George's County, now Frederick County, 1744. (Ref: Prince George's County Court Records, 1736-1748, Extracts by Patricia Abelard Andersen, *Western Maryland Genealogy*, Vol. 18, No. 1, January 2002, p. 41)

Chesley, John, appointed a Commissioner of the Peace for St. Mary's County, 1 Apr 1736. (Ref: Maryland State Archives, Governor and Council Commissioner Records, 1726-1794, p. 51)

Chesley, Robert (d. 1768), appointed a Commissioner of the Peace for St. Mary's County, 11 Jun 1739. (Ref: Maryland State Archives, Governor and Council Commissioner Records, 1726-1794, p. 63); commissioned Sheriff of St. Mary's County, 14 Jun 1748. (Ref: Maryland State Archives, Governor and Council Commissioner Records, 1726-1794, p. 106); see Negro Adam.

Cheston, Daniel, merchant, registration of the brigantine *Maryland Merchant*, 65 tons, built in Kent County, 1744. Anthony Beck, master. Daniel Cheston and William Gibbs, owners. 28 May 1744. (Ref: Maryland Commission Book No. 82, p. 110; *Maryland Historical Magazine*, Vol. XXVI, p. 252); commissioned Sheriff of Kent County, 1 Aug 1744. (Ref: Maryland State Archives, Governor and Council Commissioner Records, 1726-1794, p. 85); registration of sloop *Chester*, 15 tons, built in Maryland, 1742. John Brown, master. Daniel Cheston, owner. 21 Mar 1744/5. (Ref: Maryland Commission Book No. 82, p. 112; *Maryland Historical Magazine*, Vol. XXVI, p. 253); registration of schooner *Hollister*, 35 tons, built in Worcester County, 1745. Thomas Elmer, master. Daniel Cheston, Thomas Elmer, William Dames and Thomas Lambden, owners. 12 Sep 1746. (Ref: Maryland Commission Book No. 82, p. 122; *Maryland Historical Magazine*, Vol. XXVI, p. 257); appointed a Commissioner of the Peace for Kent County, 9 Nov 1747. (Ref: Maryland State Archives, Governor and Council Commissioner Records, 1726-1794, p. 103); see William Dames.

Cheston, James, appointed a Commissioner of the Peace for Baltimore County, 6 Mar 1775. (Ref: Maryland State Archives, Governor and Council Commissioner Records, 1726-1794, p. 288)

Chew, Benjamin, appointed a Commissioner of the Peace for Cecil County, 31 Oct 1741. (Ref: Maryland State Archives, Governor and Council Commissioner Records, 1726-1794, p. 72); see Thomas Cooper.

Chew, Joseph, appointed a Commissioner of the Peace for Prince George's County, 18 Feb 1731/2. (Ref: Maryland State Archives, Governor and Council Commissioner Records, 1726-1794, p. 21); see Thomas Norris.

Chew, Samuel (1737-1790), was appointed a Commissioner of the Peace for Calvert County, 14 Mar 1761. (Ref: Maryland State Archives, Governor and Council Commissioner Records, 1726-1794, p. 195)

Chew, Samuel (c1730-1786), was appointed a Commissioner of the Peace for Anne Arundel County, 20 Apr 1773. (Ref: Maryland State Archives, Governor and Council Commissioner Records, 1726-1794, p. 266)

Chew, Samuel, Jr., appointed a Commissioner of the Peace for Anne Arundel County, 30 May 1731. (Ref: Maryland State Archives, Governor and Council Commissioner Records, 1726-1794, p. 19); merchant, registration of snow *Henrietta* of Maryland, 80 tons, built at Wye River, 1732. Thomas Lane, master. Samuel Chew, Jr., owner. 24 Sep 1733. (Ref: Maryland Commission Book No. 82, p. 6; *Maryland Historical Magazine*, Vol. XXVI, p. 139); registration of sloop *Adventure*, formerly the *Patuxent* (forfeited by decree of Court of Vice-Admiralty), 50 tons, built at Newbury, Massachusetts, 1733. Andrew Price, master. Richard Bennett, James Heath and Samuel Chew, Jr., owners. 15 Feb 1734/5. (Ref: Maryland Commission Book No. 82, p. 26; *Maryland Historical Magazine*, Vol. XXVI, p. 143); registration of sloop *Boneta*, 6 tons, built at Wye River, 1735. William Frazer, master, Samuel Chase, Jr., owner. 12 Jul 1735. (Ref: Maryland Commission Book No. 82, p. 32; *Maryland Historical Magazine*, Vol. XXVI, p. 144); appointed a Commissioner of the Peace for Anne Arundel County, 13 Mar 1737/8 and 9 Aug 1757. (Ref: Maryland State Archives, Governor and Council Commissioner Records, 1726-1794, pp. 59, 175)

Chisem, Christopher, of Frederick County, convicted of murder, was executed on 22 Oct 1773. (Ref: Maryland State Archives, Governor and Council Commissioner Records, 1726-1794, p. 265)

Chiswell, Joseph, appointed Constable of Sugar Loaf Hundred in Frederick County, 1771. (Ref: "Frederick

County Minute Book, March 1771, Extracts by Patricia Abelard Andersen," *Western Maryland Genealogy*, Vol. 18, No. 1, January 2002, p. 25)

Christie, Charles, commissioned High Sheriff of Baltimore County, 21 Oct 1756. (Ref: Maryland State Archives, Governor and Council Commissioner Records, 1726-1794, p. 161; *Archives of Maryland*, Vol. LII, "Proceedings and Acts of the General Assembly of Maryland, 1755-1756," p. 576; *Archives of Maryland*, Vol. XXXI, "Proceedings of the Council of Maryland, 1753-1761," p. 169)

Christie, Robert, Jr., commissioned High Sheriff of Baltimore County, 27 Sep 1773. (Ref: Maryland State Archives, Governor and Council Commissioner Records, 1726-1794, p. 266)

Christopher, John, labourer, servant to Charles Baker, of Queen Anne's County, convicted felon for stealing a bay gelding from said Baker, was executed on 14 May 1756. (Ref: Maryland State Archives, Governor and Council Commissioner Records, 1726-1794, p. 153; *Archives of Maryland*, Vol. XXXI, "Proceedings of the Council of Maryland, 1753-1761," p. 1190)

Chunn, Andrew, was Sub-Sheriff of Frederick County(?), 1760. (*Calendar of Maryland State Papers, No. 1 The Black Books*, pp. 157, 160)

Claggett, Charles, appointed a Commissioner of the Peace for Calvert County, 3 Mar 1726/7. (Ref: Maryland State Archives, Governor and Council Commissioner Records, 1726-1794, p. 3); see Negro Hannah.

Claggett, John, was Constable of Mount Calvert Hundred in Prince George's County, now Frederick County, in 1733. (*Calendar of Maryland State Papers, No. 1 The Black Books*, p. 40, spelled his name Clagett); appointed a Commissioner of the Peace for Frederick County, 1 Mar 1749/50. (Ref: Maryland State Archives, Gover-nor and Council Commissioner Records, 1726-1794, p. 116); Court Justice, Frederick County, 1750; served as one of the Inspectors at Rock Creek Warehouse in 1755. (Ref: *This Was The Life: Excerpts from the Judgment Records of Frederick County, Maryland, 1748-1765*, by Millard Milburn Rice, p. 47 spelled his name Clagett, and p. 159 spelled it Claggett)

Claggett, Samuel, reverend, of Calvert County, induction into Christ Church Parish, Calvert County, 23 Feb 1748/9. (Ref: Maryland Commission Book No. 82, p. 139, did not give his first name; *Maryland Historical Magazine*, Vol. XXVI, p. 343, spelled his name Clagett and put his first name in brackets; *Directory of Ministers and the Maryland Churches They Served, 1634-1900*, by Edna Agatha Kanely, Vol. I, A-K, p. 118, spelled his name correctly); induction into William and Mary Parish, Charles County, 7 Feb 1749/50. (Ref: Maryland Commission Book No. 82, p. 142; *Maryland Historical Magazine*, Vol. XXVI, p. 345)

Claggett, Thomas, appointed Constable of the Lower Part of Potomac Hundred in Frederick County, 1760. (Ref: *This Was The Life: Excerpts from the Judgment Records of Frederick County, Maryland, 1748-1765*, by Millard Milburn Rice, p. 216, spelled his name Clagett)

Claggett, Thomas (1740-1792), was appointed a Commissioner of the Peace for Prince George's County, 26 Jul 1773. (Ref: Maryland State Archives, Governor and Council Commissioner Records, 1726-1794, p. 272)

Claggett, Thomas, Jr., appointed a Commissioner of the Peace for Prince George's County, 18 Feb 1731/2. (Ref: Maryland State Archives, Governor and Council Commissioner Records, 1726-1794, p. 21, spelled his name Clagett)

Claggett, Thomas John (1743-1816), reverend, licensed to preach in St. Anne's Parish, Anne Arundel County, vacant by the removal of Rev. Bennett Allen, but it was withdrawn on 19 Mar 1768 and induction granted to Rev. William Edmiston. (Ref: Maryland Commission Book No. 82, p. 207; *Maryland Historical Magazine*, Vol. XXVI, p. 357; licensed to preach in All Saints Parish, Calvert County, 16 Mar 1769. (Ref: Maryland Commission Book No. 82, p. 221; *Maryland Historical Magazine*, Vol. XXVI, p. 359, spelled his name Clagett; induction into All Saints Parish, Calvert County, 7 Jul 1769. (Ref: Maryland Commission Book No. 82, p. 225; *Maryland Historical Magazine*, Vol. XXVI, p. 359, spelled his name Clagett)

Clapham, John, was appointed a Commissioner for Emitting Bills of Credit, 22 Dec 1766. (Ref: Maryland Commission Book No. 82, p. 197; *Maryland Historical Magazine*, Vol. XXVI, p. 355); commissioned Commissioner for Emitting Bills of

Credit, 21 Dec 1769. (Ref: Maryland Commission Book No. 82, p. 235; *Maryland Historical Magazine*, Vol. XXVI, p. 360); commissioned High Sheriff of Anne Arundel County, 19 Oct 1769. (Ref: Maryland State Archives, Governor and Council Commissioner Records, 1726-1794, p. 236); commissioned one of two Commissioners for Emitting Bills of Credit, 29 Apr 1773. (Ref: Maryland Commission Book No. 82, p. 305; *Maryland Historical Magazine*, Vol. XXVII, p. 33)

Clare, John, appointed a Commissioner of the Peace for Calvert County, 22 Oct 1741. (Ref: Maryland State Archives, Governor and Council Commissioner Records, 1726-1794, p. 72)

Clark, Joshua, appointed a Commissioner of the Peace for Caroline County, 8 Feb 1774. (Ref: Maryland State Archives, Governor and Council Commissioner Records, 1726-1794, p. 280)

Clark, Joshua, appointed a Commissioner of the Peace for Queen Anne's County, 31 Oct 1768. (Ref: Maryland State Archives, Governor and Council Commissioner Records, 1726-1794, p. 239)

Clark, Joshua, appointed Constable of Patuxent Hundred in Prince George's County, now Frederick County, 1748. (Ref: Prince George's County Court Records, 1736-1738, Extracts by Patricia Abelard Andersen, *Western Maryland Genealogy*, Vol. 18, No. 1, January 2002, p. 46)

Clark, Philip, appointed a Commissioner of the Peace for St. Mary's County, 1 Apr 1736. (Ref: Maryland State Archives, Governor and Council Commissioner Records, 1726-1794, p. 51)

Clark, Thomas, see Osborn Sprigg.

Clarke, Caleb, see Richard Bennett.

Clarke, George (c1692-1753), was appointed a Commissioner of the Peace for St. Mary's County, 2 Mar 1726/7. (Ref: Maryland State Archives, Governor and Council Commissioner Records, 1726-1794, p. 2)

Clarke, George, commissioned Sheriff of Calvert County, 17 Aug 1729. (Ref: Maryland State Archives, Governor and Council Commissioner Records, 1726-1794, p. 10)

Clarke, James, appointed a Commissioner of the Peace for Baltimore County, 6 Mar 1775. (Ref: Maryland State Archives, Governor and Council Commissioner Records, 1726-1794, p. 288)

Clarke, John Attaway, commissioned a Coroner of St. Mary's County, 26 Dec 1766. (Ref: Maryland Commission Book No. 82, p. 198; *Maryland Historical Magazine*, Vol. XXVI, p. 355)

Clarke, Joshua, see Absalom Scott.

Clarkson, William, appointed a Commissioner of the Peace for Dorchester County, 26 Oct 1738 and 28 Feb 1742/3. (Ref: Maryland State Archives, Governor and Council Commissioner Records, 1726-1794, pp. 62, 76)

Clayton, Solomon (1685-1939), was appointed a Commissioner of the Peace for Queen Anne's County, 3 Mar 1726/7. (Ref: Maryland State Archives, Governor and Council Commissioner Records, 1726-1794, p. 2); registration of shallop *Bohemia*, 6 tons, built at Bohemia [Cecil County], 1737. William Clayton, master. Solomon and William Clayton, owners. (Ref: Maryland Commission Book No. 82, p. 73; *Maryland Historical Magazine*, Vol. XXVI, p. 154); see William Clayton.

Clayton, William, registration of the brigantine *Charming Molly*, 30 tons, built in Talbot County, 1732. Thomas Harris, master. Solomon Clayton and William Clayton, owners. 17 Jun 1736. (Ref: Maryland Commission Book No. 82, p. 44; *Maryland Historical Magazine*, Vol. XXVI, p. 147); appointed a Commissioner of the Peace for Talbot County, 16 Jan 1737/8. (Ref: Maryland State Archives, Governor and Council Commissioner Records, 1726-1794, p. 580); registration of sloop *Rachel*, 13 tons, built at Wye River, 1738. Thomas Kemp, master. Solomon Clayton and William Clayton, owners. 12 Aug 1738. (Ref: Maryland Commission Book No. 82, p. 62; *Maryland Historical Magazine*, Vol. XXVI, p. 152); appointed a Commissioner of the Peace for Queen Anne's County, 1 Dec 1746. (Ref: Maryland State Archives, Governor and Council Commissioner Records, 1726-1794, p. 95)

Clements, Francis, see Negro Jack.

Clerk, James, see Richard Floud.

Clifton, Thomas, see Thomas Williamson.

Cline (Clyne), Jacob, appointed Constable of Frederick Town Hundred in Frederick County, 1769, 1771. (Ref: "Frederick County Court Minutes November 1769 by Patricia Abelard Andersen," *Western Maryland Genealogy*, Vol. 16, No. 1, January

2000, p. 32, spelled his name Cline; "Frederick County Minute Book, March 1771, Extracts by Patricia Abelard Andersen," *Western Maryland Genealogy*, Vol. 18, No. 1, January 2002, p. 26, spelled his name Clyne)

Cockayne, Thomas, appointed a Commissioner of the Peace for Talbot County, 16 Jul 1735. (Ref: Maryland State Archives, Governor and Council Commissioner Records, 1726-1794, p. 48)

Cockey, John, appointed a Commissioner of the Peace for Baltimore County, 3 Mar 1726/7 and 22 Oct 1728. (Ref: Maryland State Archives, Governor and Council Commissioner Records, 1726-1794, pp. 2, 8)

Cocks, William, of Frederick County, was a Justice of the Peace in 1757. (Ref: *Archives of Maryland*, Vol. XXXI, "Proceedings of the Council of Maryland, 1753-1761," p. 248)

Codd, St. Leger (c1675-1730), commissioned a Provincial Justice by the Governor, 20 Oct 1729. (Ref: Maryland State Archives, Governor and Council Commissioner Record, 1726-1794, p. 12)

Cole, Charles, see Thomas Beaven.

Cole, James, see Osborn Sprigg.

Cole, Skipwith, appointed a Commissioner of the Peace for Baltimore County, 5 Dec 1739. (Ref: Maryland State Archives, Governor and Council Commissioner Records, 1726-1794, p. 66)

Cole, Skipwith, appointed a Commissioner of the Peace for Baltimore County, 9 Apr 1773. (Ref: Maryland State Archives, Governor and Council Commissioner Records, 1726-1794, p. 266)

Coleman, Peter, of Dorchester County, convicted felon, was executed on 15 May 1742. (Ref: Maryland State Archives, Governor and Council Commissioner Records, 1726-1794, p. 73)

Collier, Isaac, appointed Constable of Cumber-land Hundred in Frederick County, 1769. (Ref: "Frederick County Court Minutes, March 1769," by Patricia Abelard Andersen, *Western Maryland Genealogy*, Vol. 15, No. 2, April 1999, p. 63)

Collins, John, appointed a Commissioner of the Peace for Worcester County, 26 Jul 1773. (Ref: Maryland State Archives, Governor and Council Commissioner Records, 1726-1794, p. 271)

Collins, Joseph, appointed a Commissioner of the Peace for Worcester County, 23 Mar 1756. (Ref: Maryland State Archives, Governor and Council Commissioner Records, 1726-1794, p. 166)

Collins, Thomas, of Anne Arundel County, convicted felon, executed on 1 Nov 1734. (Ref: Maryland State Archives, Governor and Council Commissioner Records, 1726-1794, p. 45)

Colvill, John, of Virginia, registration of brigantine *The Giles*, 50 tons, built in Maryland, 1733. John Colvill, master and owner. 23 May 1734 (Ref: Maryland Commission Book No. 82, p. 19; *Maryland Historical Magazine*, Vol. XXVI, p. 141)

Colville, Thomas, appointed a Commissioner of the Peace for Kent County, 2 Jun 1732. (Ref: Maryland State Archives, Governor and Council Commissioner Records, 1726-1794, p. 23)

Comegys, John, appointed a Commissioner of the Peace for Kent County, 1 Dec 1768; appointed a Commissioner of the Peace for Cecil County, 2 Jun 1774. (Ref: Maryland State Archives, Governor and Council Commissioner Records, 1726-1794, pp. 239, 283)

Compton, John, appointed Constable of the Lower Part of Monochosey [Monocacy] Hundred in Frederick County, 1771. (Ref: "Frederick County Minute Book, March 1771, Extracts by Patricia Abelard Andersen," *Western Maryland Genealogy*, Vol. 18, No. 1, January 2002, p. 25)

Conn, James, see Negro Lie.

Conn, Thomas, was a Constable in Frederick County in 1763. (Ref: *This Was The Life: Excerpts from the Judgment Records of Frederick County, Maryland, 1748-1765*, by Millard Milburn Rice, p. 252)

Conner, Charles, see Thomas Dobbs.

Conner, Terrence, labourer, of Frederick County, convicted of murdering James Boyle, was executed on 20 Oct 1752. (Ref: Maryland State Archives, Governor and Council Commissioner Records, 1726-1794, p. 134)

Conrod, Henry, of Baltimore County, Ranger, 9 Aug 1775. (Ref: *Calendar of Maryland State Papers, The Red Books*, No. 4, Part 1, p. 5)

Constantine, Joshua, see Patrick Constantine.

Constantine, Patrick, labourer, of Baltimore County, convicted of murdering his eight-year-old son Joshua, was pardoned on 11 Oct 1768. (Ref: Maryland Commission Book No. 82, p. 216; *Maryland Historical Magazine*, Vol. XXVI, p. 358; *Archives of Maryland*, Vol. XXXII, "Proceedings of the Council of Maryland, 1761-1770," pp. 249-250)

Contee, John (1722-c1796), was appointed a Commissioner of the Peace for Prince George's County, 17 Mar 1745/6. (Ref: Maryland State Archives, Governor and Council Commissioner Records, 1726-1794, p. 91)

Contee, Thomas (c172-1811), was appointed a Commissioner of the Peace for Charles County, 17 Nov 1764. (Ref: Maryland State Archives, Governor and Council Commissioner Records, 1726-1794, p. 220)

Conway, John Span, appointed a Commissioner of the Peace for Somerset County, 20 Mar 1775. (Ref: Maryland State Archives, Governor and Council Commissioner Records, 1726-1794, p. 288)

Cooke, George, reverend, induction into Christ Church Parish, Calvert County, 7 Feb 1749/50. (Ref: Maryland Commission Book No. 82, p. 142; *Maryland Historical Magazine*, Vol. XXVI, p. 345)

Cooke, Giles, appointed a Commissioner of the Peace for Kent County, 16 Nov 1757. (Ref: Maryland State Archives, Governor and Council Commissioner Records, 1726-1794, p. 179)

Cooke, John, commissioned Sheriff of Prince George's County, 6 Aug 1744. (Ref: Maryland State Archives, Governor and Council Commissioner Records, 1726-1794, p. 85; (Ref: *Archives of Maryland*, Vol. LII, "Proceedings and Acts of the General Assembly of Maryland, 1755-1756," p. 572); late sheriff of Prince George's County, had ordinary license accounts still unpaid in 1756. (Ref: *Archives of Maryland*, Vol. LII, "Proceedings and Acts of the General Assembly of Maryland, 1755-1756," p. 568)

Cooke, Richard, appointed a Commissioner of the Peace for St. Mary's County, 29 Feb 1743/4. (Ref: Maryland State Archives, Governor and Council Commissioner Records, 1726-1794, p. 84)

Coontz, George, planter, of Baltimore County, native of High Germany, naturalized 4 Jun 1738 and also his children John, Eve and Catherine. (Ref: Maryland Commission Book No. 82, p. 57; *Maryland Historical Magazine*, Vol. XXVI, p. 151)

Cooper, John, registration of schooner *Speed-well*, 15 tons, built in Annapolis, 1747. Joseph Larey, master. John Cooper, owner. 17 Dec 1750. (Ref: Maryland Commission Book No. 82, p. 148; *Maryland Historical Magazine*, Vol. XXVI, p. 347)

Cooper, Robert, of Frederick County, convicted of murder, was executed on 21 Jun 1773. (Ref: Maryland State Archives, Governor and Council Commissioner Records, 1726-1794, p. 259)

Cooper, Thomas, labourer, of Anne Arundel County, convicted felon for breaking and entering the store house of Benjamin Chew and stealing sundry goods, was executed on 8 Oct 1762. (Ref: Maryland State Archives, Governor and Council Commissioner Records, 1726-1794, p. 190; *Archives of Maryland*, Vol. XXXII, "Proceedings of the Council of Maryland, 1761-1770," p. 42)

Copson, John, appointed a Commissioner of the Peace for Cecil County, 29 Oct 1730; captain, Provincial Commission, 8 Jul 1735; of Anne Arundel County, commissioned Judge of Oyer, Terminer and Gaol [Jail] Delivery, 21 May 1736. (Ref: Maryland State Archives, Governor and Council Commissioner Records, 1726-1794, pp. 17, 49, 52)

Corbusier, Henry, see Edward North.

Couden, Robert, appointed a Commissioner of the Peace for Anne Arundel County, 17 Nov 1762. (Ref: Maryland State Archives, Governor and Council Commissioner Records, 1726-1794, p. 208); appointed a Commissioner for Emitting Bills of Credit, 16 Dec 1766 and 21 Dec 1769. (Ref: Maryland Commission Book No. 82, pp. 197, 235; *Maryland Historical Magazine*, Vol. XXVI, pp. 355, 360)

Coughlan, William, see James Donaldson.

Coulbourn, Isaac, commissioned High Sheriff of Somerset County, 8 Oct 1767. (Ref: Maryland State Archives, Governor and Council Commissioner Records, 1726-1794, p. 222)

Coulbourn, Jacob, see William Coulbourn.

Coulbourn, William, registration of sloop *Two Brothers*, 20 tons, built in Somerset County, 1748. William Coulbourn, master and co-owner. Jacob Coulbourn, co-owner. 3 Dec 1748. (Ref: Maryland Commission Book No. 82, p. 139; *Maryland Historical Magazine*, Vol. XXVI, p. 343)

Coulter, Michael, see Charles Brown.

Coursey, William, appointed a Commissioner of the Peace for Queen Anne's County, 8 Mar 1735/6 and 6 Jun 1739. (Ref: Maryland State Archives, Governor and Council Commissioner Records, 1726-1794, pp. 51, 63)

Courtenay, Hercules, appointed a Commissioner of the Peace for Baltimore County, 30 May 1774. (Ref: Maryland State Archives, Governor and Council Commissioner Records, 1726-1794, p. 283, spelled his surname Courtnay)

Courtney, Richard, see Paul Binney.

Courts, Charles, see Negro Dick.

Coutts, Hercules, commissioned Sheriff of Cecil County, 8 Nov 1756. (Ref: Maryland State Archives, Governor and Council Commissioner Records, 1726-1794, p. 163; *Calendar of Maryland State Papers, No. 1 The Black Books*, p. 161, mistakenly stated Sheriff of Kent County in 1761 and spelled his name Coutes)

Covington, Leonard, appointed a Commissioner of the Peace for Prince George's County, 15 Jun 1739. (Ref: Maryland State Archives, Governor and Council Commissioner Records, 1726-1794, p. 64)

Covington, Leonard, appointed a Commissioner of the Peace for Prince Georges's County, 31 Mar 1773. (Ref: Maryland State Archives, Governor and Council Commissioner Records, 1726-1794, p. 266)

Covington, Nehemiah, see John Barnes.

Coward, John, appointed a Commissioner of the Peace for Talbot County, 20 Oct 1746. (Ref: Maryland State Archives, Governor and Council Commissioner Records, 1726-1794, p. 94); see Anthony Bacon, John Bartlett, John Williams and William Edmonson.

Cox, Ezekiel, appointed Constable of Fort Frederick Hundred in Frederick County, 1769, 1771. (Ref: "Frederick County Court Minutes November 1769 by Patricia Abelard Andersen," *Western Maryland Genealogy*, Vol. 16, No. 1, January 2000, p. 33; "Frederick County Minute Book, March 1771, Extracts by Patricia Abelard Andersen," *Western Maryland Genealogy*, Vol. 18, No. 1, January 2002, p. 26, misspelled his first name Eseziel); appointed a Commissioner of the Peace for Frederick County, 15 Aug 1774. (Ref: Maryland State Archives, Governor and Council Commissioner Records, 1726-1794, p. 284); Court Judge, 1774. (*Calendar of Maryland State Papers, No. 1 The Black Books*, p. 217)

Crabb, Edward, commissioned Sheriff of Prince George's County, 24 Jan 1756. (Ref: Maryland State Archives, Governor and Council Commissioner Records, 1726-1794, p. 156)

Crabb, Henry Wright (1722-1764), appointed a Commissioner of the Peace for Frederick County, 1 Mar 1749/50. (Ref: Maryland State Archives, Governor and Council Commissioner Records, 1726-1794, p. 116); Court Justice, Frederick County, 1751. (Ref: *This Was The Life: Excerpts from the Judgment Records of Frederick County, Maryland, 1748-1765*, by Millard Milburn Rice, p. 84); see Negro Coffee.

Crabb, Ralph (c1695-1733/4), appointed a Commissioner of the Peace for Prince George's County, 3 Mar 1726/7. (Ref: Maryland State Archives, Governor and Council Commissioner Records, 1726-1794, p. 3)

Crabtree, James, appointed Constable of Linton Hundred in Frederick County in 1753 and Old Town Hundred in 1763. He left the province in 1764. (Ref: *This Was The Life: Excerpts from the Judgment Records of Frederick County, Maryland, 1748-1765*, by Millard Milburn Rice, pp. 131, 249, 254)

Cradock (Craddock), John (c1749-1794), was a doctor and was appointed a Commissioner of the Peace for Baltimore County, 30 May 1774. (Ref: Maryland State Archives, Governor and Council Commissioner Records, 1726-1794, p. 283); Court Justice. 1774. (Ref: *Inhabitants of Baltimore County, 1763-1774*, by Henry C. Peden, Jr., 1989, p. 50, citing Baltimore County Court Proceedings, 1774)

Cradock (Craddock), Thomas (1718-1770), reverend, was inducted into St. Thomas' Parish, Baltimore County, 6 Dec 1744. (Ref: Maryland Commission Book No. 82, p. 111; *Maryland Historical Magazine*, Vol. XXVI, p. 253)

Craick, James, appointed a Commissioner of the Peace for Charles County, 19 Oct 1770. (Ref: Maryland State Archives, Governor and Council Commissioner Records, 1726-1794, p. 252)

Crampton, Henry, see Thomas Brown.

Crane, Jack, see Negro Jack Crane and Negro Pompey.

Crawford, David, appointed a Commissioner of the Peace for Prince George's County, 1 Nov 1729, 30 Nov 1732 and 17 Aug 1761. (Ref: Maryland State

Archives, Governor and Council Commissioner Records, 1726-1794, pp. 12, 30, 198)

Crawley, Cornelius, of Baltimore County, felon and reprieve granted in July 1743. (Ref: Maryland Commission Book No. 82, p. 103; *Maryland Historical Magazine*, Vol. XXVI, p. 249)

Crayball, John, appointed Constable of Burnt House Woods Hundred in Frederick County, 1771. (Ref: "Frederick County Minute Book, March 1771, Extracts by Patricia Abelard Andersen," *Western Maryland Genealogy*, Vol. 18, No. 1, January 2002, p. 25)

Creager, John, appointed Constable of the Upper Part of Monochosey [Monocacy] Hundred in Frederick County, 1769, 1771. (Ref: "Frederick County Court Minutes November 1769 by Patricia Abelard Andersen," *Western Maryland Genealogy*, Vol. 16, No. 1, January 2000, p. 32; "Frederick County Minute Book, March 1771, Extracts by Patricia Abelard Andersen," *Western Maryland Genealogy*, Vol. 18, No. 1, January 2002, p. 26)

Creagh, James, see Patrick Creagh.

Creagh, Patrick, merchant, registration of schooner *Hopewell*, 30 tons, built in Annapolis, 1743. John Wabby, master; Patrick Creagh, owner. 24 Oct 1743. (Ref: Maryland Commission Book No. 82, p. 104; *Maryland Historical Magazine*, Vol. XXVI, p. 250); merchant, registration of ship *Moses & Rebecca*, 200 tons, built in Anne Arundel County, 1750. James Creagh, master. Patrick Creagh, owner. 15 Jun 1750. (Ref: Maryland Commission Book No. 82, p. 144; *Maryland Historical Magazine*, Vol. XXVI, p. 345); merchant, registration of sloop *Betsy*, 30 tons, built in Anne Arundel County, 1745. William Rose, master. Patrick Creagh, owner. 28 Sep 1745. (Ref: Maryland Commission Book No. 82, p. 115; *Maryland Historical Magazine*, Vol. XXVI, p. 255); merchant, registration of sloop *Molly*, 20 tons, built in Anne Arundel County, 1735. Charles Gyles, master. Patrick Creagh, owner. 25 Aug 1746. (Ref: Maryland Commission Book No. 82, p. 122; *Maryland Historical Magazine*, Vol. XXVI, p. 257); merchant, registration of snow *Frances & Elizabeth*, 100 tons, built at Annapolis, 1747. Anthony Beck, master. Patrick Creagh, owner. 6 Apr 1747. (Ref: Maryland Commission Book No. 82, p. 128; *Maryland Historical Magazine*, Vol. XXVI, p. 259); painter(?), registration of schooner *Elizabeth*, formerly the *Mary* (forfeited by decree of the Court of Vice-Admiralty), 20 tons, built in New England, 1729. John Soare, master. Patrick Creagh, owner. 4 Feb 1734/5. (Ref: Maryland Commission Book No. 82, p. 25; *Maryland Historical Magazine*, Vol. XXVI, p. 142); registration of schooner *Annapolis*, 50 tons, formerly called *Adventure*, built at Newbury, New England, 1733, and called *Patuxent* (condemned by Admiralty Court). Richard Martyn, master. Charles Carr, surgeon, and Patrick Creagh, owners. 18 Sep 1739. (Ref: Maryland Commission Book No. 82, p. 77; *Maryland Historical Magazine*, Vol. XXVI, p. 154); registration of snow *James*, 85 tons, built in Annapolis, 1740. Thomas Askew, master. Patrick Creagh, owner. 27 Sep 1740. (Ref: Maryland Commission Book No. 82, p. 84; *Maryland Historical Magazine*, Vol. XXVI, pp. 157-158); registration of brigantine *Annapolis*, 50 tons, rebuilt in Maryland, 1747. Leonard Brook, master. Patrick Creagh, owner. 13 May 1747. (Ref: Maryland Commission Book No. 82, p. 129; *Maryland Historical Magazine*, Vol. XXVI, p. 260); registration of schooner *Elizabeth*, 20 tons, built in New England, 1729, and then called the *Mary*, was rebuilt in Annapolis, 1741. William Scandrett, master. Patrick Creagh, owner. 1742. (Ref: Maryland Commission Book No. 82, p. 92; *Maryland Historical Magazine*, Vol. XXVI, p. 246); registration of ship *Speedwell*, 100 tons, built at Annapolis, 1744. Joseph Brooke, master. Patrick Creagh, owner. 6 Aug 1744. (Ref: Maryland Commission Book No. 82, p. 110; *Maryland Historical Magazine*, Vol. XXVI, p. 252); registration of sloop *Fanny*, 20 tons, built in Annapolis, 1743. William Schandrett, master. Patrick Creagh, owner. 24 Oct 1743. (Ref: Maryland Commission Book No. 82, p. 104; *Maryland Historical Magazine*, Vol. XXVI, p. 250); registration of sloop *James*, 35 tons, built in Accomack County, Virginia, 1731. Edward Mattingly, master. Patrick Creagh, owner. 10 May 1737. (Ref: Maryland Commission Book No. 82, p. 48; *Maryland Historical Magazine*, Vol. XXVI, pp. 148-149); see Mulatto Toney.

Cresap. Daniel (b. 1727), appointed Constable of Wills Town Hundred in Frederick County, 1769. (Ref: "Frederick County Court Minutes, March 1769," by Patricia Abelard Andersen, *Western Maryland Genealogy*, Vol. 15, No. 2, April 1999, p. 63)

Cresap, Michael (1742-1775), appointed a Commissioner of the Peace for Frederick County, 2 Apr 1770 and 15 Aug 1774. (Ref: Maryland State Archives, Governor and Council Commissioner Records, 1726-1794, pp. 250 and 284)

Cresap, Thomas (c1703-1788), appointed a Commissioner of the Peace for Prince George's County, 15 Jun 1739. (Ref: Maryland State Archives, Governor and Council Commissioner Records, 1726-1794, p. 64); commissioned Deputy Surveyor of Prince George's County, 22 Apr 1747. (Ref: Maryland Commission Book No. 82, p. 128; *Maryland Historical Magazine*, Vol. XXVI, p. 260); Court Justice in Frederick County, 1748. (Ref: *This Was The Life: Excerpts from the Judgment Records of Frederick County, Maryland, 1748-1765*, by Millard Milburn Rice, p. 1); colonel, of Frederick County, Court Judge, 1774. (*Calendar of Maryland State Papers, No. 1 The Black Books*, p. 217)

Crispin, Joseph, registration of sloop *Property*, 12 tons, built in Somerset County, 1742. Joseph Crispin, master and owner. 10 Jul 1747. (Ref: Maryland Commission Book No. 82, p. 131; *Maryland Historical Magazine*, Vol. XXVI, p. 261); see Littleton Waters.

Crockett, Gilbert, see Negro Jacob.

Crompton, Thomas, a registration of the sloop *Mercury*, 10 tons, built in Virginia, 1733. Henry Filkins, master. Thomas Crompton, owner. March 1736/7. (Ref: Maryland Commission Book No. 82, p. 46; *Maryland Historical Magazine*, Vol. XXVI, p. 148); ppointed a Commissioner of the Peace for Calvert County, 22 Oct 1741. (Ref: Maryland State Archives, Governor and Council Commissioner Records, 1726-1794, p. 72)

Cromwell, Caleb, see William Cromwell.

Cromwell, John, of John, was appointed a Commissioner of the Peace for Anne Arundel County, 30 Aug 1756. (Ref: Maryland State Archives, Governor and Council Commissioner Records, 1726-1794, p. 169)

Cromwell, William, commissioned Deputy Surveyor of Anne Arundel County, 26 Oct 1742. (Ref: Maryland Commission Book No. 82, p. 98; *Maryland Historical Magazine*, Vol. XXVI, p. 247); registration of schooner *William*, 12 tons, built in Anne Arundel County, 1744. Caleb Cromwell, master. William Cromwell, owner. 6 Dec 1744. (Ref: Maryland Commission Book No. 82, p. 111; *Maryland Historical Magazine*, Vol. XXVI, p. 253)

Cron, James, appointed Constable of Eastern Branch Hundred in Prince George's County, now Frederick County, 1745. (Ref: Prince George's County Court Records, 1736-1748, Extracts by Patricia Abelard Andersen, *Western Maryland Genealogy*, Vol. 18, No. 1, January 2002, p. 43)

Crosby, Richard, alias Richard Dow or Dew, labourer, of Frederick County, convicted of murder, was executed on 28 May 1762. (Ref: Maryland State Archives, Governor and Council Commissioner Records, 1726-1794, p. 188; *Archives of Maryland*, Vol. XXXII, "Proceedings of the Council of Maryland, 1761-1770," p. 38)

Crow, James, appointed a Commissioner of the Peace for Prince George's County, 3 Dec 1766 and 26 Jul 1773. (Ref: Maryland State Archives, Governor and Council Commissioner Records, 1726-1794, pp. 230, 272)

Cruickshank, Robert, of Kent County, appointed a Commissioner of the Peace, 2 Nov 1762. (Ref: Maryland State Archives, Governor and Council Commissioner Records, 1726-1794, p. 207)

Cruickshanks, John, appointed a Commissioner of the Peace for Cecil County, 2 Jun 1774. (Ref: Maryland State Archives, Governor and Council Commissioner Records, 1726-1794, p. 283)

Cullins, Charles, labourer, of Baltimore County, convicted felon for breaking and entering an out house and stealing a considerable quantity of paper currency of Pennsylvania and pieces of eight above the value of twelve pounds, was executed by hanging at Joppa on 29 Apr 1761. (Ref: Maryland State Archives, Governor and Council Commissioner Records, 1726-1794, p. 182; *Archives of Maryland*, Vol. XXXII, "Proceedings of the Council of Maryland, 1761-1770," p. 3, spelled his name Cullens)

Culbertson, William, of Baltimore County, Ranger, 9 Aug 1775. (Ref: *Calendar of Maryland State Papers, The Red Books*, No. 4, Part 1, p. 5)

Cumberford, Mary/Margaret, see Michael Mitchell.

Cumming, Alexander, see George Steuart.

Cumming, William, of Annapolis, commissioned Clerk and Keeper of the Records of the High Court of

Appeals and Errors, 2 Feb 1733/4. (Ref: Maryland Commission Book No. 82, p. 4; *Maryland Historical Magazine*, Vol. XXVI, p. 139)

Cunliffe, Ellis, see James Bennett.

Cunliffe, Foster, see James Bennett and John Gardiner.

Cunningham, Humphrey, appointed Constable of Piney Creek Hundred in Frederick County, 1769. (Ref: "Frederick County Court Minutes November 1769 by Patricia Abelard Andersen," *Western Maryland Genealogy*, Vol. 16, No. 1, January 2000, p. 32)

Currance, George, appointed Constable of the Upper Part of Monocacy Hundred in Frederick County, 1769. (Ref: "Frederick County Court Minutes, March 1769," by Patricia Abelard Andersen, *Western Maryland Genealogy*, Vol. 15, No. 2, April 1999, p. 63)

Currey, William, of Baltimore County, Ranger, 9 Aug 1775. (Ref: *Calendar of Maryland State Papers, The Red Books*, No. 4, Part 1, p. 5)

Curtis, William, captain, see John Wright and Mulatto Toney.

Dagworthy, John, appointed a Commissioner of the Peace for Frederick County, 1 Nov 1756. (Ref: Maryland State Archives, Governor and Council Commissioner Records, 1726-1794, p. 172)

Dagworthy, John, colonel, was appointed a Commissioner of the Peace for Dorchester County, 25 Jul 1759. (Ref: Maryland State Archives, Governor and Council Commissioner Records, 1726-1794, p. 186)

Dallam, Richard (1743-1820), was appointed a Commissioner of the Peace for Baltimore County, 9 Apr 1773. (Ref: Maryland State Archives, Governor and Council Commissioner Records, 1726-1794, p. 266)

Dallam, Richard, appointed a Commissioner of the Peace for Baltimore County, 9 Feb 1748/9. (Ref: Maryland State Archives, Governor and Council Commissioner Records, 1726-1794, p. 110)

Dallam, William (1706-1761), commissioned one of the Coroners of Baltimore County, 11 Dec 1746. (Ref: Maryland Commission Book No. 82, p. 124; *Maryland Historical Magazine*, Vol. XXVI, p. 258); registration of ship *Fanny & Betsy*, 120 tons, built in Baltimore County, 1750. Charles Hargrove, master. William Dallam, owner. 12 Sep 1750. (Ref: Maryland Commission Book No. 82, p. 145; *Maryland Historical Magazine*, Vol. XXVI, p. 346)

Dalton, John, see John Handy.

Dames, William, merchant, registration of the brigantine *James and Martha*, 50 tons, built at Newcastle upon Tyne, 1738, and called the *Bon Accord*. Stephen Martin, master. William Dames, owner. 20 May 1746. (Ref: Maryland Commission Book No. 82, p. 120; *Maryland Historical Magazine*, Vol. XXVI, pp. 256-257); merchant, registration of brigantine *James and Martha*, 50 tons, built in Newcastle-upon-Tyne and called the *Bon Accord*, 1738. John Bramley, master. William Dames and James Paul Heath, owners. 24 Jul 1745. (Ref: Maryland Commission Book No. 82, p. 114; *Maryland Historical Magazine*, Vol. XXVI, p. 254); registration of schooner *Virgin*, 25 tons, built in Prince George's County, 1746. Samuel Hall, master. William Dames, owner. 11 Aug 1747. (Ref: Maryland Commission Book No. 82, p. 131; *Maryland Historical Magazine*, Vol. XXVI, p. 261); registration of ship *Duke*, of Cumberland, 100 tons, built in Kent County, 1747. Thomas Glenworth, master. William Dames, Daniel Cheston and Samuel Massey, owners. 10 Jul 1747. (Ref: Maryland Commission Book No. 82, p. 130; *Maryland Historical Magazine*, Vol. XXVI, p. 261); registration of sloop *Charming Betty*, 20 tons, built in Baltimore County, 1747. John Hall, master. William Dames, owner. 10 Jul 1747. (Ref: Maryland Commission Book No. 82, p. 131; *Maryland Historical Magazine*, Vol. XXVI, p. 261); appointed a Commissioner of the Peace for Queen Anne's County, 11 Nov 1763. (Ref: Maryland State Archives, Governor and Council Commissioner Records, 1726-1794, p. 212); see Daniel Cheston.

Darby, George, was appointed Constable of Newfoundland Hundred in Frederick County in 1753. (Ref: *This Was The Life: Excerpts from the Judgment Records of Frederick County, Maryland, 1748-1765*, by Millard Milburn Rice, p. 131)

Dare, Gideon (d. 1757), appointed a Commissioner of the Peace for Calvert County, 3 Mar 1726/7. (Ref: Maryland State Archives, Governor and Council Commissioner Records, 1726-1794, p. 3)

Dare, Nathaniel, see Negro Pompey.

Darnall, John, commissioned Sheriff of Ann Arundel

County, 25 Jun 1740, and Sheriff and Court Clerk of Frederick County, 1748. (Ref: Maryland State Archives, Governor and Council Commissioner Records, 1726-1794, p. 68; *This Was The Life: Excerpts from the Judgment Records of Frederick County, Maryland, 1748-1765*, by Millard Milburn Rice, p. 1); appointed a Commissioner of the Peace for Anne Arundel County, 8 Nov 1742. (Ref: Maryland State Archives, Governor and Council Commissioner Records, 1726-1794, p. 75); Clerk of the Court in Frederick County, 1764. (*Calendar of Maryland State Papers, No. 1 The Black Books*, p. 189); see Daniel Dunn.

Dashiell, Arthur (1715-1741), registration of the brigantine *Martha*, 35 tons, built at Clognakilly in Ireland, 1722. Arthur Dashiell, master and co-owner. Levin Gale, co-owner. 20 Mar 1736/7. (Ref: Maryland Commission Book No. 82, p. 47; *Maryland Historical Magazine*, Vol. XXVI, p. 148, spelled his surname Dashiel)

Dashiell, Clement, see George Dashiell.

Dashiell, George, appointed a Commissioner of the Peace for Somerset County, 25 Mar 1734. (Ref: Maryland State Archives, Governor and Council Commissioner Records, 1726-1794, p. 40); merchant, registration of sloop *Elizabeth*, 10 tons, built in Somerset County, 1746. Clement Dashiell, master. George Dashiell, owner. 12 Nov 1746. (Ref: Maryland Commission Book No. 82, p. 123; *Maryland Historical Magazine*, Vol. XXVI, p. 258, spelled his surname Dashiel)

Dashiell, George, of George (b. 1743), appointed a Commissioner of the Peace for Somerset County, 20 Mar 1775. (Ref: Maryland State Archives, Governor and Council Commissioner Records, 1726-1794, p. 288. spelled his surname Dashiel)

Dashiell, James, appointed a Commissioner of the Peace for Somerset County, 29 Oct 1730. (Ref: Maryland State Archives, Governor and Council Commissioner Records, 1726-1794, p. 17)

Dashiell, Joseph (1736-c1787), appointed a Commissioner of the Peace for Worcester County, 17 Nov 1766. (Ref: Maryland State Archives, Governor and Council Commissioner Records, 1726-1794, p. 229, spelled his surname Dashiel); Court Justice, Worcester County, 1774. (*Calendar of Maryland State Papers, No. 1 The Black Books*, p. 214); appointed a Commissioner of the Peace for Somerset County, 5 Jan 1775. (Ref: Maryland State Archives, Governor and Council Commissioner Records, 1726-1794, p. 286, spelled his surname Dashiel)

Dashiell, Josiah (1746-1784), commissioned High Sheriff of Somerset County, 10 Sep 1773. (Ref: Maryland State Archives, Governor and Council Commissioner Records, 1726-1794, p. 265)

Dashiell, Levin (1711-c1795), was appointed a Commissioner of the Peace for Somerset County, 20 May 1766. (Ref: Maryland State Archives, Governor and Council Commissioner Records, 1726-1794, p. 226, spelled his surname Dashiel)

Dashiell, Lowther (Louther) (1722-1765), was appointed a Commissioner of the Peace for Somerset County, 23 Mar 1756. (Ref: Maryland State Archives, Governor and Council Commissioner Records, 1726-1794, p. 166)

Dashiell, Mitchell, of Somerset County, was a Court Justice, 1753. (*Calendar of Maryland State Papers, No. 1 The Black Books*, p. 112, spelled his name Dashiel)

Dashiell, Robert, of Mitchell, was appointed a Commissioner of the Peace for Somerset County, 19 May 1774. (Ref: Maryland State Archives, Governor and Council Commissioner Records, 1726-1794, p. 282)

Davidge, John, appointed a Commissioner of the Peace for Anne Arundel County, 3 Mar 1726/7. (Ref: Maryland State Archives, Governor and Council Commissioner Records, 1726-1794, p. 3)

Davies, Allen, commissioned High Sheriff of Charles County, 17 Oct 1759. (Ref: Maryland State Archives, Governor and Council Commissioner Records, 1726-1794, p. 180, and p. 191 styled him as colonel)

Davis, Allen, appointed a Commissioner of the Peace for Charles County, 30 Oct 1732. (Ref: Maryland State Archives, Governor and Council Commissioner Records, 1726-1794, p. 27)

Davis, Benjamin, see Negro Pompey.

Davis, Clement, appointed Constable of the Upper Part of Potomac Hundred in Frederick County in 1751. (Ref: *This Was The Life: Excerpts from the Judgment Records of Frederick County, Maryland, 1748-1765*, by Millard Milburn Rice, p. 61)

Davis, Jacob, see Negro George and Negro Sam.

Davis, James, appointed Constable of Tonoloways Hundred in Prince George's County, now Frederick County, 1748. (Ref: Prince George's County Court Records, 1736-1738, Extracts by Patricia Abelard Andersen, *Western Maryland Genealogy*, Vol. 18, No. 1, January 2002, p. 46)

Davis, John, of Magotty [Magothy], appointed a Commissioner of the Peace for Anne Arundel County, 1 Nov 1761. (Ref: Maryland State Archives, Governor and Council Commissioner Records, 1726-1794, p. 201)

Davis, John, registration of sloop *Grayhound*, 50 tons, built at Pocomoke. 1738. John Davis, master and owner. 9 Jun 1739. (Ref: Maryland Commission Book No. 82, p. 74; *Maryland Historical Magazine*, Vol. XXVI, p. 154)

Davis, John, appointed Constable of Eastern Branch Hundred in Prince George's County, now Frederick County, 1739 and 1740. (Ref: Prince George's County Court Records, 1736-1748, Extracts by Patricia Abelard Andersen, *Western Maryland Genealogy*, Vol. 18, No. 1, January 2002, pp. 36, 37)

Davis, John, appointed Constable of the Lower Part of Newfoundland Hundred in Frederick County in 1751. (Ref: *This Was The Life: Excerpts from the Judgment Records of Frederick County, Maryland, 1748-1765*, by Millard Milburn Rice, p. 61)

Davis, Leonard, appointed Constable of Rock Creek Hundred in Frederick County, 1771. (Ref: "Frederick County Minute Book, March 1771, Extracts by Patricia Abelard Andersen," *Western Maryland Genealogy*, Vol. 18, No. 1, January 2002, p. 25)

Davis, Meredith, commissioned Ranger for Prince George's County from Seneca Creek upwards to the limits of said county. 30 Jun 1738. (Ref: Maryland Commission Book No. 82, p. 60; *Maryland Historical Magazine*, Vol. XXVI, p. 152)

Davis, Owen, appointed Constable of Conococheague Hundred in Frederick County in 1751. (Ref: *This Was The Life: Excerpts from the Judgment Records of Frederick County, Maryland, 1748-1765*, by Millard Milburn Rice, p. 61)

Davis, Richard, appointed a Commissioner of the Peace for Anne Arundel County, 8 Mar 1735/6 and 10 Sep 1736. (Ref: Maryland State Archives, Governor and Council Commissioner Records, 1726-1794, pp. 51, 53)

Dawkins, James, commissioner Coroner of Calvert County, 28 Apr 1770. (Ref: Maryland Commission Book No. 82, p. 240; *Maryland Historical Magazine*, Vol. XXVI, p. 361)

Dawson, Isaac, appointed Constable of Marsh Hundred in Frederick County in 1763. (Ref: *This Was The Life: Excerpts from the Judgment Records of Frederick County, Maryland, 1748-1765*, by Millard Milburn Rice, p. 249)

Dawson, Richard, appointed Constable of Streights Hundred in Dorchester County, 1744. (Ref: Dorchester County Judgment Records, 1743-1745, p. 185; *Judgment Records of Dorchester, Queen Anne's and Talbot Counties, Maryland*, by F. Edward Wright, 2001, p. 49); appointed Constable of North East Fork Hundred in Dorchester County, 1745. (Ref: Dorchester County Judgment Records, 1743-1745, p. 476; *Judgment Records of Dorchester, Queen Anne's and Talbot Counties, Maryland*, by F. Edward Wright, 2001, p. 60)

Dawson, William, of William, was appointed Constable of Bridgetown Hundred in Dorchester County, 1744, 1745. (Ref: Dorchester County Judgment Records, 1743-1745, p. 185, and p. 476 listed him without "of William;" *Judgment Records of Dorchester, Queen Anne's and Talbot Counties, Maryland*, by F. Edward Wright, 2001, p. 49, and p. 60 listed him without "of William")

Deacons, William, appointed a Commissioner of the Peace for Frederick County, 15 Aug 1774. (Ref: Maryland State Archives, Governor and Council Commissioner Records, 1726-1794, p. 284)

Deakins, William, appointed a Commissioner of the Peace for Frederick County, 20 Aug 1772. (Ref: Maryland State Archives, Governor and Council Commissioner Records, 1726-1794, p. 261)

Deans, Hugh (d. 1777), reverend, resignation from St. Margaret's Westminster Parish, Anne Arundel County, 22 Jul 1742. On same day, induction into St. John's Parish, Baltimore County. (Ref: Maryland Commission Book No. 82, pp. 91, 93; *Maryland Historical Magazine*, Vol. XXVI, p. 246)

Deason, William, appointed a Commissioner of the Peace for St. Mary's County, 29 Oct 1730. (Ref:

Maryland State Archives, Governor and Council Commissioner Records, 1726-1794, p. 12)

Deaver, John, of Baltimore County, Ranger, 9 Aug 1775. (Ref: *Calendar of Maryland State Papers, The Red Books*, No. 4, Part 1, p. 5)

DeButts, John, appointed a Commissioner of the Peace for Somerset County, 26 Jul 1773. (Ref: Maryland State Archives, Governor and Council Commissioner Records, 1726-1794, p. 272)

DeButts, Laurence (1693-1763), reverend, was inducted into William and Mary Parish, St. Mary's County, 1 Apr 1734. (Ref: Maryland Commission Book No. 82, p. 10; *Maryland Historical Magazine*, Vol. XXVI, p. 140, did not list his first name; *Directory of Ministers and the Maryland Churches They Served, 1634-1900*, by Edna Agatha Kanely, Vol. I, A-K, p. 167, listed his name as Laurence (Lawrence) DeButts)

DeButts, Robert, appointed Constable of the Upper Part of Monocacy Hundred in Prince George's County, now Frederick County, 1739 and 1740, and Lnganore Hundred in 1742. (Ref: Prince George's County Court Records, 1736-1748, Extracts by Patricia Abelard Andersen, *Western Maryland Genealogy*, Vol. 18, No. 1, January 2002, pp. 36, 37, 38)

DeCeausse, Leonard, of Anne Arundel County, naturalized 29 Apr 1735. (Ref: Maryland Commission Book No. 82, p. 29; *Maryland Historical Magazine*, Vol. XXVI, p. 143)

Delashmutt, Elias, was appointed Constable of Monocousie [Monocacy] Hundred in Prince George's County, now Frederick County, 1744. (Ref: Prince George's County Court Records, 1736-1748, Extracts by Patricia Abelard Andersen, *Western Maryland Genealogy*, Vol. 18, No. 1, January 2002, p. 41); see Thomas Ledston.

Dell, Thomas, reverend, Rector of St. Mary's Whitechappel Parish, Dorchester County. Permission granted to go to abroad for one year without loss of revenue. 20 Jun 1738. (Ref: Maryland Commission Book No. 82, p. 61; *Maryland Historical Magazine*, Vol. XXVI, p. 152)

Delleney, Edward, of Baltimore County, Ranger, 9 Aug 1775. (Ref: *Calendar of Maryland State Papers, The Red Books*, No. 4, Part 1, p. 5)

Delleney, William, of Baltimore County, Ranger, 9 Aug 1775. (Ref: *Calendar of Maryland State Papers, The Red Books*, No. 4, Part 1, p. 5)

Dennis, John, registration of sloop *Pocomoke*, 15 tons. John Dennis, master and owner. 11 Feb 1734/5. (Ref: Maryland Commission Book No. 82, p. 25; *Maryland Historical Magazine*, Vol. XXVI, p. 142: registration of sloop *Molly and Betty*, 30 tons, built in Somerset County, 1736. John Dennis, master and owner. 20 Oct 1736. (Ref: Maryland Commission Book No. 82, p. 45; *Maryland Historical Magazine*, Vol. XXVI, p. 148); registration of sloop *Catherine and Ann*, 30 tons, built in Somerset County, 1738. Duncan Murray, master. John Dennis, owner. 31 Mar 1739. (Ref: Maryland Commission Book No. 82, p. 72; *Maryland Historical Magazine*, Vol. XXVI, p. 153); see William Lane.

Dennis, John (c1724-1782), commissioned High Sheriff of Worcester County, 31 Oct 1755. (Ref: Maryland State Archives, Governor and Council Commissioner Records, 1726-1794, p. 155; *Archives of Maryland*, Vol. LII, "Proceedings and Acts of the General Assembly of Maryland, 1755-1756," p. 576); Court Justice, 1774. (*Calendar of Maryland State Papers, No. 1 The Black Books*, p. 214)

Dennis, John, Jr. (1704-1767), commissioned Sheriff of Somerset County, 16 May 1743. (Ref: Maryland State Archives, Governor and Council Commissioner Records, 1726-1794, p. 78); appointed a Commissioner of the Peace for Somerset County, 20 Oct 1746. (Ref: Maryland State Archives, Governor and Council Commissioner Records, 1726-1794, p. 94)

Dennis, John, Sr., of Somerset County, Court Justice, 1753. (*Calendar of Maryland State Papers, No. 1 The Black Books*, p. 112 listed him without the Sr.); appointed a Commissioner of the Peace for Somerset County, 1 Oct 1762 and 5 Jan 1775. (Ref: Maryland State Archives, Governor and Council Commissioner Records, 1726-1794, pp. 204, 286)

Dennis, Richard, appointed Constable of the Upper Part of Antietam Hundred in Frederick County, 1771. (Ref: "Frederick County Minute Book, March 1771, Extracts by Patricia Abelard Andersen," *Western Maryland Genealogy*, Vol. 18, No. 1, January 2002, p. 26)

Dennison, John, was commissioned one of the Coroners of Somerset County, 16 Sep 1745. (Ref:

Maryland Commission Book No. 82, p. 116; *Maryland Historical Magazine*, Vol. XXVI, p. 255)

Denom, James, of Frederick County, convicted of murder, was executed on 22 Oct 1773. (Ref: Maryland State Archives, Governor and Council Commissioner Records, 1726-1794, p. 265)

Dent, George (1690-1754), was appointed a Commissioner of the Peace for Charles County, 2 Mar 1726/7. (Ref: Maryland State Archives, Governor and Council Commissioner Records, 1726-1794, p. 2); commissioned a Provincial Justice by the Governor, 20 Oct 1729. (Ref: Maryland State Archives, Governor and Council Commissioner Records, 1726-1794, p. 12); commissioned High Sheriff of Charles County in the room of Benjamin Fendall, 17 Jun 1735 and 8 Jul 1736. (Ref: Maryland Commission Book No. 82, p. 30; *Maryland Historical Magazine*, Vol. XXVI, p. 144 Maryland State Archives, Governor and Council Commissioner Records, 1726-1794, pp. 47, 53)

Dent, George, Jr. (d. 1785), commissioned Sheriff of Charles County, 28 Apr 1753. (Ref: Maryland State Archives, Governor and Council Commissioner Records, 1726-1794, p. 140; *Calendar of Maryland State Papers, No. 1 The Black Books*, p. 132, listed him without the Jr. in 1756); appointed a Commissioner of the Peace for Charles County, 15 Oct 1774. (Ref: Maryland State Archives, Governor and Council Commissioner Records, 1726-1794, p. 284)

Dent, John, appointed a Commissioner of the Peace for Charles County, 17 Nov 1764. (Ref: Maryland State Archives, Governor and Council Commissioner Records, 1726-1794, p. 220)

Dent, Peter, appointed a Commissioner of the Peace for Prince George's County, 1 Nov 1729. (Ref: Maryland State Archives, Governor and Council Commissioner Records, 1726-1794, p. 12); commissioned Deputy Surveyor of Prince George's County, 16 Sep 1735 and 30 Aug 1742. (Ref: Maryland Commission Book No. 82, pp. 33, 93; *Maryland Historical Magazine*, Vol. XXVI, pp. 145, 246)

Dent, Peter, commissioned Deputy Surveyor of Charles County, 16 Oct 1771. (Ref: Maryland Commission Book No. 82, p. 272; *Maryland Historical Magazine*, Vol. XXVII, p. 30)

Dent, Warren (d. 1794), was appointed a Commissioner of the Peace for Charles County, 2 Oct 1771. (Ref: Maryland State Archives, Governor and Council Commissioner Records, 1726-1794, p. 258)

Dent, William, see Yellow Dick.

Deoran, William, registration of the brigantine *Revolution*, 35 tons, built in Cecil County, 1740. William Deoran, master. Susannah Bayard, James Bayard and William Deoran, owners. (Ref: Maryland Commission Book No. 82, p. 84; *Maryland Historical Magazine*, Vol. XXVI, p. 158)

Derrickson, Joseph, appointed a Commissioner of the Peace for Worcester County, 2 Mar 1754. (Ref: Maryland State Archives, Governor and Council Commissioner Records, 1726-1794, p. 142)

Derrickson, Levin, commissioned a Coroner of Worcester County, 22 May 1765. (Ref: Maryland Commission Book No. 82, p. 168; *Maryland Historical Magazine*, Vol. XXVI, p. 353)

Dew, Richard, see Richard Crosby.

Deye, Thomas Cockey (c1728-1807), appointed to represent Baltimore County in the Provincial Convention, 1775. (Ref: *Calendar of Maryland State Papers, The Red Books*, No. 4, Part 1, p. 3)

Dick, James, merchant, registration of brigantine *Sea Nymph*, 50 tons, built in Dorchester County, 1735. Archibald Johnson, master. James Dick and Daniel Campbell, owners. 16 May 1745. (Ref: Maryland Commission Book No. 82, p. 113; *Maryland Historical Magazine*, Vol. XXVI, p. 254); appointed a Commissioner of the Peace for Anne Arundel County, 28 May 1756. (Ref: Maryland State Archives, Governor and Council Commissioner Records, 1726-1794, p. 168); see William Roberts.

Dicke, Thomas, labourer, of Anne Arundel County, convicted felon for breaking into the meat houses of Beriah Mayberry and George Steuart and stealing large quantities of bacon, and the house of Samuel Chase and Richard Maccubbin and stealing sundry goods and chattels, and the warehouse of Charles Carroll, Esq., and stealing two gallons of rum belonging to Thomas Charles Williams, merchant, of Annapolis. He was pardoned, released from jail and banished on 16 Sep 1769 with the condition that he shall not stay in the city for more than twelve hours nor longer than ten days in the province, never to return again. (Ref: Maryland Commission Book No. 82, p. 228; *Maryland Historical Magazine*, Vol. XXVI, pp. 359-360; *Archives of Maryland*, Vol. XXXII, "Proceedings of the Council of Maryland, 1761-1770," p. 314)

Dickerson, John, was appointed Constable of Newfoundland Hundred in Prince George's County, now Frederick County, 1746. (Ref: Prince George's County Court Records, 1736-1748, Extracts by Patricia Abelard Andersen, *Western Maryland Genealogy*, Vol. 18, No. 1, January 2002, p. 44)

Dickinson, Charles, appointed a Commissioner of the Peace for Dorchester County, 24 May 1737 and 26 Oct 1738. (Ref: Maryland State Archives, Governor and Council Commissioner Records, 1726-1794, pp. 56, 62); commissioned one of the Coroners for Dorchester County, 18 Jun 1741. (Ref: Maryland Commission Book No. 82, p. 87; *Maryland Historical Magazine*, Vol. XXVI, p. 244, spelled his name Dickenson); appointed a Commissioner of the Peace for Caroline County, 8 Feb 1774. (Ref: Maryland State Archives, Governor and Council Commissioner Records, 1726-1794, p. 280, spelled his name Dickenson); commissioned Sheriff of Dorchester County, 29 Oct 1755. (Ref: Maryland State Archives, Governor and Council Commissioner Records, 1726-1794, p. 155)

Dickinson, James, registration of sloop *Rachel*, 40 tons, built in Baltimore County, 1748. Richard Bruff, master. James Dickinson and Robert Morris, owners. 12 Feb 1749/50. (Ref: Maryland Commission Book No. 82, p. 154; *Maryland Historical Magazine*, Vol. XXVI, pp. 350-351; registration of sloop *Rachel*, 40 tons, built in Baltimore County, 1750. Richard Bruff, master. James Dickinson, owner. 14 Sep 1750. (Ref: Maryland Commission Book No. 82, p. 146; *Maryland Historical Magazine*, Vol. XXVI, p. 346); see Anthony Bacon.

Dickinson, James (c1726-1787), commissioned High Sheriff of Talbot County, 10 Oct 1752. (Ref: Maryland State Archives, Governor and Council Commissioner Records, 1726-1794, p. 135, spelled his name Dickenson); Court Justice, Talbot County, 1774. (*Calendar of Maryland State Papers, No. 1 The Black Books*, p. 211)

Dickinson, John c1726-1789), commissioned High Sheriff of Dorchester County, 22 Sep 1764; appointed a Commissioner of the Peace for Dorchester County, 8 Apr 1770. (Ref: Maryland State Archives, Governor and Council Commissioner Records, 1726-1794, pp. 208, 250)

Dickson, Charles, appointed a Commissioner of the Peace for Dorchester County, 28 Feb 1742/3. (Ref: Maryland State Archives, Governor and Council Commissioner Records, 1726-1794, p. 76)

Dickson, George, appointed Constable of Frederick Town Hundred in Frederick County, 1769. (Ref: "Frederick County Court Minutes, March 1769," by Patricia Abelard Andersen, *Western Maryland Genealogy*, Vol. 15, No. 2, April 1999, p. 63)

Dickson, James, commissioned a Coroner of Frederick County, 20 Apr 1750. (Ref: Maryland Commission Book No. 82, p. 143; *Maryland Historical Magazine*, Vol. XXVI, p. 345; appointed a Commissioner of the Peace for Frederick County, 26 May 1756. (Ref: Maryland State Archives, Governor and Council Commissioner Records, 1726-1794, p. 168; commissioned Sheriff of Frederick County, 8 Nov 1756. (Ref: Maryland State Archives, Governor and Council Commissioner Records, 1726-1794, p. 163; *This Was The Life: Excerpts from the Judgment Records of Frederick County, Maryland, 1748-1765*, by Millard Milburn Rice, p. 179 spelled his name Dickson, and p. 180 spelled his name Dixon in 1758); appointed a Commissioner of the Peace for Frederick County, 19 Nov 1759. (Ref: Maryland State Archives, Governor and Council Commissioner Records, 1726-1794, p. 189)

Digges, William, registration of the schooner *Eleanor*, 36 tons, built at Patowmeck [Potomac], 1735. Ignatius Semmes, master. 22 May 1736. (Ref: Maryland Commission Book No. 82, p. 44; *Maryland Historical Magazine*, Vol. XXVI, p. 147)

Diggs, Edward, see Negro Anthony.

Dobbs, Thomas, of Frederick County, convicted of stealing twenty pairs of women's necklaces valued at one hundred pounds of tobacco and fifteen hundred needles valued at one hundred pounds of tobacco in 1752, the property of Charles Conner, was sentenced to be set upon the pillory for half an hour and then sent to the whipping post and receive ten stripes on his bare body. (Ref: *This Was The Life: Excerpts from the Judgment Records of Frederick County, Maryland, 1748-1765*, by Millard Milburn Rice, p. 103)

Dogan, Matthew, of Kent County, convicted felon,

was executed on 5 Oct 1759. (Ref: Maryland State Archives, Governor and Council Commissioner Records, 1726-1794, p. 175)

Donaldson, James, registration of ship *Success* of Maryland, 80 tons, built at Boston, 1733. Thomas Jenkins, master. James Donaldson, owner. 8 Feb 1733/4. (Ref: Maryland Commission Book No. 82, p. 5; *Maryland Historical Magazine*, Vol. XXVI, p. 139); registration of sloop *Biddy*, 30 tons, built at South River, 1733. William Coughlan, master. James Donaldson, owner. 9 Feb 1733/4. (Ref: Maryland Commission Book No. 82, p. 8; *Maryland Historical Magazine*, Vol. XXVI, p. 139); registration of the brigantine *Ogle*, formerly the *Success* (forfeited by decree by court of Vice-Admiralty), 80 tons, built in Boston, 1733. John Smart, master. James Donaldson, owner. 24 Mar 1734/5. (Ref: Maryland Commission Book No. 82, p. 27; *Maryland Historical Magazine*, Vol. XXVI, p. 143)

Donaldson, John, see William Whittington and Negro Andrew.

Done, John (c1747-1831), was commissioned High Sheriff of Worcester County, 10 Sep 1773. (Ref: Maryland State Archives, Governor and Council Commissioner Records, 1726-1794, p. 265)

Dorsey, Basil, Jr., appointed a Commissioner of the Peace for Frederick County, 22 Nov 1752. (Ref: Maryland State Archives, Governor and Council Commissioner Records, 1726-1794, p. 135)

Dorsey, Caleb, of Basil, was appointed a Commissioner of the Peace for Anne Arundel County, 1 Nov 1761. (Ref: Maryland State Archives, Governor and Council Commissioner Records, 1726-1794, p. 201)

Dorsey, Caleb, Jr., appointed a Commissioner of the Peace for Anne Arundel County, 13 Mar 1737/8. (Ref: Maryland State Archives, Governor and Council Commissioner Records, 1726-1794, p. 59)

Dorsey, Henry, see Negro Abraham;

Dorsey, John, appointed a Commissioner of the Peace for Baltimore County, 3 Mar 1726/7. (Ref: Maryland State Archives, Governor and Council Commissioner Records, 1726-1794, p. 2)

Dorsey, John, merchant, was appointed a Commissioner of the Peace for Anne Arundel County, 1 Aug 1768. (Ref: Maryland State Archives, Governor and Council Commissioner Records, 1726-1794, p. 234)

Dorsey, John Hammond (1718-1774), appointed a Commissioner of the Peace for Baltimore County, 23 May 1753. (Ref: Maryland State Archives, Governor and Council Commissioner Records, 1726-1794, p. 138)

Dorsey, Joshua, of Anne Arundel County, appointed a Press Master in 1774. (Ref: Anne Arundel County Court Minutes, 1725-1757, 1774)

Dorsey, Philemon, appointed a Commissioner of the Peace for Anne Arundel County, 12 Aug 1752. (Ref: Maryland State Archives, Governor and Council Commissioner Records, 1726-1794, p. 133)

Dorsey, Richard, appointed a Commissioner of the Peace for Anne Arundel County, 9 Aug 1742. (Ref: Maryland State Archives, Governor and Council Commissioner Records, 1726-1794, p. 74); Justice, Anne Arundel County Court, 1754. (Ref: Anne Arundel County Court Minutes, 1725-1757)

Dorsey, Samuel, was appointed Constable of Linganore Hundred in Frederick County in 1763. (Ref: *This Was The Life: Excerpts from the Judgment Records of Frederick County, Maryland, 1748-1765*, by Millard Milburn Rice, p. 249)

Dorsey, Thomas, appointed a Commissioner of the Peace for Anne Arundel County, 1 Aug 1768. (Ref: Maryland State Archives, Governor and Council Commissioner Records, 1726-1794, p. 234)

Dove, John, Sheriff of Worcester County, 1774. (*Calendar of Maryland State Papers, No. 1 The Black Books*, p. 214)

Dow, Richard, see Richard Crosby.

Dowell, James, appointed a Commissioner of the Peace for Frederick County, 1 Mar 1749/50. (Ref: Maryland State Archives, Governor and Council Commissioner Records, 1726-1794, p. 116); Court Justice, Frederick County, 1750. (Ref: *This Was The Life: Excerpts from the Judgment Records of Frederick County, Maryland, 1748-1765*, by Millard Milburn Rice, p. 47, spelled his name Doull)

Dowie, William, reverend, inducted into Durham Parish, Charles County, 4 Aug 1764. (Ref: Maryland Commission Book No. 82, p. 163; *Maryland Historical Magazine*, Vol. XXVI, p. 352)

Dowman, Richard, of Talbot County, convicted felon, was executed on 19 May 1729. (Ref: Maryland State Archives, Governor and Council Commissioner Records, 1726-1794, p. 10)

Downes, Charles, appointed a Commissioner of the Peace for Queen Anne's County, 16 Jul 1735. (Ref: Maryland State Archives, Governor and Council Commissioner Records, 1726-1794, p. 49)

Downes, John, appointed a Commissioner of the Peace for Queen Anne's County, 4 Nov 1749. (Ref: Maryland State Archives, Governor and Council Commissioner Records, 1726-1794, p. 114)

Downes, John, Jr., appointed a Commissioner of the Peace for Queen Anne's County, 1 Dec 1746. (Ref: Maryland State Archives, Governor and Council Commissioner Record, 1726-1794, p. 95)

Downes, Philemon (c1741-c1796), of Queen Anne's County, commissioned High Sheriff, 3 Nov 1773. (Ref: Maryland State Archives, Governor and Council Commissioner Records, 1726-1794, p. 268)

Downes, Vachel, appointed a Commissioner of the Peace for Queen Anne's County, 13 Mar 1773. (Ref: Maryland State Archives, Governor and Council Commissioner Records, 1726-1794, p. 265); Court Justice, 1774. (*Calendar of Maryland State Papers, No. 1 The Black Books*, p. 215)

Downey, Robert, appointed Constable of Salisbury Hundred in Frederick County, 1749. (Ref: *This Was The Life: Excerpts from the Judgment Records of Frederick County, Maryland, 1748-1765*, by Millard Milburn Rice, p. 7)

Downing, James, appointed Constable of Salisbury Hundred in Frederick County in 1751. (Ref: *This Was The Life: Excerpts from the Judgment Records of Frederick County, Maryland, 1748-1765*, by Millard Milburn Rice, p. 61)

Draper, Alexander, see William Draper.

Draper, William, of Somerset Co., registration of brigantine *Nanticoke*, 60 tons, built in Somerset County, 1733. Alexander Draper and William Draper, owners. 16 Oct 1733. (Ref: Maryland Commission Book No. 82, p. 7; *Maryland Historical Magazine*, Vol. XXVI, p. 139); registration of sloop *Betty*, 20 tons, built in Worcester County, 1746. Isaac Holland, master. William Draper, owner. 13 Aug 1746. (Ref: Maryland Commission Book No. 82, p. 121; *Maryland Historical Magazine*, Vol. XXVI, p. 257); appointed a Commissioner of the Peace for Worcester County, 28 Oct 1747. (Ref: Maryland State Archives, Governor and Council Commissioner Records, 1726-1794, p. 102)

Driver, Matthew (1740-1798), appointed a Commissioner of the Peace for Caroline County, 8 Feb 1774. (Ref: Maryland State Archives, Governor and Council Commissioner Records, 1726-1794, p. 280)

Driver, Matthew, Jr., appointed a Commissioner of the Peace for Caroline County, 15 Aug 1774. (Ref: Maryland State Archives, Governor and Council Commissioner Records, 1726-1794, p. 284)

Ducker, William, appointed Constable of George Town Hundred in Frederick County in 1763. (Ref: *This Was The Life: Excerpts from the Judgment Records of Frederick County, Maryland, 1748-1765*, by Millard Milburn Rice, p. 249)

Duckett, Jacob, was appointed Constable of Monocousie [Monocacy] Hundred in Prince George's County, now Frederick County, 1745. (Ref: Prince George's County Court Records, 1736-1748, Extracts by Patricia Abelard Andersen, *Western Maryland Genealogy*, Vol. 18, No. 1, January 2002, p. 43); appointed a Commissioner of the Peace for Frederick County, 3 Nov 1757. (Ref: Maryland State Archives, Governor and Council Commissioner Records, 1726-1794, p. 178); Court Justice in Frederick County in 1758. (Ref: *This Was The Life: Excerpts from the Judgment Records of Frederick County, Maryland, 1748-1765*, by Millard Milburn Rice, p. 177)

Duckett, John, of Anne Arundel Co., appointed Clerk to the Committee of Arms and Ammunition, 3 Jul 1755. (Ref: *Archives of Maryland*, Vol. LII, "Proceedings and Acts of the General Assembly of Maryland, 1755-1756," pp. 156-157)

Duckett, Richard, Jr. (1704-1788), appointed a Commissioner of the Peace for Prince George's County, 3 Dec 1766. (Ref: Maryland State Archives, Governor and Council Commissioner Records, 1726-1794, p. 230); see Negro Thomas.

Duffey, George, laborer, late of All Hallows Parish, Worcester County, pardoned and banished for burglary, 5 Jun 1771. (Ref: Maryland Commission Book No. 82, p. 257; *Maryland Historical Magazine*, Vol. XXVII, p. 30)

Duke, James, appointed a Commissioner of the Peace for Calvert County, 9 Dec 1731. (Ref: Maryland State Archives, Governor and Council Commissioner Records, 1726-1794, p. 20)

Dulany, Daniel (1685-1753), commissioned Receiver General, 29 Sep 1733. (Ref: Maryland Commission Book No. 82, p. 34; *Maryland Historical Magazine*, Vol. XXVI, p. 145); commissioned one of the Commissary Generals and Judges for Probate of Wills, 5 Feb 1733/4. (Ref: Maryland Commission Book No. 82, p. 36; *Maryland Historical Magazine*, Vol. XXVI, p. 145); commissioned Judge of Admiralty, 22 May 1734. (Ref: Maryland Commission Book No. 82, p. 14; *Maryland Historical Magazine*, Vol. XXVI, p. 141); commissioned Commissary General. 14 Oct 1742. (Ref: Maryland Commission Book No. 82, p. 96; *Maryland Historical Magazine*, Vol. XXVI, p. 247)

Dulany, Daniel, Jr. (1722-1797), commissioned one of three Agents for the Sale of His Lordship's Reserved Lands and Manors, 17 Jun 1770 and 17 Jul 1771. (Ref: Maryland Commission Book No. 82, pp. 241, 261; *Maryland Historical Magazine*, Vol. XXVI, p. 361, and Vol. XXVII, p. 30); see Charles Carroll.

Dulany, Dennis, appointed a Commissioner of the Peace for Kent County, 28 May 1756. (Ref: Maryland State Archives, Governor and Council Commissioner Records, 1726-1794, p. 168)

Dulany, Walter (d. 1773), of Annapolis, Anne Arundel County, appointed to a Committee to Inspect the Accounts and Proceedings of the Commissioners for Emitting Bills of Credit, 25 Feb 1755. (Ref: *Archives of Maryland*, Vol. LII, "Proceedings and Acts of the General Assembly of Maryland, 1755-1756," pp. 5, 46, 51); appointed to the Committee to Apportion the Public Levies, 29 May 1756. (Ref: *Archives of Maryland*, Vol. LII, "Proceedings and Acts of the General Assembly of Maryland, 1755-1756," p. 291; commissioned Naval Officer of Patuxent, 18 Jun 1765. (Ref: Maryland Commission Book No. 82, p. 168; *Maryland Historical Magazine*, Vol. XXVI, p. 353; commissioned Commissary General and Judge for Probate of Wills, 15 Jul 1767. (Ref: Maryland Commission Book No. 82, p. 201; *Maryland Historical Magazine*, Vol. XXVI, p. 355; commissioned Commissary General and Judge for Probate of Wills, 29 Apr 1773. On same day, commissioned Secretary of the Province of Maryland. (Ref: Maryland Commission Book No. 82, pp. 300-301; *Maryland Historical Magazine*, Vol. XXVII, p. 32)

Dunn, Daniel, of Frederick County, convicted "for stealing and robbing upon the high way from Mrs. Ruhamah Chaplin several goods the property of Mr. Joseph Chaplin," was executed on 28 Jan 1767. (Ref: Maryland State Archives, Governor and Council Commissioner Records, 1726-1794, p. 216; *Archives of Maryland*, Vol. XXXII, "Proceedings of the Council of Maryland, 1761-1770," p. 179)

Dunn, John, registration of sloop *George*, 20 tons, built on Gwynn's Island in Gloucester County, Virginia, 1736, and was then called the *Margaret*. John Dunn, master and owner. (Ref: Maryland Commission Book No. 82, p. 115; *Maryland Historical Magazine*, Vol. XXVI, p. 255)

Dunn, Robert (1693-1745), was appointed a Commissioner of the Peace for Kent County, 24 Nov 1735. (Ref: Maryland State Archives, Governor and Council Commissioner Records, 1726-1794, p. 50)

Dunne, John, of Baltimore County, Ranger, 9 Aug 1775. (Ref: *Calendar of Maryland State Papers, The Red Books*, No. 4, Part 1, p. 5)

Dunning, William, laborer, of Prince George's County, convicted burglar, was pardoned and then banished on 12 Apr 1771. (Ref: Maryland Commission Book No. 82, p. 256; *Maryland Historical Magazine*, Vol. XXVII, p. 30)

Durding, Joseph, see Negro Mingo.

Dutterer, Conrad, see Abraham Becraft.

Duvall, Aquilla, was appointed Constable of Newfoundland Hundred in Frederick County in 1763. (Ref: *This Was The Life: Excerpts from the Judgment Records of Frederick County, Maryland, 1748-1765*, by Millard Milburn Rice, p. 249)

Duvall, Joseph, see Negro George.

Duvall, Samuel, was appointed Constable of Monocacy Hundred in Prince George's County, now Frederick County, 1747. (Ref: Prince George's County Court Records, 1736-1748, Extracts by Patricia Abelard Andersen, *Western Maryland Genealogy*, Vol. 18, No. 1, January 2002, p. 45)

Eager, George, see Samuel Galloway.

Colonial Maryland Commissions, Appointments, and Other Proceedings, 1726-1776

Earl, James, see William Roberts.

Earle, James, Sr. (c1788-1734), appointed a Commissioner of the Peace for Queen Anne's County, 3 Mar 1726/7. (Ref: Maryland State Archives, Governor and Council Commissioner Records, 1726-1794, p. 2); commissioned Sheriff of Queen Anne's County, 27 Oct 1732. (Ref: Maryland State Archives, Governor and Council Commissioner Records, 1726-1794, p. 26); see John Fisher and William Schandrett.

Earle, Michael (1722-1787), was appointed a Commissioner of the Peace for Cecil County, 19 Dec 1751. (Ref: Maryland State Archives, Governor and Council Commissioner Records, 1726-1794, p. 131); appointed to a Committee to Inspect the Accounts and Proceedings of the Commissioners for Emitting Bills of Credit, 25 Feb 1755. (Ref: *Archives of Maryland*, Vol. LII, "Proceedings and Acts of the General Assembly of Maryland, 1755-1756," pp. 5, 51); late sheriff of Cecil County, had ordinary license accounts still unpaid in 1756. (Ref: *Archives of Maryland*, Vol. LII, "Proceedings and Acts of the General Assembly of Maryland, 1755-1756," p. 568)

Eccleston, Hugh, appointed a Commissioner of the Peace for Dorchester County, 2 Nov 1773. (Ref: Maryland State Archives, Governor and Council Commissioner Records, 1726-1794, p. 278); Court Justice, Dorchester County, 1774. (*Calendar of Maryland State Papers, No. 1 The Black Books*, p. 211)

Eccleston, John, appointed a Commissioner of the Peace for Dorchester County, 29 May 1734. (Ref: Maryland State Archives, Governor and Council Commissioner Records, 1726-1794, p. 42); major, of Dorchester County, appointed to the Committee to Enquire into Indian Complaints, 1754. (Ref: *Archives of Maryland*, Vol. XXXI, "Proceedings of the Council of Maryland, 1753-1761," p. 30)

Eccleston, John, appointed a Commissioner of the Peace for Kent County, 2 Nov 1762. (Ref: Maryland State Archives, Governor and Council Commissioner Records, 1726-1794, p. 207)

Eddis, William, was commissioned as Trustee for Emitting Bills of Credit, 22 Sep 1772. (Ref: Maryland Commission Book No. 82, p. 286; *Maryland Historical Magazine*, Vol. XXVII, p. 32); commissioned Commissioner or Trustee to Sign Bills of Credit, 29 Apr 1773. (Ref: Maryland Commission Book No. 82, p. 304; *Maryland Historical Magazine*, Vol. XXVII, p. 33); appointed a Commissioner of the Peace for Anne Arundel County, 24 Aug 1773. (Ref: Maryland State Archives, Governor and Council Commissioner Records, 1726-1794, p. 276); Court Justice, Anne Arundel County, 1774. (Ref: Anne Arundel County Court Minutes, 1725-1757, 1774)

Eden, John (c1728-1775), commissioned High Sheriff of St. Mary's County, 31 Oct 1758. (Ref: Maryland State Archives, Governor and Council Commissioner Records, 1726-1794, p. 173); appointed a Commissioner of the Peace for St. Mary's County, 26 Apr 1764. (Ref: Maryland State Archives, Governor and Council Commissioner Records, 1726-1794, p. 215)

Eden, Mr., see Negro Joe.

Eden, Robert (1741-1784), Chancellor and Keeper of the Great Seal of the Province of Maryland in 1768. (*Archives of Maryland*, Vol. XXXII, "Proceedings of the Council of Maryland, 1761-1770," p. 278); commissioned one of three Agents for the Sale of His Lordship's Reserved Lands and Manors, 17 Jun 1770 and 17 Jul 1771. (Ref: Maryland Commission Book No. 82, pp. 241, 261; *Maryland Historical Magazine*, Vol. XXVI, p. 361, and Vol. XXVII, p. 30)

Edgar, Samuel, reverend, induction into St. Anne's Parish, Anne Arundel County, 5 Jan 1743/4. (Ref: Maryland Commission Book No. 82, p. 107; *Maryland Historical Magazine*, Vol. XXVI, p. 251)

Edge, James (c1710-1757), was appointed a Commissioner of the Peace for Talbot County, 16 Jun 1741. (Ref: Maryland State Archives, Governor and Council Commissioner Records, 1726-1794, p. 70); appointed to a Committee to Inspect the Accounts and Proceedings of the Commissioners for Emitting Bills of Credit, 25 Feb 1755. (Ref: *Archives of Maryland*, Vol. LII, "Proceedings and Acts of the General Assembly of Maryland, 1755-1756," pp. 5, 51); appointed to a Committee for Enquiring into Ways and Means to Raise a Sum Sufficient for Payment of Eighty Rangers to Defend and Protect the Frontiers, 28 Jun 1755. (Ref: Maryland State Archives, Governor and Council Commissioner Records, 1726-1794, p. 151)

Edgett, Simon, see Serjeant Smythers.

Edmiston, William, reverend, induction into St. Anne's Parish, Anne Arundel County, 30 Mar 1768.

(Ref: Maryland Commission Book No. 82, p. 209; *Maryland Historical Magazine*, Vol. XXVI, p. 357); induction into St. Thomas' Parish, Baltimore County, 9 May 1770. (Ref: Maryland Commission Book No. 82, p. 241; *Maryland Historical Magazine*, Vol. XXVI, p. 361); see Thomas John Clagett.

Edmondson, James, appointed a Commissioner of the Peace for Prince George's County, 30 Nov 1741. (Ref: Maryland State Archives, Governor and Council Commissioner Records, 1726-1794, p. 72)

Edmondson, William, of Solomon, appointed Constable of Great Choptank Hundred in Dorchester County, 1744, 1745. (Ref: Dorchester County Judgment Records, 1743-1745, pp. 185, 476; *Judgment Records of Dorchester, Queen Anne's and Talbot Counties, Maryland*, by F. Edward Wright, 2001, pp. 49, 60)

Edmonson, James, was appointed Constable of Armitage Hundred in Dorchester County, 1742, 1744. (Ref: Dorchester County Judgment Records, 1742-1743, p. 84, 1743-1745, p. 185; *Judgment Records of Dorchester, Queen Anne's and Talbot Counties, Maryland*, by F. Edward Wright, 2001, pp. 30, 49)

Edmonson, James, commissioned High Sheriff of Queen Anne's County, 11 Oct 1763. (Ref: Maryland State Archives, Governor and Council Commissioner Records, 1726-1794, p. 201)

Edmonson, Peter, was commissioned Ranger of Dorchester County, 19 Jan 1741/2. (Ref: Maryland Commission Book No. 82, p. 90; *Maryland Historical Magazine*, Vol. XXVI, p. 245)

Edmonson, Solomon, commissioned a Coroner for Dorchester County, 21 Oct 1738. (Ref: Maryland Commission Book No. 82, p. 64; *Maryland Historical Magazine*, Vol. XXVI, p. 152)

Edmonson, William (Quaker), registration of the schooner *Charming Betty*, 30 tons, built in Choptank River, 1735. John Coward, master. Henry Trippe, John Anderson and William Edmonson, owners. 15 May 1735. (Ref: Maryland Commission Book No. 82, p. 30; *Maryland Historical Magazine*, Vol. XXVI, p. 143)

Edmonstone, Archibald, Jr., Constable of Eastern Branch Hundred in Prince George's County, now Frederick County, in 1733. (*Calendar of Maryland State Papers, No. 1 The Black Books*, p. 41)

Edwards, John, commissioned Deputy Surveyor of St. Mary's County, 12 Dec 1746 and 29 Apr 1747. (Ref: Maryland Commission Book No. 82, pp. 124, 129; *Maryland Historical Magazine*, Vol. XXVI, pp. 258, 260)

Edwards, Joseph, Constable of Middle River Upper Hundred in Baltimore County, 1773. (Ref: *Inhabitants of Baltimore County, 1763-1774*, by Henry C. Peden, Jr., 1989, p. 68, citing a 1773 List of Taxables)

Edwards, Stourton, commissioned one of the Coroners of St. Mary's County, 13 Apr 1744. (Ref: Maryland Commission Book No. 82, p. 109; *Maryland Historical Magazine*, Vol. XXVI, p. 252)

Eilbach, William, appointed a Commissioner of the Peace for Charles County, 22 Oct 1739. (Ref: Maryland State Archives, Governor and Council Commissioner Records, 1726-1794, p. 66, spelled his name Eilbach); Court Justice, 1756. (*Calendar of Maryland State Papers, No. 1 The Black Books*, p. 132, spelled his name Eilbeck)

Elbert, William, appointed a Commissioner of the Peace for Queen Anne's County, 15 Oct 1760. (Ref: Maryland State Archives, Governor and Council Commissioner Records, 1726-1794, p. 192)

Elbert, William, appointed a Commissioner of the Peace for Talbot County, 30 Oct 1732. (Ref: Maryland State Archives, Governor and Council Commissioner Records, 1726-1794, p. 28)

Elder, James, see Negro Coffee.

Elder, John, appointed a Commissioner of the Peace for Baltimore County, 17 Feb 1775. (Ref: Maryland State Archives, Governor and Council Commissioner Records, 1726-1794, p. 288)

Ellegood, William, Court Justice, Worcester County, 1774. (*Calendar of Maryland State Papers, No. 1 The Black Books*, p. 214); appointed a Commissioner of the Peace for Somerset County, 5 Jan 1775. (Ref: Maryland State Archives, Governor and Council Commissioner Records, 1726-1794, p. 286. spelled his name Elligood)

Elliot, John, of Frederick County, convicted of stealing a ewe valued at one hundred pounds of tobacco in 1753, sentenced to be set for half an hour at the pillory and then sent to the whipping post and receive ten lashes on his bare body. (Ref: *This Was The Life: Excerpts from the Judgment Records of*

Colonial Maryland Commissions, Appointments, and Other Proceedings, 1726-1776

Frederick County, Maryland, 1748-1765, by Millard Milburn Rice, p. 129)

Elliott, Robert, of St. Mary's County, was commissioned Deputy Surveyor of St. Mary's County, 4 Mar 1733/4. (Ref: Maryland Commission Book No. 82, p. 8; *Maryland Historical Magazine*, Vol. XXVI, p. 140)

Elliott, William (d. 1756), appointed a Commissioner of the Peace for Queen Anne's County, 9 May 1732. (Ref: Maryland State Archives, Governor and Council Commissioner Records, 1726-1794, p. 23); commissioned a Coroner for Queen Anne's County, 20 Feb 1738/9. (Ref: Maryland Commission Book No. 82, p. 66; *Maryland Historical Magazine*, Vol. XXVI, p. 153); licensed as Reader of Christ Church Parish, Queen Anne's County, 7 Jul 1747. (Ref: Maryland Commission Book No. 82, p. 130; *Maryland Historical Magazine*, Vol. XXVI, p. 261)

Elmer, Thomas, see Daniel Cheston.

Elmore, Thomas, see Thomas Lambden.

Elson, William, see Negro Charles, Negro Davey and Negro Jack Crane.

Elston, William, see Negro Abraham.

Elt, Benjamin, appointed a Commissioner of the Peace for Calvert County, 11 Jun 1760. (Ref: Maryland State Archives, Governor and Council Commissioner Records, 1726-1794, p. 191)

Eltinge, Cornelius, appointed a Commissioner of the Peace for Prince George's County, 15 Jun 1739. (Ref: Maryland State Archives, Governor and Council Commissioner Records, 1726-1794, p. 64)

Emmitt, William, appointed Constable of Upper Monocacy Hundred in Frederick County in 1751. (Ref: *This Was The Life: Excerpts from the Judgment Records of Frederick County, Maryland, 1748-1765*, by Millard Milburn Rice, p. 61)

Emory, Arthur, appointed a Commissioner of the Peace for Queen Anne's County, 3 Mar 1726/7. (Ref: Maryland State Archives, Governor and Council Commissioner Records, 1726-1794, p. 2)

Emory, John, commissioned Deputy Surveyor of Queen Anne's County, 16 Nov 1743. (Ref: Maryland Commission Book No. 82, p. 105; *Maryland Historical Magazine*, Vol. XXVI, p. 250)

Encohson(?), Enoch, appointed Constable of Conococheague Hundred in Prince George's County, now Frederick County, 1747. (Ref: Prince George's County Court Records, 1736-1748, Extracts by Patricia Abelard Andersen, *Western Maryland Genealogy*, Vol. 18, No. 1, January 2002, p. 45)

Ennalls, Bartholomew (c1700-1783), appointed a Commissioner of the Peace for Dorchester County, 29 May 1734. (Ref: Maryland State Archives, Governor and Council Commissioner Records, 1726-1794, p. 42, styled him as Jr.); appointed a Commissioner of the Peace for Dorchester County, 28 Sep 1744. (Ref: Maryland State Archives, Governor and Council Commissioner Records, 1726-1794, p. 89); commissioned Sheriff of Dorchester County, 23 Jun 1749. (Ref: Maryland State Archives, Governor and Council Commissioner Records, 1726-1794, p. 111)

Ennalls, Henry (1675-1734), was appointed a Commissioner of the Peace for Dorchester County, 1 Aug 1729 and 29 Oct 1730. (Ref: Maryland State Archives, Governor and Council Commissioner Records, 1726-1794, pp. 11, 17).

Ennalls, Henry, commissioned Deputy Surveyor of Dorchester County, 8 Nov 1743. (Ref: Maryland Commission Book No. 82, p. 106; *Maryland Historical Magazine*, Vol. XXVI, p. 250, spelled his name Ennals); appointed a Commissioner of the Peace for Dorchester County, 22 Oct 1756 and 8 Apr 1770. (Ref: Maryland State Archives, Governor and Council Commissioner Records, 1726-1794, pp. 171, 250); see Negro Stephen.

Ennalls, Joseph, appointed a Commissioner of the Peace for Dorchester County, 29 May 1734. (Ref: Maryland State Archives, Governor and Council Commissioner Records, 1726-1794, p. 42); registration of sloop *Betty*, 18 tons, built in Somerset County, 1737. Lawrence Mason, master. Ennals Hooper and Joseph Ennals, owners. 17 May 1738. (Ref: Maryland Commission Book No. 82, p. 58; *Maryland Historical Magazine*, Vol. XXVI, p. 151); see Ennals Hooper and William Hoskins.

Ennalls, Joseph (c1745-1779), at Ferry, was appointed a Commissioner of the Peace for Dorchester County, 2 Nov 1773. (Ref: Maryland State Archives, Governor and Council Commissioner Records, 1726-1794, p. 278)

Ennalls, William, (d. 1785), was a Court Justice in Dorchester County, 1774. (*Calendar of Maryland*

State Papers, No. 1 The Black Books, p. 211, spelled his name Ennals); see Negro Glasgow, Thomas Hulme and Negro Toby.

Ensor, John, commissioned one of the Coroners of Baltimore County, 14 Jun 1746. (Ref: Maryland Commission Book No. 82, p. 121; *Maryland Historical Magazine*, Vol. XXVI, p. 257)

Ensor, John, Jr., was commissioned a Coroner of Baltimore County, 25 May 1749. (Ref: Maryland Commission Book No. 82, p. 140; *Maryland Historical Magazine*, Vol. XXVI, p. 344)

Erb, Peter, Jr., appointed Constable of Piney Creek Hundred in Frederick County, 1771. (Ref: "Frederick County Minute Book, March 1771, Extracts by Patricia Abelard Andersen," *Western Maryland Genealogy*, Vol. 18, No. 1, January 2002, p. 25)

Erickson, John, was appointed Constable of Conococheague Hundred in Prince George's County, now Frederick County, 1740. (Ref: Prince George's County Court Records, 1736-1748, Extracts by Patricia Abelard Andersen, *Western Maryland Genealogy*, Vol. 18, No. 1, January 2002, p. 37)

Ervin, William, was appointed Constable of Conococheague Hundred in Frederick County in 1749. (Ref: *This Was The Life: Excerpts from the Judgment Records of Frederick County, Maryland, 1748-1765*, by Millard Milburn Rice, p. 7)

Estep, Alexander, appointed Constable of Lower Part of Newfoundland Hundred in Frederick County, 1769, 1771. (Ref: "Frederick County Court Minutes, March 1769," by Patricia Abelard Andersen, *Western Maryland Genealogy*, Vol. 15, No. 2, April 1999, p. 62; "Frederick County Minute Book, March 1771, Extracts by Patricia Abelard Andersen," *Western Maryland Genealogy*, Vol. 18, No. 1, January 2002, p. 25)

Estep, John, commissioned a Coroner for Charles County, 24 May 1740. (Ref: Maryland Commission Book No. 82, p. 81; *Maryland Historical Magazine*, Vol. XXVI, p. 157)

Evans, Henry, appointed a Commissioner of the Peace for Kent County, 29 Oct 1730 and 2 Jun 1732. (Ref: Maryland State Archives, Governor and Council Commissioner Records, 1726-1794, pp. 17, 23)

Evans, John, appointed a Commissioner of the Peace for Kent County, 3 Mar 1726/7 and 12 Jun 1729. (Ref: Maryland State Archives, Governor and Council Commissioner Records, 1726-1794, pp. 2, 11)

Evans, John (d. 1768), was appointed a Commissioner of the Peace for Worcester County, 2 Mar 1754. (Ref: Maryland State Archives, Governor and Council Commissioner Records, 1726-1794, p. 142)

Even, John, commissioned High Sheriff of St. Mary's County, 17 Oct 1759. (Ref: Maryland State Archives, Governor and Council Commissioner Records, 1726-1794, p. 180)

Everett, James, commissioned Deputy Surveyor of Baltimore County, 13 Sep 1768. (Ref: Maryland Commission Book No. 82, p. 215; *Maryland Historical Magazine*, Vol. XXVI, p. 358)

Farmer, Samuel, was appointed Constable of Newfoundland Hundred in Frederick County, 1769. (Ref: "Frederick County Court Minutes, March 1769," by Patricia Abelard Andersen, *Western Maryland Genealogy*, Vol. 15, No. 2, April 1999, p. 62)

Farrington, George, appointed a Commissioner of the Peace for Somerset County, 5 Jan 1775. (Ref: Maryland State Archives, Governor and Council Commissioner Records, 1726-1794, p. 286)

Farrington, George, appointed a Commissioner of the Peace for Worcester County, 16 Jan 1769. (Ref: Maryland State Archives, Governor and Council Commissioner Records, 1726-1794, p. 240)

Farys, Joseph, appointed Constable of the Upper Part of Monocacy Hundred in Frederick County in 1749. (Ref: *This Was The Life: Excerpts from the Judgment Records of Frederick County, Maryland, 1748-1765*, by Millard Milburn Rice, p. 7)

Faucit, William, appointed a Commissioner of the Peace for Somerset County, 29 Oct 1730. (Ref: Maryland State Archives, Governor and Council Commissioner Records, 1726-1794, p. 17)

Fearror, Leonard, planter, of Baltimore County, native of Germany, naturalized 20 May 1736. (Ref: Maryland Commission Book No. 82, p. 44; *Maryland Historical Magazine*, Vol. XXVI, p. 147)

Fendall, Benjamin, appointed a Commissioner of the Peace for Charles County, 29 Oct 1730 and 24 Jul 1748. (Ref: Maryland State Archives, Governor and Council Commissioner Records, 1726-1794, pp. 12, 108); commissioned a Coroner of Charles County, 17

Sep 1773. (Ref: Maryland Commission Book No. 82, p. 323; *Maryland Historical Magazine*, Vol. XXVII, p. 35); see George Dent.

Fendall, Henry, reverend, licensed to preach in Worcester Parish, Worcester County, vacant by the removal of Rev. Samuel Sloan, 8 Dec 1769. (Ref: Maryland Commission Book No. 82, p. 233; *Maryland Historical Magazine*, Vol. XXVI, p. 360); licensed to preach in Durham Parish, Charles County, vacant by the removal of Rev. John Scott. 14 Dec 1770. (Ref: Maryland Commission Book No. 82, p. 251; *Maryland Historical Magazine*, Vol. XXVII, p. 29); induction into Durham Parish, Charles County, 19 Sep 1772. (Ref: Maryland Commission Book No. 82, p. 286; *Maryland Historical Magazine*, Vol. XXVII, p. 32)

Fendall, John (1674-1734), was appointed a Commissioner of the Peace for Charles County, 2 Mar 1726/7. (Ref: Maryland State Archives, Governor and Council Commissioner Records, 1726-1794, p. 2); commissioned a Provincial Justice by the Governor, 20 Oct 1729. (Ref: Maryland State Archives, Governor and Council Commissioner Records, 1726-1794, p. 12)

Fendall, John, commissioned Sheriff of Charles County, 2 Oct 1756. (Ref: Maryland State Archives, Governor and Council Commissioner Records, 1726-1794, p. 160)

Ferguson, Robert, see William Graham.

Field, Joarib, mariner, of Connecticut, registered the sloop *Abigail*, formerly called *Elizabeth*, 18 tons, built at Swanzey, Rhode Island, 1733. Jaorib Field, master and owner. 13 Feb 1741/2. (Ref: Maryland Commission Book No. 82, p. 90; *Maryland Historical Magazine*, Vol. XXVI, p. 245)

Filkins, Henry, see Thomas Crompton.

Fisher, John, registration of sloop *Charming Betty*, 35 tons, built in Pocomoke, 1747. James Earle, master. John Fisher, owner. 20 Apr 1749. (Ref: Maryland Commission Book No. 82, p. 151; *Maryland Historical Magazine*, Vol. XXVI, p. 349); see William Hoskins.

Fisher, Thomas, appointed a Commissioner of the Peace for Queen Anne's County, 1 Dec 1746. (Ref: Maryland State Archives, Governor and Council Commissioner Records, 1726-1794, p. 95)

Fitz, John, registration of schooner *Two Brothers*, 25 tons, built in Somerset County, 1741. George Macclester, master. Samuel Macclester, George Macclester, Aaron Lynn and John Fitz, owners. 7 May 1741. (Ref: Maryland Commission Book No. 82, p. 86; *Maryland Historical Magazine*, Vol. XXVI, p. 244); appointed a Commissioner of the Peace for Dorchester County, 26 May 1744. (Ref: Maryland State Archives, Governor and Council Commissioner Records, 1726-1794, p. 85); registration of sloop *Molly*, 35 tons, built in Worcester County, 1751. John Fitz, master and owner. 4 May 1751. (Ref: Maryland Commission Book No. 82, p. 149; *Maryland Historical Magazine*, Vol. XXVI, p. 348)

Fitzgerald, Nicholas, laborer, of Frederick County, convicted felon for burglary, was pardoned, 11 Oct 1773. (Ref: Maryland Commission Book No. 82, p. 326; *Maryland Historical Magazine*, Vol. XXVII, p. 35)

Fitzgerald, Philip, laborer, of Dorchester County, convicted felon, was executed on 14 Dec 1768. (Ref: Maryland State Archives, Governor and Council Commissioner Records, 1726-1794, p. 228; *Archives of Maryland*, Vol. XXXII, "Proceedings of the Council of Maryland, 1761-1770," pp. 258)

Fitzhugh, George, appointed a Commissioner of the Peace for Baltimore County, 6 Mar 1775. (Ref: Maryland State Archives, Governor and Council Commissioner Records, 1726-1794, p. 288)

Fitzhugh, William (c1722-1798), was appointed a Commissioner of the Peace for Calvert County, 22 Nov 1752. (Ref: Maryland State Archives, Governor and Council Commissioner Records, 1726-1794, p. 135); commissioned Commissary General and Judge for Probate of Wills, 23 Sep 1773. (Ref: Maryland Commission Book No. 82, p. 324; *Maryland Historical Magazine*, Vol. XXVII, p. 35); commissioned Treasurer of the Western Shore, 28 Sep 1772 and 29 Apr 1773. (Ref: Maryland Commission Book No. 82, pp. 287, 306; *Maryland Historical Magazine*, Vol. XXVII, pp. 32, 33)

Fitzpatrick, Francis, of Frederick County, convicted of murdering his mistress, was executed on 1 Feb 1771 and "afterwards to hang his body in chains in some convenient place." (Ref: Maryland State Archives, Governor and Council Commissioner Records, 1726-1794, p. 245)

Fleming, John, of Talbot County, pardoned for stealing, 7 Jul 1747. (Ref: Maryland Commission Book No. 82, p. 130; *Maryland Historical Magazine*, Vol. XXVI, p. 261)

Fleming, William, appointed a Commissioner of the Peace for Somerset County, 8 Aug 1769 and 19 May 1774. (Ref: Maryland State Archives, Governor and Council Commissioner Records, 1726-1794, pp. 244, 282)

Fletchall, John, was appointed Constable of Sugarland Hundred in Frederick County in 1763 and 1769. (Ref: *This Was The Life: Excerpts from the Judgment Records of Frederick County, Maryland, 1748-1765*, by Millard Milburn Rice, p. 249; "Frederick County Court Minutes, March 1769," by Patricia Abelard Andersen, *Western Maryland Genealogy*, Vol. 15, No. 2, April 1999, p. 62)

Fletchall, Thomas, was appointed Constable of Seneca Hundred in Prince George's County, now Frederick County, 1748. (Ref: Prince George's County Court Records, 1736-1738, Extracts by Patricia Abelard Andersen, *Western Maryland Genealogy*, Vol. 18, No. 1, January 2002, p. 46); appointed Constable of Sugarland Hundred in Frederick County in 1749. (Ref: *This Was The Life: Excerpts from the Judgment Records of Frederick County, Maryland, 1748-1765*, by Millard Milburn Rice, p. 6)

Floud, Richard, of Ireland, registration of snow *Prince of Orange*, of Belfast, 98 tons, built in New England, 1733. Patrick Smith, John Gordon, James Ross, John Boyd, James Clerk, John Rainey, John Hivey and Richard Floud, owners. 14 Oct 1740. (Ref: Maryland Commission Book No. 82, p. 84; *Maryland Historical Magazine*, Vol. XXVI, p. 158)

Forbes, James, appointed a Commissioner of the Peace for Charles County, 19 Oct 1770. (Ref: Maryland State Archives, Governor and Council Commissioner Records, 1726-1794, p. 252)

Forbes, John, doctor, appointed a Commissioner of the Peace for St. Mary's County, 1 Apr 1736. (Ref: Maryland State Archives, Governor and Council Commissioner Records, 1726-1794, p. 51)

Forbes, John, reverend, licensed to preach in Queen Anne's Parish, Charles County, vacant by the death of Rev. William Brogden. 21 Dec 1770. (Ref: Maryland Commission Book No. 82, p. 251; *Maryland Historical Magazine*, Vol. XXVII, p. 29)

Ford, John, see Richard Smith.

Foreman, Ezekiel, commissioned High Sheriff of Kent County, 9 Nov 1774. (Ref: Maryland State Archives, Governor and Council Commissioner Records, 1726-1794, p. 274)

Foreman, George, see Ashbury Sutton.

Foreman, John, see Reese Williams.

Forester, George William (1722-1774), reverend, induction into Shrewsbury Parish, Kent County, 9 Sep 1735. (Ref: Maryland Commission Book No. 82, p. 33; *Maryland Historical Magazine*, Vol. XXVI, p. 145)

Forster, Ralph, commissioned High Sheriff of Prince George's County, 7 Oct 1771. (Ref: Maryland State Archives, Governor and Council Commissioner Records, 1726-1794, p. 247)

Fortune, Levi, see Levi Thompson.

Foster, Thomas, appointed a Commissioner of the Peace for Dorchester County, 26 May 1744. (Ref: Maryland State Archives, Governor and Council Commissioner Records, 1726-1794, p. 85)

Fottrell, Edward, was appointed a proctor by the Prerogative Court of Maryland, 10 May 1726. (Ref: *Abstracts of the Testamentary Proceedings and Prerogative Court of Maryland, Vol. XVII, 1724-1727*, by Vernon L. Skinner, Jr., p. 97, citing original Liber 27, f. 269)

Fountain, Marcy, appointed a Warehouse Inspector in Somerset County on 3 Sep 1750. (*Calendar of Maryland State Papers, No. 1 The Black Books*, p. 96)

Fountain, Samuel, appointed a Commissioner of the Peace for Dorchester County, 16 Jul 1735. (Ref: Maryland State Archives, Governor and Council Commissioner Records, 1726-1794, p. 48)

Fout, Bauldus, of Prince George's County, native of Germany, naturalized 4 Jun 1740, and also his children Bauldus, Maria and Catherine. (Ref: Maryland Commission Book No. 82, p. 81; *Maryland Historical Magazine*, Vol. XXVI, p. 157)

Fout, Jacob, of Prince George's County, native of Germany, naturalized 4 Jun 1740, and also his children Jacob, Henry, Bauldus, Eve, Mary, Margarett and Catherine. (Ref: Maryland Commission Book No. 82, p. 81; *Maryland Historical Magazine*, Vol. XXVI, p. 157)

Fowler, Elexis, laborer, of Frederick County, convicted felon for burglary, was pardoned on 6 May 1773. (Ref: Maryland Commission Book No. 82, p. 317; *Maryland Historical Magazine*, Vol. XXVII, p. 34)

Fraiser, John, appointed a Commissioner of the Peace for Prince George's County, 21 Feb 1735/6. (Ref: Maryland State Archives, Governor and Council Commissioner Records, 1726-1794, p. 51)

Framton, Joseph, servant of Elizabeth Hobbs, widow, of Frederick County, convicted felon, was executed on 9 Sep 1768. (Ref: *Archives of Maryland*, Vol. XXXII, "Proceedings of the Council of Maryland, 1761-1770," pp. 247-248)

Franceway, Benjamin, registration of schooner *Peggy*, 10 tons, built in Somerset County, 1745. Benjamin Franceway, master and owner. 25 Jun 1745. (Ref: Maryland Commission Book No. 82, p. 114; *Maryland Historical Magazine*, Vol. XXVI, p. 254)

Francis, Richard, of Anne Arundel County, commissioned Commissioner or Trustee for Emitting the Paper Currency, 20 Apr 1734. (Ref: Maryland Commission Book No. 82, p. 10; *Maryland Historical Magazine*, Vol. XXVI, p. 140)

Franklin, Thomas (c1706-1787), appointed a Commissioner of the Peace for Baltimore County, 5 Dec 1739. (Ref: Maryland State Archives, Governor and Council Commissioner Records, 1726-1794, p. 66); appointed a Justice in Baltimore County, 22 Feb 1773. (Ref: *Inhabitants of Baltimore County, 1763-1774*, by Henry C. Peden, Jr., 1989, p. 49, citing *Calendar of Maryland State Papers, No. 1 The Black Books*, p. 208); appointed a Commissioner of the Peace for Baltimore County, 30 May 1774. (Ref: Maryland State Archives, Governor and Council Commissioner Records, 1726-1794, p. 283)

Frazer, William, see Samuel Chase, Jr.

Frazier, Alexander (d. 1790), was appointed a Commissioner of the Peace for Dorchester County, 22 Oct 1756. (Ref: Maryland State Archives, Governor and Council Commissioner Records, 1726-1794, p. 171)

Frazier, George (d. 1764), appointed a Commissioner of the Peace for Prince George's County, 30 Nov 1741. (Ref: Maryland State Archives, Governor and Council Commissioner Records, 1726-1794, p. 72)

Freeman, Isaac, appointed a Commissioner of the Peace for Kent County, 1 Dec 1768. (Ref: Maryland State Archives, Governor and Council Commissioner Records, 1726-1794, p. 239); appointed a Commissioner of the Peace for Cecil County, 2 Jun 1774. (Ref: Maryland State Archives, Governor and Council Commissioner Records, 1726-1794, p. 283)

French, George, commissioned High Sheriff of Frederick County, 17 Nov 1775. (Ref: Maryland State Archives, Governor and Council Commissioner Records, 1726-1794, p. 279)

French, Thomas, commissioned High Sheriff of Frederick County, 11 Nov 1774. (Ref: Maryland State Archives, Governor and Council Commissioner Records, 1726-1794, p. 274)

Friend, Charles, appointed Constable of Tonol-loway Hundred in Prince George's County, now Frederick County, 1747. (Ref: Prince George's County Court Records, 1736-1748, Extracts by Patricia Abelard Andersen, *Western Maryland Genealogy*, Vol. 18, No. 1, January 2002, p. 45)

Frisby, James, appointed a Commissioner of the Peace for Kent County, 11 Nov 1763 and 1 Dec 1768. (Ref: Maryland State Archives, Governor and Council Commissioner Records, 1726-1794, pp. 212, 239)

Frisby, John, appointed a Commissioner of the Peace for Cecil County, 2 Jun 1774. (Ref: Maryland State Archives, Governor and Council Commissioner Records, 1726-1794, p. 283)

Frisby, Peregrine, see Negro Cesar.

Frisby, Richard, appointed a Commissioner of the Peace for Kent County, 2 Nov 1762. (Ref: Maryland State Archives, Governor and Council Commissioner Records, 1726-1794, p. 207)

Frisby, William, appointed a Commissioner of the Peace for Kent County, 3 Mar 1726/7 and 12 Jun 1729. (Ref: Maryland State Archives, Governor and Council Commissioner Records, 1726-1794, pp. 2, 11)

Frisby, William, commissioned a Coroner of Kent County, 16 Aug 1773. (Ref: Maryland Commission Book No. 82, p. 323; *Maryland Historical Magazine*, Vol. XXVII, p. 35)

Furney, Adam, planter, of Baltimore County, native of High Germany, naturalized 4 Jun 1738 and also his children Mark, Nicholas, Philip, Charlott, Mary and Clara. (Ref: Maryland Commission Book No. 82, p.

57; *Maryland Historical Magazine*, Vol. XXVI, p. 151)

Gaither, Basil, appointed Constable of Seneca Hundred in Frederick County, 1771. (Ref: "Frederick County Minute Book, March 1771, Extracts by Patricia Abelard Andersen," *Western Maryland Genealogy*, Vol. 18, No. 1, January 2002, p. 25)

Gaither, Henry, was appointed Constable of Newfoundland Hundred in Prince George's County, now Frederick County, 1747-1749. (Ref: Prince George's County Court Records, 1736-1748, Extracts by Patricia Abelard Andersen, *Western Maryland Genealogy*, Vol. 18, No. 1, January 2002, pp. 45, 46)

Gaither, Edward, appointed a Commissioner of the Peace for Anne Arundel County, 15 Jun 1735. (Ref: Maryland State Archives, Governor and Council Commissioner Records, 1726-1794, p. 47)

Gaitskell, William, see John Wallace.

Galaspy, George, Jr., appointed Constable of Conococheague Hundred in Frederick County, 1769. (Ref: "Frederick County Court Minutes November 1769 by Patricia Abelard Andersen," *Western Maryland Genealogy*, Vol. 16, No. 1, January 2000, p. 33)

Galbraith, William, of Baltimore County, was captain of a company of Rangers, 9 Aug 1775. (Ref: *Calendar of Maryland State Papers, The Red Books*, No. 4, Part 1, p. 5)

Gale, George, Jr., appointed a Commissioner of the Peace for Somerset County, 3 Sep 1757. (Ref: Maryland State Archives, Governor and Council Commissioner Records, 1726-1794, p. 176)

Gale, John, registration of schooner *Betty*, 60 tons, built in Somerset County, 1741. John Gale, master and owner. 16 Jun 1741. (Ref: Maryland Commission Book No. 82, p. 86; *Maryland Historical Magazine*, Vol. XXVI, p. 244); see Levin Gale.

Gale, Levin (c1704-1744), colonel, Provincial Commission, 8 Jul 1735. (Ref: Maryland State Archives, Governor and Council Commissioner Records, 1726-1794, p. 49; commissioned Judge and Register of the Land Office, 16 Dec 1738. (Ref: Maryland Commission Book No. 82, p. 64; *Maryland Historical Magazine*, Vol. XXVI, p. 152); commissioned Judge of the Land Office, 15 Oct 1742. On same day, commissioned Major General of the Eastern Shore. (Ref: Maryland Commission Book No. 82, p. 97; *Maryland Historical Magazine*, Vol. XXVI, p. 247); commissioned Naval Officer, Port of Pocomoke, 25 Jul 1733. (Ref: Maryland Commission Book No. 82, p. 2; *Maryland Historical Magazine*, Vol. XXVI, p. 139); of Anne Arundel County, commissioned Judge of Oyer, Terminer and Gaol [Jail] Delivery, 21 May 1736. (Ref: Maryland State Archives, Governor and Council Commissioner Records, 1726-1794, p. 52); registration of brigantine *Brereton*, 55 tons, built in Somerset County, 1737. Henry Smith, master. John Williams, Robert Henry and Levin Gale, owners. 3 Mar 1737/8. (Ref: Maryland Commission Book No. 82, p. 52; *Maryland Historical Magazine*, Vol. XXVI, p. 150); registration of brigantine *Leah*, 50 tons, built in Somerset County, 1736. William Murray, master. Levin Gale, owner. 27 May 1737. (Ref: Maryland Commission Book No. 82, p. 48; *Maryland Historical Magazine*, Vol. XXVI, p. 149); registration of brigantine *Ogle*, 50 tons. Henry Biglands, master. Levin Gale and John Gale, owners. 1 Mar 1734/5. (Ref: Maryland Commission Book No. 82, p. 26; *Maryland Historical Magazine*, Vol. XXVI, p. 143); registration of schooner *Bladen*, 45 tons, built in Somerset County, 1742. George Paris, master. Levin Gale, owner. Oct 1742. (Ref: Maryland Commission Book No. 82, p. 97; *Maryland Historical Magazine*, Vol. XXVI, p. 247); registration of schooner *Sarah*, 30 tons, built in Somerset County, 1739. John Ayres, master. Edward Chambers, Robert Graham, Aaron Lynn and Levin Gale, owners. 19 Dec 1739. (Ref: Maryland Commission Book No. 82, p. 78; *Maryland Historical Magazine*, Vol. XXVI, p. 155); registration of ship *Levin and Leah*, 95 tons, built in Somerset County, 1741. William Murray, master. Levin Gale and Matthias Gale, owners, 31 Aug 1741. (Ref: Maryland Commission Book No. 82, p. 87; *Maryland Historical Magazine*, Vol. XXVI, p. 245); registration of sloop *Esther*, 30 tons, built in Somerset County, 1735. John Williams, master. 29 Oct 1735. (Ref: Maryland Commission Book No. 82, p. 38; *Maryland Historical Magazine*, Vol. XXVI, p. 145); registration of sloop *Mary*, 30 tons, built in Somerset County, 1739. William Murray, master. Levin Gale, owner. 19 Dec 1739. (Ref: Maryland Commission Book No. 82, p. 78; *Maryland Historical Magazine*, Vol. XXVI, p. 155); registration of sloop *Valentine*, 12 tons, built in Somerset County, 1735. John North, master. Levin Gale, owner. 31 Mar 1736. (Ref: Maryland

Commission Book No. 82, p. 42; *Maryland Historical Magazine*, Vol. XXVI, p. 146); see Adam Muir and Arthur Dashiell.

Gale, Matthias, see Levin Gale.

Galloway, Joseph, commissioned High Sheriff of Anne Arundel County, 22 Nov 1763. (Ref: Maryland State Archives, Governor and Council Commissioner Records, 1726-1794, p. 203); see Negro Grace and Negro Jennye.S

Galloway, Samuel, registration of the schooner *Experiment*, 35 tons, built in Anne Arundel County, 1749. William Williams, master. Samuel Galloway, owner. 24 Jun 1749. (Ref: Maryland Commission Book No. 82, p. 151; *Maryland Historical Magazine*, Vol. XXVI, p. 349); registration of sloop *Greyhound*, 30 tons, built in Anne Arundel County, 1750. George Eager, master. Samuel Galloway and Kensey [Kinsey] Johns, owners. 3 Dec 1750. (Ref: Maryland Commission Book No. 82, p. 148; *Maryland Historical Magazine*, Vol. XXVI, p. 347)

Game, Levi, see Levi Thompson.

Gantt, Edward (1759-1810), reverend, licensed to preach in Queen Anne's Parish, Prince George's County, vacant by the death of Rev. William Brogden. 7 May 1771. (Ref: Maryland Commission Book No. 82, p. 257; *Maryland Historical Magazine*, Vol. XXVII, p. 30)

Gantt, George, appointed a Commissioner of the Peace for Prince George's County, 25 Nov 1751. (Ref: Maryland State Archives, Governor and Council Commissioner Records, 1726-1794, p. 129)

Gantt, Thomas, appointed a Commissioner of the Peace for Prince George's County, 3 Mar 1726/7. (Ref: Maryland State Archives, Governor and Council Commissioner Records, 1726-1794, p. 3, spelled his name Gant)

Gantt, Thomas, Jr., appointed a Commissioner of the Peace for Prince George's County, 15 Jun 1739. (Ref: Maryland State Archives, Governor and Council Commissioner Records, 1726-1794, p. 64)

Gantt, Thomas, Jr., appointed a Commissioner of the Peace for Prince George's County, 26 Jul 1773. (Ref: Maryland State Archives, Governor and Council Commissioner Records, 1726-1794, p. 272)

Garbough (or Garlough), John, was appointed Constable of Linton Hundred in Frederick County, 1769. (Ref: "Frederick County Court Minutes, March 1769," by Patricia Abelard Andersen, *Western Maryland Genealogy*, Vol. 15, No. 2, April 1999, p. 63, listed his name as Garbough; "Frederick County Court Minutes, June 1769," by Patricia Abelard Andersen, *Western Maryland Genealogy*, Vol. 15, No. 4, April 1999, p. 171, listed his name as Garlough)

Garder, Peter, planter, of Baltimore County, native of Germany, naturalized 1 May 1736. (Ref: Maryland Commission Book No. 82, p. 43; *Maryland Historical Magazine*, Vol. XXVI, p. 147)

Gardiner, John, mariner, of Liverpool, registered the ship *Upton*, 180 tons, built in Talbot County. 1749. John Gardiner, master and co-owner. Foster Cunliffe & Son, co-owners. 9 Nov 1749. (Ref: Maryland Commission Book No. 82, p. 153; *Maryland Historical Magazine*, Vol. XXVI, p. 350)

Gardiner, John, of Liverpool, registration of ship *Liverpool Merchant*, 140 tons, built in Talbot County, 1745. John Gardiner, master. John Gardiner and Foster Cunliffe & Sons, merchants in Liverpool, owners. 18 Sep 1745. (Ref: Maryland Commission Book No. 82, p. 115; *Maryland Historical Magazine*, Vol. XXVI, p. 255)

Gardiner, Richard, see Negro Ben.

Gardner, John, was Constable of Middlesex Hundred in Baltimore County, 1773. (Ref: *Inhabitants of Baltimore County, 1763-1774*, by Henry C. Peden, Jr., 1989, p. 70, citing a 1773 List of Taxables)

Garner, William, see Negro Jack.

Garnett, George, commissioned Deputy Surveyor of Kent County, 18 Nov 1743. (Ref: Maryland Commission Book No. 82, p. 105; *Maryland Historical Magazine*, Vol. XXVI, p. 250); commissioned one of the Coroner of Kent County, 3 Sep 1746. (Ref: Maryland Commission Book No. 82, p. 123; *Maryland Historical Magazine*, Vol. XXVI, p. 258)

Garnett, Thomas, of Talbot County, convicted felon, was executed on 19 May 1729. (Ref: Maryland State Archives, Governor and Council Commissioner Records, 1726-1794, p. 10)

Garnett, Thomas, appointed a Commissioner of the Peace for Kent County, 28 May 1756. (Ref: Maryland State Archives, Governor and Council Commissioner Records, 1726-1794, p. 168); commissioned a Coroner of Kent County, 26 Apr 1764. (Ref: Maryland Commission Book No. 82, p. 161; *Maryland Historical Magazine*, Vol. XXVI, p. 352)

Garrett, Amos (1723-c178), commissioned a Coroner of Baltimore County, 15 Mar 1756 and 30 Apr 1773. (Ref: Maryland Commission Book No. 82, pp. 167, 312; *Maryland Historical Magazine*, Vol. XXVI, pp. 353, and Vol. XXVII, p. 34); appointed a Commissioner of the Peace for Baltimore County, 20 Nov 1769 and 20 Feb 1774. (Ref: Maryland State Archives, Governor and Council Commissioner Records, 1726-1794, pp. 248, 281)

Garrett, John, registration of schooner *Benedict*, 20 tons, built in Baltimore County, 1749. John Garrett and Moses Garrett, owners, 10 May 1750. (Ref: Maryland Commission Book No. 82, p. 156; *Maryland Historical Magazine*, Vol. XXVI, p. 351); see Samuel Massey.

Garrett, Moses, see John Garrett.

Garrison, David, of Baltimore County, Ranger, 9 Aug 1775. (Ref: *Calendar of Maryland State Papers, The Red Books*, No. 4, Part 1, p. 5)

Garsham, Richard, appointed a Commissioner of the Peace for Cecil County, 2 Jun 1774. (Ref: Maryland State Archives, Governor and Council Commissioner Records, 1726-1794, p. 283)

Garvey, John, laborer, late of Baltimore County, convicted felon for burglary, was pardoned and banished, 3 Dec 1773. (Ref: Maryland Commission Book No. 82, p. 329; *Maryland Historical Magazine*, Vol. XXVII, p. 36)

Gassaway, John (1707-1762), was appointed a Commissioner of the Peace for Anne Arundel County, 8 Nov 1742. (Ref: Maryland State Archives, Governor and Council Commissioner Records, 1726-1794, p. 75); commissioned Sheriff of Anne Arundel County, 19 Dec 1748. (Ref: Maryland State Archives, Governor and Council Commissioner Records, 1726-1794, p. 108); Court Justice, Anne Arundel County, 1754. (Ref: Anne Arundel County Court Minutes, 1725-1757); captain, appointed to the Committee to Apportion the Public Levies, 29 May 1756. (Ref: *Archives of Maryland*, Vol. LII, "Proceedings and Acts of the General Assembly of Maryland, 1755-1756," p. 291)

Gassaway, Nicholas, commissioned a Coroner of Anne Arundel County, 18 Mar 1748/9. (Ref: Maryland Commission Book No. 82, p. 139; *Maryland Historical Magazine*, Vol. XXVI, p. 343); see Negro Daniel.

Gassaway, Nicholas, of Thomas (c1710-1745), was appointed a Commissioner of the Peace for Anne Arundel County, 21 Nov 1743. (Ref: Maryland State Archives, Governor and Council Commissioner Records, 1726-1794, p. 83)

Gassaway, Thomas, appointed a Commissioner of the Peace for Anne Arundel County, 18 Aug 1764 and 26 Jul 1773. (Ref: Maryland State Archives, Governor and Council Commissioner Records, 1726-1794, pp. 217, 272)

Gatherall, John, served as Constable in the Lower Part of Patowmack [Potomac] Hundred in Frederick County in 1754. (Ref: *This Was The Life: Excerpts from the Judgment Records of Frederick County, Maryland, 1748-1765*, by Millard Milburn Rice, p. 150)

Gaultier, John, native of France, denization, 26 Apr 1768. (Ref: Maryland Commission Book No. 82, p. 212; *Maryland Historical Magazine*, Vol. XXVI, p. 357)

Gay, Nicholas Ruxton, was appointed a Commissioner of the Peace for Baltimore County, 16 Dec 1751. (Ref: Maryland State Archives, Governor and Council Commissioner Records, 1726-1794, p. 131)

Gay, Ruxton, of Baltimore Co., a Commissioner of the Peace, served as Magistrate for several years and resigned on 2 May 1767 due to poor health including gout and other disorders. (*Archives of Maryland*, Vol. XXXII, "Proceedings of the Council of Maryland, 1761-1770," pp. 200-202)

Geoghegan, James, appointed a Commissioner of the Peace for Somerset County, 20 Mar 1775. (Ref: Maryland State Archives, Governor and Council Commissioner Records, 1726-1794, p. 288)

George, Joshua (c1695-1748), of Cecil County, commissioned Surveyor General of the Western Shore, 13 Dec 1746. (Ref: Maryland Commission Book No. 82, p. 124; *Maryland Historical Magazine*, Vol. XXVI, p. 258; *A Biographical Dictionary of the Maryland Legislature, 1635-1789*, by Edward C. Papenfuse, et al., Vol. A-H, p. 348); see William

Husbands.

George, Sidney (c1725-1774), was appointed a Commissioner of the Peace for Cecil County, 22 May 1762. (Ref: Maryland State Archives, Governor and Council Commissioner Records, 1726-1794, p. 203)

Ghiselin, Reverdy, of Anne Arundel County, commissioned Register of Court of Vice Admiralty, 1 May 1773. (Ref: Maryland Commission Book No. 82, p. 315; *Maryland Historical Magazine*, Vol. XXVII, p. 34)

Ghiselin, William, commissioned a Coroner for Anne Arundel County, 11 Aug 1734. (Ref: Maryland Commission Book No. 82, p. 20; *Maryland Historical Magazine*, Vol. XXVI, p. 141); appointed a Commissioner of the Peace for Anne Arundel County, 28 Feb 1742/3. (Ref: Maryland State Archives, Governor and Council Commissioner Records, 1726-1794, p. 77)

Giant, Richard, of Queen Anne's County, convicted felon, was executed on 13 Jun 1738. (Ref: Maryland State Archives, Governor and Council Commissioner Records, 1726-1794, p. 63)

Gibbs, James, commissioned Collector of the Port at Patuxent, 4 Apr 1764. Qualified 27 Jul 1764. (Ref: Maryland Commission Book No. 82, p. 163; *Maryland Historical Magazine*, Vol. XXVI, p. 353)

Gibbs, William, see Daniel Cheston.

Gibson, John (d. 1790), was appointed a Commissioner of the Peace for Talbot County, 2 Feb 1774. (Ref: Maryland State Archives, Governor and Council Commissioner Records, 1726-1794, p. 280); Court Justice, Talbot County, 1774. (*Calendar of Maryland State Papers, No. 1 The Black Books*, p. 211)

Gibson, Woolman (d. 1786), commissioned High Sheriff of Talbot County, 8 Oct 1761. (Ref: Maryland State Archives, Governor and Council Commissioner Records, 1726-1794, p. 190)

Gilbert, Michael, appointed a Commissioner of the Peace for Baltimore County, 23 May 1753. (Ref: Maryland State Archives, Governor and Council Commissioner Records, 1726-1794, p. 138)

Gildart, James, see Charles Slater.

Gildart, John, see Henry Smith.

Gildart, Richard, see James Sayers.

Giles, Jacob, registration of the ship *Speedwell Galley*, 140 tons, built in Baltimore County, 1749. Daniel Robinson, master. Jacob Giles, owner. 19 Oct 1749. (Ref: Maryland Commission Book No. 82, p. 153; *Maryland Historical Magazine*, Vol. XXVI, p. 350); registration of sloop *Betty*, 30 tons, built in Baltimore County, 1750. Daniel Robison, master. Jacob Giles and Daniel Robison, owners. 19 Sep 1750. (Ref: Maryland Commission Book No. 82, p. 146; *Maryland Historical Magazine*, Vol. XXVI, p. 346); registration of sloop *Hopewell*, 36 tons, built in Baltimore County, 1750. David Hughs, master. Jacob Giles and Edward Mitchell, owners. 19 Sep 1750. (Ref: Maryland Commission Book No. 82, p. 146; *Maryland Historical Magazine*, Vol. XXVI, p. 346)

Giles, John, see William Parks.

Gillespie, George, Jr., appointed Constable of Conogocheague [Conococheague] Hundred in Frederick County, 1771. (Ref: "Frederick County Minute Book, March 1771, Extracts by Patricia Abelard Andersen," *Western Maryland Genealogy*, Vol. 18, No. 1, January 2002, p. 26)

Gillis, Ezekiel, appointed a Commissioner of the Peace for Anne Arundel County, 31 Oct 1747. (Ref: Maryland State Archives, Governor and Council Commissioner Records, 1726-1794, p. 103)

Gillis, George, appointed a Commissioner of the Peace for Somerset County, 31 Oct 1770 and 19 May 1774. (Ref: Maryland State Archives, Governor and Council Commissioner Records, 1726-1794, p. 254, and p. 282 spelled his name Gilliss)

Gillis, Joseph (c1706-c1783), was appointed a Commissioner of the Peace for Somerset County, 8 Mar 1754. (Ref: Maryland State Archives, Governor and Council Commissioner Records, 1726-1794, p. 143)

Gillis, Thomas, appointed a Commissioner of the Peace for Somerset County, 25 Mar 1734. (Ref: Maryland State Archives, Governor and Council Commissioner Records, 1726-1794, p. 40)

Gilpin, Joseph (c1727-1790), registration of the sloop *Dolphin*, 14 tons, built in Cecil County, 1749. John Lackey, master. Joseph Gilpin and Samuel Gilpin, owners. 6 Feb 1749/50. (Ref: Maryland Commission Book No. 82, p. 154; *Maryland Historical Magazine*, Vol. XXVI, p. 350); appointed a Commissioner of the Peace for Cecil County, 21 Apr 1764 and 20 Feb 1774.

(Ref: Maryland State Archives, Governor and Council Commissioner Records, 1726-1794, pp. 215, 281)

Gilpin, Samuel, appointed a Commissioner of the Peace for Cecil County, 14 Jul 1740. (Ref: Maryland State Archives, Governor and Council Commissioner Records, 1726-1794, p. 68); see Joseph Gilpin.

Gilpin, Thomas, see John Lumley.

Gilpin, William, see John Lumley.

Gist, Christopher, commissioned a Coroner of Baltimore County, 17 Dec 1743. (Ref: Maryland Commission Book No. 82, p. 106; *Maryland Historical Magazine*, Vol. XXVI, p. 250); merchant, registration of sloop *Two Brothers*, 45 tons, built in Baltimore County, 1745. Richard Blakistone, master. Christopher Gist, owner. 24 Apr 1745. (Ref: Maryland Commission Book No. 82, p. 113; *Maryland Historical Magazine*, Vol. XXVI, p. 254)

Gist, Richard (1683-1741), was appointed a Commissioner of the Peace for Baltimore County, 22 Oct 1728. (Ref: Maryland State Archives, Governor and Council Commissioner Records, 1726-1794, p. 8, spelled his surname Giest)

Gist, Susannah, see Negro Caleb.

Gist, Thomas, see Negro Caleb.

Gittings, James (1735-c1823), was appointed a Commissioner of the Peace for Baltimore County, 31 Oct 1768 and 30 May 1774. (Ref: Maryland State Archives, Governor and Council Commissioner Records, 1726-1794, pp. 238, 283); appointed to represent Baltimore County in the Provincial Convention, 1775. (Ref: *Calendar of Maryland State Papers, The Red Books*, No. 4, Part 1, p. 3, misspelled his name as Giddings)

Gittings, John, appointed Constable of Western Branch Hundred in Prince George's County, now Frederick County, 1742. (Ref: Prince George's County Court Records, 1736-1748, Extracts by Patricia Abelard Andersen, *Western Maryland Genealogy*, Vol. 18, No. 1, January 2002, p. 38)

Gittings, Kinsey, appointed a Commissioner of the Peace for Frederick County, 12 Mar 1763. (Ref: Maryland State Archives, Governor and Council Commissioner Records, 1726-1794, p. 209; *This Was The Life: Excerpts from the Judgment Records of Frederick County, Maryland, 1748-1765*, by Millard Milburn Rice, p. 242, spelled his first name Kensey)

Glasgow, Patrick (d. 1753). reverend, induction into St. Margaret's Westminster Parish, Anne Arundel County, 30 Nov 1742. (Ref: Maryland Commission Book No. 82, p. 99; *Maryland Historical Magazine*, Vol. XXVI, p. 248); resignation from Parish of St. Margaret's Westminster, Anne Arundel County, 4 May 1743. On same day, induction into ---- Parish [All Hallow's Parish], Snow Hill], Somerset County. (Ref: Maryland Commission Book No. 82, p. 101; *Maryland Historical Magazine*, Vol. XXVI, p. 249)

Glenworth, Thomas, see William Harris.

Godman, Jabes, of Anne Arundel County, appointed Constable of Town Neck Hundred in 1774. (Ref: Anne Arundel County Court Minutes, 1725-1757, 1774)

Godsgrace, John, commissioned a Coroner for Calvert County in October 1739. (Ref: Maryland Commission Book No. 82, p. 77; *Maryland Historical Magazine*, Vol. XXVI, p. 155)

Godson, Mary, see Negro Dick.

Godwyn, Michael, registration of sloop *Indian Queen*, 20 tons, built in Worcester County, 1742. Cornelius Kollick, master. Michael Godwyn and Cornelius Kollick, owners. 23 Mar 1742/3. (Ref: Maryland Commission Book No. 82, p. 101; *Maryland Historical Magazine*, Vol. XXVI, p. 248)

Goldsborough, Charles, commissioned High Sheriff of Queen Anne's County, 15 Oct 1770. (Ref: Maryland State Archives, Governor and Council Commissioner Records, 1726-1794, p. 242)

Goldsborough, Charles (1707-1767), of Dorchester County, served on the Committee of Laws, 1755. (Ref: Maryland State Archives, Governor and Council Commissioner Records, 1726-1794, p. 156); appointed to the Maryland Council in July 1762. (Ref: *Archives of Maryland*, Vol. XXXII, "Proceedings of the Council of Maryland, 1761-1770," p. 38); commissioned Commissary General and Judge for Probate of Wills, 7 Dec 1764. (Ref: Maryland Commission Book No. 82, p. 166; *Maryland Historical Magazine*, Vol. XXVI, p. 353; *A Biographical Dictionary of the Maryland Legislature, 1635-1789*, by Edward C. Papenfuse, et al., Vol. A-H, pp. 356-357)

Goldsborough, John, appointed a Commissioner of the Peace for Dorchester County, 2 Aug 1766. (Ref: Maryland State Archives, Governor and Council Commissioner Records, 1726-1794, p. 226);

commissioned a Coroner of Dorchester County, 6 Oct 1766. (Ref: Maryland Commission Book No. 82, p. 181; *Maryland Historical Magazine*, Vol. XXVI, p. 354)

Goldsborough, John (1711-1778), was appointed a Commissioner of the Peace for Talbot County, 16 Jun 1741. (Ref: Maryland State Archives, Governor and Council Commissioner Records, 1726-1794, p. 70; appointed to a Committee for Enquiring into Ways and Means to Raise a Sum Sufficient for Payment of Eighty Rangers to Defend and Protect the Frontiers, 28 Jun 1755. (Ref: Maryland State Archives, Governor and Council Commissioner Records, 1726-1794, p. 151); appointed to the Committee to Apportion the Public Levies, 29 May 1756. (Ref: *Archives of Maryland*, Vol. LII, "Proceedings and Acts of the General Assembly of Maryland, 1755-1756," p. 291)

Goldsborough, Nicholas (1689-1766), appointed a Commissioner of the Peace for Talbot County, 29 Oct 1730. (Ref: Maryland State Archives, Governor and Council Commissioner Records, 1726-1794, p. 17)

Goldsborough, Nicholas (1726-1777), of Talbot County, was commissioned a Coroner on 16 Nov 1771. (Ref: Maryland Commission Book No. 82, p. 273; *Maryland Historical Magazine*, Vol. XXVII, p. 31)

Goldsborough, Robert (1660-1746), appointed a Commissioner of the Peace for Talbot County, 29 Oct 1730. (Ref: Maryland State Archives, Governor and Council Commissioner Records, 1726-1794, p. 17)

Goldsborough, Robert (1733-1788), of Dorchester County, commissioned High Sheriff on 8 Oct 1761. (Ref: Maryland State Archives, Governor and Council Commissioner Records, 1726-1794, p. 190); commissioned Attorney General, 4 Jun 1766. (Ref: Maryland Commission Book No. 82, p. 177; *Maryland Historical Magazine*, Vol. XXVI, p. 354)

Goldsmith, William, of Anne Arundel County, appointed a Constable in Annapolis in 1774. (Ref: Anne Arundel County Court Minutes, 1725-1757, 1774)

Good, Jacob, appointed Constable of Piney Creek Hundred in Frederick County, 1769. (Ref: "Frederick County Court Minutes, March 1769," by Patricia Abelard Andersen, *Western Maryland Genealogy*, Vol. 15, No. 2, April 1999, p. 63)

Good, William, appointed Constable of Sharps-burgh Hundred in Frederick County, 1769. (Ref: "Frederick County Court Minutes, March 1769," by Patricia Abelard Andersen, *Western Maryland Genealogy*, Vol. 15, No. 2, April 1999, p. 63)

Goodson, Thomas, appointed Constable of Piney Creek Hundred in Frederick County, 1760. (Ref: *This Was The Life: Excerpts from the Judgment Records of Frederick County, Maryland, 1748-1765*, by Millard Milburn Rice, p. 216)

Goodwin, Lyde, appointed a Commissioner of the Peace for Baltimore County, 15 Nov 1750. (Ref: Maryland State Archives, Governor and Council Commissioner Records, 1726-1794, p. 120)

Goodwin, William, appointed a Commissioner of the Peace for Baltimore County, 20 Nov 1769. (Ref: Maryland State Archives, Governor and Council Commissioner Records, 1726-1794, p. 248); appointed a Justice, 22 Feb 1773. (Ref: *Inhabitants of Baltimore County, 1763-1774*, by Henry C. Peden, Jr., 1989, p. 49, citing *Calendar of Maryland State Papers, No. 1 The Black Books*, p. 208)

Goodwyn, Jacob, see Jonathan Hodgson.

Gordon, George, appointed a Commissioner of the Peace for Frederick County, 12 Nov 1748. (Ref: Maryland State Archives, Governor and Council Commissioner Records, 1726-1794, p. 109; Court Justice in Frederick County, 1748. (Ref: *This Was The Life: Excerpts from the Judgment Records of Frederick County, Maryland, 1748-1765*, by Millard Milburn Rice, p. 1); Sheriff of Frederick County, 9 Jan 1749/50 to at least 1756. (Ref: Maryland State Archives, Governor and Council Commissioner Records, 1726-1794, p. 115; *Archives of Maryland*, Vol. LII, "Proceedings and Acts of the General Assembly of Maryland, 1755-1756," p. 232); see Daniel Dunn and William Graham.

Gordon, John (1717-1790), reverend, induction into St. Anne's Parish, Anne Arundel County, 25 Mar 1745. (Ref: Maryland Commission Book No. 82, p. 112; *Maryland Historical Magazine*, Vol. XXVI, p. 253); resignation from St. Anne's Parish, Anne Arundel County, on 1 Mar 1748/9. On same day, inducted to St. Michael's Parish, Talbot County. (Ref: Maryland Commission Book No. 82, p. 139; *Maryland Historical Magazine*, Vol. XXVI, p. 343); see Richard Floud.

Gordon, Robert, appointed a Commissioner of the Peace for Anne Arundel County, 3 Mar 1726/7. (Ref: Maryland State Archives, Governor and Council Commissioner Records, 1726-1794, p. 3); colonel, Provincial Commission, 8 Jul 1735. (Ref: Maryland State Archives, Governor and Council Commissioner Records, 1726-1794, p. 49); commissioned Judge of Oyer, Terminer and Gaol [Jail] Delivery, 21 May 1736. (Ref: Maryland State Archives, Governor and Council Commissioner Records, 1726-1794, p. 52)

Gordon, Samuel, convicted felon, was pardoned, 1 Jan 1738/9. (Ref: Maryland Commission Book No. 82, p. 68; *Maryland Historical Magazine*, Vol. XXVI, p. 153)

Gosnell, Samuel, of Baltimore County, Ranger, 9 Aug 1775. (Ref: *Calendar of Maryland State Papers, The Red Books*, No. 4, Part 1, p. 5)

Gott, Anthony, registration of sloop *Elizabeth and Hannah*, 15 tons, built in Maryland, 1733. Thomas Witticomb, master. Anthony Gott, owner. 17 Dec 1733. (Ref: Maryland Commission Book No. 82, p. 14; *Maryland Historical Magazine*, Vol. XXVI, p. 141)

Gott, Ezekiel, see Negro Lem.

Gough, Henry Dorsey, of Baltimore County, appointed a Commissioner of the Peace, 31 Oct 1768. (Ref: Maryland State Archives, Governor and Council Commissioner Records, 1726-1794, p. 238)

Gould, Benjamin, appointed a Commissioner of the Peace for Queen Anne's County, 2 Oct 1762. (Ref: Maryland State Archives, Governor and Council Commissioner Records, 1726-1794, p. 205); Court Justice, 1774. (*Calendar of Maryland State Papers, No. 1 The Black Books*, p. 215)

Gould, James, appointed a Commissioner of the Peace for Queen Anne's County, 30 Nov 1732. (Ref: Maryland State Archives, Governor and Council Commissioner Records, 1726-1794, p. 36)

Goulding, Robert, see Charles Ridgeley.

Govane, James, commissioned Sheriff of Anne Arundel County, 14 Dec 1727. (Ref: Maryland State Archives, Governor and Council Commissioner Records, 1726-1794, p. 6)

Govane, William (1716-1768), of Anne Arundel County, merchant, registration of the sloop *Endeavour*, 25 tons, built in Anne Arundel County, 1743. Thomas Hammond, master, and William Govane, owner, 19 Dec 1743; John Segar, master, and William Govane, owner, 2 Jan 1745/6. (Ref: Maryland Commission Book No. 82, pp. 106, 118; *Maryland Historical Magazine*, Vol. XXVI, pp. 251, 256); registration of brigantine *Industry*, 35 tons, built in Baltimore County, 1740. Richard Martyn, master. William Govane, owner. 28 Aug 1749 (Ref: Maryland Commission Book No. 82, p. 83; *Maryland Historical Magazine*, Vol. XXVI, p. 157); registration of brigantine *Endeavour*, 35 tons, built in Anne Arundel County, 1743, formerly a sloop of the same name. Robert Hamilton, master. William Govane, owner. 11 Apr 1750. (Ref: Maryland Commission Book No. 82, p. 156; *Maryland Historical Magazine*, Vol. XXVI, p. 351); registration of the sloop *Benedict*, 20 tons, built in Anne Arundel County, 1747. Thomas Hammond, master. William Govane, owner. 24 Mar 1748/9. (Ref: Maryland Commission Book No. 82, p. 150; *Maryland Historical Magazine*, Vol. XXVI, p. 348); of Baltimore County, served on the Committee of Laws, 1755. (Ref: *Archives of Maryland*, Vol. LII, "Proceedings and Acts of the General Assembly of Maryland, 1755-1756," pp. 46, 160; registration of brigantine *Industry*, 35 tons, built in Baltimore County, 1740. Richard Martyn, master. William Govane, owner. 28 Aug 1740. (Ref: Maryland Commission Book No. 82, p. 83; *Maryland Historical Magazine*, Vol. XXVI, p. 157)

Gover, Ephraim, see Negro Tida.

Gowndrill (Gowndrell), George, reverend, was licensed to preach in St. Andrew's Parish, St. Mary's County, vacant by the removal of Rev. William West, 19 Sep 1772. (Ref: Maryland Commission Book No. 82, p. 286; *Maryland Historical Magazine*, Vol. XXVII, p. 32)

Graham (Grahame), Charles (c1721-1779), appointed a Commissioner of the Peace for Calvert County, 22 Oct 1756. (Ref: Maryland State Archives, Governor and Council Commissioner Records, 1726-1794, p. 171)

Graham, Robert, see Levin Gale.

Graham, William, of North Britain, registration of ship *Caledonia*, 90 tons, built at Patowmeck [Potomac] River, 1738. William Graham, master. Robert Ferguson, George Gordon, William Lowry and William Graham, owners. 10 Apr 1738. (Ref:

Maryland Commission Book No. 82, p. 52; *Maryland Historical Magazine*, Vol. XXVI, p. 150)

Granadam, Francis, native of Germany, denization, 22 Jun 1771. (Ref: Maryland Commission Book No. 82, p. 260; *Maryland Historical Magazine*, Vol. XXVII, p. 30)

Graves, Thomas, appointed Constable of the Lower Part of Potomac Hundred in Frederick County, 1771. (Ref: "Frederick County Minute Book, March 1771, Extracts by Patricia Abelard Andersen," *Western Maryland Genealogy*, Vol. 18, No. 1, January 2002, p. 25, spelled the name Potomack)

Gray, John, see Benjamin Barrett.

Gray, Joseph Cox, appointed a Commissioner of the Peace for Dorchester County, 8 Mar 1754. (Ref: Maryland State Archives, Governor and Council Commissioner Records, 1726-1794, p. 143)

Gray, Matthias, was appointed Constable of Newfoundland Hundred in Prince George's County, now Frederick County, 1745. (Ref: Prince George's County Court Records, 1736-1748, Extracts by Patricia Abelard Andersen, *Western Maryland Genealogy*, Vol. 18, No. 1, January 2002, p. 43)

Gray, Samuel, appointed a Commissioner of the Peace for Calvert County, 12 Nov 1773. (Ref: Maryland State Archives, Governor and Council Commissioner Records, 1726-1794, p. 279)

Gray, Thomas, registration of sloop *Betty*, 20 tons, built in Somerset County, 1734. Thomas Gray, master and owner. 16 Oct 1734 (Ref: Maryland Commission Book No. 82, p. 21; *Maryland Historical Magazine*, Vol. XXVI, p. 142)

Greaves, John, see Thomas Greaves.

Greaves, Thomas, registration of the shallop *Bargain*, 5 tons, rebuilt in St. Mary's County, 1743. John Greaves, master. Thomas Greaves and John Greaves, owners. 1 Mar 1743/4. (Ref: Maryland Commission Book No. 82, p. 108; *Maryland Historical Magazine*, Vol. XXVI, p. 251)

Green, Charles, commissioned a Ranger in Charles County, 25 Oct 1748. (Ref: Maryland Commission Book No. 82, p. 137; *Maryland Historical Magazine*, Vol. XXVI, p. 342)

Green, Richard, appointed a Commissioner of the Peace for Anne Arundel County, 26 Jul 1773. (Ref: Maryland State Archives, Governor and Council Commissioner Records, 1726-1794, p. 272)

Greenfield, Thomas (c1715-1774), appointed a Commissioner of the Peace for St. Mary's County, 4 Jul 1755. (Ref: Maryland State Archives, Governor and Council Commissioner Records, 1726-1794, p. 161)

Greenfield, Thomas Truman (1682-1733), was appointed a Commissioner of the Peace for St. Mary's County, 2 Mar 1726/7. (Ref: Maryland State Archives, Governor and Council Commissioner Records, 1726-1794, p. 2); appointed a Commissioner of the Peace for Cecil County, Baltimore County, Kent County, Prince George's County, Anne Arundel County, Calvert County, Charles County, St. Mary's County, Queen Anne's County, and Talbot County, 4 Aug 1732 and 10 Aug 1732 and 20 Aug 1733. (Ref: Maryland State Archives, Governor and Council Commissioner Records, 1726-1794, pp. 32-37)

Greenleaf, Stephen, see Samuel Allyne.

Greenup, John, appointed Constable of Linga-nore Hundred in Frederick County, 1760. (Ref: *This Was The Life: Excerpts from the Judgment Records of Frederick County, Maryland, 1748-1765*, by Millard Milburn Rice, p. 216, misspelled the hundred as Linginoa)

Gregory, Henry, blacksmith, of Anne Arundel County, convicted burglar, sentenced to death in July 1766, pardoned and banished out of the province, never to return, on 9 Sep 1766. (Ref: Maryland Commission Book No. 82, p. 180; *Maryland Historical Magazine*, Vol. XXVI, p. 354; *Archives of Maryland*, Vol. XXXII, "Proceedings of the Council of Maryland, 1761-1770," pp. 159, 163)

Gresham John (c1703-1752), of Kent County, appointment as a Commissioner of the Peace renewed, 8 Jun 1727. (Ref: Maryland State Archives, Governor and Council Commissioner Records, 1726-1794, p. 4); appointed a Commissioner of the Peace for Kent County, 12 Jun 1729. (Ref: Maryland State Archives, Governor and Council Commissioner Records, 1726-1794, p. 11); commissioned Sheriff of Kent County, 19 Feb 1731/2 and High Sheriff, 17 Feb 1734/5. (Ref: Maryland Commission Book No. 82, p. 26; *Maryland Historical Magazine*, Vol. XXVI, p. 143; Maryland State Archives, Governor and Council Commissioner Records, 1726-1794, p. 22); appointed a

Commissioner of the Peace for Kent County, 1 Dec 1768. (Ref: Maryland State Archives, Governor and Council Commissioner Records, 1726-1794, p. 239); see William Harris.

Gresham, Richard (d. c1773), merchant, registered the sloop *Kent*, 20 tons, built in Kent County, 1745. James Carle, master. Richard Gresham, owner. 29 Mar 1746. (Ref: Maryland Commission Book No. 82, p. 119; *Maryland Historical Magazine*, Vol. XXVI, p. 256); registration of sloop *Dolphin*, 12 tons, built in Kent County, 1749. John Smith, master. Richard Gresham, owner. 24 May 1749. (Ref: Maryland Commission Book No. 82, p. 151; *Maryland Historical Magazine*, Vol. XXVI, p. 349; see Thomas Smith.

Griffin, Charles, appointed a Commissioner of the Peace for Anne Arundel County, 12 Jun 1739. (Ref: Maryland State Archives, Governor and Council Commissioner Records, 1726-1794, p. 63)

Griffith, Henry (c1720-1794), was appointed a Commissioner of the Peace for Anne Arundel County, 10 Aug 1755. (Ref: Maryland State Archives, Governor and Council Commissioner Records, 1726-1794, p. 162)

Griffith, Orlando, commissioned Deputy Surveyor of Anne Arundel County, 19 Sep 1765. (Ref: Maryland Commission Book No. 82, p. 172; *Maryland Historical Magazine*, Vol. XXVI, p. 353)

Griffith, William, appointed a Commissioner of the Peace for Frederick County, 12 Nov 1748. (Ref: Maryland State Archives, Governor and Council Commissioner Records, 1726-1794, p. 109); Court Justice, Frederick County, 1748. (Ref: *This Was The Life: Excerpts from the Judgment Records of Frederick County, Maryland, 1748-1765*, by Millard Milburn Rice, p. 1); commissioned Ranger of Frederick County, 25 May 1749. (Ref: Maryland Commission Book No. 82, p. 141; *Maryland Historical Magazine*, Vol. XXVI, p. 344)

Griffith, William, laborer, late of Baltimore County, convicted felon for burglary, pardoned on 30 Jan 1773. (Ref: Maryland Commission Book No. 82, p. 293; *Maryland Historical Magazine*, Vol. XXVII, p. 32)

Grimshaw, John, labourer, of Prince George's County, convicted felon, executed on on 20 May 1757. (Ref: Maryland State Archives, Governor and Council Commissioner Records, 1726-1794, p. 159)

Grindall, Christopher, registration of ship *Frederick*, built at South River by said Grindall, master, 1733. Former registration lost as appears by affidavit of Alexander Scougall, former master. Daniel Watts, John Rendell and Christopher, owners. 22 Jul 1737. (Ref: Maryland Commission Book No. 82, p. 49; *Maryland Historical Magazine*, Vol. XXVI, p. 149)

Groom, Samuel, appointed a Commissioner of the Peace for Kent County, 18 Feb 1739/40. (Ref: Maryland State Archives, Governor and Council Commissioner Records, 1726-1794, p. 66)

Gudgeon, Sutton, Constable of Gunpowder Upper Hundred in Baltimore County, 1773. (Ref: *Inhabitants of Baltimore County, 1763-1774*, by Henry C. Peden, Jr., 1989, p. 62, citing a 1773 List of Taxables)

Gunby, James, appointed a Commissioner of the Peace for Somerset County, 19 May 1774. (Ref: Maryland State Archives, Governor and Council Commissioner Records, 1726-1794, p. 282)

Guthrow, Joseph, of Baltimore County, Ranger, 9 Aug 1775. (Ref: *Calendar of Maryland State Papers, The Red Books*, No. 4, Part 1, p. 5)

Gyles, Charles, see Patrick Creagh.

Hackett, Michael, registration of schooner *Lark*, 8 tons, built in Anne Arundel County, 1744. Michael Hackett, master. Thomas Perkins, owner. 9 Nov 1745. (Ref: Maryland Commission Book No. 82, p. 117; *Maryland Historical Magazine*, Vol. XXVI, p. 256)

Hackman, James, commissioned High Sheriff of Frederick County, 16 Nov 1771. (Ref: Maryland State Archives, Governor and Council Commissioner Records, 1726-1794, p. 249)

Hagarthy, John, appointed Constable of George Town Hundred in Frederick County, 1769. (Ref: "Frederick County Court Minutes November 1769 by Patricia Abelard Andersen," *Western Maryland Genealogy*, Vol. 16, No. 1, January 2000, p. 32; "Frederick County Court Minutes, March 1769," by Patricia Abelard Andersen, *Western Maryland Genealogy*, Vol. 15, No. 2, April 1999, p. 62, spelled his name Hagathy)

Hall, Andrew, appointed a Commissioner of the Peace for Queen Anne's County, 11 Nov 1763. (Ref: Maryland State Archives, Governor and Council Commissioner Records, 1726-1794, p. 212)

Hall, Aquila (1727-1779), of Baltimore County,

appointed a Commissioner of the Peace, 3 Nov 1757. (Ref: Maryland State Archives, Governor and Council Commissioner Records, 1726-1794, p. 178); Justice, 1757-1762, 1769-1773 (Harford County, 1774), and Sheriff, Baltimore Co., 1762-1763. (*A Biographical Dictionary of the Maryland Legislature, 1635-1789*, by Edward C. Papenfuse, et al., Vol. A-H, p. 380); appointed a Commissioner of the Peace in Harford County, 20 Feb 1774. (Ref: Maryland State Archives, Governor and Council Commissioner Records, 1726-1794, p. 281)

Hall, Benedict Edward (c1744-1822), appointed a Commissioner of the Peace for Baltimore County, 31 Oct 1772. (Ref: Maryland State Archives, Governor and Council Commissioner Records, 1726-1794, p. 264); appointed a Commissioner of the Peace for Harford County, 20 Feb 1774. (Ref: Maryland State Archives, Governor and Council Commissioner Records, 1726-1794, p. 281)

Hall, Benjamin, appointed a Commissioner of the Peace for Prince George's County, 1 Jun 1750. (Ref: Maryland State Archives, Governor and Council Commissioner Records, 1726-1794, p. 118)

Hall, Benjamin, Jr., see Negro Toby.

Hall, Edward, appointed a Commissioner of the Peace for Baltimore County, 3 Mar 1726/7 and 22 Oct 1728. (Ref: Maryland State Archives, Governor and Council Commissioner Records, 1726-1794, pp. 2, 80); commissioned High Sheriff of Baltimore County, 18 Apr 1734. (Ref: Maryland Commission Book No. 82, p. 10; *Maryland Historical Magazine*, Vol. XXVI, p. 140)

Hall, Edward, appointed a Commissioner of the Peace for Calvert County, 12 Nov 1773. (Ref: Maryland State Archives, Governor and Council Commissioner Records, 1726-1794, p. 2790

Hall, Elihu (1724-c1791), appointed a Commissioner of the Peace for Cecil County, 26 May 1756. (Ref: Maryland State Archives, Governor and Council Commissioner Records, 1726-1794, p. 167)

Hall, Elisha, appointed a Commissioner of the Peace for Cecil County, 8 Mar 1754. (Ref: Maryland State Archives, Governor and Council Commissioner Records, 1726-1794, p. 143)

Hall, Elizabeth, see Negro Sharper.

Hall, Henry, Jr. (1727-1770), was appointed a Commissioner of the Peace for Anne Arundel County, 12 Aug 1752. (Ref: Maryland State Archives, Governor and Council Commissioner Records, 1726-1794, p. 133); major, served on the Committee of Laws, 1755. (Ref: *Archives of Maryland*, Vol. LII, "Proceedings and Acts of the General Assembly of Maryland, 1755-1756," pp. 46, 74 styled him without the Jr.)

Hall, Isaac, appointed a Commissioner of the Peace for Anne Arundel County, 26 Jul 1773. (Ref: Maryland State Archives, Governor and Council Commissioner Records, 1726-1794, p. 272

Hall, John, alias John Philby, laborer, of Baltimore County, convicted felon for stealing a horse, was pardoned 7 Jul 1773. (Ref: Maryland Commission Book No. 82, p. 320; *Maryland Historical Magazine*, Vol. XXVII, p. 34)

Hall, John, appointed a Commissioner of the Peace for Cecil County, 22 Apr 1758. (Ref: Maryland State Archives, Governor and Council Commissioner Records, 1726-1794, p. 180)

Hall, John, appointed a Commissioner of the Peace for Cecil County, Baltimore County, Kent County, Prince George's County, Anne Arundel County, Calvert County, Charles County, St. Mary's County, Queen Anne's County, and Talbot County, 4 Aug 1732 and 10 Aug 1732 and 20 Aug 1733. (Ref: Maryland State Archives, Governor and Council Commissioner Records, 1726-1794, pp. 32-37)

Hall, John, commissioned Sheriff of Baltimore County, 18 Apr 1732. (Ref: Maryland State Archives, Governor and Council Commissioner Records, 1726-1794, p. 22)

Hall, John, of Cranberry, appointed a Commissioner of the Peace for Baltimore County, 8 Nov 1752. (Ref: Maryland State Archives, Governor and Council Commissioner Records, 1726-1794, p. 135)

Hall, John, of Spesutia, appointed a Commissioner of the Peace for Baltimore County, 23 May 1753. (Ref: Maryland State Archives, Governor and Council Commissioner Records, 1726-1794, p. 138)

Hall, John, see Richard Smith, William Dames and William Hammond.

Hall, John, Jr., appointed a Commissioner of the Peace for Baltimore County, 2 Mar 1754. (Ref: Maryland State Archives, Governor and Council

Colonial Maryland Commissions, Appointments, and Other Proceedings, 1726-1776

Commissioner Records, 1726-1794, p. 142)

Hall, John, Jr., appointed a Commissioner of the Peace for Baltimore County, 22 Oct 1728. (Ref: Maryland State Archives, Governor and Council Commissioner Records, 1726-1794, p. 8)

Hall, John, Jr., commissioned High Sheriff of Baltimore County, 18 Jan 1734/5. (Ref: Maryland Commission Book No. 82, p. 25; *Maryland Historical Magazine*, Vol. XXVI, p. 142; Maryland State Archives, Governor and Council Commissioner Records, 1726-1794, p. 45)

Hall, John, Jr., of Swan Creek, appointed a Commissioner of the Peace for Baltimore County [now Harford County] on 31 Oct 1768. (Ref: Maryland State Archives, Governor and Council Commissioner Records, 1726-1794, p. 238)

Hall, Joseph, appointed a Commissioner of the Peace for Calvert County, 9 Dec 1731. (Ref: Maryland State Archives, Governor and Council Commissioner Records, 1726-1794, p. 20)

Hall, Parker, appointed a Commissioner of the Peace for Baltimore County, 24 Nov 1732. (Ref: Maryland State Archives, Governor and Council Commissioner Records, 1726-1794, p. 39)

Hall, Ralph, laborer, of Prince George's County, pardoned for felony, 17 Jun 1735. (Ref: Maryland Commission Book No. 82, p. 31; *Maryland Historical Magazine*, Vol. XXVI, p. 144)

Hall, Robert, appointed a Commissioner of the Peace for Dorchester County, 4 Aug 1757. (Ref: Maryland State Archives, Governor and Council Commissioner Records, 1726-1794, p. 175)

Hall, Robert, appointed a Commissioner of the Peace for Talbot County, 19 Dec 1751. (Ref: Maryland State Archives, Governor and Council Commissioner Records, 1726-1794, p. 131)

Hall, Samuel, see Francis Lee and William Dames.

Hall(?), Henry, of Calvert County, convicted felon, ordered on 28 Jan 1731/2 to be executed. (Ref: Maryland State Archives, Governor and Council Commissioner Records, 1726-1794, p. 21)

Hallam, John, was appointed Constable of Conococheague Hundred in Prince George's County, now Frederick County, 1745. (Ref: Prince George's County Court Records, 1736-1748, Extracts by Patricia Abelard Andersen, *Western Maryland Genealogy*, Vol. 18, No. 1, January 2002, p. 43)

Hambleton, Mary, see Mulatto James.

Hamett, John, commissioned a Coroner of Charles County, 21 Apr 1766. (Ref: Maryland Commission Book No. 82, p. 177; *Maryland Historical Magazine*, Vol. XXVI, p. 354)

Hamilton, George, appointed a Commissioner of the Peace for Prince George's County, 1 Jun 1750. (Ref: Maryland State Archives, Governor and Council Commissioner Records, 1726-1794, p. 118)

Hamilton, John, commissioned High Sheriff of Cecil County, 16 Sep 1772. (Ref: Maryland State Archives, Governor and Council Commissioner Records, 1726-1794, p. 252)

Hamilton, John (d. 1756), reverend, induction into Somerset Parish, Somerset County, 10 Dec 1745. (Ref: Maryland Commission Book No. 82, p. 118; *Maryland Historical Magazine*, Vol. XXVI, p. 256)

Hamilton, John, see John Seegar, Negro Rachel and William Thompson.

Hamilton, Patrick, appointed a Commissioner of the Peace for Queen Anne's County, 18 May 1758. (Ref: Maryland State Archives, Governor and Council Commissioner Records, 1726-1794, p. 180)

Hamilton, Robert, see Robert Swan and William Govane.

Hamilton, Thomas, appointed Constable of New Scotland Hundred in Prince George's County, now Frederick County, 1742. (Ref: Prince George's County Court Records, 1736-1748, Extracts by Patricia Abelard Andersen, *Western Maryland Genealogy*, Vol. 18, No. 1, January 2002, p. 38)

Hamilton, William (c1682-1759), appointed a Commissioner of the Peace for Baltimore County, 22 Oct 1728. (Ref: Maryland State Archives, Governor and Council Commissioner Records, 1726-1794, p. 8)

Hammett, McKelvie, commissioned a Coroner of St. Mary's County, 24 Dec 1773. (Ref: Maryland Commission Book No. 82, p. 333; *Maryland Historical Magazine*, Vol. XXVII, p. 36)

Hammit, Robert, appointed a Commissioner of the Peace for St. Mary's County, 6 Nov 1758. (Ref: Maryland State Archives, Governor and Council Commissioner Records, 1726-1794, p. 183)

Hammitt, Robert, appointed a Commissioner of the Peace for Cecil County, 10 May 1757. (Ref: Maryland State Archives, Governor and Council Commissioner Records, 1726-1794, p. 174)

Hammond, Charles, appointed a Commissioner of the Peace for Calvert County, 2 Mar 1731/2. (Ref: Maryland State Archives, Governor and Council Commissioner Records, 1726-1794, p. 22)

Hammond, Charles (1692-1772), of Anne Arundel County, commissioned Commissioner for Emitting Bills of Credit, 29 Jan 1733/4. (Ref: Maryland Commission Book No. 82, p. 3; *Maryland Historical Magazine*, Vol. XXVI, p. 139); colonel, Provincial Commission, 8 Jul 1735. (Ref: Maryland State Archives, Governor and Council Commissioner Records, 1726-1794, p. 49); of Anne Arundel County, commissioned Treasurer of the Western Shore, 23 Oct 1736. (Ref: Maryland Commission Book No. 82, p. 46; *Maryland Historical Magazine*, Vol. XXVI, p. 148; *A Biographical Dictionary of the Maryland Legislature, 1635-1789*, by Edward C. Papenfuse, et al., Vol. A-H, pp. 392-393); colonel, commissioned Treasurer of the Western Shore, 29 Sep 1742. On same day, commissioned to be one of the Commissioners of the Paper Currency Office. (Ref: Maryland Commission Book No. 82, p. 95; *Maryland Historical Magazine*, Vol. XXVI, pp. 246-247); appointed a Privy Council on 10 May 1753. (Ref: *Archives of Maryland*, Vol. XXXI, "Proceedings of the Council of Maryland, 1753-1761," p. 8)

Hammond, John, appointed a Commissioner of the Peace for Cecil County, 29 Oct 1730 and 30 Nov 1732. (Ref: Maryland State Archives, Governor and Council Commissioner Records, 1726-1794, pp. 17, 30)

Hammond, John, appointed a Commissioner of the Peace for Kent County, 2 Jun 1732. (Ref: Maryland State Archives, Governor and Council Commissioner Records, 1726-1794, p. 23)

Hammond, John, of Nicholas, of Anne Arundel County, appointed Constable of Town Neckr Hundred in 1774. (Ref: Anne Arundel County Court Minutes, 1725-1757, 1774)

Hammond, Mordecai, appointed Commissioner of the Peace for Anne Arundel County, 3 Mar 1726/7. (Ref: Maryland State Archives, Governor and Council Commissioner Records, 1726-1794, p. 3); registration of schooner *Mulberry*, 55 tons, built in Anne Arundel County, 1742. George Hammond, master. Mordecai Hammond, owner. 30 Sep 1742. (Ref: Maryland Commission Book No. 82, p. 96; *Maryland Historical Magazine*, Vol. XXVI, p. 247)

Hammond, Mordecai, commissioned a Coroner of Baltimore County, 5 Jan 1771. (Ref: Maryland Commission Book No. 82, p. 251; *Maryland Historical Magazine*, Vol. XXVII, p. 29)

Hammond, Nathan (1708-1762), major, was commissioned Sheriff of Anne Arundel County, 23 Dec 1751. (Ref: Maryland State Archives, Governor and Council Commissioner Records, 1726-1794, p. 130; *A Biographical Dictionary of the Maryland Legislature, 1635-1789*, by Edward C. Papenfuse, et al., Vol. A-H, p. 395)

Hammond Nathan (1731-1811), sheriff, of Anne Arundel County, 1753-1754. Trustee of the Poor, 1772. (*A Biographical Dictionary of the Maryland Legislature, 1635-1789*, by Edward C. Papenfuse, et al., Vol. A-H, pp. 393-394)

Hammond, Philip (1697-1760), esquire, of Anne Arundel County, served on the Committee of Laws, 1755. (Ref: *Archives of Maryland*, Vol. LII, "Proceedings and Acts of the General Assembly of Maryland, 1755-1756," pp. 46, 97); appointed to a Committee for Enquiring into Ways and Means to Raise a Sum Sufficient for Payment of Eighty Rangers to Defend and Protect the Frontiers, 28 Jun 1755. (Ref: Maryland State Archives, Governor and Council Commissioner Records, 1726-1794, p. 151); appointed to the Committee to Apportion the Public Levies, 29 May 1756. (Ref: *Archives of Maryland*, Vol. LII, "Proceedings and Acts of the General Assembly of Maryland, 1755-1756," p. 291); see Mulatto Jack and Negro Frank.

Hammond, Rezin (d. 1783), was appointed a Commissioner of the Peace for Baltimore County on 30 May 1774. (Ref: Maryland State Archives, Governor and Council Commissioner Records, 1726-1794, p. 284 spelled his first name Reasin, and p. 288 spelled it Rezin)

Hammond, Thomas, appointed a Commissioner of the Peace for Anne Arundel County, 15 Nov 1770 and 26 Jul 1773. (Ref: Maryland State Archives, Governor and Council Commissioner Records, 1726-1794, pp. 255 and p. 272); see William Govane.

Colonial Maryland Commissions, Appointments, and Other Proceedings, 1726-1776

Hammond, William, appointed a Commissioner of the Peace for Baltimore County, 1 Nov 1729. (Ref: Maryland State Archives, Governor and Council Commissioner Records, 1726-1794, p. 12); commissioned High Sheriff of Baltimore County in the room of John Hall, 3 Nov 1735. (Ref: Maryland Commission Book No. 82, p. 38; *Maryland Historical Magazine*, Vol. XXVI, p. 145); see Negro Phil.

Hands, Bedingfield, appointed a Commissioner of the Peace for Queen Anne's County, 4 Aug 1732. (Ref: Maryland State Archives, Governor and Council Commissioner Records, 1726-1794, p. 25); of Kent County, was a Justice of Assize, Oyer and Terminer, and Gaol [Jail] Delivery, 1757. (Ref: *Archives of Maryland*, Vol. XXXI, "Proceedings of the Council of Maryland, 1753-1761," p. 205); commissioned High Sheriff of Kent County, 4 Nov 1760. (Ref: Maryland State Archives, Governor and Council Commissioner Records, 1726-1794, p. 185); esquire, commissioned Treasurer of the Eastern Shore, 14 Oct 1766. (Ref: Maryland Commission Book No. 82, p. 182; *Maryland Historical Magazine*, Vol. XXVI, p. 354); see George Steuart and John Wallace.

Handy, Benjamin (d. c1763), was appointed a Commissioner of the Peace for Worcester County, 21 Dec 1747. (Ref: Maryland State Archives, Governor and Council Commissioner Records, 1726-1794, p. 105); commissioned High Sheriff of Worcester County, 4 Nov 1758. (Ref: Maryland State Archives, Governor and Council Commissioner Records, 1726-1794, p. 174); see William Outten.

Handy, Charles, merchant, of Somerset County, registration of schooner *Charming Esther*, built in Somerset County. George Handy, master. Charles Handy and George Handy, owners. 12 Mar 1747/8. (Ref: Maryland Commission Book No. 82, p. 133; *Maryland Historical Magazine*, Vol. XXVI, p. 262)

Handy, Ebenezer, appointed a Commissioner of the Peace for Worcester County, 26 Jul 1773. (Ref: Maryland State Archives, Governor and Council Commissioner Records, 1726-1794, p. 271); Court Justice, Worcester County, 1774. (*Calendar of Maryland State Papers, No. 1 The Black Books*, p. 214); appointed a Commissioner of the Peace for Somerset County, 5 Jan 1775. (Ref: Maryland State Archives, Governor and Council Commissioner Records, 1726-1794, p. 286)

Handy, George, see Charles Handy and Isaac Handy.

Handy, Isaac (c1700-1762), was appointed a Commissioner of the Peace for Somerset County, 25 Mar 1734. (Ref: Maryland State Archives, Governor and Council Commissioner Records, 1726-1794, p. 40); merchant, registration of sloop *Sally & Molly*, 30 tons, built in Worcester County, 1748. George Handy, master. Isaac Handy and George Handy, owners. 6 Apr 1748. (Ref: Maryland Commission Book No. 82, p. 133; *Maryland Historical Magazine*, Vol. XXVI, p. 262); Court Justice, 1753. (*Calendar of Maryland State Papers, No. 1 The Black Books*, p. 112); see John Blewer.

Handy, John (c1724-1756), was appointed a Commissioner of the Peace for Somerset County, 29 Oct 1730. (Ref: Maryland State Archives, Governor and Council Commissioner Records, 1726-1794, p. 17); registration of sloop *Polly*, 38 tons, built in Somerset County, 1749. John West, master. John West, John Carlisle, Richard Jackson and John Dalton, owners. 31 Jan 1749/50. (Ref: Maryland Commission Book No. 82, p. 142; *Maryland Historical Magazine*, Vol. XXVI, p. 344); appointed a Commissioner of the Peace for Somerset County, 14 Dec 1751. (Ref: Maryland State Archives, Governor and Council Commissioner Records, 1726-1794, p. 131); Court Justice, 1753. (*Calendar of Maryland State Papers, No. 1 The Black Books*, p. 112); captain, appointed to a Committee to Inspect the Accounts and Proceedings of the Commissioners for Emitting Bills of Credit, 25 Feb 1755. (Ref: *Archives of Maryland*, Vol. LII, "Proceedings and Acts of the General Assembly of Maryland, 1755-1756," pp. 5, 51)

Handy, John, appointed a Commissioner of the Peace for Worcester County, 30 Apr 1770. (Ref: Maryland State Archives, Governor and Council Commissioner Records, 1726-1794, p. 250)

Handy, Nehemiah, appointed a Commissioner of the Peace for Somerset County, 8 Mar 1754. (Ref: Maryland State Archives, Governor and Council Commissioner Records, 1726-1794, p. 143)

Handy, Robert, appointed a Commissioner of the Peace for Worcester County, 17 Oct 1764. (Ref: Maryland State Archives, Governor and Council Commissioner Records, 1726-1794, p. 218)

Handy, Samuel, appointed a Commissioner of the Peace for Somerset County, 5 Jan 1775. (Ref:

Maryland State Archives, Governor and Council Commissioner Records, 1726-1794, p. 286)

Handy, Samuel, commissioned Sheriff of Somer-set County, 1 Jul 1746. (Ref: Maryland State Archives, Governor and Council Commissioner Records, 1726-1794, p. 92)

Handy, Thomas, appointed a Commissioner of the Peace for Somerset County, 19 May 1774. (Ref: Maryland State Archives, Governor and Council Commissioner Records, 1726-1794, p. 282)

Handy, Thomas, appointed a Commissioner of the Peace for Worcester County, 26 Jul 1754. (Ref: Maryland State Archives, Governor and Council Commissioner Records, 1726-1794, p. 156)

Handy, William, see Ephraim Waggaman.

Hanmash, John, laborer, of Baltimore County, pardoned for horse stealing, 17 Jan 1771. (Ref: Maryland Commission Book No. 82, p. 251; *Maryland Historical Magazine*, Vol. XXVII, p. 29)

Hanson, Frederick, of Kent County, sheriff, 1726. (Ref: *Abstracts of the Testamentary Proceedings and Prerogative Court of Maryland, Vol. XVII, 1724-1727*, by Vernon L. Skinner, Jr., p. 125, citing original Liber 27, f. 321); appointed a Commissioner of the Peace for Kent County, 3 Mar 1726/7, and Queen Anne's County, 29 Oct 1730. (Ref: Maryland State Archives, Governor and Council Commissioner Records, 1726-1794, pp. 2, 17)

Hanson, John, was commissioned High Sheriff of Frederick County, 2 Oct 1771. (Ref: Maryland State Archives, Governor and Council Commissioner Records, 1726-1794, p. 246); commissioned Deputy Surveyor of Frederick County, 3 Oct 1771 and 5 May 1773. (Ref: Maryland Commission Book No. 82, pp. 270, 316; *Maryland Historical Magazine*, Vol. XXVII, pp. 30, 34)

Hanson, John (1721-1783), late sheriff of Charles County, had ordinary license accounts still unpaid in 1756. (Ref: *Archives of Maryland*, Vol. LII, "Proceedings and Acts of the General Assembly of Maryland, 1755-1756," p. 568)

Hanson, Jonathan, commissioned Inspector of Flour in Baltimore Town, 13 Sep 1768. (Ref: Maryland Commission Book No. 82, p. 216; *Maryland Historical Magazine*, Vol. XXVI, p. 358)

Hanson, Robert (c1680-1748), was appointed a Commissioner of the Peace for Charles County, 2 Mar 1726/7. (Ref: Maryland State Archives, Governor and Council Commissioner Records, 1726-1794, p. 2)

Hanson, Samuel (1716-1794), commissioned Sheriff of Charles County, 17 Sep 1744; appointed a Commissioner of the Peace for Somerset County, 26 May 1755. (Ref: Maryland State Archives, Governor and Council Commissioner Records, 1726-1794, pp. 85, 159); Court Justice, 1756. (*Calendar of Maryland State Papers, No. 1 The Black Books*, p. 132); late sheriff of Charles County, had ordinary license accounts still unpaid in 1756. (Ref: *Archives of Maryland*, Vol. LII, "Proceedings and Acts of the General Assembly of Maryland, 1755-1756," p. 568; styled him as Jr.)

Hanson, Samuel (c1685-1740), of Charles County, appointed a Deputy Commissary [government official who had certain duties to perform] on 11 Jul 1727. (Ref: *Abstracts of the Testamentary Proceedings and Prerogative Court of Maryland, Vol. XVII, 1724-1727*, by Vernon L. Skinner, Jr., p. 203, citing original Liber 28, f. 77, listed him without the Jr.); appointed a Commissioner of the Peace for Charles County, 31 Mar 1736 and 1 May 1739. (Ref: Maryland State Archives, Governor and Council Commissioner Records, 1726-1794, pp. 51, 63)

Hanson, Shadrick, appointed a Commissioner of the Peace for Kent County, 12 Jun 1729. (Ref: Maryland State Archives, Governor and Council Commissioner Records, 1726-1794, p. 11)

Hanson, Theophilus, was commissioned Deputy Surveyor of Charles County, 6 Feb 1767. (Ref: Maryland Commission Book No. 82, p. 199; *Maryland Historical Magazine*, Vol. XXVI, p. 355)

Hanson, Walter (1711-1794), was commissioned High Sheriff of Charles County, 12 Apr 1738. (Ref: Maryland State Archives, Governor and Council Commissioner Records, 1726-1794, p. 59); appointed a Commissioner of the Peace for Charles County, 15 Oct 1741. (Ref: Maryland State Archives, Governor and Council Commissioner Records, 1726-1794, p. 71); late sheriff of Charles County, had ordinary license accounts still unpaid in 1756. Ref: (Ref: *Archives of Maryland*, Vol. LII, "Proceedings and Acts of the General Assembly of Maryland, 1755-1756," p. 568); Court Justice, 1756. (*Calendar of Maryland State Papers, No. 1 The Black Books*, p. 132)

Hanson, William, commissioned Deputy Surveyor of Charles County, 4 Mar 1733/4. (Ref: Maryland Commission Book No. 82, p. 8; *Maryland Historical Magazine*, Vol. XXVI, p. 140); commissioned Deputy Surveyor of Charles County, 19 May 1743 and 29 Apr 1747. (Ref: Maryland Commission Book No. 82, pp. 102, 129; *Maryland Historical Magazine*, Vol. XXVI, pp. 249, 260)

Hardman John, see Christopher Lowndes.

Hardy, George, appointed a Commissioner of the Peace for Prince George's County, 3 Dec 1766. (Ref: Maryland State Archives, Governor and Council Commissioner Records, 1726-1794, p. 230)

Hargrove, Charles, see William Dallam.

Harris, Benjamin, appointed Constable of Rock Creek Hundred in Prince George's County, now Frederick County, 1742 and 1744, and Middle Hundred, 1745. (Ref: Prince George's County Court Records, 1736-1748, Extracts by Patricia Abelard Andersen, *Western Maryland Genealogy*, Vol. 18, No. 1, January 2002, pp. 38, 41, 43)

Harris, Benton (c1716-1777), was appointed a Commissioner of the Peace for Worcester County, 22 May 1762. (Ref: Maryland State Archives, Governor and Council Commissioner Records, 1726-1794, p. 202); appointed a Commissioner of the Peace for Somerset County, 5 Jan 1775. (Ref: Maryland State Archives, Governor and Council Commissioner Records, 1726-1794, p. 286); Court Justice, Worcester County, 1774. (*Calendar of Maryland State Papers, No. 1 The Black Books*, p. 214)

Harris, Edward, see Negro Judith.

Harris, James (1682-1743), was appointed a Commissioner of the Peace for Kent County, 30 Nov 1732. (Ref: Maryland State Archives, Governor and Council Commissioner Records, 1726-1794, p. 33); commissioned Surveyor General of the Eastern Shore, 23 Aug 1737. (Ref: Maryland Commission Book No. 82, p. 50; *Maryland Historical Magazine*, Vol. XXVI, p. 150); colonel, commissioned Surveyor General of the Eastern Shore. 29 Sep 1742. (Ref: Maryland Commission Book No. 82, p. 96; *Maryland Historical Magazine*, Vol. XXVI, p. 247)

Harris, John, appointed a Commissioner of the Peace for Baltimore County, 17 May 1764. (Ref: Maryland State Archives, Governor and Council Commissioner Records, 1726-1794, p. 216)

Harris, John, appointed a Press Master in Dorchester County in 1745. (Ref: Dorchester County Judgment Records, 1743-1745, p. 476; *Judgment Records of Dorchester, Queen Anne's and Talbot Counties, Maryland*, by F. Edward Wright, 2001, p. 60)

Harris, Lloyd, commissioned a Coroner for Baltimore County, 4 Nov 1735. (Ref: Maryland Commission Book No. 82, p. 38; *Maryland Historical Magazine*, Vol. XXVI, p. 145); commissioned Ranger for Baltimore County, 26 Oct 1737. (Ref: Maryland Commission Book No. 82, p. 51; *Maryland Historical Magazine*, Vol. XXVI, p. 150)

Harris, Matthias, commissioned Receiver of the Manor Rents in Kent County. 23 Dec 1743. (Ref: Maryland Commission Book No. 82, p. 107; *Maryland Historical Magazine*, Vol. XXVI, p. 251)

Harris, Matthias (1718-1773), reverend, was inducted into Christ Church Parish, Queen Anne's County, 11 Aug 1769. (Ref: Maryland Commission Book No. 82, p. 225; *Maryland Historical Magazine*, Vol. XXVI, p. 359); induction into Chester Parish, Kent County, 11 Feb 1773. (Ref: Maryland Commission Book No. 82, p. 294; *Maryland Historical Magazine*, Vol. XXVII, p. 32

Harris, Thomas (d. 1760), commissioned Sheriff of Queen Anne's County, 29 Oct 1751. (Ref: Maryland State Archives, Governor and Council Commissioner Records, 1726-1794, p. 129)

Harris, William (1704-1748), commissioned High Sheriff of Kent County in the room of John Gresham, 20 Aug 1735, and on 22 Jul 1741. (Ref: Maryland Commission Book No. 82, p. 33; *Maryland Historical Magazine*, Vol. XXVI, p. 144; Maryland State Archives, Governor and Council Commissioner Records, 1726-1794, p. 71); merchant, registration of schooner *Mulberry*, built in Kent County, 1746. Thomas Glenworth, master. William Harris, owner. 6 Oct 1746. (Ref: Maryland Commission Book No. 82, p. 123; *Maryland Historical Magazine*, Vol. XXVI, p. 258)

Harrison, Benjamin, appointed a Commissioner of the Peace for Anne Arundel County, 12 Aug 1752. (Ref: Maryland State Archives, Governor and Council Commissioner Records, 1726-1794, p. 133); Court Justice, Anne Arundel County, 1755. (Ref: Anne Arundel County Court Minutes, 1725-1757)

Harrison, Elisha, appointed a Commissioner of the Peace for Anne Arundel County, 18 Aug 1764 and 26 Jul 1773. (Ref: Maryland State Archives, Governor and Council Commissioner Records, 1726-1794, p. 217); Maryland State Archives, Governor and Council Commissioner Records, 1726-1794, p. 272)

Harrison, James, appointed Constable of Seneca Hundred in Prince George's County, now Frederick County, 1746. (Ref: Prince George's County Court Records, 1736-1748, Extracts by Patricia Abelard Andersen, *Western Maryland Genealogy*, Vol. 18, No. 1, January 2002, p. 44)

Harrison, John, alias John Stewart, of Frederick County, convicted felon for stealing a horse and mare from Andrew Rench. He petitioned to Gov. Horatio Sharpe on 29 Apr 1760 stating that he was "at this time enlisted in his Majesty's service" and prayed for a pardon, but he was executed on 17 Oct 1760. (Ref: Maryland State Archives, Governor and Council Commissioner Records, 1726-1794, p. 178; *Archives of Maryland*, Vol. XXXI, "Proceedings of the Council of Maryland, 1753-1761," pp. 412-413)

Harrison, John, appointed a Commissioner of the Peace for Prince George's County, 3 Dec 1766. (Ref: Maryland State Archives, Governor and Council Commissioner Records, 1726-1794, p. 230)

Harrison, Joseph Hanson (d. 1785), appointed a Commissioner of the Peace for Charles County, 30 Apr 1759. (Ref: Maryland State Archives, Governor and Council Commissioner Records, 1726-1794, p. 185)

Harrison, Rachel, see Negro Ben.

Harrison, Richard, appointed a Commissioner of the Peace for Anne Arundel County, 16 Mar 1748/9. (Ref: Maryland State Archives, Governor and Council Commissioner Records, 1726-1794, p. 110)

Harrison, Richard (d. 1780), appointed a Commissioner of the Peace for Charles County, 22 Oct 1739. (Ref: Maryland State Archives, Governor and Council Commissioner Records, 1726-1794, p. 66); Court Justice, 1756. (*Calendar of Maryland State Papers, No. 1 The Black Books*, p. 132); see Hugh Neil and John Barclay.

Harrison, Richard, reverend, induction into St. Margaret's Westminster, Anne Arundel County, 30 Aug 1742. (Ref: Maryland Commission Book No. 82, p. 95; *Maryland Historical Magazine*, Vol. XXVI, p. 246); resignation from St. Margaret's Westminster Parish, Anne Arundel County, 29 Nov 1742. On same day, inducted to St. Luke's Parish, Queen Anne's County. (Ref: Maryland Commission Book No. 82, p. 98; *Maryland Historical Magazine*, Vol. XXVI, p. 248)

Harrison, Robert (1740-1802), commissioned High Sheriff of Dorchester County, 31 Oct 1767. (Ref: Maryland State Archives, Governor and Council Commissioner Records, 1726-1794, p. 223)

Harrison, Samuel, appointed a Commissioner of the Peace for Anne Arundel County, 26 Jul 1773. (Ref: Maryland State Archives, Governor and Council Commissioner Records, 1726-1794, p. 272)

Harrison, Thomas (d. 1782), appointed to represent Baltimore County in the Provincial Convention, 1775. (Ref: *Calendar of Maryland State Papers, The Red Books*, No. 4, Part 1, p. 3)

Harrison, Thomas, appointed Constable of the Lower Part of Andietam [Antietam] Hundred in Frederick County, 1769. (Ref: "Frederick County Court Minutes November 1769 by Patricia Abelard Andersen," *Western Maryland Genealogy*, Vol. 16, No. 1, January 2000, p. 33)

Hartley, George, appointed Constable of the Lower Part of Antietam Hundred in Frederick County, 1769. (Ref: "Frederick County Court Minutes, March 1769," by Patricia Abelard Andersen, *Western Maryland Genealogy*, Vol. 15, No. 2, April 1999, p. 63)

Harts, John, commissioned Measurer of Grain, Salt, and Flax Seed in Baltimore Town, 13 Sep 1768. (Ref: Maryland Commission Book No. 82, p. 216; *Maryland Historical Magazine*, Vol. XXVI, p. 358)

Harvey, John, see Robert Harvey.

Harvey, Robert, of Bermuda, registration of the schooner *Betty*, 35 tons, built in Worcester County, 1748. Stephen Mitchell, master. Robert Harvey, John Harvey, Jeremiah Burk, and Cornelius Williams, owners. 10 Apr 1748. (Ref: Maryland Commission Book No. 82, p. 133; *Maryland Historical Magazine*, Vol. XXVI, p. 262)

Harwood, Benjamin, see Negro Charles and Negro James.

Harwood, Richard, appointed a Commissioner of the Peace for Anne Arundel County, 16 Dec 1769 and 26

Jul 1773. (Ref: Maryland State Archives, Governor and Council Commissioner Records, 1726-1794, pp. 249, 272)

Harwood, Richard, appointed a Commissioner of the Peace for Anne Arundel County, 28 Feb 1742/3. (Ref: Maryland State Archives, Governor and Council Commissioner Records, 1726-1794, p. 77)

Harwood, Richard, Jr. (1738-1826), Court Justice, Anne Arundel County, 1774. (Ref: Anne Arundel County Court Minutes, 1725-1757, 1774)

Harwood, Thomas, of Annapolis, commissioned a Coroner of Anne Arundel County, 15 Mar 1764. (Ref: Maryland Commission Book No. 82, p. 161; *Maryland Historical Magazine*, Vol. XXVI, p. 352)

Haskins, Thomas, appointed a Commissioner of the Peace for Anne Arundel County, 30 Nov 1732. (Ref: Maryland State Archives, Governor and Council Commissioner Records, 1726-1794, p. 34)

Haskins, William, appointed a Commissioner of the Peace for Dorchester County, 19 Mar 1764 and 8 Apr 1770. (Ref: Maryland State Archives, Governor and Council Commissioner Records, 1726-1794, pp. 215, 250)

Hatherly, Elizabeth, see Jeremiah Swift.

Hawkins, George Frazer (Fraser) (1741-1785), appointed a Commissioner of the Peace for Prince George's County, 15 Mar 1769. (Ref: Maryland State Archives, Governor and Council Commissioner Records, 1726-1794, p. 241)

Hawkins, Henry Holland (1683-1751), was appointed a Commissioner of the Peace for Charles County, 29 Oct 1730 and 25 Apr 1735. (Ref: Maryland State Archives, Governor and Council Commissioner Records, 1726-1794, pp. 12, 47)

Hawkins, John, see Negro Jacob.

Hawkins, John Frazer, appointed a Commissioner of the Peace for Prince George's County, 26 Jul 1773. (Ref: Maryland State Archives, Governor and Council Commissioner Records, 1726-1794, p. 272)

Hawkins, John, Jr., Constable of Upper Piscat-away Hundred in Prince George's County, now Frederick County, 1733. (*Calendar of Maryland State Papers, No. 1 The Black Books*, p. 39)

Hawkins, John Stone (1734-1764), appointed a Commissioner of the Peace for Prince George's County, 26 Sep 1759. (Ref: Maryland State Archives, Governor and Council Commissioner Records, 1726-1794, p. 187)

Hawkins, Josias (1735-1789), was appointed a Commissioner of the Peace for Charles County, 2 Oct 1762 and 17 Nov 1764. (Ref: Maryland State Archives, Governor and Council Commissioner Records, 1726-1794, pp. 205, 220)

Hawkins, Samuel, appointed a Commissioner of the Peace for Prince George's County, 22 Oct 1747. (Ref: Maryland State Archives, Governor and Council Commissioner Records, 1726-1794, p. 101)

Hawkins, William, appointed a Commissioner of the Peace for Caroline County, 8 Feb 1774. (Ref: Maryland State Archives, Governor and Council Commissioner Records, 1726-1794, p. 280)

Haymond, Calder, appointed Constable of the Upper Part of Newfoundland Hundred in Frederick County, 1769, 1771. (Ref: "Frederick County Court Minutes November 1769 by Patricia Abelard Andersen," *Western Maryland Genealogy*, Vol. 16, No. 1, January 2000, p. 32; "Frederick County Minute Book, March 1771, Extracts by Patricia Abelard Andersen," *Western Maryland Genealogy*, Vol. 18, No. 1, January 2002, p. 25)

Hayes, John, see John Hayse.

Haynes, Martain, of Baltimore County, Ranger, 9 Aug 1775. (Ref: *Calendar of Maryland State Papers, The Red Books*, No. 4, Part 1, p. 5)

Haynes, Thomas, of Frederick Co., magistrate, 1766. (Ref: *Archives of Maryland*, Vol. XXXII, "Proceedings of the Council of Maryland, 1761-1770," p. 166)

Hayse, John, appointed Constable of Willis Town Hundred in Frederick County, 1771. (Ref: "Frederick County Minute Book, March 1771, Extracts by Patricia Abelard Andersen," *Western Maryland Genealogy*, Vol. 18, No. 1, January 2002, p. 26)

Hayton, Richard, see Morris Mongall.

Hayward, Francis, registration of sloop *Diana*, 40 tons, built in Baltimore County, 1749. Francis Hayward, master and owner. 6 Oct 1749. (Ref: Maryland Commission Book No. 82, p. 153; *Maryland Historical Magazine*, Vol. XXVI, p. 350)

Hayward, Thomas, appointed a Commissioner of the Peace for Somerset County, 29 May 1750. (Ref:

Colonial Maryland Commissions, Appointments, and Other Proceedings, 1726-1776

Maryland State Archives, Governor and Council Commissioner Records, 1726-1794, p. 117); Court Justice, 1753. (*Calendar of Maryland State Papers, No. 1 The Black Books*, p. 112)

Hayward, Thomas, Jr., see Negro Robin.

Hayward, William (d. 1791), of Talbot County, Court Justice, 1766. (*Calendar of Maryland State Papers, No. 1 The Black Books*, p. 199); commissioned Rent Roll Keeper of the Western Shore, 4 Jul 1772. (Ref: Maryland Commission Book No. 82, p. 281; *Maryland Historical Magazine*, Vol. XXVII, p. 31)

Heath, Daniel Charles (d. after 1783), appointed a Commissioner of the Peace for Cecil County, 3 Mar 1772. (Ref: Maryland State Archives, Governor and Council Commissioner Records, 1726-1794, p. 260)

Heath, James, see John Wallace.

Heath, James Paul, see William Dames.

Hebb, William, appointed a Commissioner of the Peace for St. Mary's County, 25 Jan 1745/6. (Ref: Maryland State Archives, Governor and Council Commissioner Records, 1726-1794, p. 90)

Hedge, Charles, appointed Constable of the Middle Part of Monocacy Hundred in Frederick County, 1760. (Ref: *This Was The Life: Excerpts from the Judgment Records of Frederick County, Maryland, 1748-1765*, by Millard Milburn Rice, p. 216)

Hedges, Joseph, appointed Constable of the Middle Part of Monocacy Hundred in Frederick County, 1769. (Ref: "Frederick County Court Minutes November 1769 by Patricia Abelard Andersen," *Western Maryland Genealogy*, Vol. 16, No. 1, January 2000, p. 32)

Hedges, William, commissioned Sheriff of Cecil County, 8 Nov 1755. (Ref: Maryland State Archives, Governor and Council Commissioner Records, 1726-1794, p. 155; *Archives of Maryland*, Vol. LII, "Proceedings and Acts of the General Assembly of Maryland, 1755-1756," p. 577)

Heigh (Heighe), James (d. 1757), appointed a Commissioner of the Peace for Calvert County, 29 May 1734. (Ref: Maryland State Archives, Governor and Council Commissioner Records, 1726-1794, p. 42)

Hellen, Peter, was commissioned a Coroner of Calvert County, 9 Dec 1773. On same day, commissioned Deputy Surveyor of Calvert County. (Ref: Maryland Commission Book No. 82, pp. 331-332; *Maryland Historical Magazine*, Vol. XXVII, p. 36)

Hellen, Peter, commissioned a Deputy Surveyor of St. Mary's County, 9 Mar 1772. (Ref: Maryland Commission Book No. 82, p. 274; *Maryland Historical Magazine*, Vol. XXVII, p. 31)

Hellen, Richard, see Negro Charles.

Helmes, John, appointed Constable of the Middle Part of Monocacy Hundred in Frederick County in 1763. (Ref: *This Was The Life: Excerpts from the Judgment Records of Frederick County, Maryland, 1748-1765*, by Millard Milburn Rice, p. 249)

Hemersly, William, see Negro Bob.

Hemmett, Robert, commissioned a Coroner of St. Mary's County. 2 Nov 1748. (Ref: Maryland Commission Book No. 82, p. 138; *Maryland Historical Magazine*, Vol. XXVI, p. 343); appointed a Commissioner of the Peace for St. Mary's County, 4 Jul 1755. (Ref: Maryland State Archives, Governor and Council Commissioner Records, 1726-1794, p. 161)

Hemsley, William (1703-1736), of Queen Anne's County, sheriff, 1726. (Ref: *Abstracts of the Testamentary Proceedings and Prerogative Court of Maryland, Vol. XVII, 1724-1727*, by Vernon L. Skinner, Jr., p. 124, citing original Liber 27, f. 319); appointed a Commissioner of the Peace for Queen Anne's County, 29 Oct 1730. (Ref: Maryland State Archives, Governor and Council Commissioner Records, 1726-1794, p. 17)

Hemsley, William (1736-1812), of Queen Anne's County, commissioned Treasurer of the Eastern Shore, 29 Apr 1773. (Ref: Maryland Commission Book No. 82, p. 306; *Maryland Historical Magazine*, Vol. XXVII, p. 33); see Negro Davy and Thomas Marsh.

Henderson, Richard, appointed a Commissioner of the Peace for Prince George's County, 24 Aug 1773. (Ref: Maryland State Archives, Governor and Council Commissioner Records, 1726-1794, p. 273)

Henney, Thomas, registration of the schooner *Susannah*, 12 tons, built in Kent County, 1741. Thomas Henney, owner. 30 Dec 1742. (Ref: Maryland Commission Book No. 82, p. 100; *Maryland Historical Magazine*, Vol. XXVI, p. 248)

Henry, John (c1714-1781), was commissioned Sheriff of Somerset, 5 May 1737. (Ref: Maryland State Archives, Governor and Council Commissioner Records, 1726-1794, p. 55); appointed a Commissioner of the Peace for Worcester County, 11 Dec 1742. (Ref: Maryland State Archives, Governor and Council Commissioner Records, 1726-1794, p. 75); commissioned Deputy Surveyor of Worcester County, 23 Nov 1743. (Ref: Maryland Commission Book No. 82, p. 106; *Maryland Historical Magazine*, Vol. XXVI, p. 250); merchant, registration of sloop *Esther and Dolly*, 20 tons, built in Worcester County, 1747. Samuel Wise, master, John Henry and Isaac Morris, owners. 17 Aug 1747. (Ref: Maryland Commission Book No. 82, p. 132; *Maryland Historical Magazine*, Vol. XXVI, p. 261)colonel, of Worcester County, appointed to a Committee to Inspect the Accounts and Proceedings of the Commissioners for Emitting Bills of Credit, 25 Feb 1755. (Ref: *Archives of Maryland*, Vol. LII, "Proceedings and Acts of the General Assembly of Maryland, 1755-1756," pp. 5, 46, 51); appointed to the Committee for Enquiring into the Accounts and Vouchers Relating to the Disposal of the Sum of £6000 Granted by Act of Assembly for His Majesty's Service, 14 Mar 1755. (Ref: *Archives of Maryland*, Vol. LII, "Proceedings and Acts of the General Assembly of Maryland, 1755-1756," p. 81); appointed to a Committee for Enquiring into Ways and Means to Raise a Sum Sufficient for Payment of Eighty Rangers to Defend and Protect the Frontiers, 28 Jun 1755. (Ref: Maryland State Archives, Governor and Council Commissioner Records, 1726-1794, p. 151); see Robert Jenckins Henry.

Henry, Robert Jenckins (1712-1766), Clerk of Indictments, Somerset County, 1732, 1737. (Ref: *A Biographical Dictionary of the Maryland Legislature, 1635-1789*, by Edward C. Papenfuse, et al., Vol. A-H, p. 438); registration of sloop *Sea Nymph*, 1742 ... [information incomplete]. (Ref: Maryland Commission Book No. 82, p. 97; *Maryland Historical Magazine*, Vol. XXVI, p. 247); merchant, registration of sloop *Dolly*, 30 tons, built in Somerset County, 1745. Clement Bailey, master. Robert Jenckins Henry, owner. 6 Aug 1745. (Ref: Maryland Commission Book No. 82, p. 115; *Maryland Historical Magazine*, Vol. XXVI, pp. 254-255); registration of sloop *Charles*, 60 tons, built in Dorchester County, 1749. Samuel Wise, master. Robert Jenckins Henry, Isaac Morris, John Henry and Robert King, Jr., owners. 14 Apr 1750. (Ref: Maryland Commission Book No. 82, p. 156; *Maryland Historical Magazine*, Vol. XXVI, p. 351); registration of sloop *Gertrude*, 30 tons, built in Somerset County, 1751. John Webb, master. Robert Jenckins Henry, owner. 11 Jun 1751. (Ref: Maryland Commission Book No. 82, p. 149; *Maryland Historical Magazine*, Vol. XXVI, p. 348); of Kent County, was a Justice of Assize, Oyer and Terminer, and Gaol [Jail] Delivery, 1757. (Ref: *Archives of Maryland*, Vol. XXXI, "Proceedings of the Council of Maryland, 1753-1761," p. 205); see Negro Ned.

Henry, Robert, see Levin Gale.

Hepbourn, John, appointed a Commissioner of the Peace for Prince George's County, 21 Feb 1735/6. (Ref: Maryland State Archives, Governor and Council Commissioner Records, 1726-1794, p. 51); commissioned Sheriff of Prince George's County, 10 Jul 1740. (Ref: Maryland State Archives, Governor and Council Commissioner Records, 1726-1794, p. 68, spelled his name Hepburn)

Heron, Robert, Collector of Customs at the Port of Pocomoke [Somerset County], 1764. (*Calendar of Maryland State Papers, No. 1 The Black Books*, p. 191)

Hess, Jacob, appointed Constable of George Town Hundred in Frederick County, 1771. (Ref: "Frederick County Minute Book, March 1771, Extracts by Patricia Abelard Andersen," *Western Maryland Genealogy*, Vol. 18, No. 1, January 2002, p. 25)

Heugh, Andrew (c1727-c1789), appointed a Commissioner of the Peace for Frederick County, 3 Jul 1754. (Ref: Maryland State Archives, Governor and Council Commissioner Records, 1726-1794, p. 155, spelled his name Heughes); served as a Court Justice in Frederick County in 1758 and as a Coroner in 1762 and 1773. (Ref: *This Was The Life: Excerpts from the Judgment Records of Frederick County, Maryland, 1748-1765*, by Millard Milburn Rice, pp. 177, 252); Maryland Commission Book No. 82, p. 318; *Maryland Historical Magazine*, Vol. XXVII, p. 34); appointed a Commissioner of the Peace for Frederick County, 15 Aug 1774. (Ref: Maryland State Archives, Governor and Council Commissioner Records, 1726-1794, p. 284); Court Judge, 1774. (*Calendar of Maryland State Papers, No. 1 The Black*

Books, 217, misspelled name as Hough)

Hewitt, Michael, see Michael Mitchell.

Heyman, James, of Baltimore County, Ranger, 9 Aug 1775. (Ref: *Calendar of Maryland State Papers, The Red Books*, No. 4, Part 1, p. 5)

Hickes, Henry, see Henry Travers.

Hickman, Arthur, appointed Constable of Sugarland Hundred in Frederick County, 1760. (Ref: *This Was The Life: Excerpts from the Judgment Records of Frederick County, Maryland, 1748-1765*, by Millard Milburn Rice, p. 216)

Hickman, Henry, was appointed Constable of Sugarland Hundred in Frederick County in 1753. (Ref: *This Was The Life: Excerpts from the Judgment Records of Frederick County, Maryland, 1748-1765*, by Millard Milburn Rice, p. 131)

Hickman, William, was commissioned one of the Coroners of Calvert County, 12 Mar 1747/8. (Ref: Maryland Commission Book No. 82, p. 133; *Maryland Historical Magazine*, Vol. XXVI, p. 262); see Negro Samuel.

Hicks, Denwood, see Negro Sampson and Negro Booze.

Hicks, John, appointed a Commissioner of the Peace for St. Mary's County, 29 Oct 1730. (Ref: Maryland State Archives, Governor and Council Commissioner Records, 1726-1794, p. 12); commissioned Sheriff of St. Mary's County, 16 Jun 1733. (Ref: Maryland State Archives, Governor and Council Commissioner Records, 1726-1794, p. 31, and p. 45 called him captain)

Hicks, Levin, appointed a Commissioner of the Peace for Dorchester County, 22 Oct 1747. (Ref: Maryland State Archives, Governor and Council Commissioner Records, 1726-1794, p. 101)

Hicks, Stephen, see Basil Noell.

Higginson, Charles, of Anne Arundel County, reprieve for ----, 21 Sep 1748. (Ref: Maryland Commission Book No. 82, p. 136; *Maryland Historical Magazine*, Vol. XXVI, p. 342)

Hill, Joshua, appointed a Commissioner of the Peace for Somerset County, 5 Jan 1775. (Ref: Maryland State Archives, Governor and Council Commissioner Records, 1726-1794, p. 286)

Hill, Joshua, appointed a Commissioner of the Peace for Worcester County, 30 Apr 1770. (Ref: Maryland State Archives, Governor and Council Commissioner Records, 1726-1794, p. 250)

Hill, Richard, see William Loyall.

Hill, Thomas, see Negro Abraham.

Hillhouse, William, see Negro Hannah.

Hindman, Jacob (c1710-1766), was commissioned Sheriff of Talbot County, 22 Oct 1747. (Ref: Maryland State Archives, Governor and Council Commissioner Records, 1726-1794, p. 100); appointed a Commissioner of the Peace for Talbot County, 2 Oct 1751 and 6 Nov 1758. (Ref: Maryland State Archives, Governor and Council Commissioner Records, 1726-1794, pp. 124, 183)

Hindman, Jacob, reverend, licensed to preach in St. Andrew's Parish, St. Mary's County, 8 May 1772; induction into St. Peter's Parish. Talbot County. 19 Sep 1772. (Ref: Maryland Commission Book No. 82, pp. 280, 286; *Maryland Historical Magazine*, Vol. XXVII, pp. 31, 32; *Directory of Ministers and the Maryland Churches They Served, 1634-1900*, by Edna Agatha Kanely, Vol. I, A-H, p. 323, stated his full name was Jacob Henderson Hindman and he died after 1783)

Hindman, William, commissioned High Sheriff of Queen Anne's County, 30 Oct 1767. (Ref: Maryland State Archives, Governor and Council Commissioner Records, 1726-1794, p. 222)

Hivey, John, see Richard Floud.

Hobb, Vernon, appointed a Commissioner of the Peace for St. Mary's County, 11 May 1769. (Ref: Maryland State Archives, Governor and Council Commissioner Records, 1726-1794, p. 241)

Hobbs, Elizabeth, see Joseph Framton.

Hobbs, John, see Dennis Igoe & James Johnson.

Hodges, Thomas Ramsay, see Negro Scipio.

Hodgkin, Thomas, merchant, registration of brigantine *Lucy and Jannett*, 80 tons, built in Prince George's County, 1748. Richard Russell, master. Thomas Hodgkins and Stephen Jermain, owners. 13 Sep 1748. (Ref: Maryland Commission Book No. 82, p. 136; *Maryland Historical Magazine*, Vol. XXVI, p. 342)

Hodgkin, Thomas Brooke, was appointed a Commissioner of the Peace for Anne Arundel County, 24 Aug 1773. (Ref: Maryland State Archives,

Governor and Council Commissioner Records, 1726-1794, p. 276); Court Justice, 1774. (Ref: Anne Arundel County Court Minutes, 1725-1757, 1774)

Hodgkiss, Michael, appointed Constable of Pipe Creek Hundred in Frederick County in 1751 and Constable of Burnt Woods Hundred in 1760. (Ref: *This Was The Life: Excerpts from the Judgment Records of Frederick County, Maryland, 1748-1765*, by Millard Milburn Rice, pp. 61, 216)

Hodgson, Jonathan, registration of the sloop *Speedwell*, 50 tons, built in Cecil County, 1750. Jonathan Hodgson, master and co-owner. Jacob Goodwyn and William Whittill, owners. 17 Jul 1750. (Ref: Maryland Commission Book No. 82, p. 144; *Maryland Historical Magazine*, Vol. XXVI, p. 346)

Hodson, James, appointed Constable of Nanti-coke Hundred in Dorchester County, 1742. (Ref: Dorchester County Judgment Records, 1742-1743, p. 84; *Judgment Records of Dorchester, Queen Anne's and Talbot Counties, Maryland*, by F. Edward Wright, 2001, p. 30)

Hodson, John 3rd, appointed a Press Master in Dorchester County in 1744. (Ref: Dorchester County Judgment Records, 1743-1745, p. 129; *Judgment Records of Dorchester, Queen Anne's and Talbot Counties, Maryland*, by F. Edward Wright, 2001, p. 46)

Hodson, Levin, see Joseph Bailey.

Hoggins, Peter, commissioned Ranger for Prince George's County, 6 Dec 1748. (Ref: Maryland Commission Book No. 82, p. 139; *Maryland Historical Magazine*, Vol. XXVI, p. 343)

Holbrooke, Thomas, appointed a Commissioner of the Peace for Somerset County, 1 Oct 1762. (Ref: Maryland State Archives, Governor and Council Commissioner Records, 1726-1794, p. 204)

Holland, Isaac, see William Draper.

Holland, James, was appointed Constable of Newfoundland Hundred in Prince George's County, now Frederick County, 1744. (Ref: Prince George's County Court Records, 1736-1748, Extracts by Patricia Abelard Andersen, *Western Maryland Genealogy*, Vol. 18, No. 1, January 2002, p. 41)

Holland, Nehemiah (d. 1788), was appointed a Commissioner of the Peace for Worcester County, 1 Oct 1768. (Ref: Maryland State Archives, Governor and Council Commissioner Records, 1726-1794, p. 238); Court Justice, Worcester County, 1774. (*Calendar of Maryland State Papers, No. 1 The Black Books*, p. 214); appointed a Commissioner of the Peace for Somerset County, 5 Jan 1775. (Ref: Maryland State Archives, Governor and Council Commissioner Records, 1726-1794, p. 286)

Holland, Thomas, appointed a Commissioner of the Peace for Calvert County, 9 Dec 1731. (Ref: Maryland State Archives, Governor and Council Commissioner Records, 1726-1794, p. 20)

Holland, William, appointed a Commissioner of the Peace for Calvert County, 3 Mar 1726/7. (Ref: Maryland State Archives, Governor and Council Commissioner Records, 1726-1794, p. 3)

Holland, William, appointed a Commissioner of the Peace for Worcester County, 16 Jan 1769 and 26 Oct 1773. (Ref: Maryland State Archives, Governor and Council Commissioner Records, 1726-1794, pp. 240, 278); Court Justice, Worcester County, 1774. (*Calendar of Maryland State Papers, No. 1 The Black Books*, p. 214)

Holliday, James, Provincial Commission [styled Mister, but rank and/or position not stated], 8 Jul 1735. (Ref: Maryland State Archives, Governor and Council Commissioner Records, 1726-1794, p. 49); of Anne Arundel County, commissioned Judge of Oyer, Terminer and Gaol [Jail] Delivery, 21 May 1736. (Ref: Maryland State Archives, Governor and Council Commissioner Records, 1726-1794, p. 52)

Holliday, John Robert, Sheriff of Baltimore County, 1773. (Ref: *Inhabitants of Baltimore County, 1763-1774*, by Henry C. Peden, Jr., 1989, p. 49, citing *Calendar of Maryland State Papers, No. 1 The Black Books*, p. 208)

Holliday, Leonard, appointed a Commissioner of the Peace for Prince George's County, 30 Nov 1732. (Ref: Maryland State Archives, Governor and Council Commissioner Records, 1726-1794, p. 30)

Holliday, Thomas, see Negro Jacob.

Hollingsworth, Jesse (1732-1810), appointed a Commissioner of the Peace for Cecil County, 1 Oct 1768. (Ref: Maryland State Archives, Governor and Council Commissioner Records, 1726-1794, p. 240, spelled his first name Jessey)

Hollingsworth, Stephen (d. after 1760), appointed a

Commissioner of the Peace for Cecil County, 3 Mar 1726/7. (Ref: Maryland State Archives, Governor and Council Commissioner Records, 1726-1794, p. 2)

Hollyday, Henry (c1725-1789), was commissioned Sheriff of Queen Anne's County, 27 Oct 1748. (Ref: Maryland State Archives, Governor and Council Commissioner Records, 1726-1794, p. 108); Deputy Naval Officer of Port Oxford, 1762. (Ref: *Archives of Maryland*, Vol. XXXII, "Proceedings of the Council of Maryland, 1761-1770," p. 48); see Negro Ben.

Hollyday, James (1696-1747), appointed a Commissioner of the Peace for Talbot County, 29 Oct 1730. (Ref: Maryland State Archives, Governor and Council Commissioner Records, 1726-1794, p. 17); (Hon.), commissioned Naval Officer of the Port of Oxford, 23 Aug 1737. (Ref: Maryland Commission Book No. 82, p. 50; *Maryland Historical Magazine*, Vol. XXVI, p. 150); colonel, commissioned Naval Officer of the Port of Oxford, 29 Sep 1742. (Ref: Maryland Commission Book No. 82, p. 96; *Maryland Historical Magazine*, Vol. XXVI, p. 247); commissioned Sheriff of Queen Anne's County, 29 Oct 1747. (Ref: Maryland State Archives, Governor and Council Commissioner Records, 1726-1794, p. 102)

Hollyday, James, Jr. (1722-1786), commissioned Sheriff of Anne Arundel County, 16 Sep 1745. (Ref: Maryland State Archives, Governor and Council Commissioner Records, 1726-1794, p. 89)

Hollyday, John Robert, commissioned High Sheriff of Baltimore County, 16 Sep 1772. (Ref: Maryland State Archives, Governor and Council Commissioner Records, 1726-1794, p. 252)

Hollyday, Leonard, appointed a Commissioner of the Peace for Prince George's County, 3 Mar 1726/7. (Ref: Maryland State Archives, Governor and Council Commissioner Records, 1726-1794, p. 3)

Hollyday, Leonard, commissioned High Sheriff of Calvert County, 27 Dec 1762. (Ref: Maryland State Archives, Governor and Council Commissioner Records, 1726-1794, p. 199, and p. 204 styled him as doctor); see Negro Jack.

Hollyday, Robert, commissioned High Sheriff of Baltimore County, 15 Oct 1770. (Ref: Maryland State Archives, Governor and Council Commissioner Records, 1726-1794, p. 242)

Holt, Arthur, commissioned a Coroner of Queen Anne's County, 12 Apr 1771 and 26 Jul 1773. (Ref: Maryland Commission Book No. 82, pp. 254, 321; *Maryland Historical Magazine*, Vol. XXVII, pp. 29, 35)

Holt, Arthur, reverend, induction into All Faith's Parish, St. Mary's County, 26 Jan 1733/4. (Ref: Maryland Commission Book No. 82, p. 4; *Maryland Historical Magazine*, Vol. XXVI, p. 139); induction into St. Luke's Parish, Queen Anne's County, 14 Sep 1734. (Ref: Maryland Commission Book No. 82, pp. 20, 23; *Maryland Historical Magazine*, Vol. XXVI, p. 141)

Holt, Susanna, spinster, convicted of infanticide, was pardoned on 23 Dec 1734. (Ref: Maryland Commission Book No. 82, p. 23; *Maryland Historical Magazine*, Vol. XXVI, p. 142)

Homewood, Thomas, appointed a Commissioner of the Peace for Anne Arundel County, 8 Mar 1735/6. (Ref: Maryland State Archives, Governor and Council Commissioner Records, 1726-1794, p. 51)

Hood, John, Jr. (d. c1795), was appointed a Commissioner of the Peace for Anne Arundel County, 24 Aug 1773. (Ref: Maryland State Archives, Governor and Council Commissioner Records, 1726-1794, p. 276)

Hood, William, appointed a Commissioner of the Peace for Anne Arundel County, 17 Nov 1749. (Ref: Maryland State Archives, Governor and Council Commissioner Records, 1726-1794, p. 114)

Hooe, Robert, commissioned Deputy Surveyor of Charles County, 7 Jul 1766. (Ref: Maryland Commission Book No. 82, p. 178; *Maryland Historical Magazine*, Vol. XXVI, p. 354)

Hook, James, of John, appointed Constable of the Lower Part of Kittocton [Catoctin] Hundred in Frederick County, 1771. (Ref: "Frederick County Minute Book, March 1771, Extracts by Patricia Abelard Andersen," *Western Maryland Genealogy*, Vol. 18, No. 1, January 2002, p. 26)

Hooke, John, appointed Constable of Monocacy Hundred in Prince George's County, now Frederick County, 1748. (Ref: Prince George's County Court Records, 1736-1738, Extracts by Patricia Abelard Andersen, *Western Maryland Genealogy*, Vol. 18, No. 1, January 2002, p. 46)

Hooper, Ennalls (d. c1763), registration of sloop

Betty, 30 tons, built in Somerset County, 1737. Lawrence Mason, master. Joseph Ennals and Ennals Hooper, owners. 2 Dec 1737. (Ref: Maryland Commission Book No. 82, p. 51; *Maryland Historical Magazine*, Vol. XXVI, p. 150); commissioned Sheriff of Dorchester County, 19 Oct 1748. (Ref: Maryland State Archives, Governor and Council Commissioner Records, 1726-1794, p. 107); see Joseph Ennals.

Hooper, Henry, appointed a Commissioner of the Peace for Anne Arundel County, 17 Oct 1734. (Ref: Maryland State Archives, Governor and Council Commissioner Records, 1726-1794, p. 44); of Anne Arundel County, commissioned Judge of Oyer, Terminer and Gaol [Jail] Delivery, 21 May 1736. (Ref: Maryland State Archives, Governor and Council Commissioner Records, 1726-1794, p. 52)

Hooper, Henry (c1687-1767), appointed a Commissioner of the Peace for Dorchester County, 9 May 1732. (Ref: Maryland State Archives, Governor and Council Commissioner Records, 1726-1794, p. 23); colonel, Provincial Commission, 8 Jul 1735. (Ref: Maryland State Archives, Governor and Council Commissioner Records, 1726-1794, p. 49); colonel, of Dorchester County, appointed to the Committee to Enquire into Indian Complaints, 1754. (Ref: *Archives of Maryland*, Vol. XXXI, "Proceedings of the Council of Maryland, 1753-1761," p. 30)

Hooper, Henry, Jr. (c1727-1790), appointed a Commissioner of the Peace for Dorchester County, 8 Mar 1754. (Ref: Maryland State Archives, Governor and Council Commissioner Records, 1726-1794, p. 143)

Hooper, John, appointed a Commissioner of the Peace for Dorchester County, 21 Apr 1735. (Ref: Maryland State Archives, Governor and Council Commissioner Records, 1726-1794, p. 46)

Hopewell, Hugh (d. 1777), was appointed a Commissioner of the Peace for St. Mary's County, 5 Mar 1761. (Ref: Maryland State Archives, Governor and Council Commissioner Records, 1726-1794, p. 195); commissioned High Sheriff of St. Mary's County, 29 Oct 1773. (Ref: Maryland State Archives, Governor and Council Commissioner Records, 1726-1794, p. 267)

Hopewell, Richard (c1680-c1745), appointed a Commissioner of the Peace for St. Mary's County, 29 Oct 1730. (Ref: Maryland State Archives, Governor and Council Commissioner Records, 1726-1794, p. 12); commissioned Sheriff of St. Mary's County, 5 Jun 1736. (Ref: Maryland State Archives, Governor and Council Commissioner Records, 1726-1794, p. 52)

Hopewell, Thomas, colonel, commissioned High Sheriff of St. Mary's County, 25 Jun 1735. (Ref: Maryland Commission Book No. 82, p. 31; *Maryland Historical Magazine*, Vol. XXVI, p. 144)

Hopkins, Hampton, see Isaac Morris.

Hopkins, James, registration of the snow *Three Brothers*, 90 tons, built in Kent County, 1750. James Hopkins, master and co-owner. John Luxon and Thomas Kenney, co-owners. 24 Sep 1750. (Ref: Maryland Commission Book No. 82, p. 147; *Maryland Historical Magazine*, Vol. XXVI, p. 347)

Hopkins, Matthew, commissioned one of the Coroners of Prince George's County, 1 Feb 1745/6. (Ref: Maryland Commission Book No. 82, p. 119; *Maryland Historical Magazine*, Vol. XXVI, p. 256); commissioned a Coroner of Frederick County, 25 May 1749. (Ref: Maryland Commission Book No. 82, p. 141; *Maryland Historical Magazine*, Vol. XXVI, p. 344)

Hopkins, Samuel (1668-1744), was appointed a Commissioner of the Peace for Somerset County, 29 Oct 1730. (Ref: Maryland State Archives, Governor and Council Commissioner Records, 1726-1794, p. 17); of Sinapuxent, appointed a Commissioner of the Peace for Somerset County, 23 May 1738. (Ref: Maryland State Archives, Governor and Council Commissioner Records, 1726-1794, p. 60); appointed a Commissioner of the Peace for Worcester County, 11 Dec 1742. (Ref: Maryland State Archives, Governor and Council Commissioner Records, 1726-1794, p. 75

Hopper, William (1707-1772), was appointed a Commissioner of the Peace for Queen Anne's County, 24 Jun 1743. (Ref: Maryland State Archives, Governor and Council Commissioner Records, 1726-1794, p. 80); commissioned Sheriff of Queen Anne's County, 5 Nov 1754. (Ref: Maryland State Archives, Governor and Council Commissioner Records, 1726-1794, p. 149; *Archives of Maryland*, Vol. LII, "Proceedings and Acts of the General Assembly of Maryland, 1755-1756," p. 569)

Hopper, William (c1745-1806), was appointed a Commissioner of the Peace for Queen Anne's County, 13 Mar 1773. (Ref: Maryland State Archives,

Governor and Council Commissioner Records, 1726-1794, p. 265); commissioned High Sheriff of Caroline County, 26 Dec 1775. (Ref: Maryland State Archives, Governor and Council Commissioner Records, 1726-1794, p. 279)

Hornebrooke, Thomas, of Baltimore County, convicted felon, executed on 6 May 1752. (Ref: Maryland State Archives, Governor and Council Commissioner Records, 1726-1794, p. 132)

Horner, Elizabeth, spinster, of Somerset County, convicted felon for stealing a dark bay colored mare valued at ten pounds from Levin Ballard's pasture, was pardoned on 20 Oct 1769 and banished from the province on or before 1 Jan 1770, never to return again, or giving security before two Justices of Peace for her good behavior for seven years. (Ref: Maryland Commission Book No. 82, p. 230; *Maryland Historical Magazine*, Vol. XXVI, p. 360; *Archives of Maryland*, Vol. XXXII, "Proceedings of the Council of Maryland, 1761-1770," p. 315)

Horner, James, labourer, of Dorchester County, convicted felon "for a rape committed by him on one Mary Satchell, a girl of about fourteen years old," was executed on 2 May 1760. (Ref: Maryland State Archives, Governor and Council Commissioner Records, 1726-1794, p. 178; *Archives of Maryland*, Vol. XXXI, "Proceedings of the Council of Maryland, 1753-1761," p. 405)

Horner, Robert, captain, was appointed a Commissioner of the Peace for Charles County, 25 Jul 1759. (Ref: Maryland State Archives, Governor and Council Commissioner Records, 1726-1794, p. 186)

Horsey, Ouchterbridge (Outherbridge) (c1718-1788), registration of the schooner *Endeavour*, 50 tons, built in Somerset Co., 1745. Ouchterbridge Horsey, master and owner. 18 Jul 1745. (Ref: Maryland Commission Book No. 82, p. 114; *Maryland Historical Magazine*, Vol. XXVI, p. 254); merchant, registration of schooner *Industry*, 80 tons, built in Somerset County, 1746. Ouchterbridge Horsey, master and co-owner. Jonathan Birr Ouchterbridge, co-owner. 25 Feb 1746/7. (Ref: Maryland Commission Book No. 82, p. 125; *Maryland Historical Magazine*, Vol. XXVI, p. 259); registration of sloop *Speedwell*, 65 tons, built in Somerset County, 1749. William Townshend, master. Outherbridge Horsey and William Smith, owners. 12 Jul 1749. (Ref: Maryland Commission Book No. 82, p. 152; *Maryland Historical Magazine*, Vol. XXVI, p. 349)

Horsey, William (c1745-1786), was appointed a Commissioner of the Peace for Somerset County, 8 Aug 1769 and 19 May 1774. (Ref: Maryland State Archives, Governor and Council Commissioner Records, 1726-1794, pp. 244), 282

Hoskins, William, registration of brigantine *Free Mason*, 50 tons, built at Newcastle-upon-Tyne, 1738. John Fisher, master. William Hoskins, John Fisher, Joseph Ennalls and Thomas Price, owners. 16 Jul 1750. (Ref: Maryland Commission Book No. 82, p. 144; *Maryland Historical Magazine*, Vol. XXVI, pp. 345-346)

Hough, Edmund, see Isaac Morris.

House, William, appointed Constable of Kittoctin [Catoctin] Hundred in Frederick County in 1753. (Ref: *This Was The Life: Excerpts from the Judgment Records of Frederick County, Maryland, 1748-1765*, by Millard Milburn Rice, p. 131)

How, Robert, was a Justice of Dorchester County in 1765. (Ref: *Archives of Maryland*, Vol. XXXII, "Proceedings of the Council of Maryland, 1761-1770," p. 117)

Howard, Ephraim, appointed a Commissioner of the Peace for Anne Arundel County, 10 Aug 1755. (Ref: Maryland State Archives, Governor and Council Commissioner Records, 1726-1794, p. 162)

Howard, Ephraim, commissioned a Coroner in Frederick County, 14 Jan 1767. (Ref: Maryland Commission Book No. 82, p. 198; *Maryland Historical Magazine*, Vol. XXVI, p. 355)

Howard, Henry, appointed a Commissioner of the Peace for Anne Arundel County, 16 Mat 1748/9 and 10 Aug 1755. (Ref: Maryland State Archives, Governor and Council Commissioner Records, 1726-1794, pp. 110, 162)

Howard, James, commissioned a Coroner of Anne Arundel County, 30 Sep 1766. (Ref: Maryland Commission Book No. 82, p. 180; *Maryland Historical Magazine*, Vol. XXVI, p. 354)

Howard, John, appointed a Commissioner of the Peace for Baltimore County, 21 Feb 1753. (Ref: Maryland State Archives, Governor and Council Commissioner Records, 1726-1794, p. 137)

Howard, John, commissioned a Coroner of Anne Arundel County, 14 Mar 1743/4; commissioned a Ranger on 18 Mar 1748/9. (Ref: Maryland Commission Book No. 82, pp. 108, 139; *Maryland Historical Magazine*, Vol. XXVI, pp. 251, 343)

Howard, John, merchant, registration of sloop *Sea Flower*, 14 tons, built at Hampton, Virginia, 1746. John Howard, master and owner. 1 May 1746. (Ref: Maryland Commission Book No. 82, p. 120; *Maryland Historical Magazine*, Vol. XXVI, p. 256); of Kent County, registration of sloop *Sea Flower*, 14 tons, built in Virginia, 1746. Patrick Byrne, master. John Howard, owner. 14 Dec 1747. (Ref: Maryland Commission Book No. 82, p. 132; *Maryland Historical Magazine*, Vol. XXVI, p. 262)

Howard, John, of Charles County, sheriff, 1726. (Ref: *Abstracts of the Testamentary Proceedings and Prerogative Court of Maryland, Vol. XVII, 1724-1727*, by Vernon L. Skinner, Jr., p. 135, citing original Liber 27, f. 334); appointment as a Commissioner of the Peace renewed, 17 Mar 1726/7 and 29 Oct 1730. (Ref: Maryland State Archives, Governor and Council Commissioner Records, 1726-1794, pp. 4, 12)

Howard, John, registration of sloop *Nancy*, 15 tons, built in Somerset County, 1741. John Howard, owner. 25 Mar 1745. (Ref: Maryland Commission Book No. 82, p. 112; *Maryland Historical Magazine*, Vol. XXVI, p. 253)

Howard, John, of Benjamin, was appointed a Commissioner of the Peace for Anne Arundel County, 8 Nov 1742. (Ref: Maryland State Archives, Governor and Council Commissioner Records, 1726-1794, p. 75)

Howard, John Beale (c1739-1799), appointed a Commissioner of the Peace for Baltimore County, 31 Oct 1768. (Ref: Maryland State Archives, Governor and Council Commissioner Records, 1726-1794, p. 238); appointed a Commissioner of the Peace for Harford County, 20 Feb 1774. (Ref: Maryland State Archives, Governor and Council Commissioner Records, 1726-1794, p. 281)

Howard, Joseph, was commissioned a Coroner in Anne Arundel County, 5 Dec 1767. (Ref: Maryland Commission Book No. 82, p. 205; *Maryland Historical Magazine*, Vol. XXVI, p. 356)

Howard, Michael, appointed a Commissioner of the Peace for Cecil County, Baltimore County, Kent County, Prince George's County, Anne Arundel County, Calvert County, Charles County, St. Mary's County, Queen Anne's County, and Talbot County, 4 Aug 1732 and 10 Aug 1732 and 20 Aug 1733. (Ref: Maryland State Archives, Governor and Council Commissioner Records, 1726-1794, pp. 32-37); commissioned Naval Officer, Port of Oxford, 25 Jul 1733. (Ref: Maryland Commission Book No. 82, p. 1; *Maryland Historical Magazine*, Vol. XXVI, p. 139)

Howard, Samuel, of Anne Arundel County, appointed Constable in Elk Ridge Hundred in 1774. (Ref: Anne Arundel County Court Minutes, 1725-1757, 1774)

Howard, Samuel, reverend, licensed to preach in Christ Church Parish, Calvert County, vacant by the death of Rev. Dingle. 4 Jun 1767; induction into Christ Church Parish, Queen Anne's County, 25 Apr 1768. (Ref: Maryland Commission Book No. 82, pp. 177, 211; *Maryland Historical Magazine*, Vol. XXVI, pp. 354, 357)

Howard, Thomas Gassaway, doctor, appointed a Commissioner of the Peace for Baltimore County, 30 May 1774. (Ref: Maryland State Archives, Governor and Council Commissioner Records, 1726-1794, p. 283)

Howell, Thomas, see Negro James.

Hoy, Paul, appointed Constable of the Upper Part of Newfoundland Hundred in Frederick County, 1771. (Ref: "Frederick County Minute Book, March 1771, Extracts by Patricia Abelard Andersen," *Western Maryland Genealogy*, Vol. 18, No. 1, January 2002, p. 25)

Hubbert, John, of ---- County, convicted of murder, was executed on 4 Oct 1765. (Ref: *Archives of Maryland*, Vol. XXXII, "Proceedings of the Council of Maryland, 1761-1770," p. 108)

Hudson, John, Secundus (c1680-1745), appointed a Commissioner of the Peace for Dorchester County, 1 Aug 1729 and 29 Oct 1730. (Ref: Maryland State Archives, Governor and Council Commissioner Records, 1726-1794, pp. 11, 17)

Hughes, Philip, reverend, licensed to preach in Worcester Parish, Worcester County, 5 Jan 1767; induction into Coventry Parish in Somerset and Worcester Counties, 5 Dec 1767. (Ref: Maryland Commission Book No. 82, pp. 198, 205; *Maryland Historical Magazine*, Vol. XXVI, pp. 355, 356, spelled his name Hughs); reverend doctor, induction into Great Choptank Parish, Dorchester County, 11 Feb 1773. (Ref: Maryland Commission Book No. 82, p. 294; *Maryland Historical Magazine*, Vol. XXVII, p. 32); induction into Coventry Parish circa 1767-1768. (*Archives of Maryland*, Vol. XXXII, "Proceedings of the Council of Maryland, 1761-1770," p. 224); resignation from Coventry Parish, 15 Jul 1769. On same day, induction into Chester Parish, Kent County. (Ref: Maryland Commission Book No. 82, p. 225; *Maryland Historical Magazine*, Vol. XXVI, p. 359)

Hughes, Thomas, appointed a Commissioner of the Peace for Cecil County, 20 Feb 1774. (Ref: Maryland State Archives, Governor and Council Commissioner Records, 1726-1794, p. 281)

Hughs, David, see Jacob Giles.

Hulme, Thomas, joiner, of Dorchester County, convicted of breaking open and robbing the house of William Ennalls and stealing fifty pounds of sugar and fifty pounds of coffee, was executed on 26 Jun 1767. (Ref: Maryland State Archives, Governor and Council Commissioner Records, 1726-1794, p. 216; *Archives of Maryland*, Vol. XXXII, "Proceedings of the Council of Maryland, 1761-1770," p. 200)

Humbert, William, appointed Constable of the Upper Part of Kittocton [Catoctin] Hundred in Frederick County in 1763. (Ref: *This Was The Life: Excerpts from the Judgment Records of Frederick County, Maryland, 1748-1765*, by Millard Milburn Rice, p. 249)

Humphreys, Thomas, appointed Constable of Old Town Hundred in Frederick County, 1771. (Ref: "Frederick County Minute Book, March 1771, Extracts by Patricia Abelard Andersen," *Western Maryland Genealogy*, Vol. 18, No. 1, January 2002, p. 26)

Hungerford, Thomas, commissioned Sheriff of Charles County, 30 Sep 1747. (Ref: Maryland State Archives, Governor and Council Commissioner Records, 1726-1794, p. 100); late sheriff of Charles County, had ordinary license accounts still unpaid in 1756. (Ref: *Archives of Maryland*, Vol. LII, "Proceedings and Acts of the General Assembly of Maryland, 1755-1756," p. 568)

Hunt, Henry, commissioned High Sheriff of Calvert County, 9 Dec 1775. (Ref: Maryland State Archives, Governor and Council Commissioner Records, 1726-1794, p. 279)

Hunter, Henry, reverend, induction into Christ Church Parish, Queen Anne's County, 19 Feb 1738/9. (Ref: Maryland Commission Book No. 82, p. 66; *Maryland Historical Magazine*, Vol. XXVI, p. 153)

Hunter, Samuel, commissioned Reader of Christ Church in Queen Anne's County, 8 Oct 1741, salary 10,000 pounds of tobacCounty (Ref: Maryland Commission Book No. 82, p. 88; *Maryland Historical Magazine*, Vol. XXVI, p. 245); induction into Christ Church Parish, Queen Anne's County, 5 Feb 1744/5. (Ref: Maryland Commission Book No. 82, p. 112; *Maryland Historical Magazine*, Vol. XXVI, p. 253); resignation from Christ Church Parish in Queen Anne's County, 11 Dec 1746. On same day, induction into All Saint's Parish in Prince George's County. (Ref: Maryland Commission Book No. 82, p. 124; *Maryland Historical Magazine*, Vol. XXVI, p. 258)

Husbands, Herman, see John Seegar.

Husbands, William, registration of sloop *Sarah*, 30 tons, built at Free Town in New England, 1729. William Husbands, master. Joshua George, Sarah Moody and William Husbands, owners. 3 Aug 1734. (Ref: Maryland Commission Book No. 82, p. 21; *Maryland Historical Magazine*, Vol. XXVI, p. 142); appointed a Commissioner of the Peace for Baltimore County, 3 Nov 1757. (Ref: Maryland State Archives, Governor and Council Commissioner Records, 1726-1794, p. 178); see Charles Brown.

Huse, Joseph, registration of snow *Prince of Orange*, 70 tons, built at Sunderland, Great Britain. Richard Chambers, master. Joseph Huse, owner. 15 May 1739. (Ref: Maryland Commission Book No. 82, p. 72; *Maryland Historical Magazine*, Vol. XXVI, p. 153)

Hust, Joseph, appointed Constable of Fort Frederick Hundred in Frederick County, 1769. (Ref: "Frederick County Court Minutes, March 1769," by Patricia Abelard Andersen, *Western Maryland Genealogy*, Vol. 15, No. 2, April 1999, p. 63)

Hussey, John, laborer, of Prince George's County, pardoned and banished for burglary, 12 Apr 1771. (Ref: Maryland Commission Book No. 82, p. 255; *Maryland Historical Magazine*, Vol. XXVII, p. 29)

Hutchings, James, Sr., commissioned a Coroner of Queen Anne's County, 9 Feb 1770. (Ref: Maryland Commission Book No. 82, p. 236; *Maryland*

Historical Magazine, Vol. XXVI, p. 360)

Hutson, William, Constable of Back River Upper Hundred in Baltimore County, 1773. (Ref: *Inhabitants of Baltimore County, 1763-1774*, by Henry C. Peden, Jr., 1989, p. 50, citing a 1773 List of Taxables)

Hyatt, Hezekiah, appointed Constable of Old Town Hundred in Frederick County, 1769. (Ref: "Frederick County Court Minutes, March 1769," by Patricia Abelard Andersen, *Western Maryland Genealogy*, Vol. 15, No. 2, April 1999, p. 63)

Hyatt, Meshech, appointed Constable of Linga-nore Hundred in Frederick County, 1769 and 1771. (Ref: "Frederick County Court Minutes November 1769 by Patricia Abelard Andersen," *Western Maryland Genealogy*, Vol. 16, No. 1, January 2000, p. 32; "Frederick County Minute Book, March 1771, Extracts by Patricia Abelard Andersen," *Western Maryland Genealogy*, Vol. 18, No. 1, January 2002, p. 25)

Hyde, Samuel, see Daniel Watts.

Hyland, Nicholas (c1710-1774), was appointed a Commissioner of the Peace for Cecil County, 14 Jul 1740. (Ref: Maryland State Archives, Governor and Council Commissioner Records, 1726-1794, p. 68)

Hyland, Stephen (1744-1806), was appointed a Commissioner of the Peace for Cecil County, 20 Feb 1774. (Ref: Maryland State Archives, Governor and Council Commissioner Records, 1726-1794, p. 281)

Hynson, Charles (1692-1748), was appointed a Commissioner of the Peace for Kent County, 2 Jun 1732. (Ref: Maryland State Archives, Governor and Council Commissioner Records, 1726-1794, p. 23)

Hynson, James, of Eastern Neck, appointed a Commissioner of the Peace for Cecil County, 1 Dec 1768 and 2 Jun 1774. (Ref: Maryland State Archives, Governor and Council Commissioner Records, 1726-1794, pp. 239, 283)

Hynson, John Carvill, commissioned a Coroner of Kent County, 28 Feb 1770 and 25 Sep 1773. (Ref: Maryland Commission Book No. 82, p. 236; *Maryland Historical Magazine*, Vol. XXVI, pp. 360, 326; *Maryland Historical Magazine*, Vol. XXVII, p. 35, spelled his middle name Carville)

Hynson, Nathaniel, commissioned one of the Coroners of Kent County, 30 Mar 1747. (Ref: Maryland Commission Book No. 82, p. 128; *Maryland Historical Magazine*, Vol. XXVI, p. 259)

Hynson, Thomas, Jr., appointed a Commissioner of the Peace for Kent County, 24 Nov 1735. (Ref: Maryland State Archives, Governor and Council Commissioner Records, 1726-1794, p. 50)

Hynson, William, appointed a Commissioner of the Peace for Kent County, 10 Aug 1748. (Ref: Maryland State Archives, Governor and Council Commissioner Records, 1726-1794, p. 106)

Idlesberry, Francis, native of Germany, denization, 12 Feb 1773. (Ref: Maryland Commission Book No. 82, p. 294; *Maryland Historical Magazine*, Vol. XXVII, p. 32)

Igoe, Dennis, servant of John Hobbs, of Frederick County, convicted felon, was executed on 9 Sep 1768. (Ref: *Archives of Maryland*, Vol. XXXII, "Proceedings of the Council of Maryland, 1761-1770," pp. 247-248)

Ijams, John, appointed a Commissioner of the Peace for Anne Arundel County, 12 Aug 1752. (Ref: Maryland State Archives, Governor and Council Commissioner Records, 1726-1794, p. 133); Court Justice, Anne Arundel County, 1754. (Ref: Anne Arundel County Court Minutes, 1725-1757, spelled his name Jiams)

Indian Jack, of Charles County, convicted felon, executed on 1 Jun 1737. (Ref: Maryland State Archives, Governor and Council Commissioner Records, 1726-1794, p. 55)

Ingram, Job, appointed a Commissioner of the Peace for Somerset County, 5 Jan 1775. (Ref: Maryland State Archives, Governor and Council Commissioner Records, 1726-1794, p. 286)

Innes, Amos, appointed a Commissioner of the Peace for Frederick County, 16 Nov 1763. (Ref: Maryland State Archives, Governor and Council Commissioner Records, 1726-1794, p. 213)

Innis, Enoch, of Frederick County, Court Justice, 1764. (Ref: *This Was The Life: Excerpts from the Judgment Records of Frederick County, Maryland, 1748-1765*, by Millard Milburn Rice, pp. 255)

Ireland, Gilbert, mariner, of Liverpool, registered the ship *Hamilton*, 120 tons, built at Patowmeck [Potomac] River, 1735. Gilbert Ireland, master and owner. March, 1735/6. (Ref: Maryland Commission Book No. 82, p. 42; *Maryland Historical Magazine*, Vol. XXVI, p. 146); appointed a Commissioner of the

Peace for St. Mary's County on 11 Jun 1739. (Ref: Maryland State Archives, Governor and Council Commissioner Records, 1726-1794, p. 63); commissioned Sheriff of St. Mary's County, 21 Oct 1747. (Ref: Maryland State Archives, Governor and Council Commissioner Records, 1726-1794, p. 100)

Ireland, John, of Anne Arundel County, was pardoned for killing Negro Frank, 17 Aug 1765. (Ref: Maryland Commission Book No. 82, p. 169; *Maryland Historical Magazine*, Vol. XXVI, p. 353)

Ireland, Thomas, Jr., appointed a Commissioner of the Peace for Calvert County, 22 Oct 1741. (Ref: Maryland State Archives, Governor and Council Commissioner Records, 1726-1794, p. 72); appointed a Commissioner of the Peace for Calvert County, 281 Oct 1744. (Ref: Maryland State Archives, Governor and Council Commissioner Records, 1726-1794, p. 89)

Ireland, William (c1714-1775), Clerk of Calvert County in 1768. (*Archives of Maryland*, Vol. XXXII, "Proceedings of the Council of Maryland, 1761-1770," p. 237); appointed a Commissioner of the Peace for Calvert County, 26 Jul 1773. (Ref: Maryland State Archives, Governor and Council Commissioner Records, 1726-1794, p. 272)

Ireland, William, Jr. (c1742 – d. after 1787), appointed a Commissioner of the Peace for Calvert County, 24 Aug 1773. (Ref: Maryland State Archives, Governor and Council Commissioner Records, 1726-1794, p. 275)

Isaac, Jacob, commissioned a Coroner for Calvert County, 14 Feb 1750/1. (Ref: Maryland Commission Book No. 82, p. 148; *Maryland Historical Magazine*, Vol. XXVI, p. 347)

Isaac, Richard, Jr., appointed Constable of Eastern Branch Hundred in Prince George's County, now Frederick County, 1744. (Ref: Prince George's County Court Records, 1736-1748, Extracts by Patricia Abelard Andersen, *Western Maryland Genealogy*, Vol. 18, No. 1, January 2002, p. 41)**, Sutton**, appointed a Commissioner of the Peace for Calvert County, 22 Oct 1741. (Ref: Maryland State Archives, Governor and Council Commissioner Records, 1726-1794, p. 72)

Jack, John, of Frederick County, appointed Constable of Conococheague Hundred in 1753. (Ref: *This Was The Life: Excerpts from the Judgment Records of Frederick County, Maryland, 1748-1765*, by Millard Milburn Rice, p. 131)

Jackson, Edward, appointed a Commissioner of the Peace for Cecil County, 3 Mar 1726/7 and 30 Nov 1732. (Ref: Maryland State Archives, Governor and Council Commissioner Records, 1726-1794, pp. 2, 30)

Jackson, John, doctor, appointed a Commissioner of the Peace for Queen Anne's County, 18 May 1758. (Ref: Maryland State Archives, Governor and Council Commissioner Records, 1726-1794, p. 180)

Jackson, John, registration of the schooner *Mulberry*, 15 tons, built in Cecil County, 1746. John Jackson, master and co-owner. John Jackson, Sr., co-owner. 8 Aug 1749. (Ref: Maryland Commission Book No. 82, p. 152; *Maryland Historical Magazine*, Vol. XXVI, p. 349)

Jackson, Richard, planter, late of St. Luke's Parish, Queen Anne's County, pardoned for felony. 18 May 1739. (Ref: Maryland Commission Book No. 82, p. 73; *Maryland Historical Magazine*, Vol. XXVI, p. 153); see John Handy.

Jacob, Mordecai (1714-1771), was appointed a Commissioner of the Peace for Prince George's County, 12 Nov 1748. (Ref: Maryland State Archives, Governor and Council Commissioner Records, 1726-1794, p. 109)

Jacobs, John, appointed Constable of the Lower Part of Monocacy Hundred in Frederick County in 1753. (Ref: *This Was The Life: Excerpts from the Judgment Records of Frederick County, Maryland, 1748-1765*, by Millard Milburn Rice, p. 131)

Jacobs, Joseph, appointed a Commissioner of the Peace for Anne Arundel County, 9 Aug 1757. (Ref: Maryland State Archives, Governor and Council Commissioner Records, 1726-1794, p. 175)

Jacques, Lancelot, commissioned High Sheriff of Anne Arundel County, 30 May 1763. (Ref: Maryland State Archives, Governor and Council Commissioner Records, 1726-1794, p. 200)

James, Daniel, appointed Constable of Burnt House Woods Hundred in Frederick County in 1763. (Ref: *This Was The Life: Excerpts from the Judgment Records of Frederick County, Maryland, 1748-1765*, by Millard Milburn Rice, p. 249)

James, Walter, Constable of Middle River Lower Hundred in Baltimore County, 1773. (Ref: *Inhabitants of Baltimore County, 1763-1774*, by Henry C. Peden,

Jr., 1989, p. 65, citing a 1773 List of Taxables)

James, William, of Baltimore County, convicted felon, was executed on 31 May 1749. (Ref: Maryland State Archives, Governor and Council Commissioner Records, 1726-1794, p. 111)

Jaoul(?), Cornelius, of Frederick County, was convicted of murder and executed on 22 Oct 1773. (Ref: Maryland State Archives, Governor and Council Commissioner Records, 1726-1794, p. 265)

Jenifer, Daniel (c1725-1795), appointed a Commissioner of the Peace for Charles County, 26 May 1756. (Ref: Maryland State Archives, Governor and Council Commissioner Records, 1726-1794, p. 168); Court Justice, 1756. (*Calendar of Maryland State Papers, No. 1 The Black Books*, p. 132); commissioned High Sheriff of Charles County, 3 Dec 1763. (Ref: Maryland State Archives, Governor and Council Commissioner Records, 1726-1794, p. 204)

Jenifer, Daniel of St. Thomas (1723-1790), was appointed a Commissioner of the Peace for Charles County, 24 Jul 1748. (Ref: Maryland State Archives, Governor and Council Commissioner Records, 1726-1794, p. 109); commissioned Chief Agent, Escheater, and Receiver of Rents, 9 Sep 1771 and 1773. (Ref: Maryland Commission Book No. 82, pp. 266, 298; *Maryland Historical Magazine*, Vol. XXVII, pp. 30, 32)

Jenifer, Samuel, commissioned a Coroner of St. Mary's County, 13 Apr 1744. (Ref: Maryland Commission Book No. 82, p. 109; *Maryland Historical Magazine*, Vol. XXVI, p. 252)

Jenings, Edmund, commissioned a Coroner of Anne Arundel Co, 5 Sep 1767. (Ref: Maryland Commission Book No. 82, p. 203; *Maryland Historical Magazine*, Vol. XXVI, p. 355)

Jenings, Edmund (d. 1756), esquire, appointed a Commissioner of the Peace for Cecil County, Baltimore County, Kent County, Prince George's County, Anne Arundel County, Calvert County, Charles County, St. Mary's County, Queen Anne's County, and Talbot County, 4 Aug 1732 and 10 Aug 1732 and 20 Aug 1733. (Ref: Maryland State Archives, Governor and Council Commissioner Records, 1726-1794, pp. 32-37); appointed a Privy Council on 10 May 1753. (Ref: *Archives of Maryland*, Vol. XXXI, "Proceedings of the Council of Maryland, 1753-1761," pp. 8, 14)

Jenings, Thomas, appointed a Commissioner of the Peace for Prince George's County, 14 Mar 1736/7 and 29 Mar 1738. (Ref: Maryland State Archives, Governor and Council Commissioner Records, 1726-1794, pp. 53, 59)

Jenings, Thomas (1736-1796), commissioned Attorney General, 27 Oct 1768 and 29 Apr 1773. (Ref: Maryland Commission Book No. 82, pp. 220;, 302 *Maryland Historical Magazine*, Vol. XXVI, p. 358, and Vol. XXVII, p. 33)

Jenkins, Thomas, see James Donaldson.

Jennings, Joseph, reverend, induction into All Saint's Parish, Prince George's County, 23 Nov 1742. (Ref: Maryland Commission Book No. 82, p. 98; *Maryland Historical Magazine*, Vol. XXVI, p. 248)

Jennings, Thomas, Court Justice, Anne Arundel County, 1754. (Ref: Anne Arundel County Court Minutes, 1725-1757); Justice of the Peace in 1757. (Ref: *Archives of Maryland*, Vol. XXXI, "Proceedings of the Council of Maryland, 1753-1761," p. 253)

Jennings, Thomas, appointed Constable of George Town Hundred in Frederick County, 1771. (Ref: "Frederick County Minute Book, March 1771, Extracts by Patricia Abelard Andersen," *Western Maryland Genealogy*, Vol. 18, No. 1, January 2002, p. 25)

Jermain, Stephen, see Thomas Hodgkin.

Jewell, George, appointed Constable of Sugarland Hundred in Frederick County in 1751. (Ref: *This Was The Life: Excerpts from the Judgment Records of Frederick County, Maryland, 1748-1765*, by Millard Milburn Rice, p. 61)

Jiams, John, see John Ijams.

Joel, Henry, appointed Constable of Sharpsburgh Hundred in Frederick County, 1769, 1771. (Ref: "Frederick County Court Minutes November 1769 by Patricia Abelard Andersen," *Western Maryland Genealogy*, Vol. 16, No. 1, January 2000, p. 33, misspelled his name as Joce; "Frederick County Minute Book, March 1771, Extracts by Patricia Abelard Andersen," *Western Maryland Genealogy*, Vol. 18, No. 1, January 2002, p. 26, spelled it correctly as Joel)

Johns, Kinsey, appointed a Commissioner of the Peace for Anne Arundel County, 8 Mar 1754. (Ref: Maryland State Archives, Governor and Council

Commissioner Records, 1726-1794, p. 143); Court Justice, Anne Arundel County, 1754. (Ref: Anne Arundel County Court Minutes, 1725-1757); commissioned High Sheriff of Anne Arundel County, 22 Nov 1760. (Ref: Maryland State Archives, Governor and Council Commissioner Records, 1726-1794, p. 186, and p. 198 styled him as captain); Justice, Anne Arundel County Court, 1754. (Ref: Anne Arundel County Court Minutes, 1725-1757); see Samuel Galloway.

Johnson, Archibald, see James Dick and William Govane.

Johnson, Barnet, of Frederick Co., magistrate, 1766. (Ref: *Archives of Maryland*, Vol. XXXII, "Proceedings of the Council of Maryland, 1761-1770," p. 166)

Johnson, David, appointed a Commissioner of the Peace for Worcester County, 2 Oct 1751. (Ref: Maryland State Archives, Governor and Council Commissioner Records, 1726-1794, p. 124)

Johnson, Edward (c1737-1797), doctor, was appointed a Commissioner of the Peace for Calvert County, 26 Jul 1773. (Ref: Maryland State Archives, Governor and Council Commissioner Records, 1726-1794, p. 272)

Johnson, George, appointed a Commissioner of the Peace for Cecil County, 20 Feb 1774. (Ref: Maryland State Archives, Governor and Council Commissioner Records, 1726-1794, p. 281)

Johnson, Henry, Clerk of Worcester County, 1756. (Ref: *Archives of Maryland*, Vol. LII, "Proceedings and Acts of the General Assembly of Maryland, 1755-1756," p. 232)

Johnson, James, servant of John Hobbs, of Frederick County, convicted felon, was executed on 9 Sep 1768. (Ref: *Archives of Maryland*, Vol. XXXII, "Proceedings of the Council of Maryland, 1761-1770," pp. 247-248); see Robert Swan, Alexander Lawson, and James Russell.

Johnson, Jeremiah, of Baltimore County, now Harford County, was Deputy Sheriff under Aquila Hall, 1764-1771. (Ref: *Inhabitants of Baltimore County, 1763-1774*, by Henry C. Peden, Jr., 1989, p. 4)

Johnson, Martin, see Gamaliel Butler and William Savory.

Johnson, Thomas, of Anne Arundel Co., convicted felon, was executed on 1 Nov 1734. (Ref: Maryland State Archives, Governor and Council Commissioner Records, 1726-1794, p. 45)

Johnson, Thomas, the Younger, shoemaker, of Frederick County, pardoned for theft, 30 Jan 1773. (Ref: Maryland Commission Book No. 82, p. 292; *Maryland Historical Magazine*, Vol. XXVII, p. 32)

Johnson, Thomas, Jr. (d. 1738/9), appointed a Commissioner of the Peace for Cecil County, 30 Nov 1732. (Ref: Maryland State Archives, Governor and Council Commissioner Records, 1726-1794, p. 30)

Johnson, William, appointed Constable of Kittocton [Catoctin] Hundred in Frederick County in 1751. (Ref: *This Was The Life: Excerpts from the Judgment Records of Frederick County, Maryland, 1748-1765*, by Millard Milburn Rice, p. 61)

Johnstone, John, was appointed Constable of Kittoctin [Catoctin] Hundred in Frederick County in 1749. (Ref: *This Was The Life: Excerpts from the Judgment Records of Frederick County, Maryland, 1748-1765*, by Millard Milburn Rice, p. 7)

Jones, Charles, appointed Constable of Potomack [Potomac] Hundred in Prince George's County, now Frederick County, 1747, 1748. (Ref: Prince George's County Court Records, 1736-1748, Extracts by Patricia Abelard Andersen, *Western Maryland Genealogy*, Vol. 18, No. 1, January 2002, pp. 45, 46); appointed Constable of Lower Potomac Hundred in Frederick County in 1749. (Ref: *This Was The Life: Excerpts from the Judgment Records of Frederick County, Maryland, 1748-1765*, by Millard Milburn Rice, p. 6; appointed a Commissioner of the Peace for Frederick County, 3 Jul 1754. (Ref: Maryland State Archives, Governor and Council Commissioner Records, 1726-1794, p. 155); Court Justice, 1754. (Ref: *This Was The Life: Excerpts from the Judgment Records of Frederick County, Maryland, 1748-1765*, by Millard Milburn Rice, p. 145); appointed to a Special Commission to hear cases involving convicted felons on 31 Aug 1768. (Ref: *Archives of Maryland*, Vol. XXXII, "Proceedings of the Council of Maryland, 1761-1770," p. 247); appointed a Commissioner of the Peace for Frederick County, 15 Aug 1774. (Ref: Maryland State Archives, Governor and Council Commissioner Records, 1726-1794, p. 284)

Jones, Jacob, gentleman, commissioned High Sheriff of Kent County, 18 Jan 1734/5. (Ref: Maryland

Commission Book No. 82, p. 25; *Maryland Historical Magazine*, Vol. XXVI, p. 142; Maryland State Archives, Governor and Council Commissioner Records, 1726-1794, p. 45); appointed a Commissioner of the Peace for Kent County, 20 Oct 1746. (Ref: Maryland State Archives, Governor and Council Commissioner Records, 1726-1794, p. 94); commissioned Sheriff of Kent County, 9 Nov 1747. (Ref: Maryland State Archives, Governor and Council Commissioner Records, 1726-1794, p. 103)

Jones, John, appointed Constable of Conococheague Hundred in Prince George's County, now Frederick County, 1739 and 1742. (Ref: Prince George's County Court Records, 1736-1748, Extracts by Patricia Abelard Andersen, *Western Maryland Genealogy*, Vol. 18, No. 1, January 2002, pp. 36, 38)

Jones, John, appointed a Commissioner of the Peace for Dorchester County, 20 May 1736. (Ref: Maryland State Archives, Governor and Council Commissioner Records, 1726-1794, p. 52); commissioned one of the Coroners for Dorchester County, 18 Jun 1741. (Ref: Maryland Commission Book No. 82, p. 87; *Maryland Historical Magazine*, Vol. XXVI, p. 244)

Jones, John, appointed a Commissioner of the Peace for Somerset County, 29 Oct 1730. (Ref: Maryland State Archives, Governor and Council Commissioner Records, 1726-1794, p. 17)

Jones, John, of Baltimore County, Ranger, 9 Aug 1775. (Ref: *Calendar of Maryland State Papers, The Red Books*, No. 4, Part 1, p. 5)

Jones, John, of ---- County, convicted felon, was executed on 15 May 1741. (Ref: Maryland State Archives, Governor and Council Commissioner Records, 1726-1794, p. 70)

Jones, Michael, appointed Constable of Senecear [Seneca] Hundred in Prince George's County, now Frederick County, 1744. (Ref: Prince George's County Court Records, 1736-1748, Extracts by Patricia Abelard Andersen, *Western Maryland Genealogy*, Vol. 18, No. 1, January 2002, p. 41)

Jones, Philip, appointed a Commissioner of the Peace for Baltimore County, 18 Feb 1731/2 and 24 Nov 1732. (Ref: Maryland State Archives, Governor and Council Commissioner Records, 1726-1794, pp. 21, 39)

Jones, Philip, commissioned a Coroner of Anne Arundel County, 19 Mar 1749/50. (Ref: Maryland Commission Book No. 82, p. 143; *Maryland Historical Magazine*, Vol. XXVI, p. 345)

Jones, Ralph, of Anne Arundel Co., convicted felon, was executed on 23 Feb 1738/9. (Ref: Maryland State Archives, Governor and Council Commissioner Records, 1726-1794, p. 255)

Jones, Thomas, appointed a Commissioner of the Peace for Somerset County, 4 Nov 1758 and 25 Sep 1761. (Ref: Maryland State Archives, Governor and Council Commissioner Records, 1726-1794, pp. 18, 1982)

Jones, William, of Goose Creek, was appointed a Warehouse Inspector in Somerset County on 3 Sep 1750. (*Calendar of Maryland State Papers, No. 1 The Black Books*, p. 96)

Jordan, James (d. 1787), commissioned Deputy Surveyor of St. Mary's County, 8 Dec 1766. (Ref: Maryland Commission Book No. 82, p. 196; *Maryland Historical Magazine*, Vol. XXVI, p. 355)

Jordan, Jeremiah (c1733-1806), appointed a Commissioner of the Peace for St. Mary's County, 15 Feb 1760. (Ref: Maryland State Archives, Governor and Council Commissioner Records, 1726-1794, p. 190); commissioned High Sheriff of St. Mary's County, 30 Oct 1764. (Ref: Maryland State Archives, Governor and Council Commissioner Records, 1726-1794, p. 209)

Jordan, John Morton, of Annapolis, Anne Arundl County, was commissioned Chief Agent, Escheater, and Receiver General, 30 Nov 1769. (Ref: Maryland Commission Book No. 82, p. 230; *Maryland Historical Magazine*, Vol. XXVI, p. 360); commissioned one of three Agents for the Sale of His Lordship's Reserved Lands and Manors, Jun 1770 and 17 Jul 1771. (Ref: Maryland Commission Book No. 82, pp. 241, 261; *Maryland Historical Magazine*, Vol. XXVI, p. 361, and Vol. XXVII, p. 30)

Jordan, Justinian (c1686-1749), was appointed a Commissioner of the Peace for St. Mary's County, 2 Mar 1726/7. (Ref: Maryland State Archives, Governor and Council Commissioner Records, 1726-1794, p. 2, spelled his name Jourdan)

Jordan, Justinian, Jr. (c1686-1759), appointed a Commissioner of the Peace for St. Mary's County, 25 Jan 1745/6. (Ref: Maryland State Archives, Governor and Council Commissioner Records, 1726-1794, p. 90)

Jordan, William, appointed a Commissioner of the Peace for St. Mary's County, 15 Feb 1760. (Ref: Maryland State Archives, Governor and Council Commissioner Records, 1726-1794, p. 190); commissioned a Deputy Surveyor of St. Mary's County, 25 Mar 1768, 15 Feb 1772 and 1 Dec 1773. (Ref: Maryland Commission Book No. 82, pp. 207, 274, 333; *Maryland Historical Magazine*, Vol. XXVII, pp. 31, 36, 357)

Joseph, William, of St. Mary's County, *noli prosequi* ordered to stop all Proceedings against him, being a Papist indicted for keeping school contrary to law. 28 Oct 1767. (Ref: Maryland Commission Book No. 82, p. 205; *Maryland Historical Magazine*, Vol. XXVI, p. 356)

Julian, Stephen, appointed Constable of the Middle Part of Monocacy Hundred in Frederick County, 1748, 1749 and 1771. (Ref: *This Was The Life: Excerpts from the Judgment Records of Frederick County, Maryland, 1748-1765*, by Millard Milburn Rice, p. 7; "Frederick County Minute Book, March 1771, Extracts by Patricia Abelard Andersen," *Western Maryland Genealogy*, Vol. 18, No. 1, January 2002, p. 26, misspelled name of the hundred as Monochosey, and p. 46)

Jump, William, appointed a Commissioner of the Peace for Queen Anne's County, 9 May 1732. (Ref: Maryland State Archives, Governor and Council Commissioner Records, 1726-1794, p. 23)

Jump, William, appointed a Commissioner of the Peace for Queen Anne's County, 16 Jun 1773. (Ref: Maryland State Archives, Governor and Council Commissioner Records, 1726-1794, p. 266)

Jumpe. George, was appointed Constable of Monocacy Hundred [downward] to Shannandore [Shenandoah] in Prince George's County, now Frederick County, 1736. (Ref: Prince George's County Court Records, 1736-1748, Extracts by Patricia Abelard Andersen, *Western Maryland Genealogy*, Vol. 18, No. 1, January 2002, p. 35)

Justice, Maunce (or Mounts), wasvappointed Constable of Pipe Creek Hundred in Frederick County in 1749 and served on a Grand Jury in 1755. (Ref: *This Was The Life: Excerpts from the Judgment Records of Frederick County, Maryland, 1748-1765*, by Millard Milburn Rice, pp. 37, 170)

Kankey, John, see George Rock.

Keene, Benjamin, appointed a Commissioner of the Peace for Dorchester County, 21 Apr 1735. (Ref: Maryland State Archives, Governor and Council Commissioner Records, 1726-1794, p. 46, spelled his name Keen); see Negro Glasgow.

Keene, Richard, appointed a Commissioner of the Peace for Dorchester County, 2 Aug 1766. (Ref: Maryland State Archives, Governor and Council Commissioner Records, 1726-1794, p. 226)

Keene, Samuel (1734-1810), reverend, licensed to preach in St. Paul's Parish, Queen Anne's County, vacant by the death of Rev. Alexander Malcolm, 8 Jul 1763; induction into St. Luke's Parish, Queen Anne's County, 1 Jan 1767. (Ref: Maryland Commission Book No. 82, pp. 160, 198; *Maryland Historical Magazine*, Vol. XXVI, pp. 352, 355)

Keene, Travers Benjamin (Hon.), appointed a Commissioner of the Peace for Dorchester County, 17 Oct 1734. (Ref: Maryland State Archives, Governor and Council Commissioner Records, 1726-1794, p. 44)

Kelby, William, see Henry Lowes.

Kell, Henry, Court Justice, Anne Arundel County, 1754. (Ref: Anne Arundel County Court Minutes, 1725-1757)

Keller, Conrad, of Prince George's County, native of Germany, naturalized 3 May 1740, and also his children Matthias, Gasparus, Susanna and Barbara. (Ref: Maryland Commission Book No. 82, p. 80; *Maryland Historical Magazine*, Vol. XXVI, p. 156)

Kellet, Roger, registration of sloop *Betty and Ann*, 30 tons, built in Maryland, 1738. Roger Kellet and David Wilson, owners. 27 Feb 1738/9. (Ref: Maryland Commission Book No. 82, p. 67; *Maryland Historical Magazine*, Vol. XXVI, p. 153)

Kelley, William, Jr., Constable of Pipe Creek Hundred in Baltimore County, 1773. (Ref: *Inhabitants of Baltimore County, 1763-1774*, by Henry C. Peden, Jr., 1989, p. 82, citing a 1773 List of Taxables)

Kelly, Bridget, alias Sullivan, of Frederick Co., convicted felon, along with Patrick Sullivan, for stealing the pocketbook of Stephen Ransberg in 1760, were sentenced to be set upon the pillory for one-half hour and then sent to the whipping post and receive twenty lashes on each of their bare bodies. (Ref: *This Was The Life: Excerpts from the Judgment Records of Frederick County, Maryland, 1748-1765*, by Millard Milburn Rice, p. 208)

Kemp, Thomas, see George Steuart and William Clayton.

Kennard, Philip, appointed a Commissioner of the Peace for Kent County, 12 Jun 1729. (Ref: Maryland State Archives, Governor and Council Commissioner Records, 1726-1794, p. 11)

Kennedy, Daniel, appointed Constable of the Upper Part of Potomac Hundred in Frederick County in 1753. (Ref: *This Was The Life: Excerpts from the Judgment Records of Frederick County, Maryland, 1748-1765*, by Millard Milburn Rice, p. 131); and he transported Gen. Braddock's soldiers and wagons over Manockasy [Monocacy] Ferry, but the Maryland Assembly rejected his account [no reason given] on 20 Mar 1756. (Ref: *Archives of Maryland*, Vol. LII, "Proceedings and Acts of the General Assembly of Maryland, 1755-1756," pp. 234, 342)

Kenny, Thomas, of Biddeford, registration of ship *Juliana*, 100 tons, built in Maryland, 1738. Thomas Kenny, master and owner. 8 May 1739. (Ref: Maryland Commission Book No. 82, p. 72; *Maryland Historical Magazine*, Vol. XXVI, p. 153); see Henry Young and James Hopkins.

Kent, James, appointed a Commissioner of the Peace for Queen Anne's County, 13 Mar 1773. (Ref: Maryland State Archives, Governor and Council Commissioner Records, 1726-1794, p. 265)

Kephemond, Edward, appointed Constable of Burnt House Woods Hundred in Frederick County, 1771. (Ref: "Frederick County Minute Book, March 1771, Extracts by Patricia Abelard Andersen," *Western Maryland Genealogy*, Vol. 18, No. 1, January 2002, p. 25)

Kerr, David (1749-1814), appointed a Commissioner of the Peace for Anne Arundel County, 24 Aug 1773. (Ref: Maryland State Archives, Governor and Council Commissioner Records, 1726-1794, p. 276); Court Justice, Anne Arundel County, 1774. (Ref: Anne Arundel County Court Minutes, 1725-1757, 1774)

Kerr, John, appointed a Commissioner of the Peace for Queen Anne's County, 13 Mar 1773. (Ref: Maryland State Archives, Governor and Council Commissioner Records, 1726-1794, p. 265)

Key, Edmund (d. 1766), of Annapolis, Anne Arundel County, commissioned Attorney General, 26 Dec 1763. (Ref: Maryland Commission Book No. 82, p. 160; *Maryland Historical Magazine*, Vol. XXVI, p. 352)

Key, John, see Negro Harry and Negro Cork.

Key, Philip (1696-1764), commissioned Sheriff of St. Mary's County, 25 Apr 1745. (Ref: Maryland State Archives, Governor and Council Commissioner Records, 1726-1794, p. 87); see Negro Harry and Negro Cork.

Key, Philip Barton, (d. 1756), Sheriff of St. Mary's County, 1754. (Ref: *Archives of Maryland*, Vol. LII, "Proceedings and Acts of the General Assembly of Maryland, 1755-1756," p. 573)

Kilby, Christopher, see Daniel Wolstenholme.

Kilby, John, appointed a Commissioner of the Peace for Worcester County, 11 Dec 1742. (Ref: Maryland State Archives, Governor and Council Commissioner Records, 1726-1794, p. 75)

Kimboll, John (b. 1698), appointed Constable of Linganoree Hundred in Prince George's County, now Frederick County, 1746. (Ref: Prince George's County Court Records, 1736-1748, Extracts by Patricia Abelard Andersen, *Western Maryland Genealogy*, Vol. 18, No. 1, January 2002, p. 44); of Frederick County, appointed Constable in the Upper Part of Monocacy Hundred in 1758 and Constable of Frederick Town Hundred in 1760. (Ref: *This Was The Life: Excerpts from the Judgment Records of Frederick County, Maryland, 1748-1765*, by Millard Milburn Rice, pp. 185, 216, and p. 221 spelled his name Kimbol and stated he was age 63 or thereabouts in 1761)

Kimboll, William, was appointed Constable of Frederick Town Hundred in Frederick County in 1763. (Ref: *This Was The Life: Excerpts from the Judgment Records of Frederick County, Maryland, 1748-1765*, by Millard Milburn Rice, p. 249)

King, Ephraim, appointed a Commissioner of the Peace for Cecil County, 10 May 1757. (Ref: Maryland State Archives, Governor and Council Commissioner Records, 1726-1794, p. 174)

King, John, appointed a Commissioner of the Peace for Charles County, 2 Mar 1726/7. (Ref: Maryland

State Archives, Governor and Council Commissioner Records, 1726-1794, p. 2)

King, Nehemiah, commissioned Sheriff of Somerset County, 23 Jun 1749. (Ref: Maryland State Archives, Governor and Council Commissioner Records, 1726-1794, p. 111); appointed a Commissioner of the Peace for Somerset County, 30 Jul 1754. (Ref: Maryland State Archives, Governor and Council Commissioner Records, 1726-1794, p. 156); see Robert King.

King, Robert (1689-1755), was appointed a Commissioner of the Peace for Somerset County, 29 Oct 1730. (Ref: Maryland State Archives, Governor and Council Commissioner Records, 1726-1794, p. 17); registration of schooner *Two Brothers*, 20 tons, built in Somerset County, 1751. Nehemiah King, master and co-owner. Robert King and Robert King, Jr., co-owners. 20 May 1751. (Ref: Maryland Commission Book No. 82, p. 149; *Maryland Historical Magazine*, Vol. XXVI, p. 348)

King, Robert, Jr., see Robert Jenckins Henry and Robert King.

Kipps, Francis, see William Alexander.

Kirk, Thomas, of Frederick County, convicted felon for stealing a pair of black worsted stockings valued at twenty pounds of tobacco in 1759, was sentenced to be set upon the pillory for fifteen minutes and then sent to the whipping post and receive fifteen lashes on his bare back. (Ref: *This Was The Life: Excerpts from the Judgment Records of Frederick County, Maryland, 1748-1765*, by Millard Milburn Rice, p. 193)

Kitteridge, William Serjeant, doctor, appointed a Commissioner of the Peace for Queen Anne's County, 18 May 1758. (Ref: Maryland State Archives, Governor and Council Commissioner Records, 1726-1794, p. 180)

Kloss, Swishorn(?), of Baltimore County, was appointed a Ranger, 9 Aug 1775. (Ref: *Calendar of Maryland State Papers, The Red Books*, No. 4, Part 1, p. 5)

Knight, John Leach, appointed a Commissioner of the Peace for Cecil County, 20 Feb 1774. (Ref: Maryland State Archives, Governor and Council Commissioner Records, 1726-1794, p. 281)

Knight, Stephen, appointed a Commissioner of the Peace for Kent County, 30 Nov 1732. (Ref: Maryland State Archives, Governor and Council Commissioner Records, 1726-1794, p. 33)

Knight, Stephen, of Anne Arundel County, commissioned Judge of Oyer, Terminer and Gaol [Jail] Delivery, 21 May 1736. (Ref: Maryland State Archives, Governor and Council Commissioner Records, 1726-1794, p. 52)

Knowles, Samuel, alias Samuel Nollar, of Charles County, convicted felon for store breaking and stealing sundry goods, ordered to be hung on 24 May 1754, but pardoned on 28 May 1754 because he was very young and this was his first offense. (Ref: *Archives of Maryland*, Vol. XXXI, "Proceedings of the Council of Maryland, 1753-1761," pp. 32-33)

Knowsley, Catharine, see Negro George.

Kollock, Cornelius, appointed a Commissioner of the Peace for Worcester County, 16 Jan 1769. (Ref: Maryland State Archives, Governor and Council Commissioner Records, 1726-1794, p. 240); see Mchael Godwyn.

Kollock, Simon, appointed a Commissioner of the Peace for Worcester County, 26 Jul 1773. (Ref: Maryland State Archives, Governor and Council Commissioner Records, 1726-1794, p. 271)

Lackey, John, see Joseph Gilpin.

Lake, Charles, reverend, was inducted into Dorchester Parish, Dorchester County, 18 Jul 1739. (Ref: Maryland Commission Book No. 82, p. 76; *Maryland Historical Magazine*, Vol. XXVI, p. 154); resignation from Dorchester Parish, Dorchester County, 29 Sep 1740. On same day, induction into St. Anne's Parish, Anne Arundel County. (Ref: Maryland Commission Book No. 82, p. 84; *Maryland Historical Magazine*, Vol. XXVI, p. 157); resignation from St. Anne's Parish, 4 Jan 1743/4. On same day, induction into Christ Church Parish, Calvert County. (Ref: Maryland Commission Book No. 82, p. 107; *Maryland Historical Magazine*, Vol. XXVI, p. 251); of Anne Arundel County, induction into St. James Parish, Anne Arundel Parish, 23 Feb 1748/9. (Ref: Maryland Commission Book No. 82, p. 139; *Maryland Historical Magazine*, Vol. XXVI, p. 343, listed his first name in brackets; *Directory of Ministers and the Maryland Churches They Served, 1634-1900*, by Edna Agatha Kanely, Vol. II, L-Z, p. 2)

Lamar, Alexander, see Elizabeth Weaver.

Lamb, Pierce, appointed Constable of Pipe Creek

Hundred in Frederick County, 1769. (Ref: "Frederick County Court Minutes, March 1769," by Patricia Abelard Andersen, *Western Maryland Genealogy*, Vol. 15, No. 2, April 1999, p. 63, misspelled his first name Pence; "Frederick County Court Minutes, June 1769," by Patricia Abelard Andersen, *Western Maryland Genealogy*, Vol. 15, No. 4, April 1999, p. 171)

Lamb, Thomas, of Prince George's County, convicted of murder, was executed on 13 May 1747 "on the north side of Rock Creek on the top of a hill near Holmead's mill in said county." (Ref: Maryland State Archives, Governor and Council Commissioner Records, 1726-1794, p. 99)

Lambden, Thomas, merchant, registration of schooner *Hollister*, 35 tons, built in Worcester County, 1745. Thomas Elmore, master. Thomas Lampden, owner. (Ref: Maryland Commission Book No. 82, p. 113; *Maryland Historical Magazine*, Vol. XXVI, p. 254, spelled his name Lampden); commissioned Sheriff of Worcester County, 20 May 1746. (Ref: Maryland State Archives, Governor and Council Commissioner Records, 1726-1794, p. 92, misspelled his name as Lampden, and p. 100 spelled it Lambden on 11 Sep 1747); registration of sloop *Ogle*, 50 tons, built at Indian River, 1747. Thomas Elmore, master. Thomas Lambden and Aaron Lynn, owners. 12 Jan 1747/8. (Ref: Maryland Commission Book No. 82, p. 132; *Maryland Historical Magazine*, Vol. XXVI, p. 262); merchant, registration of ship *Polly*, 150 tons, built in Worcester County, 1749. Thomas Elmore, master. (Ref: Maryland Commission Book No. 82, p. 140; *Maryland Historical Magazine*, Vol. XXVI, p. 344, spelled his name Lamden); see Daniel Cheston.

Lamon, John, planter, of Baltimore County, native of High Germany, naturalized 4 Jun 1738 and his children John, George, Louisa, Leonora, Catherine, and Margarett also. (Ref: Maryland Commission Book No. 82, p. 58; *Maryland Historical Magazine*, Vol. XXVI, p. 151)

Lancaster, John, see Joseph Lancaster.

Lancaster, Joseph, registration of the schooner *Catherine*, 35 tons, built in Potowmeck [Potomac] River, 1734. John Lancaster and Joseph Lancaster, owners. 26 Jun 1734. (Ref: Maryland Commission Book No. 82, p. 17; *Maryland Historical Magazine*, Vol. XXVI, p. 141)

Lancaster, Thomas, see Negro Will, Negro Charles and Negro James.

Lane, Richard, of Calvert County, convicted of murder, was executed in February 1727/8. (Ref: Maryland State Archives, Governor and Council Commissioner Records, 1726-1794, p. 6)

Lane, Richard, appointed Constable of Andietam [Antietam] Hundred in Prince George's County, now Frederick County, 1742. (Ref: Prince George's County Court Records, 1736-1748, Extracts by Patricia Abelard Andersen, *Western Maryland Genealogy*, Vol. 18, No. 1, January 2002, p. 38)

Lane, Samuel, appointed a Commissioner of the Peace for Anne Arundel County, 24 Aug 1773. (Ref: Maryland State Archives, Governor and Council Commissioner Records, 1726-1794, p. 276); Court Justice, 1774. (Ref: Anne Arundel County Court Minutes, 1725-1757, 1774)

Lane, William, was commissioned one of the Coroners of Somerset County on 6 May 1737 and appointed a Commissioner of the Peace for Worcester County, 11 Dec 1742 and 30 Mar 1747. (Ref: Maryland Commission Book No. 82, pp. 48, 99, 128; *Maryland Historical Magazine*, Vol. XXVI, pp. 149, 248, 259; Maryland State Archives, Governor and Council Commissioner Records, 1726-1794, p. 75; registration of sloop Sally and Leah, 35 tons, built in Worcester County, 1749. William Townshend, master. William Lane and John Dennis, owners. 11 Feb 1748/9. (Ref: Maryland Commission Book No. 82, p. 140; *Maryland Historical Magazine*, Vol. XXVI, p. 344); appointed a Commissioner of the Peace for Somerset County, 5 Jan 1775. (Ref: Maryland State Archives, Governor and Council Commissioner Records, 1726-1794, p. 286)

Lang, John, reverend, induction into St. James Parish, Anne Arundel County, 18 May 1734. (Ref: Maryland Commission Book No. 82, p. 10; *Maryland Historical Magazine*, Vol. XXVI, p. 140)

Lanham, Aaron, appointed Constable of the Lower Part of Potomac Hundred in Frederick County in 1763. (Ref: *This Was The Life: Excerpts from the Judgment Records of Frederick County, Maryland, 1748-1765*, by Millard Milburn Rice, p. 249)

Lansdale, Thomas, was a Constable in Frederick County in 1763. (Ref: *This Was The Life: Excerpts from the Judgment Records of Frederick County, Maryland, 1748-1765*, by Millard Milburn Rice, p.

252)

Lant, Lawrence, commissioned Deputy Surveyor of St. Mary's County in Sep/Oct 1737 and on 10 Dec 1742. (Ref: Maryland Commission Book No. 82, pp. 50, 99; *Maryland Historical Magazine*, Vol. XXVI, pp. 150, 248)

Larey, Joseph, see John Cooper.

Lauder, Francis, reverend, induction into St. Andrew's Parish, St. Mary's County, 18 Feb 1764; induction into Christ Church Parish, Calvert County, 25 Oct 1765. (Ref: Maryland Commission Book No. 82, pp. 161, 175; *Maryland Historical Magazine*, Vol. XXVI, pp. 352, 353)

Lawes, Elijah, appointed a Commissioner of the Peace for Somerset County, 5 Jan 1775. (Ref: Maryland State Archives, Governor and Council Commissioner Records, 1726-1794, p. 286)

Lawes, John, Jr., appointed a Commissioner of the Peace for Somerset County, 5 Jan 1775. (Ref: Maryland State Archives, Governor and Council Commissioner Records, 1726-1794, p. 286)

Lawrence, Levin, of Anne Arundel County, appointed Constable in Upper Part of ----(?) Hundred in 1774. (Ref: Anne Arundel County Court Minutes, 1725-1757, 1774)

Laws, John, appointed a Commissioner of the Peace for Worcester County, 4 Jul 1755. (Ref: Maryland State Archives, Governor and Council Commissioner Records, 1726-1794, p. 161)

Laws, Panther, see Negro Jack.

Lawson, Alexander, registration of ship *Dorothy*, 160 tons, built in Baltimore County, 1748. James Lucas, master. Alexander Lawson and James Johnson, owners. 22 Oct 1748. (Ref: Maryland Commission Book No. 82, p. 150; *Maryland Historical Magazine*, Vol. XXVI, p. 348); see Negro Tomboy.

Lawson, John, Constable of Mattapany Hundred in Prince George's County, now Frederick County, in 1733. (*Calendar of Maryland State Papers, No. 1 The Black Books*, p. 44)

Layfield, George, appointed a Commissioner of the Peace for Worcester County, 25 Sep 1761. (Ref: Maryland State Archives, Governor and Council Commissioner Records, 1726-1794, p. 198); see Negro Simon.

Layfield, Isaac, appointed a Commissioner of the Peace for Worcester County, 26 Jul 1773. (Ref: Maryland State Archives, Governor and Council Commissioner Records, 1726-1794, p. 271)

Lazier, Joseph, Jr., appointed Constable of Old Town Hundred in Frederick County, 1769 and 1771. (Ref: "Frederick County Court Minutes November 1769 by Patricia Abelard Andersen," *Western Maryland Genealogy*, Vol. 16, No. 1, January 2000, p. 33, spelled his name Lazier; "Frederick County Minute Book, March 1771, Extracts by Patricia Abelard Andersen," *Western Maryland Genealogy*, Vol. 18, No. 1, January 2002, p. 26, spelled his name Lazear)

Leaphart, Henry, planter, of Baltimore County, native of Germany, naturalized 1 May 1736. (Ref: Maryland Commission Book No. 82, p. 43; *Maryland Historical Magazine*, Vol. XXVI, p. 147)

Lecompte, John (1686-1754), was appointed a Commissioner of the Peace for Dorchester County on 1 Aug 1729 and 29 Oct 1730. (Ref: Maryland State Archives, Governor and Council Commissioner Records, 1726-1794, pp. 11, 17)

Ledsom, Thomas, see Thomas Ledston.

Ledston, Thomas, alias Thomas Ledsom, laborer, of Frederick County, convicted felon "for stealing and leading away a bay gelding, the goods and chattels of one Elias Delashmutt," was pardoned on 28 Oct 1758. (Ref: *Archives of Maryland*, Vol. XXXI, "Proceedings of the Council of Maryland, 1753-1761," p. 296)

Lee, Arthur (d. 1760), appointed a Commissioner of the Peace for Charles County, 7 Oct 1744. (Ref: Maryland State Archives, Governor and Council Commissioner Records, 1726-1794, p. 89); Court Justice, 1756. (*Calendar of Maryland State Papers, No. 1 The Black Books*, p. 132)

Lee, Francis (d. 1749), appointed a Commissioner of the Peace for Dorchester County on 1 Jun 1743. (Ref: Maryland State Archives, Governor and Council Commissioner Records, 1726-1794, p. 78); merchant, who registered the sloop *Elizabeth*, 13 tons, built in Wye River, 1738, and called the Rachel. Samuel Hall, master. Francis Lee, owner. 28 Jun 1746. (Ref: Maryland Commission Book No. 82, p. 120; *Maryland Historical Magazine*, Vol. XXVI, p. 257)

Lee, George (1736-1807), appointed a Commissioner of the Peace for Charles County, 17 Nov 1764. (Ref:

Maryland State Archives, Governor and Council Commissioner Records, 1726-1794, p. 220); commissioned High Sheriff of Charles County, 2 Oct 1771. (Ref: Maryland State Archives, Governor and Council Commissioner Records, 1726-1794, p. 246)

Lee, James, Jr., planter, Baltimore County, pardoned for killing Negro slave Nase, 12 Sep 1764. (Ref: Maryland Commission Book No. 82, p. 165; *Maryland Historical Magazine*, Vol. XXVI, p. 353)

Lee, Philip (c1681-1744), was commissioned a Provincial Justice by the Governor, 20 Oct 1729. (Ref: Maryland State Archives, Governor and Council Commissioner Records, 1726-1794, p. 12); appointed a Commissioner of the Peace for Cecil County, Baltimore County, Kent County, Prince George's County, Anne Arundel County, Calvert County, Charles County, St. Mary's County, Queen Anne's County, and Talbot County, 4 Aug 1732 and 10 Aug 1732 and 20 Aug 1733. (Ref: Maryland State Archives, Governor and Council Commissioner Records, 1726-1794, pp. 32-37); commissioned Naval Officer of the Port of North Patowmeck [Potomac], 25 Jul 1733 and Port of Patowmeck [Potomac], 29 Sep 1742. (Ref: Maryland Commission Book No. 82, pp. 1, 96; *Maryland Historical Magazine*, Vol. XXVI, pp. 139, 247)

Lee, Richard (c1707-1787), was commissioned Sheriff of Prince George's County, 27 May 1728. (Ref: Maryland State Archives, Governor and Council Commissioner Records, 1726-1794, p. 7); commission renewed for High Sheriff of Prince George's County, 28 Aug 1735. (Ref: Maryland Commission Book No. 82, p. 33; *Maryland Historical Magazine*, Vol. XXVI, p. 145); appointed Privy Council on 10 May 1753. (Ref: *Archives of Maryland*, Vol. XXXI, "Proceedings of the Council of Maryland, 1753-1761," p. 8); esquire, of Charles County, appointed to a Committee to Inspect the Accounts and Proceedings of the Commissioners of the Paper Currency Office, 25 Feb 1755. (Ref: *Archives of Maryland*, Vol. LII, "Proceedings and Acts of the General Assembly of Maryland, 1755-1756," pp. 5, 53); see William Ostroe.

Lee, Richard, of Charles County, commissioned Naval Officer of Patowmeck [Potomac] on 28 Aug 1769 and again on 29 Apr 1773. (Ref: Maryland Commission Book No. 82, pp. 226, 307; *Maryland Historical Magazine*, Vol. XXVI, p 359, and Vol. XXVI p. 33)

Lee, Richard, Jr., commissioned High Sheriff of Charles County, 10 Oct 1768. (Ref: Maryland State Archives, Governor and Council Commissioner Records, 1726-1794, p. 225)

Lee, Robert, appointed Constable of Sugar Loaf Hundred in Frederick County, 1769, 1771. (Ref: "Frederick County Court Minutes November 1769 by Patricia Abelard Andersen," *Western Maryland Genealogy*, Vol. 16, No. 1, January 2000, pp. 25, 32)

Lee, Samuel, appointed a Commissioner of the Peace for Charles County, 12 May 1769. (Ref: Maryland State Archives, Governor and Council Commissioner Records, 1726-1794, p. 241)

Leeds, John, appointed a Commissioner of the Peace for Talbot County, 17 Oct 1734. (Ref: Maryland State Archives, Governor and Council Commissioner Records, 1726-1794, p. 44); commissioned Treasurer of the Eastern Shore, 29 Apr 1766. (Ref: Maryland Commission Book No. 82, p. 180; *Maryland Historical Magazine*, Vol. XXVI, p. 354); Court Justice, Somerset County, 1766. (*Calendar of Maryland State Papers, No. 1 The Black Books*, p. 199); commissioned Naval Officer of Pocomoke, 14 Oct 1766, 14 Sep 1769 and 29 Apr 1773. (Ref: Maryland Commission Book No. 82, pp. 181, 309; *Maryland Historical Magazine*, Vol. XXVI, pp. 354, 359; *Maryland Historical Magazine*, Vol. XXVII, p. 33; *Calendar of Maryland State Papers, No. 1 The Black Books*, p. 206)

Leeke, Frank, commissioned High Sheriff of Prince George's County, 30 Nov 1774. (Ref: Maryland State Archives, Governor and Council Commissioner Records, 1726-1794, p. 275, spelled his surname Leak and p. 278 spelled it Leeke)

Leigh, John, appointed a Commissioner of the Peace for St. Mary's County, 2 Mar 1726/7. (Ref: Maryland State Archives, Governor and Council Commissioner Records, 1726-1794, p. 2)

Leith, Alexander, was commissioned one of the Corders of Wood in Baltimore Town. (Ref: Maryland Commission Book No. 82, p. 216; *Maryland Historical Magazine*, Vol. XXVI, p. 358)

Leitzing, Peter, native of Germany, denization, 26 Apr 1768. (Ref: Maryland Commission Book No. 82, p. 212; *Maryland Historical Magazine*, Vol. XXVI, p.

357)

Lendrum, Andrew, reverend, induction into St. Anne's Parish, Anne Arundel County, 25 Mar 1749. (Ref: Maryland Commission Book No. 82, p. 140; *Maryland Historical Magazine*, Vol. XXVI, p. 344)

Lendrum, Thomas, reverend, induction into Christ Church Parish, Queen Anne's County, 26 May 1773. (Ref: Maryland Commission Book No. 82, p. 318; *Maryland Historical Magazine*, Vol. XXVII, p. 34)

Leonard, Benedict, of Calvert County, was Commissioner of Assize, Oyer and Terminer and Gaol [Jail] Delivery, 11 Aug 1727. (Ref: Maryland State Archives, Governor and Council Commissioner Records, 1726-1794, p. 5)

Levett, John, appointed Constable of Marl-borough Hundred in Prince George's County, now Frederick County, 1744. (Ref: Prince George's County Court Records, 1736-1748, Extracts by Patricia Abelard Andersen, *Western Maryland Genealogy*, Vol. 18, No. 1, January 2002, p. 41)

Lewis, William, was Constable in Pipe Creek Hundred in Frederick County in 1758. (Ref: *This Was The Life: Excerpts from the Judgment Records of Frederick County, Maryland, 1748-1765*, by Millard Milburn Rice, p. 185); see Negro Caleb.

Lillie, Jeremiah, of Somerset County, convicted felon, was executed on 10 Nov 1736. (Ref: Maryland State Archives, Governor and Council Commissioner Records, 1726-1794, p. 54)

Lilliston, John, of Anne Arundel County, convicted burglar, executed on 15 Jun 1743. (Ref: Maryland State Archives, Governor and Council Commissioner Records, 1726-1794, p. 79)

Linchcomb, Eli, see Negro Toby.

Lingam, Thomas, see Negro George and Negro Sam.

Linn, David, appointed a Commissioner of the Peace for Frederick County, 3 Jul 1754. (Ref: Maryland State Archives, Governor and Council Commissioner Records, 1726-1794, p. 155); Court Justice, 1754. (Ref: *This Was The Life: Excerpts from the Judgment Records of Frederick County, Maryland, 1748-1765*, by Millard Milburn Rice, p. 145); see David Lynn.

Little, James, appointed Constable of Salisbury Hundred in Frederick County in 1763. (Ref: *This Was The Life: Excerpts from the Judgment Records of Frederick County, Maryland, 1748-1765*, by Millard Milburn Rice, p. 249)

Litton, Caleb, appointed Constable of Fort Frederick Hundred in Frederick County in 1763. (Ref: *This Was The Life: Excerpts from the Judgment Records of Frederick County, Maryland, 1748-1765*, by Millard Milburn Rice, p. 249)

Lloyd, Edward (1711-1770), appointed a Privy Council on 10 May 1753. (Ref: *Archives of Maryland*, Vol. XXXI, "Proceedings of the Council of Maryland, 1753-1761," p. 8); see Negro Ben

Lloyd, James, appointed a Commissioner of the Peace for Talbot County, 19 Dec 1751. (Ref: Maryland State Archives, Governor and Council Commissioner Records, 1726-1794, p. 131)

Lloyd, John, commissioned a Coroner for Baltimore County, 1 Apr 1741. (Ref: Maryland Commission Book No. 82, p. 85; *Maryland Historical Magazine*, Vol. XXVI, p. 158)

Lloyd, Richard (c1717-1786), was appointed a Commissioner of the Peace for Kent County, 18 Oct 1744; colonel, appointed a Commissioner of the Peace, 2 Jun 1774. (Ref: Maryland State Archives, Governor and Council Commissioner Records, 1726-1794, pp. 86. 283)

Lloyd, Robert (c1712-1770), of Queen Anne's County, served on the Committee of Laws, 1755. (Ref: *Archives of Maryland*, Vol. LII, "Proceedings and Acts of the General Assembly of Maryland, 1755-1756," pp. 46, 62); appointed to a Committee for Enquiring into Ways and Means to Raise a Sum Sufficient for Payment of Eighty Rangers to Defend and Protect the Frontiers, 28 Jun 1755. (Ref: Maryland State Archives, Governor and Council Commissioner Records, 1726-1794, p. 151); appointed to the Committee to Apportion the Public Levies, 29 May 1756. (Ref: *Archives of Maryland*, Vol. LII, "Proceedings and Acts of the General Assembly of Maryland, 1755-1756," p. 291)

Lochman, Jacob, planter, of Baltimore County, native of Germany, naturalized 20 May 1736. (Ref: Maryland Commission Book No. 82, p. 43; *Maryland Historical Magazine*, Vol. XXVI, p. 147)

Lock, Meverel, commissioned Sheriff of St. Mary's County, 27 Oct 1755, and appointed a Commissioner of the Peace, 6 Nov 1758. (Ref: Maryland State

Archives, Governor and Council Commissioner Records, 1726-1794, pp. 154, 183; *Archives of Maryland*, Vol. LII, "Proceedings and Acts of the General Assembly of Maryland, 1755-1756," p. 572)

Lock, William, appointed a Commissioner of the Peace for Anne Arundel County, 17 Nov 1749. (Ref: Maryland State Archives, Governor and Council Commissioner Records, 1726-1794, p. 114)

Lock, Williamson, commissioned a Provincial Justice by the Governor, 20 Oct 1729. (Ref: Maryland State Archives, Governor and Council Commissioner Records, 1726-1794, p. 12)

Lockwood, Samuel, registration of the sloop *William*, 7 tons, built in Anne Arundel County, 1746. William Strachan, master. Samuel Lockwood, owner. 23 Jul 1748. (Ref: Maryland Commission Book No. 82, p. 135; *Maryland Historical Magazine*, Vol. XXVI, p. 263)

Lomar, John, appointed a Commissioner of the Peace for Prince George's County, 30 Nov 1741. (Ref: Maryland State Archives, Governor and Council Commissioner Records, 1726-1794, p. 72)

Loockerman, Govert, see Christopher Lowndes.

Loockerman, Jacob, of Jacob, commissioned Sheriff of Dorchester County, 29 Jan 1728/9. (Ref: Maryland State Archives, Governor and Council Commissioner Records, 1726-1794, p. 9)

Loockerman, Thomas (d. 1753), was appointed Constable of Fishing Creek Hundred in Dorchester County, 1742, 1744. (Ref: Dorchester County Judgment Records, 1742-1743, p. 84, and 1743-1745, p. 185; *Judgment Records of Dorchester, Queen Anne's and Talbot Counties, Maryland*, by F. Edward Wright, 2001, pp. 30, 49); appointed Constable of Nanticoke Hundred in Dorchester County, 1745. (Ref: Dorchester County Judgment Records, 1743-1745, p. 476; *Judgment Records of Dorchester, Queen Anne's and Talbot Counties, Maryland*, by F. Edward Wright, 2001, p. 60)

Louttit, John, appointed a Commissioner of the Peace for Cecil County, 21 Apr 1764. (Ref: Maryland State Archives, Governor and Council Commissioner Records, 1726-1794, p. 215)

Love, Charles, of Charles County, appointed one of the inspectors of Piles' Warehouse, 1756. (Ref: *Archives of Maryland*, Vol. LII, "Proceedings and Acts of the General Assembly of Maryland, 1755-1756," p. 638)

Love, David, reverend, inducted into All Hallows Parish, Anne Arundel County. 29 Oct 1765. (Ref: Maryland Commission Book No. 82, p. 175; *Maryland Historical Magazine*, Vol. XXVI, p. 354)

Love, Samuel (b. 1745/46), was appointed a Commissioner of the Peace for Charles County, 2 Oct 1771. (Ref: Maryland State Archives, Governor and Council Commissioner Records, 1726-1794, p. 258)

Lowe, Nicholas, commissioned Sheriff of Talbot County, 5 Aug 1728. (Ref: Maryland State Archives, Governor and Council Commissioner Records, 1726-1794, p. 7); appointed a Commissioner of the Peace for Talbot County, 9 May 1732. (Ref: Maryland State Archives, Governor and Council Commissioner Records, 1726-1794, p. 23)

Lowe, Richard, commissioned Sheriff of Talbot County, 5 Aug 1728. (Ref: Maryland State Archives, Governor and Council Commissioner Records, 1726-1794, p. 7)

Lowes, Henry (d. 1767), registration of the sloop *Esther*, 25 tons, built in Somerset County, 1739. William Kelby, master. Henry Lowes, owner. 20 Feb 1739/40. (Ref: Maryland Commission Book No. 82, p. 79; *Maryland Historical Magazine*, Vol. XXVI, p. 155); registration of the brigantine *Cookson*, 70 tons, built in Somerset County, 1746. John Richardson, master. Henry Lowes, Anthony Bacon and John Williams, owners. 25 Feb 1746/7. (Ref: Maryland Commission Book No. 82, p. 125; *Maryland Historical Magazine*, Vol. XXVI, p. 259); merchant, registration of the brigantine *Douglass & Arbuckle*, 80 tons, built in Worcester County, 1747. Henry Lowes, master and co-owner. Anthony Bacon and Aaron Lynn, co-owners. 27 Oct 1747. (Ref: Maryland Commission Book No. 82, p. 132; *Maryland Historical Magazine*, Vol. XXVI, pp. 261-262); registration of schooner *Ogle*, 40 tons, built in Somerset County, 1747. John Richardson, master. Henry Lowes, owner, 26 Sep 1748. (Ref: Maryland Commission Book No. 82, p. 136; *Maryland Historical Magazine*, Vol. XXVI, p. 342); registration of schooner *Industry*, 50 tons, built in Somerset County, 1751. John Caldwell, master. Henry Lowes, owner. 6 Jun 1751. (Ref: Maryland Commission Book No. 82, p. 149; *Maryland Historical Magazine*, Vol.

XXVI, p. 348)

Lowndes, Christopher, merchant, registration of ship *Bladensburg*, 200 tons, built in Virginia, 1746. Govert Loockerman, master. Christopher Lowndes, John Hardman, William Whalley and Edward Lowndes, of Great Britain, owners. 13 Dec 1746. (Ref: Maryland Commission Book No. 82, p. 124; *Maryland Historical Magazine*, Vol. XXVI, p. 258); registration of schooner *Tasker*, 45 tons, built in Prince George's County, 1749. Henry Parr, master. Christopher Lowndes, owner. 22 Mar 1749/50. (Ref: Maryland Commission Book No. 82, p. 155; *Maryland Historical Magazine*, Vol. XXVI, p. 351); appointed a Commissioner of the Peace for Prince George's County, 8 Mar 1754. (Ref: Maryland State Archives, Governor and Council Commissioner Records, 1726-1794, p. 144)

Lowndes, Edward, see Christopher Lowndes.

Lowry, William, see William Graham.

Loyall, William, registration of sloop *Elizabeth*, 70 tons, formerly called *Spadille*, a French vessel captured by H.M.S. *Bellona* on 22 Aug 1748 and condemned as a lawful prize. William Loyall, and Richard Hill and Rees Meredith of Pennsylvania, owners, 3 Sep 1748. (Ref: Maryland Commission Book No. 82, p. 138; *Maryland Historical Magazine*, Vol. XXVI, p. 343)

Lucas, Barton, commissioned a Coroner of Prince George's County, 5 Jan 1769. (Ref: Maryland Commission Book No. 82, p. 221; *Maryland Historical Magazine*, Vol. XXVI, p. 359)

Lucas, James, see Aaron Lynn and Alexander Lawson.

Lucas, Onisophorus, of Anne Arundel County, convicted burglar, executed 26 Jun 1751. (Ref: Maryland State Archives, Governor and Council Commissioner Records, 1726-1794, p. 123)

Luckett, William (1711-c1783), appointed a Commissioner of the Peace for Frederick County, 3 Nov 1757. (Ref: Maryland State Archives, Governor and Council Commissioner Records, 1726-1794, p. 178); magistrate, 1766. (Ref: *Archives of Maryland*, Vol. XXXII, "Proceedings of the Council of Maryland, 1761-1770," p. 176); Court Justice, 1769. (Ref: "Frederick County Court Minutes, March 1769," by Patricia Abelard Andersen, *Western Maryland Genealogy*, Vol. 15, No. 2, April 1999, p. 62); appointed a Commissioner of the Peace, 15 Aug 1774. (Ref: Maryland State Archives, Governor and Council Commissioner Records, 1726-1794, p. 284); Court Judge, 1774. (*Calendar of Maryland State Papers, No. 1 The Black Books*, p. 217)

Luke(?), Matthew, appointed a Commissioner of the Peace for Kent County, 8 Mar 1754. (Ref: Maryland State Archives, Governor and Council Commissioner Records, 1726-1794, p. 143)

Lumley, John, of Whitehaven, registration of the brigantine *William and Thomas*, 70 tons, brought into Maryland as a wreck by John Rigby and purchased under Court of Admiralty. William and Thomas Gilpin, of Whitehaven, and John Lumley, owners. 14 Jun 1746. (Ref: Maryland Commission Book No. 82, p. 121; *Maryland Historical Magazine*, Vol. XXVI, p. 257)

Lusby, Thomas, commissioned Receiver of His Lordship's Quit Rents for Cecil County, 6 Apr 1741. (Ref: Maryland Commission Book No. 82, p. 85; *Maryland Historical Magazine*, Vol. XXVI, p. 158)

Lux, Darby (d. 1795), appointed a Commissioner of the Peace for Baltimore County, 9 Feb 1748/9. (Ref: Maryland State Archives, Governor and Council Commissioner Records, 1726-1794, p. 110); registration of sloop *Baltimore Town*, 36 tons, built in Baltimore County, 1746. James Saunders, master. Darby Lux, owner. 9 May 1750. (Ref: Maryland Commission Book No. 82, p. 155; *Maryland Historical Magazine*, Vol. XXVI, p. 351); appointed a Commissioner of the Peace for Baltimore County, 30 May 1774. (Ref: Maryland State Archives, Governor and Council Commissioner Records, 1726-1794, p. 283); appointed to represent Baltimore County in the Provincial Convention, 1775. (Ref: *Calendar of Maryland State Papers, The Red Books*, No. 4, Part 1, p. 3)

Lux, William (c1730-1778), was appointed a Commissioner of the Peace for Baltimore County, 21 Feb 1753. (Ref: Maryland State Archives, Governor and Council Commissioner Records, 1726-1794, p. 137); of Elk Ridge, appointed a Commissioner of the Peace for Anne Arundel County, 25 May 1764. (Ref: Maryland State Archives, Governor and Council Commissioner Records, 1726-1794, p. 216)

Luxon, John, see Henry Young and James Hopkins.

Lyddel, Thomas, registration of sloop *Victory*, 12 tons, built in Somerset County, 1744. Thomas Lyddel, master and owner. 26 Feb 1744/5. (Ref: Maryland Commission Book No. 82, p. 112; *Maryland Historical Magazine*, Vol. XXVI, p. 253)

Lyle (Lyles), William (d. 1790), appointed a Commissioner of the Peace for Calvert County on 11 Jun 1760. (Ref: Maryland State Archives, Governor and Council Commissioner Records, 1726-1794, p. 191)

Lynch, Charles, of Anne Arundel County, convicted felon, executed on 1 Nov 1734. (Ref: Maryland State Archives, Governor and Council Commissioner Records, 1726-1794, p. 45)

Lynn, Aaron, registration of sloop *Elizabeth*, built in Somerset County, 1741. John Windsor, master. Aaron Lynn, owner. 25 Jul 1741. (Ref: Maryland Commission Book No. 82, p. 86; *Maryland Historical Magazine*, Vol. XXVI, p. 244); merchant, registration of ship *William and Mary*, 150 tons, built in Somerset County, 1745. James Lucas, master. 26 Apr 1745. (Ref: Maryland Commission Book No. 82, p. 113; *Maryland Historical Magazine*, Vol. XXVI, p. 254; registration of ship *Johnson*, 200 tons, built in Somerset County, 1747. Moses Lynn, master. Aaron Lynn and Moses Lynn, owners. 31 Oct 1747. (Ref: Maryland Commission Book No. 82, p. 132; *Maryland Historical Magazine*, Vol. XXVI, p. 262); see Henry Lowes, John Fitz, Levin Gale, Thomas Lambden and William Roberts.

Lynn, David, of Frederick County, Court Justice, 1769. (Ref: "Frederick County Court Minutes, March 1769," by Patricia Abelard Andersen, *Western Maryland Genealogy*, Vol. 15, No. 2, April 1999, p. 62); appointed a Commissioner of the Peace, 15 Aug 1774. (Ref: Maryland State Archives, Governor and Council Commissioner Records, 1726-1794, p. 284); Court Judge, 1774. (*Calendar of Maryland State Papers, No. 1 The Black Books*, p. 217)

Lynn, Moses, see Aaron Lynn.

Lynthicum, Ely, see Negro Toby.

Lyon, John George, of Prince George's County, native of Germany, naturalized 3 May 1740, and also his children Mary, Jacob and Elizabeth. (Ref: Maryland Commission Book No. 82, p. 80; *Maryland Historical Magazine*, Vol. XXVI, p. 156)

Lyon, William, appointed a Commissioner of the Peace for Baltimore County, 21 Feb 1753. (Ref: Maryland State Archives, Governor and Council Commissioner Records, 1726-1794, p. 137)

Lytle, George, Constable of Mine Run Hundred in Baltimore County, 1773. (Ref: *Inhabitants of Baltimore County, 1763-1774*, by Henry C. Peden, Jr., 1989, p. 72, citing a 1773 List of Taxables)

Macarthen, James, see Hugh Campbell.

Macclester, George, commissioned Sheriff of Somerset County, 23 May 1734. (Ref: Maryland State Archives, Governor and Council Commissioner Records, 1726-1794, p. 41, also spelled his surname McClester); registration of sloop *Sally and Betty*, 16 tons, built in Somerset County, 1748. George Macclester, master and co-owner. Samuel Macclester, co-owner. (Ref: Maryland Commission Book No. 82, p. 136; *Maryland Historical Magazine*, Vol. XXVI, p. 342); see John Fitz.

Macclester, Joseph, of Somerset County, sheriff, 1727, and commission renewed for High Sheriff of Somerset County, 29 Jul 1735. (Ref: Maryland Commission Book No. 82, p. 33; *Maryland Historical Magazine*, Vol. XXVI, p. 144; *Abstracts of the Testamentary Proceedings and Prerogative Court of Maryland, Vol. XVII, 1724-1727*, by Vernon L. Skinner, Jr., p. 192, citing original Liber 27, f. 348)

Macclester, Samuel, see George Macclester and John Fitz.

Maccubbin, Moses, appointed a Commissioner of the Peace for Anne Arundel County, 3 Mar 1726/7. (Ref: Maryland State Archives, Governor and Council Commissioner Records, 1726-1794, p. 3)

Maccubbin, Nicholas, commission renewed for High Sheriff of Anne Arundel County, 27 Jun 1735. (Ref: Maryland Commission Book No. 82, p. 32; *Maryland Historical Magazine*, Vol. XXVI, p. 144); appointed a Commissioner of the Peace for Anne Arundel County, 10 Sep 1736. (Ref: Maryland State Archives, Governor and Council Commissioner Records, 1726-1794, p. 53)

Maccubbin, Nicholas, of Anne Arundel County, appointed a Commissioner of the Peace, 20 Apr 1773. (Ref: Maryland State Archives, Governor and Council Commissioner Records, 1726-1794, p. 266)

Maccubbin, Richard, see Thomas Dicke.

Maccubbin, William, appointed Constable of Burnt House Woods Hundred in Frederick County in 1753. (Ref: *This Was The Life: Excerpts from the Judgment Records of Frederick County, Maryland, 1748-1765*, by Millard Milburn Rice, p. 131)

Maccubbin, William, of Moses, of Anne Arundel County, appointed Constable in Middle Neck Hundred in 1774. (Ref: Anne Arundel County Court Minutes, 1725-1757, 1774)

Maccubbin, Zachariah, of Anne ArundelCo., appointed a Commissioner of the Peace, 3 Mar 1726/7. (Ref: Maryland State Archives, Governor and Council Commissioner Records, 1726-1794, p. 3); commissioned Sheriff of Anne Arundel County, 11 Nov 1730. (Ref: Maryland State Archives, Governor and Council Commissioner Records, 1726-1794, p. 20)

Maccubbin, Zachariah, Jr., commissioned a Coroner for Anne Arundel County, 17 Jun 1735. (Ref: Maryland Commission Book No. 82, p. 30; *Maryland Historical Magazine*, Vol. XXVI, p. 144)

Maccullum, Neill ot Nevill, reverend, induction into Dorchester Parish, Dorchester County, 6 Apr 1741. (Ref: Maryland Commission Book No. 82, p. 85, and *Maryland Historical Magazine*, Vol. XXVI, p. 158, both gave his first name as Neill. but *Directory of Ministers and the Maryland Churches They Served, 1634-1900*, by Edna Agatha Kanely, Vol. II, L-Z, p. 47, listed him as Nevill MacCullum)

Macdowell, James, alias John Nicholson, of Charles County, convicted felon for store breaking and stealing sundry goods, pardoned on 13 May 1754. (Ref: *Archives of Maryland*, Vol. XXXI, "Proceedings of the Council of Maryland, 1753-1761," p. 32)

Mackall, Benjamin (1675-1761), appointed a Commissioner of the Peace for Calvert County, 3 Mar 1726/7. (Ref: Maryland State Archives, Governor and Council Commissioner Records, 1726-1794, p. 3)

Mackall, Benjamin [Jr.] (c1723-1795), was appointed a Commissioner of the Peace for Calvert County, 3 Nov 1766. (Ref: Maryland State Archives, Governor and Council Commissioner Records, 1726-1794, p. 229)

Mackall, Thomas (1751-1799), was appointed a Commissioner of the Peace for Calvert County, 26 Jul 1773. (Ref: Maryland State Archives, Governor and Council Commissioner Records, 1726-1794, p. 272)

Mackdowel, Hugh, see John Carlyle.

Mackeel, Thomas, was commissioned one of the Coroners for Dorchester County, 18 Jun 1741. (Ref: Maryland Commission Book No. 82, p. 87; *Maryland Historical Magazine*, Vol. XXVI, p. 244); appointed Constable of Little Choptank Hundred in Dorchester County, 1744. (Ref: Dorchester County Judgment Records, 1743-1745, p. 185; *Judgment Records of Dorchester, Queen Anne's and Talbot Counties, Maryland*, by F. Edward Wright, 2001, p. 49)

Mackenzy, Patrick, of Baltimore County, convicted felon for stealing a gelding from John Guyton on 10 Sep 1766, was executed on 15 Oct 1766. (Ref: Maryland State Archives, Governor and Council Commissioner Records, 1726-1794, p. 211; *Archives of Maryland*, Vol. XXXII, "Proceedings of the Council of Maryland, 1761-1770," p. 164)

Mackey, David, appointed a Commissioner of the Peace for Cecil County, 3 Mar 1772 and 20 Feb 1774. (Ref: Maryland State Archives, Governor and Council Commissioner Records, 1726-1794, p. 260, and p. 281 spelled his name Mackie)

Mackey, John, appointed a Commissioner of the Peace for Cecil County, 30 Nov 1756. (Ref: Maryland State Archives, Governor and Council Commissioner Records, 1726-1794, p. 172)

Mackie, Ebenezer, appointed a Commissioner of the Peace for Baltimore County, 6 Mar 1775. (Ref: Maryland State Archives, Governor and Council Commissioner Records, 1726-1794, p. 288)

Mackleraith, John, see William Roberts.

Macnamar, John, was appointed Constable of Streights Hundred in Dorchester County, 1745. (Ref: Dorchester County Judgment Records, 1743-1745, p. 476; *Judgment Records of Dorchester, Queen Anne's and Talbot Counties, Maryland*, by F. Edward Wright, 2001, p. 60)

Macknaul, Mary, of Frederick County, convicted of stealing a snuff box valued at ten pounds from Nicholas Bundrick on 10 Feb 1750/51, was sentenced to be set upon the pillory for five minutes and then taken to the whipping post and receive five lashes on her bare back. (Ref: *This Was The Life: Excerpts from the Judgment Records of Frederick County, Maryland, 1748-1765*, by Millard Milburn Rice, pp. 43-44)

Macrombie, John, appointed a Commissioner of the Peace for Charles County, 22 Oct 1739. (Ref: Maryland State Archives, Governor and Council Commissioner Records, 1726-1794, p. 66)

MacWilliams, William, appointed Commissioner of the Peace for St. Mary's County, 26 May 1755. (Ref: Maryland State Archives, Governor and Council Commissioner Records, 1726-1794, p. 159)

Maddox, John, appointed a Warehouse Inspector in Somerset County on 3 Sep 1750. (*Calendar of Maryland State Papers, No. 1 The Black Books*, p. 96)

Magowan, Walter (1736-1786), reverend, was inducted into St. James' Parish, Anne Arundel County, on 21 Jun 1769. (Ref: Maryland Commission Book No. 82, p. 225; *Maryland Historical Magazine*, Vol. XXVI, p. 359)

Magruder, Alexander, appointed Commissioner of the Peace for Prince George's County, 29 Oct 1730. (Ref: Maryland State Archives, Governor and Council Commissioner Records, 1726-1794, p. 12)

Magruder, Alexander, Jr., was appointed a Commissioner of the Peace for Prince George's County, 26 Jul 1773. (Ref: Maryland State Archives, Governor and Council Commissioner Records, 1726-1794, p. 272)

Magruder, Alexander Howard (1745-1782), was appointed a Commissioner of the Peace for Prince George's County, 29 Jul 1773. (Ref: Maryland State Archives, Governor and Council Commissioner Records, 1726-1794, p. 272)

Magruder, Jeremiah (1731-1798), appointed a Commissioner of the Peace for Prince George's County, 29 Jul 1773. (Ref: Maryland State Archives, Governor and Council Commissioner Records, 1726-1794, p. 272)

Magruder, John (1694-1750), was appointed a Commissioner of the Peace for Prince George's County, 3 Mar 1726/7. (Ref: Maryland State Archives, Governor and Council Commissioner Records, 1726-1794, p. 3)

Magruder, John, appointed a Commissioner of the Peace for Prince George's County, 15 Mar 1769. (Ref: Maryland State Archives, Governor and Council Commissioner Records, 1726-1794, p. 241)

Magruder, John Read, appointed Commissioner of the Peace for Prince George's County, 26 Jul 1773. (Ref: Maryland State Archives, Governor and Council Commissioner Records, 1726-1794, p. 272)

Magruder, Nathan (c1718-1786), was appointed a Commissioner of the Peace for Frederick County, 17 Nov 1749. (Ref: Maryland State Archives, Governor and Council Commissioner Records, 1726-1794, p. 115); Court Justice, Frederick County, 1751. (Ref: *This Was The Life: Excerpts from the Judgment Records of Frederick County, Maryland, 1748-1765*, by Millard Milburn Rice, p. 61); appointed a Commissioner of the Peace for Prince George's County, 22 Nov 1752. (Ref: Maryland State Archives, Governor and Council Commissioner Records, 1726-1794, p. 135)

Magruder, Nathaniel, of Alexander, appointed a Commissioner of the Peace for Frederick County, 6 Nov 1758. (Ref: Maryland State Archives, Governor and Council Commissioner Records, 1726-1794, p. 183)

Magruder, Ninian, Jr., appointed Constable of Potomac Hundred in Prince George's County, now Frederick County, 1739 and 1740. (Ref: Prince George's County Court Records, 1736-1748, Extracts by Patricia Abelard Andersen, *Western Maryland Genealogy*, Vol. 18, No. 1, January 2002, pp. 36, 37)

Magruder, Samuel, was Constable of Western Branch Hundred in Prince George's County, now Frederick County, 1733. (*Calendar of Maryland State Papers, No. 1 The Black Books*, p. 37, listed him once as Samuel Magruder and once as Samuel Magruder, Jr.); appointed Constable of the Lower Part of Kittoctin [Catoctin] Hundred in Frederick County, 1760. (Ref: *This Was The Life: Excerpts from the Judgment Records of Frederick County, Maryland, 1748-1765*, by Millard Milburn Rice, p. 216)

Magruder, Samuel III, Constable of Potowmack [Potomac] Hundred in Prince George's County, now Frederick County, in 1733. (*Calendar of Maryland State Papers, No. 1 The Black Books*, p. 42)

Magruder, Zadock (1730-1811), was appointed a Commissioner of the Peace for Frederick County, 12 Mar 1763. (Ref: Maryland State Archives, Governor and Council Commissioner Records, 1726-1794, p. 209)

Mail, John, convicted felon for the destruction of tobacco [county not stated], was pardoned on 22 Nov 1735. (Ref: Maryland Commission Book No. 82, p.

40; *Maryland Historical Magazine*, Vol. XXVI, p. 146)

Malcolm, Alexander, see Samuel Keene.

Mansfield, Richard, labourer, late of Baltimore County, convicted felon for stealing the horse of Richard Rogers, was pardoned on 29 Apr 1768 because he had only taken the horse to get home to his sick wife who had just delivered a child without assistance. (Ref: Maryland Commission Book No. 82, p. 213; *Maryland Historical Magazine*, Vol. XXVI, p. 357; *Archives of Maryland*, Vol. XXXII, "Proceedings of the Council of Maryland, 1761-1770," p. 221)

Marbury, Francis, appointed a Commissioner of the Peace for Prince George's County, 3 Mar 1726/7. (Ref: Maryland State Archives, Governor and Council Commissioner Records, 1726-1794, p. 3, misspelled his name Marlberry)

Marbury, Luke (1710-1758), was appointed a Commissioner of the Peace for Prince George's County, 22 Mar 1742/3, 21 Nov 1743 and 1 Jun 1750. (Ref: Maryland State Archives, Governor and Council Commissioner Records, 1726-1794, pp. 77, 83, 118)

Marbury, Luke (c1745-1809), was appointed a Commissioner of the Peace for Prince George's County, 26 Jul 1773. (Ref: Maryland State Archives, Governor and Council Commissioner Records, 1726-1794, p. 272)

Marbury, William, was appointed a Press Master in Prince George's County, now Frederick County, 1748. (Ref: Prince George's County Court Records, 1736-1738, Extracts by Patricia Abelard Andersen, *Western Maryland Genealogy*, Vol. 18, No. 1, January 2002, p. 46)

Mariarte, Daniel (c1676-1727), of Anne Arundel County, sheriff, 1726. (Ref: *Abstracts of the Testamentary Proceedings and Prerogative Court of Maryland, Vol. XVII, 1724-1727*, by Vernon L. Skinner, Jr., p. 16, citing original Liber 27, f. 311)

Mariarte, Ninian (1701-1748/9), commissioned a Ranger of Prince George's County, 16 Mar 1736/7. (Ref: Maryland Commission Book No. 82, p. 47; *Maryland Historical Magazine*, Vol. XXVI, p. 148)

Markland, Matthew, was appointed Constable of New Scotland Hundred in Prince George's County, now Frederick County, 1738. (Ref: Prince George's County Court Records, 1736-1748, Extracts by Patricia Abelard Andersen, *Western Maryland Genealogy*, Vol. 18, No. 1, January 2002, p. 35)

Marr, John, alias Thomas Soper, laborer, late of Anne Arundel County, pardoned and banished for horse stealing, 19 Oct 1773. (Ref: Maryland Commission Book No. 82, p. 327; *Maryland Historical Magazine*, Vol. XXVII, p. 35)

Marriott, Silvanus, of Anne Arundel County, was appointed Constable of Severn Hundred in 1774. (Ref: Anne Arundel County Court Minutes, 1725-1757, 1774)

Marsden, Thomas, of Liverpool, registration of sloop *Martha*, 35 tons, built in Somerset County, 1737. Thomas Marsden, master and owner. 8 Sep 1740. (Ref: Maryland Commission Book No. 82, p. 83; *Maryland Historical Magazine*, Vol. XXVI, p. 157)

Marsh, Thomas, appointed a Commissioner of the Peace for Kent County, 2 Nov 1762. (Ref: Maryland State Archives, Governor and Council Commissioner Records, 1726-1794, p. 207)

Marsh, Thomas, appointed a Commissioner of the Peace for Queen Anne's County, 18 May 1758. (Ref: Maryland State Archives, Governor and Council Commissioner Records, 1726-1794, p. 180); of Queen Anne's County, registration of schooner *Swallow*, 30 tons, built at Wye River, 1734. Thomas Marsh, master. William Hemsley and Thomas Marsh, owners. 1 Oct 1734 (Ref: Maryland Commission Book No. 82, p. 21; *Maryland Historical Magazine*, Vol. XXVI, p. 142); see George Robins.

Marshall, Thomas, appointed a Commissioner of the Peace for Prince George's County, 15 Jun 1739. (Ref: Maryland State Archives, Governor and Council Commissioner Records, 1726-1794, p. 64)

Marshall, Thomas Hanson (1731-1801), was appointed a Commissioner of the Peace for Prince George's County, 17 Nov 1764. (Ref: Maryland State Archives, Governor and Council Commissioner Records, 1726-1794, p. 220)

Martin, Edmond, appointed Constable of Linton Hundred in Frederick County in 1749. (Ref: *This Was The Life: Excerpts from the Judgment Records of Frederick County, Maryland, 1748-1765*, by Millard Milburn Rice, p. 7)

Martin, George, Jr., commissioned High Sheriff of Worcester County, 8 Oct 1761. (Ref: Maryland State

Archives, Governor and Council Commissioner Records, 1726-1794, p. 190)

Martin, James (d. 1747/48), was commissioned Sheriff of Worcester County, 11 Dec 1742. (Ref: Maryland State Archives, Governor and Council Commissioner Records, 1726-1794, p. 75)

Martin, John, appointed Constable of Manor Hundred in Frederick County in 1749. (Ref: *This Was The Life: Excerpts from the Judgment Records of Frederick County, Maryland, 1748-1765*, by Millard Milburn Rice, p. 6); see Nathaniel Whitaker.

Martin, Robert, see Negro David.

Martin, Stephen, see William Dames.

Martin, William, the Elder, was appointed a Commissioner of the Peace for Talbot County, 8 Aug 1769. (Ref: Maryland State Archives, Governor and Council Commissioner Records, 1726-1794, p. 245)

Martyn, Richard, see Patrick Creagh and William Govane.

Martyn, Samuel, see Richard Bennett.

Mason, John, of Baltimore County, convicted felon, was executed on 26 May 1738. (Ref: Maryland State Archives, Governor and Council Commissioner Records, 1726-1794, p. 60)

Mason, Lawrence, see Joseph Ennals.

Mason, Richard (d. 1781), was appointed a Commissioner of the Peace for Queen Anne's County, 31 Oct 1768, and a Commissioner of the Peace for Caroline County, 8 Feb 1774. (Ref: Maryland State Archives, Governor and Council Commissioner Records, 1726-1794, pp. 239, 280)

Massey, Samuel, merchant, of Kent County, registration of the sloop *Ann*, 40 tons, built at Wiccocomoco in Somerset County, 1737. John Garrett, master. Samuel Massey, owner. 30 Sep 1745. (Ref: Maryland Commission Book No. 82, p. 117; *Maryland Historical Magazine*, Vol. XXVI, p. 255); merchant, registration of schooner *Charming Polly*, 30 tons, built in Kent County, 1747. John Birstall, master. Samuel Massey, Evan Watkins and Theophilus Randall, owners. 11 Aug 1747. (Ref: Maryland Commission Book No. 82, p. 131; *Maryland Historical Magazine*, Vol. XXVI, p. 261); see William Dames.

Masters, Nathan, appointed Constable from the mouth of Seneca to the mouth of Monocacy in Prince George's County, now Frederick County, 1738. (Ref: Prince George's County Court Records, 1736-1748, Extracts by Patricia Abelard Andersen, *Western Maryland Genealogy*, Vol. 18, No. 1, January 2002, p. 35)

Matthews (Mathews), Chidley, was appointed Constable of part of Eastern Branch Hundred in Prince George's County, now Frederick County, 1736. (Ref: Prince George's County Court Records, 1736-1748, Extracts by Patricia Abelard Andersen, *Western Maryland Genealogy*, Vol. 18, No. 1, January 2002, p. 35)

Matthews (Mathews), Jacob, planter, of Prince George's County, native of Germany, naturalized 4 Jun 1740, and his children George, Margarett, Maudlin and Catherine. (Ref: Maryland Commission Book No. 82, p. 81; *Maryland Historical Magazine*, Vol. XXVI, p. 157)

Matthews (Mathews), John (1714-1783), was appointed a Commissioner of the Peace for Baltimore County, 9 Feb 1748/9, and appointed a Commissioner of the Peace for Harford County, 20 Feb 1774. (Ref: Maryland State Archives, Governor and Council Commissioner Records, 1726-1794, pp. 110, 281)

Matthews (Mathews), Roger (c1685-1740), was appointed a Commissioner of the Peace for Baltimore County, 3 Mar 1726/7 and 22 Oct 1728. (Ref: Maryland State Archives, Governor and Council Commissioner Records, 1726-1794, pp. 2, 8)

Mattingley, Edward, registration of the sloop *Pembroke*, 30 tons, built at Pembroke in New England, 1735. Edward Mattingley, master. Edward Neal, Raphael Faulkner and Edward Mattingley, owners. 25 Jun 1739. (Ref: Maryland Commission Book No. 82, p. 75; *Maryland Historical Magazine*, Vol. XXVI, p. 154); see Patrick Creagh.

Mauduit, William, commissioned High Sheriff of Prince George's County, 18 Nov 1746. (Ref: Maryland State Archives, Governor and Council Commissioner Records, 1726-1794, p. 95); late sheriff of Prince George's County, had ordinary license accounts still unpaid in 1756. (Ref: *Archives of Maryland*, Vol. LII, "Proceedings and Acts of the General Assembly of Maryland, 1755-1756," p. 568, misspelled his name as Manduit); see Michael Taylor.

Mauldin, Francis (d. 1734/35), was appointed a

Commissioner of the Peace for Cecil County, 3 Mar 1726/27. (Ref: Maryland State Archives, Governor and Council Commissioner Records, 1726-1794, p. 2)

Maulester, John, appointed a Commissioner of the Peace for Somerset County, 29 Oct 1730. (Ref: Maryland State Archives, Governor and Council Commissioner Record, 1726-1794, p. 17)

Maxwell, George, appointed a Commissioner of the Peace for Charles County, 8 Jun 1751. (Ref: Maryland State Archives, Governor and Council Commissioner Records, 1726-1794, p. 123)

Maxwell, James, appointed a Commissioner of the Peace for Baltimore County, 3 Mar 1726/7. (Ref: Maryland State Archives, Governor and Council Commissioner Records, 1726-1794, p. 2)

Maxwell, John, appointed a Commissioner of the Peace for Cecil County, 2 Jun 1774. (Ref: Maryland State Archives, Governor and Council Commissioner Records, 1726-1794, p. 283)

Maxwell, John (1726-c1778), was appointed a Commissioner of the Peace for Kent County, 16 Jun 1764. (Ref: Maryland State Archives, Governor and Council Commissioner Records, 1726-1794, p. 217)

Maxwell, Robert (1736-1787), commissioned a Coroner of Kent County, 16 Aug 1773. (Ref: Maryland Commission Book No. 82, p. 323; *Maryland Historical Magazine*, Vol. XXVII, p. 35)

Mayberry, Beriah, see Thomas Dicke.

Maynadier, Daniel, reverend, was inducted into Great Choptank Parish, Dorchester County, 29 Oct 1765. (Ref: Maryland Commission Book No. 82, p. 175; *Maryland Historical Magazine*, Vol. XXVI, p. 353); *Directory of Ministers and the Maryland Churches They Served, 1634-1900*, by Edna Agatha Kanely, Vol. II, L-Z, p. 57, styled him as Jr. and stated he died in 1772 or 1773)

Maynard, James, of Anne Arundel County, appointed a Constable in Annapolis in 1774. (Ref: Anne Arundel County Court Minutes, 1725-1757, 1774)

Maynard, Thomas, appointed Constable of Linganore Hundred in Frederick County in 1749. (Ref: *This Was The Life: Excerpts from the Judgment Records of Frederick County, Maryland, 1748-1765*, by Millard Milburn Rice, p. 6)

Mayo, Thomas, was commissioned a Coroner of Anne Arundel County, 7 Aug 1773. (Ref: Maryland Commission Book No. 82, p. 321; *Maryland Historical Magazine*, Vol. XXVII, p. 35)

McCall, James, appointed Constable of the Lower Part of Monochosey [Monocacy] Hundred in Frederick County, 1771. (Ref: "Frederick County Minute Book, March 1771, Extracts by Patricia Abelard Andersen," *Western Maryland Genealogy*, Vol. 18, No. 1, January 2002, p. 25)

McCallum, Neil, reverend, resigned from Dorset Parish, Dorchester County, 30 May 1772. (Ref: Maryland Commission Book No. 82, p. 280; *Maryland Historical Magazine*, Vol. XXVII, p. 31); see Neil or Nevil Maccullum.

McCleland, George, appointed a Commissioner of the Peace for Prince George's County, 25 Nov 1751. (Ref: Maryland State Archives, Governor and Council Commissioner Records, 1726-1794, p. 129)

McClellan, David, was commissioned the Culler, Garbler, and Counter of Staves and Shingles in Baltimore Town, 13 Sep 1768. (Ref: Maryland Commission Book No. 82, p. 216; *Maryland Historical Magazine*, Vol. XXVI, p. 358)

McClemmy, William, was appointed a Warehouse Inspector in Somerset County on 3 Sep 1750. (*Calendar of Maryland State Papers, No. 1 The Black Books*, p. 96)

McClester, George, see Edward Rumney.

McCoy, Morris, of Anne Arundel County, was convicted of murder, executed on 23 Jan 1771 and "afterwards to hang his body in chains on some eminence near the place where the murder for which he was condemned was perpetrated within sight of the road to Baltimore." (Ref: Maryland State Archives, Governor and Council Commissioner Records, 1726-1794, p. 244)

McCoy (Mecoy), William, of Baltimore County, was appointed a Ranger, 9 Aug 1775. (Ref: *Calendar of Maryland State Papers, The Red Books*, No. 4, Part 1, p. 5)

McCullock, David, was commissioned Sheriff of Baltimore County, 3 Sep 1757. (Ref: Maryland State Archives, Governor and Council Commissioner Records, 1726-1794, p. 167)

McDermot, John, see Negro Caroline.

MacDonald, Enoch, and wife Rebecca, of Baltimore County, convicted felons for severely beating to death Charity Stroble on 7 Oct 1774, were sentenced to be hanged, but a pardon was granted because they never intended to kill the child and they were recommended as fit objects of mercy by the justices and foreman of the jury. (Ref: *Inhabitants of Baltimore County, 1763-1774*, by Henry C. Peden, Jr., 1989, p. 49, citing Baltimore County Court Proceedings, 1774)

McGaughley, William, was appointed Constable of Linton Hundred in Frederick County, 1771. (Ref: "Frederick County Minute Book, March 1771, Extracts by Patricia Abelard Andersen," *Western Maryland Genealogy*, Vol. 18, No. 1, January 2002, p. 26)

McKennie, Donald, see David alias Daniel Sulivane.

McKinley, John, appointed Constable of Piney Creek Hundred in Frederick County in 1763. (Ref: *This Was The Life: Excerpts from the Judgment Records of Frederick County, Maryland, 1748-1765*, by Millard Milburn Rice, p. 249)

McLachlan, James, appointed a Commissioner of the Peace for Kent County, 11 Nov 1763. (Ref: Maryland State Archives, Governor and Council Commissioner Records, 1726-1794, p. 212)

McMechan, Alexander, see Thomas Robinson.

McMullen, Thomas, of Frederick Co., convicted felon for stealing a rifle in 1763, was sentenced to be set on the pillory for fifteen minutes and then get fifteen lashes. (Ref: *This Was The Life: Excerpts from the Judgment Records of Frederick County, Maryland, 1748-1765*, by Millard Milburn Rice, p. 246)

McPherson, Alexander (1738-1805), of Charles County, was commissioned a Coroner on 7 Aug 1773. (Ref: Maryland Commission Book No. 82, p. 321; *Maryland Historical Magazine*, Vol. XXVII, p. 35)

McPherson, Thomas, commissioned Deputy Surveyor of Charles County, 2 Sep 1772 and 20 Jul 1773. (Ref: Maryland Commission Book No. 82, p. 322; *Maryland Historical Magazine*, Vol. XXVII, pp. 32, 35)

Mead, Samuel, of Anne Arundel County, was appointed Constable of Lyons Creek Hundred in 1774. (Ref: Anne Arundel County Court Minutes, 1725-1757, 1774)

Meek, Francis, was commissioned one of the Coroners of Charles County, 12 Mar 1747/8. (Ref: Maryland Commission Book No. 82, p. 133; *Maryland Historical Magazine*, Vol. XXVI, p. 262)

Meek, Joshua, of Frederick County, magistrate, 1766. (Ref: *Archives of Maryland*, Vol. XXXII, "Proceedings of the Council of Maryland, 1761-1770," p. 166)

Mercier, Francis, laborer, late of Baltimore County, pardoned and banished for burglary (stealing surgical instruments from the house of Dr. John Boyd), 3 Dec 1773. (Ref: Maryland Commission Book No. 82, p. 329; *Maryland Historical Magazine*, Vol. XXVII, pp. 35-36)

Meredith, Rees, see William Loyall.

Merrikin, John, appointed a Commissioner of the Peace for Anne Arundel County, 1 Aug 1768. (Ref: Maryland State Archives, Governor and Council Commissioner Records, 1726-1794, p. 234)

Merriman, John, appointed a Commissioner of the Peace for Baltimore County, 23 May 1753. (Ref: Maryland State Archives, Governor and Council Commissioner Records, 1726-1794, p. 138)

Michael, Daniel, of Frederick County, convicted felon for stealing a cutting knife valued at forty pounds of tobacco in 1759 [but no sentence was recorded]. (Ref: *This Was The Life: Excerpts from the Judgment Records of Frederick County, Maryland, 1748-1765*, by Millard Milburn Rice, p. 201)

Middaugh, John, was appointed a Press Master for Frederick County in 1757. (Ref: *This Was The Life: Excerpts from the Judgment Records of Frederick County, Maryland, 1748-1765*, by Millard Milburn Rice, p. 176)

Middlemore, Josias, appointed a Commissioner of the Peace for Baltimore County, 22 Oct 1728. (Ref: Maryland State Archives, Governor and Council Commissioner Records, 1726-1794, p. 8)

Middleton, Horatio Samuel, see Ashbury Sutton.

Middleton, William (1686-1769), was appointed a Commissioner of the Peace for Charles County, 22 Oct 1739. (Ref: Maryland State Archives, Governor and Council Commissioner Records, 1726-1794, p. 66)

Milhouse, William, see Negro Hannah.

Mill, William, of Biddeford, registration of ship *Bohemia*, 95 tons, built in Cecil County, 1735.

William Mill, master and owner. 24 May 1735. (Ref: Maryland Commission Book No. 82, p. 230 *Maryland Historical Magazine*, Vol. XXVI, p. 143); mariner, of Biddeford, registration of ship *Revolution*, 90 tons, built at Bohemia [Cecil County], 1742. William Mill, master. George Strange, merchant, and William Mill, owners. 12 Jun 1742. (Ref: Maryland Commission Book No. 82, p. 92; *Maryland Historical Magazine*, Vol. XXVI, p. 246)

Millard, Joshua, see Mulatto James.

Millegan, George, commissioned High Sheriff of Cecil County, 4 Dec 1758. (Ref: Maryland State Archives, Governor and Council Commissioner Records, 1726-1794, p. 176)

Miller, Abraham, of Prince George's County, native of Germany, naturalized 3 May 1740, and also his children Jacob, Abraham, Isaac, Barbara and Louisa. (Ref: Maryland Commission Book No. 82, p. 81; *Maryland Historical Magazine*, Vol. XXVI, p. 156)

Miller, John, appointed a Commissioner of the Peace for Worcester County, 11 Dec 1742. (Ref: Maryland State Archives, Governor and Council Commissioner Records, 1726-1794, p. 75)

Miller, John, chimney sweeper, of Frederick County, pardoned for burglary, 7 Jul 1772. (Ref: Maryland Commission Book No. 82, p. 281; *Maryland Historical Magazine*, Vol. XXVII, p. 31)

Miller, John, of Seaside, was appointed a Commissioner of the Peace for Somerset County, 6 Jun 1740. (Ref: Maryland State Archives, Governor and Council Commissioner Records, 1726-1794, p. 67)

Miller, Joseph, appointed a Commissioner of the Peace for Worcester County, 28 Oct 1747. (Ref: Maryland State Archives, Governor and Council Commissioner Records, 1726-1794, p. 102)

Miller, Michael, appointed Constable of the Upper Part of Andiatum [Antietam] Hundred in Frederick County in 1760. (Ref: *This Was The Life: Excerpts from the Judgment Records of Frederick County, Maryland, 1748-1765*, by Millard Milburn Rice, p. 216)

Miller, Thomas, commissioned High Sheriff of Harford County, 13 Jan 1774. (Ref: Maryland State Archives, Governor and Council Commissioner Records, 1726-1794, p. 269)

Miller, William, commissioned one of the Coroners of Calvert County, 23 Mar 1742/3 and 10 Apr 1747. (Ref: Maryland Commission Book No. 82, pp. 101, 128; *Maryland Historical Magazine*, Vol. XXVI, pp. 249, 260)

Miller, William, Jr., commissioned a Coroner for Calvert County in October 1739. (Ref: Maryland Commission Book No. 82, p. 77; *Maryland Historical Magazine*, Vol. XXVI, p. 155)

Milligan, George, appointed a Commissioner of the Peace for Cecil County, 26 May 1756 and 20 Feb 1774. (Ref: Maryland State Archives, Governor and Council Commissioner Records, 1726-1794, pp. 167, 281); see George Millegan.

Millikin, Hugh, see John Pagan.

Mills, James (d. 1764), appointed a Commissioner of the Peace for St. Mary's County, 1 Aug 1746 and 28 Oct 1747. (Ref: Maryland State Archives, Governor and Council Commissioner Records, 1726-1794, pp. 93, 102)

Mills, James, Jr., commissioned a Coroner of St. Mary's County, 18 Jan 1765. (Ref: Maryland Commission Book No. 82, p. 167; *Maryland Historical Magazine*, Vol. XXVI, p. 353)

Mills, John, registration of sloop *Bohemia Batchelor*, 18 tons, built in Dorchester County, 1745. John Mills, master and co-owner with James MacLachlan. (Ref: Maryland Commission Book No. 82, p. 122; *Maryland Historical Magazine*, Vol. XXVI, p. 257)

Mills, Levi, was appointed Constable of Fort Frederick Hundred in Frederick County, 1771. (Ref: "Frederick County Minute Book, March 1771, Extracts by Patricia Abelard Andersen," *Western Maryland Genealogy*, Vol. 18, No. 1, January 2002, p. 26)

Minskie, Emmanuel, of Anne Arundel County, was pardoned for robbery and burglary, September 1748. (Ref: Maryland Commission Book No. 82, p. 135; *Maryland Historical Magazine*, Vol. XXVI, p. 263)

Minspaker, Henry, Constable of Westminster Hundred in Baltimore County, 1773. (Ref: *Inhabitants of Baltimore County, 1763-1774*, by Henry C. Peden, Jr., 1989, p. 83, citing a 1773 List of Taxables)

Mitchell, Edward, appointed a Commissioner of the Peace for Cecil County, 22 May 1762 and 20 Feb 1774. (Ref: Maryland State Archives, Governor and

Council Commissioner Records, 1726-1794, pp. 203, 281); commissioned High Sheriff of Cecil County, 6 Oct 1766. (Ref: Maryland State Archives, Governor and Council Commissioner Records, 1726-1794, p. 217); see Jacob Giles and John Seegar.

Mitchell, Joseph, appointed a Commissioner of the Peace for Worcester County, 26 Jul 1754. (Ref: Maryland State Archives, Governor and Council Commissioner Records, 1726-1794, p. 156)

Mitchell, Joshua, appointed a Commissioner of the Peace for Worcester County, 2 Mar 1754. (Ref: Maryland State Archives, Governor and Council Commissioner Records, 1726-1794, p. 142); Court Justice, Worcester County, 1774. (*Calendar of Maryland State Papers, No. 1 The Black Books*, p. 214); appointed a Commissioner of the Peace for Somerset County, 5 Jan 1775. (Ref: Maryland State Archives, Governor and Council Commissioner Records, 1726-1794, p. 286)

Mitchell, Michael, alias Michael Heweitt, labourer, of Anne Arundel County, convicted murderer of Mary or Margaret Cumberford, was pardoned on 20 Dec 1769 and banished from the province immediately upon his release from prison, never to return again. (Ref: Maryland Commission Book No. 82, p. 234, and *Maryland Historical Magazine*, Vol. XXVI, p. 360, called her Margaret, but *Archives of Maryland*, Vol. XXXII, "Proceedings of the Council of Maryland, 1761-1770," pp. 332-333, called her Mary)

Mitchell, Stephen, see Robert Harvey.

Moale, John (c1731-1798), of Baltimore Town, appointed a Commissioner of the Peace, 20 Nov 1769 and 30 May 1774. (Ref: Maryland State Archives, Governor and Council Commissioner Records, 1726-1794, pp. 248, 283); appointed a Justice, 22 Feb 1773. (Ref: *Inhabitants of Baltimore County, 1763-1774*, by Henry C. Peden, Jr., 1989, p. 49, citing *Calendar of Maryland State Papers, No. 1 The Black Books*, p. 208); appointed to represent Baltimore County in the Provincial Convention, 1775. (Ref: *Calendar of Maryland State Papers, The Red Books*, No. 4, Part 1, p. 3)

Mockbee, Roger, of Frederick County, convicted felon for house breaking, was executed on 1 Feb 1771. (Ref: Maryland State Archives, Governor and Council Commissioner Records, 1726-1794, p. 245)

Moffet, Thomas, of Baltimore County, was appointed a Ranger, 9 Aug 1775. (Ref: *Calendar of Maryland State Papers, The Red Books*, No. 4, Part 1, p. 5)

Moloany, Michael, of Baltimore County, was appointed a Ranger, 9 Aug 1775. (Ref: *Calendar of Maryland State Papers, The Red Books*, No. 4, Part 1, p. 5)

Money, Francis, appointed a Commissioner of the Peace for Dorchester County, 29 May 1734. (Ref: Maryland State Archives, Governor and Council Commissioner Records, 1726-1794, p. 42)

Mongall, Morris, labourer, of Baltimore County, convicted felon "for breaking and entering the store house of a certain Richard Hayton (the said store house not being contiguous to or used with any mansion house) and stealing and taking thereout, and carrying away sundry goods and chattels, the property of the said Richard Hayton to above the value of five shillings current money," was executed on Wednesday seven night next" [30 Oct 1758]. (Ref: Maryland State Archives, Governor and Council Commissioner Records, 1726-1794, p. 168; *Archives of Maryland*, Vol. XXXI, "Proceedings of the Council of Maryland, 1753-1761," pp. 296-297)

Montgomerie (Montgomery), John, reverend, licensed to preach in Worcester Parish, Worcester County, vacant by the removal of Rev. Samuel Sloan. 26 Nov 1770; induction into Worcester Parish, Worcester County, 13 Apr 1771; induction into St. Anne's Parish, Anne Arundel County, 11 Nov 1771. (Ref: Maryland Commission Book No. 82, pp. 251, 257, 273; *Maryland Historical Magazine*, Vol. XXVII, pp. 29, 30, 31, spelled his name Montgomerie, but; *Directory of Ministers and the Maryland Churches They Served, 1634-1900*, by Edna Agatha Kanely, Vol. II, L-Z, p. 98, spelled his name Montgomery)

Montgomery, Walter, see James Russell.

Moody, Benjamin, appointed a Commissioner of the Peace for Cecil County, 4 Jan 1757 and 22 Apr 1758. (Ref: Maryland State Archives, Governor and Council Commissioner Records, 1726-1794, pp. 173, 180)

Moody, Sarah, see William Husbands.

Moor, Thomas, appointed a Commissioner of the Peace for Somerset County, 8 Jun 1763. (Ref: Maryland State Archives, Governor and Council Commissioner Records, 1726-1794, p. 210)

Moor, William, appointed Constable of Cumber-land

Hundred in Frederick County, 1771. (Ref: "Frederick County Minute Book, March 1771, Extracts by Patricia Abelard Andersen," *Western Maryland Genealogy*, Vol. 18, No. 1, January 2002, p. 26)

Moore, George, reverend, induction into Christ Church Parish, Queen Anne's County, 16 Feb 1739/40. (Ref: Maryland Commission Book No. 82, p. 78; *Maryland Historical Magazine*, Vol. XXVI, p. 155)

Moore, George, was appointed Constable of Conococheague Hundred in Prince George's County, now Frederick County, 1748. (Ref: Prince George's County Court Records, 1736-1738, Extracts by Patricia Abelard Andersen, *Western Maryland Genealogy*, Vol. 18, No. 1, January 2002, p. 46)

Moore, George, Sr., appointed Constable of Monocacy Hundred from Shanandore Mtn [Shenandoah Mountains] upwards in Prince George's County, now Frederick County, 1738. (Ref: Prince George's County Court Records, 1736-1748, Extracts by Patricia Abelard Andersen, *Western Maryland Genealogy*, Vol. 18, No. 1, January 2002, p. 35)

Moore, Sm (sic), appointed Constable of Cumberland Hundred in Frederick County, 1769. (Ref: "Frederick County Court Minutes November 1769 by Patricia Abelard Andersen," *Western Maryland Genealogy*, Vol. 16, No. 1, January 2000, p. 33)

Morell, William, reverend, induction into William and Mary Parish Parish, Charles County, 25 Nov 1734. (Ref: Maryland Commission Book No. 82, p. 23; *Maryland Historical Magazine*, Vol. XXVI, p. 142)

Morgan, Henry, late sheriff of Baltimore County, had ordinary license accounts still unpaid in 1756. (Ref: *Archives of Maryland*, Vol. LII, "Proceedings and Acts of the General Assembly of Maryland, 1755-1756," p. 568)

Morgan, Job, of Kent County, convicted burglar, executed on 5 Mar 1740/41. (Ref: Maryland State Archives, Governor and Council Commissioner Records, 1726-1794, p. 69)

Morningstar, John, planter, of Baltimore County, native of High Germany, naturalized 4 Jun 1738 and also his children Philip, Elizabeth and Joanna. (Ref: Maryland Commission Book No. 82, p. 57; *Maryland Historical Magazine*, Vol. XXVI, p. 151)

Morris, Isaac (Quaker), of Somerset County, registration of sloop *John Williams*, 40 tons, built in Maryland, 1734. Isaac Morris, master. Isaac Morris, Luke Morris and Edmund Hough, owners. 1 Mar 1734/5. (Ref: Maryland Commission Book No. 82, p. 26; *Maryland Historical Magazine*, Vol. XXVI, p. 143); merchant, registration of sloop *Eagle*, 20 tons, built in Somerset County, 1743. Hampton Hopkins, master. Isaac Morris, owner. 30 Oct 1743. (Ref: Maryland Commission Book No. 82, p. 105; *Maryland Historical Magazine*, Vol. XXVI, p. 250); see John Henry and Robert Jenckins Henry.

Morris, Luke, see Isaac Morris.

Morris, Randolph, gentleman, commissioned Sheriff of Charles County, 4 Jun 1729. (Ref: Maryland State Archives, Governor and Council Commissioner Records, 1726-1794, p. 10)

Morris, Robert, see Anthony Bacon and James Dickinson.

Morrison, Robert, see David Ross and John Pagan.

Morrow, David, doctor, appointed a Commissioner of the Peace for Cecil County, 3 Mar 1772. (Ref: Maryland State Archives, Governor and Council Commissioner Records, 1726-1794, p. 260)

Motley, John, registration of shallop *Henry and Mockey*, 10 tons, built in Prince George's County, 1736. John Motley, master and owner. 4 May 1736. (Ref: Maryland Commission Book No. 82, p. 43; *Maryland Historical Magazine*, Vol. XXVI, p. 147)

Mouat, James, appointed a Commissioner of the Peace for Anne Arundel County, 10 Sep 1736. (Ref: Maryland State Archives, Governor and Council Commissioner Records, 1726-1794, p. 53); Chief Justice, Anne Arundel County Court, 1754. (Ref: Anne Arundel County Court Minutes, 1725-1757)

Mounts, Joseph, appointed Constable of Cumberland Hundred in Frederick County in 1763. (Ref: *This Was The Life: Excerpts from the Judgment Records of Frederick County, Maryland, 1748-1765*, by Millard Milburn Rice, p. 249)

Muir, Adam, appointed a Commissioner of the Peace for Dorchester County, 17 Oct 1734. (Ref: Maryland State Archives, Governor and Council Commissioner Records, 1726-1794, p. 44); registration of brigantine *Sea Nymph*, 50 tons, built in Dorchester County, 1735. Lawrence Draper, master. 17 Jun 1735. (Ref: Maryland Commission Book No. 82, p. 31; *Maryland*

Historical Magazine, Vol. XXVI, p. 144); registration of sloop *Lucky Nancy*, 30 tons, built in Norfolk, Virginia, 1738. Levin Gale and Adam Muir, owners. 7 May 1741. (Ref: Maryland Commission Book No. 82, p. 86; *Maryland Historical Magazine*, Vol. XXVI, p. 244); registration of snow *St. Andrew*, formerly called *Port Glasgow*, 60 tons, built at Philadelphia, 1730, rebuilt in Maryland in 1741. Adam Muir, master and owner. 31 Aug 1741. (Ref: Maryland Commission Book No. 82, p. 88; *Maryland Historical Magazine*, Vol. XXVI, p. 245)

Muir, James, appointed a Commissioner of the Peace for Dorchester County, 8 Apr 1770. (Ref: Maryland State Archives, Governor and Council Commissioner Records, 1726-1794, p. 250); Court Justice, Dorchester County, 1774. (*Calendar of Maryland State Papers, No. 1 The Black Books*, p. 211)

Muir, Thomas, of Dorchester County, commissioned Receiver, Bailiff and Collector of Quit Rents for Dorchester County on 27 Nov 1735. On same day commissioned Supervisor of Nanticoke Manor. (Ref: Maryland Commission Book No. 82, p. 39; *Maryland Historical Magazine*, Vol. XXVI, p. 146)

Mulatto Charles, see Negro Charles.

Mulatto Dick, also called Yellow Dick, of Charles County, slave of William Dent, convicted felon for store breaking and stealing sundry goods, ordered to be hung on 24 May 1754, was pardoned on 28 May 1754 because he was very young and this was his first offense. (Ref: *Archives of Maryland*, Vol. XXXI, "Proceedings of the Council of Maryland, 1753-1761," pp. 32-33)

Mulatto Jack, slave of Philip Hammond, of Anne Arundel County, convicted felon and burglar, was executed on 13 Jul 1743. (Ref: Maryland State Archives, Governor and Council Commissioner Records, 1726-1794, p. 81); see Negro Jack.

Mulatto James, slave of Joshua Millard, of St. Mary's County, convicted of rape and murder of Mary Hambleton, sentenced to death on 24 Apr 1754 and his body "to be hung in chains on Friday the third day of May next upon the publick road as conveniently as conveniently can be to the place were the fact was committed." (Ref: *Archives of Maryland*, Vol. XXXI, "Proceedings of the Council of Maryland, 1753-1761," p. 31)

Mulatto Joe, slave of Edward Taylor, of Cecil County, convicted felon, ordered on 23 Jan 1750/1 that "his right hand cut off, to be hanged by the neck until he be dead, his head to be severed from his body, his body to be divided into four quarters, and his head and quarters to be set up at the most publick places in the said county," execution to be conducted on 1 Feb 1750/1. (Ref: Maryland State Archives, Governor and Council Commissioner Records, 1726-1794, p. 121)

Mulatto Roger, slave of James Weems, Jr., of Calvert County, convicted felon for breaking into the store house of said Weems and stealing sundry goods and chattels, was executed on 31 May 1761. (Ref: Maryland State Archives, Governor and Council Commissioner Records, 1726-1794, p. 184; *Archives of Maryland*, Vol. XXXII, "Proceedings of the Council of Maryland, 1761-1770," p. 15)

Mulatto Toney, slave of Patrick Creagh, of Anne Arundel County, convicted with John Wright of murdering Capt. William Curtis, ordered on 13 Jul 1754 to be executed "at the common gallows and afterwards hung in chains at Kings Point." (Ref: Maryland State Archives, Governor and Council Commissioner Records, 1726-1794, p. 143; *Archives of Maryland*, Vol. XXXI, "Proceedings of the Council of Maryland, 1753-1761," p. 46)

Mullin, Patrick Keen, labourer, late of Baltimore County, under sentence of death for stealing a horse, was pardoned and banished to Pensacola or some of the West India Islands on 5 Dec 1767. (Ref: Maryland Commission Book No. 82, p. 206; *Maryland Historical Magazine*, Vol. XXVI, p. 356; *Archives of Maryland*, Vol. XXXII, "Proceedings of the Council of Maryland, 1761-1770," pp. 212-214, also spelled his name Patrick Cane Mullen)

Munday, Henry, appointed a Commissioner of the Peace for Prince George's County, 12 Jun 1746. (Ref: Maryland State Archives, Governor and Council Commissioner Records, 1726-1794, p. 92); Court Justice, Frederick County, 1748. (Ref: *This Was The Life: Excerpts from the Judgment Records of Frederick County, Maryland, 1748-1765*, by Millard Milburn Rice, p. 1)

Murdock, George, see Alexander Williamson.

Murdock, William (c1710-1769), was appointed a Commissioner of the Peace for Prince George's County, 18 Feb 1731/2. (Ref: Maryland State Archives, Governor and Council Commissioner

Records, 1726-1794, p. 21); commissioned Sheriff of Prince George's County, 16 Aug 1737. (Ref: Maryland State Archives, Governor and Council Commissioner Records, 1726-1794, p. 57); served on the Maryland Council Committee of Grievance, 1755. (Ref: *Archives of Maryland*, Vol. LII, "Proceedings and Acts of the General Assembly of Maryland, 1755-1756," p. 82); appointed to a Committee for Enquiring into Ways and Means to Raise a Sum Sufficient for Payment of Eighty Rangers to Defend and Protect the Frontiers, 28 Jun 1755. (Ref: Maryland State Archives, Governor and Council Commissioner Records, 1726-1794, p. 151)

Murphey, Henry, of Charles County, convicted felon, was executed on 16 Nov 1737. (Ref: Maryland State Archives, Governor and Council Commissioner Records, 1726-1794, p. 58)

Murphy, John, of Frederick County, convicted felon, was executed on 15 Dec 1749. (Ref: Maryland State Archives, Governor and Council Commissioner Records, 1726-1794, p. 116)

Murray, Duncan, registration of schooner *Isaac and Murray*, 22 tons, built in Somerset County, 1735. Duncan Murray, master and owner. 11 Jun 1735. (Ref: Maryland Commission Book No. 82, p. 30; *Maryland Historical Magazine*, Vol. XXVI, p. 144); registration of sloop *Argyle*, formerly *The Dolphin*, 12 tons, built at Cohansie, Pennsylvania, 1738. Duncan Murray, master and owner. 29 Aug 1741. (Ref: Maryland Commission Book No. 82, p. 87; *Maryland Historical Magazine*, Vol. XXVI, p. 244); see John Dennis.

Murray, Duncan, Jr., registration of the sloop *George*, 10 tons, built in New Jersey, 1741. Thomas Robins, master. Duncan Murray and Duncan Murray, Sr., owners. 7 Mar 1746/7. (Ref: Maryland Commission Book No. 82, p. 125; *Maryland Historical Magazine*, Vol. XXVI, p. 259)

Murray, James (d. 1784), was appointed a Commissioner of the Peace for Dorchester County, 2 Nov 1773. (Ref: Maryland State Archives, Governor and Council Commissioner Records, 1726-1794, p. 278)

Murray, William, appointed a Commissioner of the Peace for Dorchester County, 29 May 1734 and 16 Oct 1750. (Ref: Maryland State Archives, Governor and Council Commissioner Records, 1726-1794, pp. 42, 119); commissioned Supervisor of His Lordship's Manor in Somerset County in October 1739. (Ref: Maryland Commission Book No. 82, p. 77; *Maryland Historical Magazine*, Vol. XXVI, p. 155); doctor, of Dorchester County, appointed to the Committee to Enquire into Indian Complaints, 1754. (Ref: *Archives of Maryland*, Vol. XXXI, "Proceedings of the Council of Maryland, 1753-1761," p. 30); see Edward Scott, Levin Gale and Negro Jack.

Neale, Edward, registration of schooner *Polly*, 50 tons, built at Pamunkie, 1736. Ignatius Simmes, master. Edward Neale, owner. 3 Aug 1736. (Ref: Maryland Commission Book No. 82, p. 45; *Maryland Historical Magazine*, Vol. XXVI, p. 147)

Neale, William, see Negro Robert Rustain.

Needham, John, appointed a Commissioner of the Peace for Frederick County, 17 Nov 1749. (Ref: Maryland State Archives, Governor and Council Commissioner Records, 1726-1794, p. 115); Court Justice, Frederick County, 1750. (Ref: *This Was The Life: Excerpts from the Judgment Records of Frederick County, Maryland, 1748-1765*, by Millard Milburn Rice, p. 47)

Needles, Edward, appointed a Commissioner of the Peace for Talbot County, 12 Jun 1739. (Ref: Maryland State Archives, Governor and Council Commissioner Records, 1726-1794, p. 64)

Negro Abigail, of Calvert County, convicted felon, along with Negro Samuel and Negro Rachel, attempted to poison Mrs. Smith, was pardoned on 14 Oct 1761. (Ref: *Archives of Maryland*, Vol. XXXII, "Proceedings of the Council of Maryland, 1761-1770," pp. 16-17)

Negro Abraham, slave of Henry Dorsey, of Anne Arundel County, convicted felon and burglar, was executed on 26 Mar 1740. (Ref: Maryland State Archives, Governor and Council Commissioner Records, 1726-1794, p. 67)

Negro Abraham, slave of William Elston, of Talbot of County, convicted felon for attempting to burn the kitchen of Thomas Hill, was pardoned on 15 Dec 1762. (Ref: *Archives of Maryland*, Vol. XXXII, "Proceedings of the Council of Maryland, 1761-1770," p. 47)

Negro Abraham, slave of Capt. Thomas Bond, of St. Mary's County, convicted felon for breaking open the house and bar of Elias Smith, tavern keeper, and stealing sundry bills of credit and pieces of money, and attempting to ravish and carnally know Miss Eleanor Bryan against her will, was sentenced to death on 29 Jun 1770. It was stated that Negro Abraham had been whipped by said Bond and then confessed, but Miss Bryan could not swear to his identity and said Smith essentially felt the same. He was therefore pardoned and ordered out of the province within ten days. (*Archives of Maryland*, Vol. XXXII, "Proceedings of the Council of Maryland, 1761-1770," pp. 368-370)

Negro Adam, slave of Capt. Robert Chesley, of St. Mary's County, convicted felon for consulting to murder his master and for consulting and attempting to his burn his store house, was executed on 8 Oct 1762. (Ref: Maryland State Archives, Governor and Council Commissioner Records, 1726-1794, p. 195; *Archives of Maryland*, Vol. XXXII, "Proceedings of the Council of Maryland, 1761-1770," p. 55)

Negro Anthony, slave of Edward Diggs, of Charles County, convicted of "conspiring [with Negro Jenny] and feloniously poisoning Jeremiah Chase, deceased, and afterwards to be hung in chains on a gibbet as near to the place where the fact was committed as conveniently can be," executed 4 Jul 1755. (Ref: Maryland State Archives, Governor and Council Commissioner Records, 1726-1794, p. 147; *Archives of Maryland*, Vol. XXXI, "Proceedings of the Council of Maryland, 1753-1761," p. 69)

Negro Babb, of Kent County, convicted felon, was executed on 17 Jun 1729. (Ref: Maryland State Archives, Governor and Council Commissioner Records, 1726-1794, p. 10)

Negro Ben, of Prince George's County, convicted felon, was executed on 10 Nov 1732. (Ref: Maryland State Archives, Governor and Council Commissioner Records, 1726-1794, p. 26)

Negro Ben, of St. Mary's County, convicted felon and burglar, was executed on 6 Dec 1751. (Ref: Maryland State Archives, Governor and Council Commissioner Records, 1726-1794, p. 130)

Negro Ben, slave of James Calder, of Baltimore County, convicted felon, was executed on 30 Apr 1773. (Ref: Maryland State Archives, Governor and Council Commissioner Records, 1726-1794, p. 256)

Negro Ben, slave of Elizabeth Oldham, of Talbot County, convicted of breaking open the store house of Col. Edward Lloyd and Henry Hollyday, and stealing one stock and stock buckle, was pardoned on 11 Dec 1761. (Ref: *Archives of Maryland*, Vol. XXXII, "Proceedings of the Council of Maryland, 1761-1770," p. 18)

Negro Ben, slave of Rachel Harrison, of Talbot County, convicted of assaulting with intent to ravish Eve Shanahan, was pardoned on 10 Apr 1769 because "the fellow before bore a good character, the attempt but small, and the evidence not so clear." (Ref: *Archives of Maryland*, Vol. XXXII, "Proceedings of the Council of Maryland, 1761-1770," pp. 270-271)

Negro Ben, slave of Richard Gardiner, convicted felon, was ordered on 26 Aug 1756 to be executed. (Ref: *Archives of Maryland*, Vol. XXXI, "Proceedings of the Council of Maryland, 1753-1761," p. 157)

Negro Ben, slave of Walter Bowie, of Prince George's County, convicted felon, was executed on 5 Oct 1772. (Ref: Maryland State Archives, Governor and Council Commissioner Records, 1726-1794, p. 251)

Negro Betty, slave of William Hamilton Smith, of Calvert County, convicted felon who attempted to poison William Hamilton Smith and his wife Barbara Smith, was executed on 20 Jun 1764. (Ref: Maryland State Archives, Governor and Council Commissioner Records, 1726-1794, p. 201; *Archives of Maryland*, Vol. XXXII, "Proceedings of the Council of Maryland, 1761-1770," pp. 91-92

Negro Bob, slave of William Hemersly, of St. Mary's County, convicted felon and burglar, was executed on 19 Sep 1755. (Ref: Maryland State Archives, Governor and Council Commissioner Records, 1726-1794, p. 148)

Negro Booze, slave of Denwood Hicks, of Dorchester County, convicted of house breaking, was pardoned on 30 Mar 1757. (Ref: *Archives of Maryland*, Vol. XXXI, "Proceedings of the Council of Maryland, 1753-1761," p. 182)

Negro Caleb, slave of William Lewis, of Baltimore County, convicted felon, "for advising a certain Negro Moll, slave of a certain Thomas Gist, to poison Susannah Gist the wife of him the said Thomas, was executed on 2 Sep 1757. (Ref: Maryland State Archives, Governor and Council Commissioner Records, 1726-1794, p. 161)

Negro Caroline, slave of John McDermot, of Cecil

County, convicted felon for burning several of her master's out houses, was executed on 22 Dec 1749 "by hanging in chains in Frederick Town on Sassafras River." (Ref: Maryland State Archives, Governor and Council Commissioner Records, 1726-1794, p. 116)

Negro Cato, of Talbot County, convicted of murder, ordered on 26 Jun 1745 "to be hanged, to have his head severed from his body, his body to be divided into four quarters, and the said head and quarters to be hung up in the most publick places in the said county." (Ref: Maryland State Archives, Governor and Council Commissioner Records, 1726-1794, p. 88)

Negro Cesar, of Anne Arundel County, convicted felon, was executed on 3 Jul 1754. (Ref: Maryland State Archives, Governor and Council Commissioner Records, 1726-1794, p. 142)

Negro Cesar, slave of Benjamin Rogers, of Baltimore County, convicted felon for setting fire to the barn of James Bosley, was executed on 27 Dec 1765. (Ref: Maryland State Archives, Governor and Council Commissioner Records, 1726-1794, p. 210; *Archives of Maryland*, Vol. XXXII, "Proceedings of the Council of Maryland, 1761-1770," pp. 114-115)

Negro Cesar, slave of Peregrine Frisby, of Baltimore County, convicted felon, was executed on 21 Dec 1739. (Ref: Maryland State Archives, Governor and Council Commissioner Records, 1726-1794, p. 66)

Negro Charles, otherwise called Young Charles Butler, slave of James Campbell, of Prince George's County, convicted felon "for taking and leading away one black mare of the price of five pounds, the goods and chattels of a certain William Elson," was ordered executed on 14 May 1756, but was pardoned on 5 May 1756. (Ref: Maryland State Archives, Governor and Council Commissioner Records, 1726-1794, p. 152; *Archives of Maryland*, Vol. XXXI, "Proceedings of the Council of Maryland, 1753-1761," p. 119, called him Mulatto Charles)

Negro Charles, slave of Margaret Brown, of Charles County, convicted felon, sentenced to death, but was pardoned in July 1763. (Ref: *Archives of Maryland*, Vol. XXXII, "Proceedings of the Council of Maryland, 1761-1770," p. 62)

Negro Charles, slave of Thomas Lancaster, of Prince George's County, convicted felon, with Negro James, for breaking open the meat house of Benjamin Harwood and stealing a large quantity of bacon, pardoned 27 Sep 1765. (Ref: *Archives of Maryland*, Vol. XXXII, "Proceedings of the Council of Maryland, 1761-1770," pp. 107-108)

Negro Charles, slave of James Calder, of Baltimore County, convicted felon, was executed on 30 Apr 1773. (Ref: Maryland State Archives, Governor and Council Commissioner Records, 1726-1794, p. 256)

Negro Charles, slave of Richard Hellen, of Calvert County, convicted felon, was executed on 20 Jun 1773. (Ref: Maryland State Archives, Governor and Council Commissioner Records, 1726-1794, p. 245)

Negro Cloe, of Anne Arundel County, convicted felon, was executed on 27 May 1737. (Ref: Maryland State Archives, Governor and Council Commissioner Records, 1726-1794, p. 55)

Negro Coroko(?), of Prince George's County, convicted felon, executed on 25 Nov 1730. (Ref: Maryland State Archives, Governor and Council Commissioner Records, 1726-1794, p. 13)

Negro Coffee, labourer, of Anne Arundel County, convicted felon, executed in August 1750. (Ref: Maryland State Archives, Governor and Council Commissioner Records, 1726-1794, p. 118)

Negro Coffee, slave of James Elder, of Anne Arundel County, convicted of murder, was executed on 5 May 1762. (Ref: Maryland State Archives, Governor and Council Commissioner Records, 1726-1794, p. 188; *Archives of Maryland*, Vol. XXXII, "Proceedings of the Council of Maryland, 1761-1770," p. 36)

Negro Coffee, slave of Henry Wright Crabb, of Frederick County, convicted felon for breaking and entering the meat house of said Crabb and stealing twenty-five pounds of bacon, sentenced to death, but was reprieved on 15 Dec 1762. (Ref: *Archives of Maryland*, Vol. XXXII, "Proceedings of the Council of Maryland, 1761-1770," p. 47)

Negro Cork, slave of Phillip Key, of St. Mary's County, convicted felon for conspiring with Negro Harry and attempting to poison John Key, was executed on 12 Nov 1755 at Choptico "and afterwards to be hung in chains at Budds Creek." (Ref: Maryland State Archives, Governor and Council Commissioner Records, 1726-1794, p. 149; *Archives of Maryland*, Vol. XXXI, "Proceedings of the Council of Maryland, 1753-1761," pp. 79-80)

Negro Corra, of Baltimore County, convicted of

murder, was executed on and hung in chains on 16 May 1729. (Ref: Maryland State Archives, Governor and Council Commissioner Records, 1726-1794, p. 9)

Negro Daniel, slave of James Adams, of Dorchester County, convicted burglar, was executed on 9 Sep 1768. (Ref: Maryland State Archives, Governor and Council Commissioner Records, 1726-1794, p. 224; *Archives of Maryland*, Vol. XXXII, "Proceedings of the Council of Maryland, 1761-1770," p. 247)

Negro Daniel, slave of Nicholas Gassaway, of Nicholas, of Anne Arundel County, convicted felon and burglar, was executed on 23 Jan 1771. (Ref: Maryland State Archives, Governor and Council Commissioner Records, 1726-1794, p. 244)

Negro Davey, slave of Stephen West, of Prince George's County, convicted with Negro Jack Crane and Negro Jack Wood, for murdering William Ellson, had their right hands cut off and then were executed on 4 Jul 1770. (Ref: Maryland State Archives, Governor and Council Commissioner Records, 1726-1794, p. 240; *Archives of Maryland*, Vol. XXXII, "Proceedings of the Council of Maryland, 1761-1770," pp. 370-371)

Nero David, see Negro Robin.

Negro David, slave of Juliana Simson, of Charles County, convicted felon, was executed on 19 Oct 1770. (Ref: Maryland State Archives, Governor and Council Commissioner Records, 1726-1794, p. 241)

Negro David, slave of Robert Martin, of Charles County, convicted felon for raping Sarah Smith, was executed on 9 Aug 1769. (*Archives of Maryland*, Vol. XXXII, "Proceedings of the Council of Maryland, 1761-1770," p. 266)

Negro Davy, see Andrew Windfield.

Negro Davy, slave of Joseph Halton, of Prince George's County, convicted felon, was executed on 14 Jul 1740. (Ref: Maryland State Archives, Governor and Council Commissioner Records, 1726-1794, p. 69)

Negro Davy, slave of William Hemsley, of Queen Anne's County, convicted of murder, was executed on 25 Jul 1764. (Ref: Maryland State Archives, Governor and Council Commissioner Records, 1726-1794, p. 202)

Negro Dick, slave of Charles Courts, of Charles County, convicted felon "for breaking and entering the out house of a certain George Keech and stealing therefrom thirty pounds of bacon, and it appearing to this Board that he had been a notorious offender and lately pardoned for an offence of the same kind, ordered [on 24 Jun 1755] that Death Warrant issue for his execution," which was done on 4 Jul 1755. (Ref: Maryland State Archives, Governor and Council Commissioner Records, 1726-1794, pp. 147-148; *Archives of Maryland*, Vol. XXXI, "Proceedings of the Council of Maryland, 1753-1761," p. 69)

Negro Dick, slave of William Russell, of Baltimore County, convicted felon for assaulting Mary Godson and stealing money and various articles from her on 8 Oct 1774, was sentenced to be hanged. (Ref: *Inhabitants of Baltimore County, 1763-1774*, by Henry C. Peden, Jr., 1989, p. 50, citing Baltimore County Court Proceedings, 1774)

Negro Eve, slave of James Lloyd Chamberlaine, of Talbot County, convicted felon, was executed on 15 Mar 1771. (Ref: Maryland State Archives, Governor and Council Commissioner Records, 1726-1794, p. 245)

Negro Frank, slave of Philip Hammond, of Anne Arundel County, convicted felon and burglar, was executed on 22 Jul 1743. (Ref: Maryland State Archives, Governor and Council Commissioner Records, 1726-1794, p. 81); see John Ireland.

Negro George, slave of Mrs. Deborah Nicols, of Talbot County, convicted felon for breaking and entering the store house of William Nicholls and stealing sundry goods and chattels, was sentenced to death on 15 Dec 1762. (Ref: *Archives of Maryland*, Vol. XXXII, "Proceedings of the Council of Maryland, 1761-1770," p. 47)

Negro George, slave of Henry Brent, of Charles County, convicted felon for robbing the house of William Beck in June 1766, broke out of jail in August 1766 and a reward was offered for his apprehension. He was executed on 24 Jul 1766. (Ref: *Archives of Maryland*, Vol. XXXII, "Proceedings of the Council of Maryland, 1761-1770," p. 159, and p. 163 called him Negro George Rustin)

Negro George, slave of Joseph Duvall, of Prince George's County, convicted felon for breaking open the meat house of William Waters, Jr. and stealing a quantity of bacon in March 1767, was pardoned in April 1767. (Ref: *Archives of Maryland*, Vol. XXXII,

"Proceedings of the Council of Maryland, 1761-1770," pp. 197-198)

Negro George, slave of Thomas Lingam, of Baltimore County, convicted with Negro Sam of breaking open and robbing the meat house of Jacob Davis, pardoned 10 Apr 1769. (Ref: *Archives of Maryland*, Vol. XXXII, "Proceedings of the Council of Maryland, 1761-1770," p. 271)

Negro George, slave of Thomas Wright, of Anne Arundel County, convicted felon for breaking into the house of Catharine Knowsley and stealing sundry goods and chattels, was pardoned on 20 Nov 1769. (*Archives of Maryland*, Vol. XXXII, "Proceedings of the Council of Maryland, 1761-1770," pp. 331-332)

Negro Glasgow, slave of Benjamin Keene, of Dorchester County, convicted felon for attempting to poison Negro Quomony, slave of William Ennals, was executed on 6 May 1767. (Ref: Maryland State Archives, Governor and Council Commissioner Records, 1726-1794, p. 220; *Archives of Maryland*, Vol. XXXII, "Proceedings of the Council of Maryland, 1761-1770," p. 188)

Negro Grace, slave of Joseph Galloway, of Anne Arundel County, convicted with Negro Jennye for burning their master's house, executed on 12 Apr 1751. (Ref: Maryland State Archives, Governor and Council Commissioner Records, 1726-1794, p. 121)

Negro Hannah, slave of Charles Clagget, of Calvert County, convicted felon for breaking open the house of William Hillhouse and stealing several goods and chattels owned by said Hillhouse and Mary Parran, but this being the first crime she has ever committed and promising to be honest and faithful for the future, was pardoned in December 1763. (Ref: *Archives of Maryland*, Vol. XXXII, "Proceedings of the Council of Maryland, 1761-1770," p. 90)

Negro Hannibal, of Charles County, convicted of rape, was executed on 26 Dec 1740. (Ref: Maryland State Archives, Governor and Council Commissioner Records, 1726-1794, p. 69)

Negro Harry, of Marlborough, Prince George's County, convicted felon, was executed on 1 Jul 1743. (Ref: Maryland State Archives, Governor and Council Commissioner Records, 1726-1794, p. 79)

Negro Harry, of Prince George's County, convicted felon, executed on 14 Nov 1733. (Ref: Maryland State Archives, Governor and Council Commissioner Records, 1726-1794, p. 39)

Negro Harry, slave of Phillip Key, the Younger, of St. Mary's County, convicted felon for attempting to poison John Key, was executed on 31 Oct 1755 at Choptico "and afterwards to be hung in chains." (Ref: Maryland State Archives, Governor and Council Commissioner Records, 1726-1794, p. 149; *Archives of Maryland*, Vol. XXXI, "Proceedings of the Council of Maryland, 1753-1761," pp. 79-80)

Negro Harry, of Anne Arundel County, convicted felon for burning Dorsey's barn in 1774 [sentence not stated]. (Ref: Anne Arundel County Court Minutes, 1725-1757, 1774)

Negro Jack, of ---- County, convicted felon, was executed on 7 Dec 1728. (Ref: Maryland State Archives, Governor and Council Commissioner Records, 1726-1794, p. 9)

Negro Jack, of Kent County, convicted felon for breaking into the store house of William Murray, was executed on 14 May 1756. (Ref: Maryland State Archives, Governor and Council Commissioner Records, 1726-1794, p. 153)

Negro Jack, of Marlborough, Prince George's County, convicted felon, was executed on 1 Jul 1743. (Ref: Maryland State Archives, Governor and Council Commissioner Records, 1726-1794, p. 79)

Negro Jack, slave, of St. Mary's County, convicted for making a false key and stealing goods from the store of Hugh Hopewell, was pardoned on 2 Aug 1766. (Ref: *Archives of Maryland*, Vol. XXXII, "Proceedings of the Council of Maryland, 1761-1770," pp. 157-158)

Negro Jack, slave of Constant Chapman, of Charles County, convicted of murdering William Garner, was executed on 30 Apr 1766. (Ref: Maryland State Archives, Governor and Council Commissioner Records, 1726-1794, p. 210; *Archives of Maryland*, Vol. XXXII, "Proceedings of the Council of Maryland, 1761-1770," pp. 126-127)

Negro Jack, slave of Francis Clements, of Charles County, convicted of "wickedly, feloniously and traitorously conspire and attempt to poison the said Clements, his master, to poison," executed 4 Jul 1755. (Ref: Maryland State Archives, Governor and Council Commissioner Records, 1726-1794, p. 147; *Archives of Maryland*, Vol. XXXI, "Proceedings of the Council of Maryland, 1753-1761," p. 69)

Negro Jack, slave of Joseph Nicholson, of Queen Anne's County, convicted felon for breaking into the store house of William Murray and taking a piece of corded dimothy, was executed on 14 May 1756. (Ref: *Archives of Maryland*, Vol. XXXI, "Proceedings of the Council of Maryland, 1753-1761," p. 199)

Negro Jack, slave of Leonard Hollyday, of Calvert County, convicted felon, was executed on 13 Dec 1749 by hanging in chains. (Ref: Maryland State Archives, Governor and Council Commissioner Records, 1726-1794, p. 116)

Negro Jack, slave of Panther Laws, of Somerset County, convicted "for feloniously, wickedly and attempting to raise an insurrection and to murder, kill and destroy sundry and many liege subjects of Our Lord the King that is now within the County of Somerset and Province of Maryland residing," executed 13 Jun 1753. (Ref: Maryland State Archives, Governor and Council Commissioner Records, 1726-1794, p. 136)

Negro Jack, slave of John Selby, of Prince George's County, convicted felon for poisoning Negro Clair, slave of Thomas Holliday, "ordered reprieve issue for the said Negro on condition of his not continuing in Prince George's County for the space of five days from the date of the reprieve which issued on the 8th day of January 1765 accordingly." (Ref: *Archives of Maryland*, Vol. XXXII, "Proceedings of the Council of Maryland, 1761-1770," p. 101)

Negro Jack, slave of Zachariah Offutt, of Frederick County, convicted felon for burglary and rape, was executed on 8 Sep 1769. (Ref: Maryland State Archives, Governor and Council Commissioner Records, 1726-1794, p. 234; *Archives of Maryland*, Vol. XXXII, "Proceedings of the Council of Maryland, 1761-1770," pp. 312-313, called him Mulatto Jack)

Negro Jack Crane, slave of Stephen West, of Prince George's County, convicted with Negro Davey and Negro Jack Wood of murdering William Ellson, had their right hands cut off and then executed on 4 Jul 1770. (Ref: Maryland State Archives, Governor and Council Commissioner Records, 1726-1794, p. 240; *Archives of Maryland*, Vol. XXXII, "Proceedings of the Council of Maryland, 1761-1770," pp. 370-371)

Negro Jack Wood, slave of Stephen West, of Prince George's County, convicted with Negro Davey and Negro Jack Crane of murdering William Ellson, had their right hands cut off and then were executed on 4 Jul 1770. (Ref: Maryland State Archives, Governor and Council Commissioner Records, 1726-1794, p. 240; *Archives of Maryland*, Vol. XXXII, "Proceedings of the Council of Maryland, 1761-1770," pp. 370-371)

Negro Jacob, slave of John Hawkins, of Baltimore County, convicted felon for breaking and entering the store house of Gilbert Crockett and stealing several goods, was executed on 18 May 1764. (Ref: *Archives of Maryland*, Vol. XXXII, "Proceedings of the Council of Maryland, 1761-1770," p. 91)

Negro Jacob, slave of Roger Boyce, of Baltimore County, convicted felon, was executed on 16 Oct 1771. (Ref: Maryland State Archives, Governor and Council Commissioner Records, 1726-1794, p. 247)

Negro Jago, of Anne Arundel County, convicted felon, was executed on 27 May 1737. (Ref: Maryland State Archives, Governor and Council Commissioner Records, 1726-1794, p. 55)

Negro James, slave of Dr. George Riddell, of Charles County, convicted felon, was executed on 6 Jun 1743. (Ref: Maryland State Archives, Governor and Council Commissioner Records, 1726-1794, p. 85)

Negro James, slave of Ledstone Smallwood, of Charles County, convicted felon and burglar, was executed on 15 Dec 1749. (Ref: Maryland State Archives, Governor and Council Commissioner Records, 1726-1794, p. 120)

Negro James, slave of Thomas Howell, of Dorchester County, convicted felon, was pardoned on 21 Apr 1762. (Ref: *Archives of Maryland*, Vol. XXXII, "Proceedings of the Council of Maryland, 1761-1770," p. 36)

Negro James, slave of Robert Tyler, of Prince George's County, convicted felon, with Negro Charles, for breaking open the meat house of Benjamin Harwood and stealing a large quantity of bacon, pardoned 27 Sep 1765. (Ref: *Archives of Maryland*, Vol. XXXII, "Proceedings of the Council of Maryland, 1761-1770," pp. 107-108)

Negro Jenny, slave of Betty Wilkinson, of Calvert County, convicted of murder, was executed on 17 Nov 1774. (Ref: Maryland State Archives, Governor and Council Commissioner Records, 1726-1794, p. 277)

Negro Jenny, slave of the late Jeremiah Chase, of

Charles County, convicted of "conspiring [with Negro Anthony] and feloniously poisoning the said Chase, her master, and afterwards to be hung in chains on a gibbet as near to the place where the fact was committed as conveniently can be," on 11 Jul 1755. (Ref: Maryland State Archives, Governor and Council Commissioner Records, 1726-1794, p. 147; *Archives of Maryland*, Vol. XXXI, "Proceedings of the Council of Maryland, 1753-1761," p. 69)

Negro Jennye, slave of Joseph Galloway, of Anne Arundel County, convicted with Negro Grace for burning their master's house, was executed on 12 Apr 1751. (Ref: Maryland State Archives, Governor and Council Commissioner Records, 1726-1794, p. 121)

Negro Job, see Negro Tom.

Negro Joe, of St. Mary's County, convicted felon and burglar for "breaking the store house of Mr. Eden and taken from thence several goods," case recorded 5 Jan 1756 and the "execution on Fryday seven night." (Ref: Maryland State Archives, Governor and Council Commissioner Records, 1726-1794, p. 151)

Negro Joe, slave of James Weems, of Anne Arundel County, convicted of murdering Richard Price, his overseer, ordered on 11 Mar 1755 that he be executed and "hung in chains as near the place where the fact was committed as conveniently can be." (Ref: Maryland State Archives, Governor and Council Commissioner Records, 1726-1794, p. 146, stated hung 27 Mar 1755; *Archives of Maryland*, Vol. XXXI, "Proceedings of the Council of Maryland, 1753-1761," p. 58, stated hung 19 Mar 1755)

Negro Joe, slave of Richard Marsh Warrin, of Calvert County, convicted felon who attempted to poison William Hamilton Smith and his wife Barbara, was executed on 20 Jun 1764. (Ref: Maryland State Archives, Governor and Council Commissioner Records, 1726-1794, p. 201; *Archives of Maryland*, Vol. XXXII, "Proceedings of the Council of Maryland, 1761-1770," pp. 91-92, misspelled his name Toe)

Negro Joe, slave of Sarah Perkins, of Talbot County, convicted felon and burglar, was executed on 20 Oct 1752. (Ref: Maryland State Archives, Governor and Council Commissioner Records, 1726-1794, p. 134)

Negro Jonathan, slave of Basil Smith, of Charles County, convicted felon for robbing the house of Smallwood Thompson, ordered in August 1762 to be reprieved for one month and set at liberty as long as he behaves well or he will be called to his former sentence. He was again a convicted felon, broke jail in August 1766 and a reward was offered for his apprehension. He was executed on 24 Aug 1766. (Ref: *Archives of Maryland*, Vol. XXXII, "Proceedings of the Council of Maryland, 1761-1770," pp. 41, 158-159, 163)

Negro Judith, slave of Edward Harris, of Queen Anne's County, convicted of the murder of said Edward Harris in December Court 1740, ordered that "her right hand to be cut off, then to be hanged, her head to be severed from her body, her body to be cut into four quarters, and the said head and quarters to be hanged up in the most publick places in Queen Anne's County, execution to be on 13th March instant" [1740/1]. (Ref: Maryland State Archives, Governor and Council Commissioner Records, 1726-1794, p. 69)

Negro Judy, slave of George Plater, esquire, of St. Mary's County, convicted felon, was executed on 30 Mar 1739. (Ref: Maryland State Archives, Governor and Council Commissioner Records, 1726-1794, p. 255)

Negro Jupiter, of ---- County, convicted felon, was executed on 7 Dec 1728. (Ref: Maryland State Archives, Governor and Council Commissioner Records, 1726-1794, p. 9)

Negro Jupiter, of St. Mary's County, convicted felon, was executed on 25 Jul 1738. (Ref: Maryland State Archives, Governor and Council Commissioner Records, 1726-1794, p. 64)

Negro Kildare, of Anne Arundel County, convicted felon, executed on 10 Nov 1736. (Ref: Maryland State Archives, Governor and Council Commissioner Records, 1726-1794, p. 54)

Negro Lem, slave of Ezekiel Gott [of Anne Arundel County], not quite eighteen years old, convicted for burglary of the house of Boardley Bowers, was pardoned on 26 Aug 1768. (*Archives of Maryland*, Vol. XXXII, "Proceedings of the Council of Maryland, 1761-1770," pp. 246-247)

Negro Lie, slave of James Conn, of Frederick County, convicted felon for stealing a meal bag and some flour in 1763, was sent to the whipping post and received thirty lashes on his bare back. (Ref: *This Was The Life: Excerpts from the Judgment Records of Frederick County, Maryland, 1748-1765*, by Millard Milburn

Rice, p. 246)

Negro London, of St. Mary's County, convicted felon, was executed on 27 Dec 1754. (Ref: Maryland State Archives, Governor and Council Commissioner Records, 1726-1794, p. 146)

Negro London, slave of James Weems, son of David, of Calvert County, convicted felon and burglar, was executed on 2 Sep 1757. (Ref: Maryland State Archives, Governor and Council Commissioner Records, 1726-1794, p. 161)

Negro man, slave of Prince George's County, name not given, convicted of an insurrection in March 1740, ordered to be executed on 4 Apr 1740 "and afterwards to be hung in chains." (Ref: Maryland State Archives, Governor and Council Commissioner Records, 1726-1794, p. 67)

Negro Mary, slave of James Plant, of Charles County, convicted felon and burglar, executed on 2 Jul 1742. (Ref: Maryland State Archives, Governor and Council Commissioner Records, 1726-1794, p. 73)

Negro Miall, slave of Thomas Blake, of Calvert County, convicted of rape, executed on 17 Nov 1774. (Ref: Maryland State Archives, Governor and Council Commissioner Records, 1726-1794, p. 277)

Negro Mingo, slave of Joseph Durding, of Kent County, convicted felon, was executed on 3 Feb 1742/3. (Ref: Maryland State Archives, Governor and Council Commissioner Records, 1726-1794, p. 75)

Negro Moll, see Negro Caleb.

Negro Nase, see James Lee, Jr.

Negro Ned, slave of Robert Jenckins Henry, of Somerset County, convicted felon, executed on 11 Jul 1746. (Ref: Maryland State Archives, Governor and Council Commissioner Records, 1726-1794, p. 91)

Negro Park, of Anne Arundel County, convicted felon, was executed on 27 May 1737. (Ref: Maryland State Archives, Governor and Council Commissioner Records, 1726-1794, p. 55)

Negro Parraway, of Prince George's County, convicted felon, executed on 18 Apr 1729. (Ref: Maryland State Archives, Governor and Council Commissioner Records, 1726-1794, p. 10)

Negro Peter, slave of John Booth, of St. Mary's County, convicted felon for murdering the wife and child of said Booth, was executed on 5 Jun 1761 "on the Main Road near the place where the fact was committed he being found guilty of murder and afterwards to be there hung in chains." (Ref: Maryland State Archives, Governor and Council Commissioner Records, 1726-1794, p. 183; *Archives of Maryland*, Vol. XXXII, "Proceedings of the Council of Maryland, 1761-1770," p. 3)

Negro Peter, slave of Prothesia Wheeler, of St. Mary's County, convicted felon and burglar, was executed on 22 Nov 1743. (Ref: Maryland State Archives, Governor and Council Commissioner Records, 1726-1794, p. 82)

Negro Peter, slave of James Wardrop, of Frederick County, convicted for stealing a narrow axe and a hat from Richard Smith in 1749, received thirty lashes on his bare back at the whipping post. (Ref: *This Was The Life: Excerpts from the Judgment Records of Frederick County, Maryland, 1748-1765*, by Millard Milburn Rice, p. 22)

Negro Phil, slave of William Hammond, of Anne Arundel County, convicted felon, was executed on 27 Mar 1754. (Ref: Maryland State Archives, Governor and Council Commissioner Records, 1726-1794, p. 141)

Negro Pompey, of ---- County, convicted felon, was executed on 7 Dec 1728. (Ref: Maryland State Archives, Governor and Council Commissioner Records, 1726-1794, p. 9)

Negro Pompey, of Anne Arundel County, convicted felon for breaking and entering an out house belonging to Nathaniel Dare with Negro Sambo (Pompey's young son who was influenced by the authority of his father) and Negro Jack, ordered on 14 Sep 1754 that Pompey be executed on 20 Sep 1754 and the other two pardoned. (Ref: *Archives of Maryland*, Vol. XXXI, "Proceedings of the Council of Maryland, 1753-1761," p. 49)

Negro Pompey, slave of Benjamin Davis, of Charles County, convicted for attempting to poison Leonard Burch, was executed on 6 Oct 1769. (Ref: Maryland State Archives, Governor and Council Commissioner Records, 1726-1794, p. 234; *Archives of Maryland*, Vol. XXXII, "Proceedings of the Council of Maryland, 1761-1770," p. 313)

Negro Pompey, slave of George Plater, esquire, of St. Mary's County, convicted felon, was executed on 30 Mar 1739. (Ref: Maryland State Archives, Governor and Council Commissioner Records, 1726-1794, p. 255)

Negro Quomony, see Negro Glasgow.

Negro Rachel, slave of John Hamilton, of Calvert County, convicted felon for attempting to poison Mrs. Smith, was executed on 7 Oct 1761. (Ref: Maryland State Archives, Governor and Council Commissioner Records, 1726-1794, p. 185; *Archives of Maryland*, Vol. XXXII, "Proceedings of the Council of Maryland, 1761-1770," p. 16)

Negro Robert Rustain, slave of William Neale, of Charles County, convicted felon and burglar, was executed on 15 Dec 1749. (Ref: Maryland State Archives, Governor and Council Commissioner Records, 1726-1794, p. 120)

Negro Robin, slave of John Wamsley, of Anne Arundel County, convicted felon, ordered on 29 Aug 1739 "to be hung in a gibbet to be erected fifty yards from the gallows and the common road on a straight line from the said gallows." (Ref: Maryland State Archives, Governor and Council Commissioner Records, 1726-1794, p. 64)

Negro Robin, slave of Mrs. Elizabeth Beale, of Anne Arundel County, convicted felon, was executed on 29 Aug 1739. (Ref: Maryland State Archives, Governor and Council Commissioner Records, 1726-1794, p. 64)

Negro Robin, slave of Thomas Hayward, Jr., of Somerset County, convicted felon who allegedly assisted Negro David in the murder of Henry Selby, was pardoned on 14 Apr 1766. (Ref: *Archives of Maryland*, Vol. XXXII, "Proceedings of the Council of Maryland, 1761-1770," pp. 130-131)

Negro Ruben, slave of James Weems, son of David, of Ca0lvert County, convicted felon and burglar, was executed on 2 Sep 1757. (Ref: Maryland State Archives, Governor and Council Commissioner Records, 1726-1794, p. 161)

Negro Sam Banning, slave of Edward Tilghman, of Queen Anne's County, convicted felon, was executed on 12 Jul 1771. (Ref: Maryland State Archives, Governor and Council Commissioner Records, 1726-1794, p. 246)

Negro Sam, of ---- County, convicted felon, was executed on 15 May 1741. (Ref: Maryland State Archives, Governor and Council Commissioner Records, 1726-1794, p. 70)

Negro Sam, slave of George Steuart, Esq., of Annapolis, Anne Arundel County, convicted felon, was executed on 7 Sep 1768. (Ref: Maryland State Archives, Governor and Council Commissioner Records, 1726-1794, p. 224; *Archives of Maryland*, Vol. XXXII, "Proceedings of the Council of Maryland, 1761-1770," p. 247)

Negro Sam, slave of Thomas Lingam, of Baltimore County, convicted with Negro George of breaking open and robbing the meat house of Jacob Davis, pardoned 10 Apr 1769. (Ref: *Archives of Maryland*, Vol. XXXII, "Proceedings of the Council of Maryland, 1761-1770," p. 271)

Negro Sambo, see Negro Pompey.

Negro Sambo, slave of William Hamilton Smith, of Calvert County, convicted felon who attempted to poison William Hamilton Smith and his wife Barbara Smith, was executed on 20 Jun 1764. (Ref: Maryland State Archives, Governor and Council Commissioner Records, 1726-1794, p. 201; *Archives of Maryland*, Vol. XXXII, "Proceedings of the Council of Maryland, 1761-1770," pp. 91-92)

Negro Sampson, slave of Denwood Hicks, of Dorchester County, convicted of house breaking, was pardoned on 30 Mar 1757. (Ref: *Archives of Maryland*, Vol. XXXI, "Proceedings of the Council of Maryland, 1753-1761," p. 182)

Negro Samuel, slave of William Hickman, of Calvert County, convicted felon for attempting to poison Mrs. Smith, was executed on 7 Oct 1761. (Ref: Maryland State Archives, Governor and Council Commissioner Records, 1726-1794, p. 185; *Archives of Maryland*, Vol. XXXII, "Proceedings of the Council of Maryland, 1761-1770," p. 16)

Negro Sango, of Prince George's County, convicted felon, was executed on 10 Nov 1736. (Ref: Maryland State Archives, Governor and Council Commissioner Records, 1726-1794, p. 54)

Negro Scipio, slave of Thomas Ramsay Hodges, of Prince George's County, convicted felon for breaking into the meat house of Stephen West and stealing a quantity of bacon, was pardoned on 5 May 1769. (*Archives of Maryland*, Vol. XXXII, "Proceedings of the Council of Maryland, 1761-1770," pp. 268, 272)

Negro Scipio, see Levi Thompson.

Negro Sharper, of Dorchester County, convicted felon for ravishing Elizabeth Hall, "and his body to be hung in chains near the place where the rape was committed," was executed on the Wednesday after 15 Apr 1751. (Ref: Maryland State Archives, Governor and Council Commissioner Records, 1726-1794, p. 122)

Negro Shephon, slave of Dr. William Stevenson, of Baltimore County, convicted felon, was executed on 27 Jul 1764. (Ref: Maryland State Archives, Governor and Council Commissioner Records, 1726-1794, p. 202)

Negro Siladdy, slave of Elizabeth Trippe, of Dorchester County, convicted of house breaking, was pardoned on 30 Mar 1757. (Ref: Archives of Maryland, Vol. XXXI, "Proceedings of the Council of Maryland, 1753-1761," p. 182)

Negro Simon, slave of George Layfield, of Worcester County, convicted felon and burglar, was executed on 20 Jan 1757. (Ref: Maryland State Archives, Governor and Council Commissioner Records, 1726-1794, p. 158)

Negro Stephen, slave of Henry Ennalls, of Dorchester County, convicted felon for breaking and entering the dwelling house of said Ennalls and stealing four gallons of brandy, was sentenced on 15 Dec 1762 to be executed. (Ref: Archives of Maryland, Vol. XXXII, "Proceedings of the Council of Maryland, 1761-1770," p. 47)

Negro Stepney, of Charles County, convicted felon, was executed on and hung in chains on 16 May 1733. (Ref: Maryland State Archives, Governor and Council Commissioner Records, 1726-1794, p. 31)

Negro Thomas, slave of John Prather, of Prince George's County, convicted felon for attempting to poison Richard Duckett, the Younger, ordered to be executed on 11 Jul 1755 and "hung in chains as near the publick road as conveniently can be where the fact was committed," but was subsequently pardoned. (Ref: Archives of Maryland, Vol. XXXI, "Proceedings of the Council of Maryland, 1753-1761," pp. 79-80)

Negro Tida, slave of Ephraim Gover, of Anne Arundel County, convicted felon for attempting to poison her said master, was executed on 6 Apr 1757. (Ref: Archives of Maryland, Vol. XXXI, "Proceedings of the Council of Maryland, 1753-1761," p. 182)

Negro Toby, slave of William Ennalls, of Dorchester County, convicted felon for breaking open and robbing the house of said Ennalls, taking a purse valued at five shillings and four hundred Spanish milled dollars valued at 120 pounds, was sentenced to death on 2 Apr 1767 and to be executed on 6 May 1767, was granted a reprieve on 17 Apr 1767, and then executed on 26 Jun 1767. (Ref: Maryland State Archives, Governor and Council Commissioner Records, 1726-1794, p. 216; Archives of Maryland, Vol. XXXII, "Proceedings of the Council of Maryland, 1761-1770," pp. 188, 200)

Negro Toby, slave of Benjamin Hall, Jr., of Frederick County, convicted felon for the murder of Ely Lynthicumb [also spelled Eli Linchcomb] on 25 Dec 1763, was put in prison and ordered to be hung, but being only nine years old the Court deemed him to be an object of mercy and pardoned him on 12 Apr 1764. (Ref: Archives of Maryland, Vol. XXXII, "Proceedings of the Council of Maryland, 1761-1770," p. 91; This Was The Life: Excerpts from the Judgment Records of Frederick County, Maryland, 1748-1765, by Millard Milburn Rice, p. 253)

Negro Tom, of Anne Arundel County, convicted felon, was executed on 3 Oct 1733. (Ref: Maryland State Archives, Governor and Council Commissioner Records, 1726-1794, p. 38)

Negro Tom, of Anne Arundel County, convicted felon, was executed on 6 Aug 1754. (Ref: Maryland State Archives, Governor and Council Commissioner Records, 1726-1794, p. 142)

Negro Tom, of Cecil County, convicted of murder, was executed in November 1728. (Ref: Maryland State Archives, Governor and Council Commissioner Records, 1726-1794, p. 8)

Negro Tom, slave of John Smith Prather, of Prince George's County, convicted of murder, was executed on 23 Dec 1748 "by hanging in chains near to the place where the fact was committed." (Ref: Maryland State Archives, Governor and Council Commissioner Records, 1726-1794, p. 110)

Negro Tom, slave of Richard Snowden, of Anne Arundel County, convicted felon and burglar, was executed on 24 Jun 1747. (Ref: Maryland State Archives, Governor and Council Commissioner Records, 1726-1794, p. 100)

Negro Tom, slave of Samuel Swearingen, of Prince

George's County, convicted of murder, was executed on 2 Sep 1765. (Ref: Maryland State Archives, Governor and Council Commissioner Records, 1726-1794, p. 209)

Negro Tom, slave of Jane or Sarah Strawbridge, of Somerset County, convicted of murdering Negro Job, slave of John Williams, in November 1769, was sentenced to be executed on 4 Apr 1770, but was reprieved on 20 Mar 1770 and then executed on 11 Apr 1770. It was indicated that Negro Tom was a notorious character who had always been "a villain of the blackest dye." (Ref: Maryland State Archives, Governor and Council Commissioner Records, 1726-1794, p. 238, gave her name as Sarah Strawbridge, spinster, but *Archives of Maryland*, Vol. XXXII, "Proceedings of the Council of Maryland, 1761-1770," pp. 333-335, gave her name as Mrs. Jane Strawbridge)

Negro Tomboy, slave of Alexander Lawson & County, of Baltimore County, convicted felon, was executed on 25 Aug 1759. (Ref: Maryland State Archives, Governor and Council Commissioner Records, 1726-1794, p. 173)

Negro Tony, slave of Thomas Sandsbury, of Prince George's County, carpenter, convicted felon for breaking and entering the store house of James Russell, merchant, of the City of London, and stealing sundry goods and chattels, was executed on 23 Oct 1761. (Ref: Maryland State Archives, Governor and Council Commissioner Records, 1726-1794, p. 187; *Archives of Maryland*, Vol. XXXII, "Proceedings of the Council of Maryland, 1761-1770," p. 17)

Negro Wapping, slave of Benjamin Brooke, of Prince George's County, convicted felon who attempted to poison his master, was executed on 20 Sep 1762. (Ref: Maryland State Archives, Governor and Council Commissioner Records, 1726-1794, p. 195)

Negro Will, slave of Thomas Lancaster, of Prince George's County, convicted felon, was executed on 17 Aug 1743. (Ref: Maryland State Archives, Governor and Council Commissioner Records, 1726-1794, p. 85)

Negro York, slave of Thomas Pierce, of Anne Arundel County, convicted felon, was executed on 9 Dec 1747. (Ref: Maryland State Archives, Governor and Council Commissioner Records, 1726-1794, p. 105)

Negro, Andrew, slave of John Donaldson, of St. Mary's County, convicted felon, was reprieved on 27 May 1727 and ordered out of the province within the next three months. (Ref: Maryland State Archives, Governor and Council Commissioner Records, 1726-1794, p. 4)

Neill, Hugh, reverend, licensed to preach in St. Luke's Parish, Queen Anne's County, vacant by the death of Rev. Richard Harrison. 27 Oct 1766; inducted into St. Paul's Parish, Queen Anne's County, 1 Jan 1767. (Ref: Maryland Commission Book No. 82, pp. 183, 198; *Maryland Historical Magazine*, Vol. XXVI, p. 355; *Directory of Ministers and the Maryland Churches They Served, 1634-1900*, by Edna Agatha Kanely, Vol. II, L-Z, p. 120, stated he died in 1781 or 1782)

Nelson, Arthur, was appointed Constable of Monocasie [Monocacy] in Prince George's County, now Frederick County, in 1746 and Constable in the Lower Part of Monocacy Hundred in Frederick County in 1760. (Ref: *This Was The Life: Excerpts from the Judgment Records of Frederick County, Maryland, 1748-1765*, by Millard Milburn Rice, p. 216); appointed Constable of Middle Hundred in Prince George's County, now Frederick County, 1746. (Ref: Prince George's County Court Records, 1736-1748, Extracts by Patricia Abelard Andersen, *Western Maryland Genealogy*, Vol. 18, No. 1, January 2002, p. 44)

Nelson, John, appointed Constable of the Lower Part of Monocacy Hundred in Prince George's County, now Frederick County, 1739. (Ref: Prince George's County Court Records, 1736-1748, Extracts by Patricia Abelard Andersen, *Western Maryland Genealogy*, Vol. 18, No. 1, January 2002, p. 36)

Nevett, Thomas, appointed a Commissioner of the Peace for Dorchester County, 4 Aug 1732 and 20 May 1736. (Ref: Maryland State Archives, Governor and Council Commissioner Records, 1726-1794, pp. 25, 52); registration of sloop *Elizabeth*, 40 tons, built at Amesbury, Massa-chusetts, 1734. Robert Wing, master. Thomas Nevett, owner. 12 Jul 1735. (Ref: Maryland Commission Book No. 82, p. 32; *Maryland Historical Magazine*, Vol. XXVI, p. 144)

Nevison, James, appointed a Commissioner of the Peace for Charles County, 8 Jun 1751. (Ref: Maryland State Archives, Governor and Council Commissioner Records, 1726-1794, p. 123, spelled his name Niveson); Court Justice, 1756. (*Calendar of Maryland*

State Papers, No. 1 The Black Books, p. 132, spelled his name Nevison)

Newbold, John, registration of sloop *Catherine and Ann*, 25 tons, built in Accomac, Virginia. John Newbold, master and owner. 11 May 1744; registration of sloop *Catherine & Ann*, 15 tons, built in Virginia, 1745. William Newbold, master. John Newbold, owner. 15 Mar 1749/50. (Ref: Maryland Commission Book No. 82, pp. 110, 155; *Maryland Historical Magazine*, Vol. XXVI, pp. 252, 351)

Newbold, William, see John Newbold.

Nicholls, John, appointed Constable of Linton Hundred in Frederick County in 1751. (Ref: *This Was The Life: Excerpts from the Judgment Records of Frederick County, Maryland, 1748-1765*, by Millard Milburn Rice, p. 61)

Nicholls, William, see Negro George.

Nichols, Isaac, appointed a Commissioner of the Peace for Dorchester County, 20 May 1736 and 28 Sep 1744. (Ref: Maryland State Archives, Governor and Council Commissioner Records, 1726-1794, pp. 52, 89)

Nichols, Jeremiah, appointed a Commissioner of the Peace for Cecil County, 2 Jun 1774. (Ref: Maryland State Archives, Governor and Council Commissioner Records, 1726-1794, p. 283)

Nichols, Jeremiah, appointed a Commissioner of the Peace for Talbot County, 23 Oct 1742, 1 Jun 1743 and 27 Oct 1744. (Ref: Maryland State Archives, Governor and Council Commissioner Records, 1726-1794, pp. 74, 79, and p. 87 spelled his name Nicols)

Nichols, Jonathan, appointed a Commissioner of the Peace for Queen Anne's County, 17 May 1746. (Ref: Maryland State Archives, Governor and Council Commissioner Records, 1726-1794, p. 92); see Jonathan Nicolls.

Nichols, Joseph, commissioned High Sheriff of Talbot County, 18 Oct 1739. (Ref: Maryland State Archives, Governor and Council Commissioner Records, 1726-1794, p. 65)

Nicholson, John, see James Macdowell.

Nicholson, Joseph, appointed a Commissioner of the Peace for Cecil County, 2 Jun 1774. (Ref: Maryland State Archives, Governor and Council Commissioner Records, 1726-1794, p. 283)

Nicholson, Joseph (d. 1786), commissioned High Sheriff of Queen Anne's County, 25 Nov 1762. (Ref: Maryland State Archives, Governor and Council Commissioner Records, 1726-1794, p. 198); see Negro Jack.

Nicolls, John, appointed Constable of Great Choptank Hundred in Dorchester County, 1742 and 1744. (Ref: Dorchester County Judgment Records, 1742-1743, p. 84, 1743-1745, p. 185; *Judgment Records of Dorchester, Queen Anne's and Talbot Counties, Maryland*, by F. Edward Wright, 2001, p. 30, styled him as Jr., but p. 49 did not)

Nicolls, Jonathan, commissioned High Sheriff of Queen Anne's County, 3 Nov 1757. (Ref: Maryland State Archives, Governor and Council Commissioner Records, 1726-1794, p. 170); appointed a Commissioner of the Peace for Talbot County, 26 May 1761. (Ref: Maryland State Archives, Governor and Council Commissioner Records, 1726-1794, p. 197)

Nicolls, Moses, appointed Constable of Bridge Town Hundred in Dorchester County, 1742. (Ref: Dorchester County Judgment Records, 1742-1743, p. 84; *Judgment Records of Dorchester, Queen Anne's and Talbot Counties, Maryland*, by F. Edward Wright, 2001, p. 30)

Nicols, Deborah, see Negro George.

Nisbet, Nathaniel, was appointed Constable of Conococheague Hundred in Frederick County, 1769. (Ref: "Frederick County Court Minutes, March 1769," by Patricia Abelard Andersen, *Western Maryland Genealogy*, Vol. 15, No. 2, April 1999, p. 63)

Noble, George, appointed a Commissioner of the Peace for Prince George's County, 3 Mar 1726/7. (Ref: Maryland State Archives, Governor and Council Commissioner Records, 1726-1794, p. 3; commissioned Deputy Surveyor of Prince George's County, 8 Feb 1733/4. (Ref: Maryland Commission Book No. 82, p. 5; *Maryland Historical Magazine*, Vol. XXVI, p. 139)

Noble, Joseph, was commissioned a Coroner of Prince George's County 2 Nov 1748. (Ref: Maryland Commission Book No. 82, p. 138; *Maryland Historical Magazine*, Vol. XXVI, p. 343)

Noble, Robert, appointed a Commissioner of the Peace for Talbot County, 29 Oct 1730. (Ref: Maryland State Archives, Governor and Council Commissioner

Records, 1726-1794, p. 17)

Noell, Basil, appointed a Commissioner of the Peace for Dorchester County, 21 Apr 1735. (Ref: Maryland State Archives, Governor and Council Commissioner Records, 1726-1794, p. 46); registration of sloop *The Roe*, 15 tons, built in Dorchester County, 1746. Stephen Hicks, master. Basil Noell, owner. 20 Jul 1747. (Ref: Maryland Commission Book No. 82, p. 131; *Maryland Historical Magazine*, Vol. XXVI, p. 261, spelled his first name Bazil); see John Parran.

Noell, Edward, see John Parran.

Noell, Septimus, see Daniel Campbell.

Noke, William, commissioned High Sheriff of Anne Arundel County, 16 Sep 1772. (Ref: Maryland State Archives, Governor and Council Commissioner Records, 1726-1794, p. 252)

Nollar, Samuel, see Samuel Knowles.

Norris, John, appointed Constable of Sugar Loaf Hundred in Frederick County in 1749. (Ref: *This Was The Life: Excerpts from the Judgment Records of Frederick County, Maryland, 1748-1765*, by Millard Milburn Rice, p. 6)

Norris, John, of Benjamin, appointed Constable of Seneca Hundred in Prince George's County, now Frederick County, 1747. (Ref: Prince George's County Court Records, 1736-1748, Extracts by Patricia Abelard Andersen, *Western Maryland Genealogy*, Vol. 18, No. 1, January 2002, p. 45)

Norris, Thomas, of Pipe Creek, was appointed a Commissioner of the Peace for Frederick County, 3 Nov 1757. (Ref: Maryland State Archives, Governor and Council Commissioner Records, 1726-1794, p. 178); Court Justice in Frederick County in 1758. (Ref: *This Was The Life: Excerpts from the Judgment Records of Frederick County, Maryland, 1748-1765*, by Millard Milburn Rice, p. 177)

Norris, Thomas, shipwright, registration of sloop *Essex*, 30 tons, built in Anne Arundel County, 1746. Thomas Norris, master and owner. 14 May 1747; ship carpenter, registration of sloop *Aurora*, 25 tons, built at West River [Anne Arundel County]. 1750. Joseph Chew, master. Thomas Norris, owner. (Ref: Maryland Commission Book No. 82, pp. 130, 146; *Maryland Historical Magazine*, Vol. XXVI, pp. 260, 346-347)

Norris, William, of Benjamin, appointed Constable of Sugar Loaf Hundred in Frederick County, 1760. (Ref: *This Was The Life: Excerpts from the Judgment Records of Frederick County, Maryland, 1748-1765*, by Millard Milburn Rice, p. 216)

Norris, William Stier, appointed Constable of Sugar Loaf Hundred in Frederick County, 1769. (Ref: "Frederick County Court Minutes, March 1769," by Patricia Abelard Andersen, *Western Maryland Genealogy*, Vol. 15, No. 2, April 1999, p. 63)

North, Edward, of Bermuda, registration of sloop *Endeavour*, 40 tons, built in Somerset County, 1748. John Smith, master. Edward North, Henry Corbusier and Samuel Trott, of Bermuda, owners. 12 Jul 1748. (Ref: Maryland Commission Book No. 82, p. 135; *Maryland Historical Magazine*, Vol. XXVI, p. 263)

North, John, see Levin Gale.

Northcraft, Richard, appointed Constable of Sugar Loaf Hundred in Frederick County, 1763. (Ref: *This Was The Life: Excerpts from the Judgment Records of Frederick County, Maryland, 1748-1765*, by Millard Milburn Rice, p. 249)

Northey, Samuel, registration of sloop *Ann*, 15 tons, built in South Carolina, 1739 and called the *Sea Flower*. Samuel Northey, master and owner. 7 Aug 1744. (Ref: Maryland Commission Book No. 82, p. 110; *Maryland Historical Magazine*, Vol. XXVI, p. 252)

Nutter, Charles, appointed a Commissioner of the Peace for Dorchester County, 1 Aug 1729 and 29 Oct 1730. (Ref: Maryland State Archives, Governor and Council Commissioner Records, 1726-1794, pp. 11, 17)

O'Neal, Lawrence, commissioned High Sheriff of Frederick County, 29 Apr 1773. (Ref: Maryland State Archives, Governor and Council Commissioner Records, 1726-1794, p. 260)

O'Neil, Mary, spinster, of Baltimore County, convicted felon, was pardoned, 17 May 1738. (Ref: Maryland Commission Book No. 82, p. 58; *Maryland Historical Magazine*, Vol. XXVI, p. 151)

Offutt, James, appointed Constable of Upper Potomac Hundred in Frederick County in 1749. (Ref: *This Was The Life: Excerpts from the Judgment Records of Frederick County, Maryland, 1748-1765*, by Millard Milburn Rice, p. 6)

Offutt, Nathaniel, appointed a Commissioner of the Peace for Prince George's County, 22 Nov 1752. (Ref:

Maryland State Archives, Governor and Council Commissioner Records, 1726-1794, p. 135)

Offutt, Samuel, appointed Constable of Patuxent Hundred in Prince George's County, now Frederick County, 1736. (Ref: Prince George's County Court Records, 1736-1748, Extracts by Patricia Abelard Andersen, *Western Maryland Genealogy*, Vol. 18, No. 1, January 2002, p. 34)

Offutt, Zachariah, see Negro Jack.

Ogle, Henry, reverend, induction into St. John's Parish, Baltimore County [now part of Harford County], 24 Jul 1739; resignation from St. John's Parish, Baltimore County, 21 Jul 1742. On same day, induction into Port Tobacco Parish, Charles County. (Ref: Maryland Commission Book No. 82, pp. 76, 92; *Maryland Historical Magazine*, Vol. XXVI, pp. 154, 246)

Ogle, Joseph, appointed a Commissioner of the Peace for Frederick County, 12 Nov 1748. (Ref: Maryland State Archives, Governor and Council Commissioner Records, 1726-1794, p. 109)

Ogle, Thomas, appointed Constable of the Upper Part of Monochosey [Monocacy] Hundred in Frederick County, 1771. (Ref: "Frederick County Minute Book, March 1771, Extracts by Patricia Abelard Andersen," *Western Maryland Genealogy*, Vol. 18, No. 1, January 2002, p. 26)

Oldham, Edward (1709-1773), was appointed a Commissioner of the Peace for Talbot County, 2 Oct 1751. (Ref: Maryland State Archives, Governor and Council Commissioner Records, 1726-1794, p. 124)

Oldham, Elizabeth, see Negro Ben.

Oroonoko, Michael, of Cecil County, convicted of murder, was executed on 7 May 1762. (Ref:; *Archives of Maryland*, Vol. XXXII, "Proceedings of the Council of Maryland, 1761-1770," p. 36; Maryland State Archives, Governor and Council Commissioner Records, 1726-1794, p. 188, spelled his name Oranoka)

Orrick, Nicholas, appointed a Commissioner of the Peace for Baltimore County, 2 Mar 1754. (Ref: Maryland State Archives, Governor and Council Commissioner Records, 1726-1794, p. 142)

Ostroe, William, servant of Richard Lee, of Prince George's County, pardoned for burglary, 4 Jun 1743. (Ref: Maryland Commission Book No. 82, p. 102; *Maryland Historical Magazine*, Vol. XXVI, p. 249)

Otley, William, appointed a Commissioner of the Peace for Baltimore County, 31 Oct 1768. (Ref: Maryland State Archives, Governor and Council Commissioner Records, 1726-1794, p. 238, listed him as Otty or Otly); appointed a Justice in Baltimore County, 22 Feb 1773. (Ref: *Inhabitants of Baltimore County, 1763-1774*, by Henry C. Peden, Jr., 1989, p. 49, citing *Calendar of Maryland State Papers, No. 1 The Black Books*, p. 208 spelled his name Otley)

Ouchterbridge, Jonathan Birr, see Ouchterbridge Horsey.

Outten, Abraham (d. 1747), commissioned one of the Coroners of Worcester County, 16 Sep 1745. (Ref: Maryland Commission Book No. 82, p. 116; *Maryland Historical Magazine*, Vol. XXVI, p. 255)

Outten, Isaac, appointed a Commissioner of the Peace for Somerset County, 20 Mar 1775. (Ref: Maryland State Archives, Governor and Council Commissioner Records, 1726-1794, p. 288)

Outten, William, of Worcester County, Sub Sheriff to Major Benjamin Handy, the late Sheriff, 1759. (Ref: *Archives of Maryland*, Vol. XXXI, "Proceedings of the Council of Maryland, 1753-1761," p. 323)

Owen, Edward, Jr., appointed Constable of Rock Creek Hundred in Frederick County, 1769, 1771. (Ref: "Frederick County Court Minutes November 1769 by Patricia Abelard Andersen," *Western Maryland Genealogy*, Vol. 16, No. 1, January 2000, p. 32; "Frederick County Minute Book, March 1771, Extracts by Patricia Abelard Andersen," *Western Maryland Genealogy*, Vol. 18, No. 1, January 2002, p. 25)

Owen, John, of Talbot County, convicted felon for horse stealing, was pardoned on 15 Apr 1751. (Ref: Maryland Commission Book No. 82, p. 149; *Maryland Historical Magazine*, Vol. XXVI, p. 348)

Owen, Lawrence, appointed Constable of Middle Hundred in Prince George's County, now Frederick County, 1746, and Constable of the Middle Part of Rock Creek Hundred, 1747. (Ref: Prince George's County Court Records, 1736-1748, Extracts by Patricia Abelard Andersen, *Western Maryland Genealogy*, Vol. 18, No. 1, January 2002, pp. 44, 45); appointed a Press Master for Frederick County in 1757. (Ref: *This Was The Life: Excerpts from the*

Colonial Maryland Commissions, Appointments, and Other Proceedings, 1726-1776

Judgment Records of Frederick County, Maryland, 1748-1765, by Millard Milburn Rice, p. 176)

Owen, Thomas (d. 1751), was appointed a Commissioner of the Peace for Prince George's County, 15 Jun 1739. (Ref: Maryland State Archives, Governor and Council Commissioner Records, 1726-1794, p. 64)

Owings, Christopher, appointed a Commissioner of the Peace for Baltimore County, 17 Feb 1775. (Ref: Maryland State Archives, Governor and Council Commissioner Records, 1726-1794, p. 288)

Owings, Samuel (1702-1775), was appointed a Commissioner of the Peace for Baltimore County, 29 Feb 1743/4. (Ref: Maryland State Archives, Governor and Council Commissioner Records, 1726-1794, p. 84)

Owings, Samuel, Jr. (1733-1803), appointed a Commissioner of the Peace for Baltimore County, 31 Oct 1768 and 6 Mar 1775. (Ref: Maryland State Archives, Governor and Council Commissioner Records, 1726-1794, pp. 238, 288)

Ozier, John, planter, of Cecil County, native of France, naturalized 30 Apr 1736 and also his sons Jacob, William and John,. (Ref: Maryland Commission Book No. 82, p. 42; *Maryland Historical Magazine*, Vol. XXVI, pp. 146-147)

Paca, Aquila (1703-1743/4), was appointed a Commissioner of the Peace for Baltimore County, 24 Nov 1732. (Ref: Maryland State Archives, Governor and Council Commissioner Records, 1726-1794, p. 39)

Paca, Aquila (1738-1788), appointed a Commissioner of the Peace for Harford County, 20 Feb 1774. (Ref: Maryland State Archives, Governor and Council Commissioner Records, 1726-1794, p. 281)

Paca, John (c1712-1785), appointed a Commissioner of the Peace for Baltimore County, 29 Feb 1743/4. (Ref: Maryland State Archives, Governor and Council Commissioner Records, 1726-1794, p. 84); commissioned a Ranger for Baltimore County, 9 Jun 1743. (Ref: Maryland Commission Book No. 82, p. 102; *Maryland Historical Magazine*, Vol. XXVI, p. 249); appointed a Commissioner of the Peace for Harford County, 20 Feb 1774. (Ref: Maryland State Archives, Governor and Council Commissioner Records, 1726-1794, p. 281)

Pagan, John, of Virginia, registration of schooner *Cameron*, 25 tons, built in Charles County, 1749. Robert Morrison, master. John Pagan, John Brown, John Nelson, Hugh Millikin, William Wallace and Thomas Wallace, owners. 6 Nov 1749. (Ref: Maryland Commission Book No. 82, p. 153; *Maryland Historical Magazine*, Vol. XXVI, p. 350)

Page, Ralph, appointed a Commissioner of the Peace for Kent County, 28 May 1756. (Ref: Maryland State Archives, Governor and Council Commissioner Records, 1726-1794, p. 168)

Pairpoint, Francis, appointed Constable of Wills Town Hundred in Frederick County, 1669, 1771. (Ref: "Frederick County Court Minutes November 1769 by Patricia Abelard Andersen," *Western Maryland Genealogy*, Vol. 16, No. 1, January 2000, p. 33, misspelled his name Panpoint); "Frederick County Minute Book, March 1771, Extracts by Patricia Abelard Andersen," *Western Maryland Genealogy*, Vol. 18, No. 1, January 2002, p. 26)

Palmer, Charles, registration of sloop *Two Brothers*, built at Chester River, 1730. John Tenant, master. Charles Palmer and Daniel Palmer, owners. (Ref: Maryland Commission Book No. 82, p. 46; *Maryland Historical Magazine*, Vol. XXVI, p. 148); registration of schooner *Tryall*, 30 tons, built in Maryland, 1735. Nathaniel Palmer, master. Nathaniel Palmer and Charles Palmer, owners. 23 Jan 1738/9. (Ref: Maryland Commission Book No. 82, p. 65; *Maryland Historical Magazine*, Vol. XXVI, p. 152); registration of brigantine *Hercules*, 40 tons, built in Somerset County, 1736. Charles Palmer, master. Nathaniel Palmer and Charles Palmer, owners. 26 Jan 1738/9. (Ref: Maryland Commission Book No. 82, p. 65; *Maryland Historical Magazine*, Vol. XXVI, p. 153); see Nathaniel Palmer.

Palmer, Daniel, see Charles Palmer.

Palmer, Nathaniel (Quaker), registration of sloop *Flying Fish*, 15 tons, built at Bohemia [Cecil County], 1730. Charles Palmer, master. Nathaniel Palmer, owner. 26 May 1736. (Ref: Maryland Commission Book No. 82, p. 44; *Maryland Historical Magazine*, Vol. XXVI, p. 147)

Palmer, Nathaniel, see Charles Palmer.

Paris, George, see Levin Gale.

Parker, Gabriel, appointed a Commissioner of the

Peace for Calvert County, 3 Mar 1726/7. (Ref: Maryland State Archives, Governor and Council Commissioner Records, 1726-1794, p. 3); commissioned Sheriff of Calvert County, 19 Jun 1732, 2 Jul 1741 and 24 Dec 1748. (Ref: Maryland State Archives, Governor and Council Commissioner Records, 1726-1794, pp. 24, 71, 109)

Parker, Hugh, appointed a Commissioner of the Peace for Frederick County, 17 Nov 1749. (Ref: Maryland State Archives, Governor and Council Commissioner Records, 1726-1794, p. 115)

Parks, William, printer, of Annapolis, registered the sloop *Tryal*, 10 tons, built in Ware River on Mockjack Bay in Virginia, 1733. John Giles, master. William Parks, owner. 1 Jul 1734 (Ref: Maryland Commission Book No. 82, p. 19; *Maryland Historical Magazine*, Vol. XXVI, p. 141)

Parr, Henry, see Christopher Lowndes.

Parran, John, appointed a Commissioner of the Peace for Calvert County, 9 Dec 1731. (Ref: Maryland State Archives, Governor and Council Commissioner Records, 1726-1794, p. 20); commissioned Sheriff of Calvert County, 28 Sep 1738 and 25 Sep 1740. (Ref: Maryland State Archives, Governor and Council Commissioner Records, 1726-1794, pp. 61, 68); registration of sloop *Charming Betty*, 10 tons, built at Choptank, 1737. Edward Noell, master. "The said Basil Noell" and John Parran, owners. (Ref: Maryland Commission Book No. 82, p. 89; *Maryland Historical Magazine*, Vol. XXVI, p. 245); late sheriff of Calvert County, had ordinary license accounts still unpaid in 1756. (Ref: *Archives of Maryland*, Vol. LII, "Proceedings and Acts of the General Assembly of Maryland, 1755-1756," p. 568, misspelled his name as Paran)

Parran, Mary, see Negro Hannah.

Parran, Nathan, appointed a Commissioner of the Peace for Calvert County, 18 Sep 1759. (Ref: Maryland State Archives, Governor and Council Commissioner Records, 1726-1794, p. 187)

Parran, Richard (d. c178), was appointed a Commissioner of the Peace for Calvert County, 26 Jul 1773. (Ref: Maryland State Archives, Governor and Council Commissioner Records, 1726-1794, p. 272)

Parran, Young (1711-1772), commissioned High Sheriff of Calvert County, 20 Aug 1739. (Ref: Maryland State Archives, Governor and Council Commissioner Records, 1726-1794, p. 64); appointed a Commissioner of the Peace for Charles County, 19 May 1743 and 2 Oct 1751. (Ref: Maryland State Archives, Governor and Council Commissioner Records, 1726-1794, pp. 78, 126)

Parris, George, registration of sloop *Elizabeth*, 30 tons, built in Somerset County, 150. George Parris, master and owner. 31 Oct 1750. (Ref: Maryland Commission Book No. 82, p. 147; *Maryland Historical Magazine*, Vol. XXVI, p. 347)

Partridge, Buckler, chyrurgeon, registration of the brigantine *Baltimore*, 40 tons, built in Baltimore County, 1732. Paul Whichcote, master. Buckler Partridge, owner. 17 Sep 1734. (Ref: Maryland Commission Book No. 82, p. 47; *Maryland Historical Magazine*, Vol. XXVI, p. 148)

Partridge, Dominick B., was Constable of Back River Lower Hundred in Baltimore County, 1773. (Ref: *Inhabitants of Baltimore County, 1763-1774*, by Henry C. Peden, Jr., 1989, p. 54, citing a 1773 List of Taxables)

Patten, Richard, see John Seegar.

Patterson, John, reverend, induction into Worcester Parish, Worcester County, 11 Nov 1771. (Ref: Maryland Commission Book No. 82, p. 273; *Maryland Historical Magazine*, Vol. XXVII, p. 31); induction into Chester Parish, Kent County, 11 May 1773. (Ref: Maryland Commission Book No. 82, p. 318; *Maryland Historical Magazine*, Vol. XXVII, p. 34)

Payne, Flail, appointed Constable of the Lower Part of Monocacy Hundred in Prince George's County, now Frederick County, 1740. (Ref: Prince George's County Court Records, 1736-1748, Extracts by Patricia Abelard Andersen, *Western Maryland Genealogy*, Vol. 18, No. 1, January 2002, p. 37)

Pearce, Benjamin, appointed a Commissioner of the Peace for Cecil County, 3 Mar 1726/7. (Ref: Maryland State Archives, Governor and Council Commissioner Records, 1726-1794, p. 2)

Pearce, Gideon, appointed a Commissioner of the Peace for Kent County, 30 Nov 1732. (Ref: Maryland State Archives, Governor and Council Commissioner Records, 1726-1794, p. 33)

Pearce, Henry Ward, commissioned a Coroner of

Cecil County, 6 Aug 1764. (Ref: Maryland Commission Book No. 82, p. 163; *Maryland Historical Magazine*, Vol. XXVI, p. 352); appointed a Commissioner of the Peace for Cecil County, 20 Feb 1774. (Ref: Maryland State Archives, Governor and Council Commissioner Records, 1726-1794, p. 281)

Pearce, James, was appointed a Commissioner of the Peace for Cecil County, 2 Jun 1774. (Ref: Maryland State Archives, Governor and Council Commissioner Records, 1726-1794, p. 283)

Pearce, James (d. 1802), was appointed a Commissioner of the Peace for Kent County, 21 Mar 1760. (Ref: Maryland State Archives, Governor and Council Commissioner Records, 1726-1794, p. 190)

Pearce, William, commissioned a Coroner for Cecil County, 9 Jun 1740 and 20 Feb 1746/7. (Ref: Maryland Commission Book No. 82, p. 82; *Maryland Historical Magazine*, Vol. XXVI, pp. 157, 259)

Peck, Michael, labourer, of Frederick County, convict felon for the murder of George Jacob Poe in August 1762, was executed 2 Oct 1762. (Ref: Maryland State Archives, Governor and Council Commissioner Records, 1726-1794, p. 190; *Archives of Maryland*, Vol. XXXII, "Proceedings of the Council of Maryland, 1761-1770," p. 42; *This Was The Life: Excerpts from the Judgment Records of Frederick County, Maryland, 1748-1765*, by Millard Milburn Rice, p. 239)

Peele, Roger, registration of schooner *Dolphin*, 25 tons, built in New England, 1729. Thomas Airy, master. Roger Peele, owner. 17 Apr 1741. (Ref: Maryland Commission Book No. 82, p. 85; *Maryland Historical Magazine*, Vol. XXVI, p. 158)

Pelton, Samuel, of Frederick County, convicted felon for murdering Abraham Kellor, was executed on 25 May 1770. (*Archives of Maryland*, Vol. XXXII, "Proceedings of the Council of Maryland, 1761-1770," p. 368)

Pemberton, Grundy (d. 1768), was appointed a Commissioner of the Peace for Queen Anne's County, 17 Oct 1734. (Ref: Maryland State Archives, Governor and Council Commissioner Records, 1726-1794, p. 44)

Pemberton, Grundy, appointed a Commissioner of the Peace for Queen Anne's County, 16 Jun 1773. (Ref: Maryland State Archives, Governor and Council Commissioner Records, 1726-1794, p. 266)

Pemberton, Isaac, carpenter, late of Baltimore County, convicted of burglary, was pardoned and then banished on 18 Apr 1772. (Ref: Maryland Commission Book No. 82, p. 276; *Maryland Historical Magazine*, Vol. XXVII, p. 31)

Penn, William, appointed a Commissioner of the Peace for Charles County, 22 Oct 1739. (Ref: Maryland State Archives, Governor and Council Commissioner Records, 1726-1794, p. 66)

Penson, William, appointed a Commissioner of the Peace for Prince George's County, 29 Oct 1730. (Ref: Maryland State Archives, Governor and Council Commissioner Records, 1726-1794, p. 12)

Perkins, Daniel, registration of schooner *Ranger*, 15 tons, built in Anne Arundel County, 1744. Daniel Perkins, master and owner. 5 Feb 1744/5. (Ref: Maryland Commission Book No. 82, p. 112; *Maryland Historical Magazine*, Vol. XXVI, p. 253)

Perkins, Sarah, see Negro Joe.

Perkins, Thomas, see Michael Hackett.

Perrie, Samuel (d. 1729), was appointed a Commissioner of the Peace for Prince George's County, 3 Mar 1726/7. (Ref: Maryland State Archives, Governor and Council Commissioner Records, 1726-1794, p. 3)

Perrigo, Nathan, was Constable of Patapsco Lower Hundred in Baltimore County in 1773. (Ref: *Inhabitants of Baltimore County, 1763-1774*, by Henry C. Peden, Jr., 1989, p. 77, citing a 1773 List of Taxables)

Perry, Alexander, appointed Constable of Sugar Loaf Hundred in Frederick County in 1751. (Ref: *This Was The Life: Excerpts from the Judgment Records of Frederick County, Maryland, 1748-1765*, by Millard Milburn Rice, p. 61)

Perry, Benjamin, appointed Constable of Rock Creek Hundred in Prince George's County, now Frederick County, 1740. (Ref: Prince George's County Court Records, 1736-1748, Extracts by Patricia Abelard Andersen, *Western Maryland Genealogy*, Vol. 18, No. 1, January 2002, p. 37)

Perry, Charles, was Constable of Rock Creek Hundred in Prince George's County, now Frederick County, 1733. (*Calendar of Maryland State Papers, No. 1 The Black Books*, p. 43)

Perry, James, appointed Constable of Potomack [Potomac] Hundred in Prince George's County, now Frederick County, 1745. (Ref: Prince George's County Court Records, 1736-1748, Extracts by Patricia Abelard Andersen, *Western Maryland Genealogy*, Vol. 18, No. 1, January 2002, p. 43)

Perry, James, Jr., appointed Constable of George Town Hundred in Frederick County, 1769. (Ref: "Frederick County Court Minutes November 1769 by Patricia Abelard Andersen," *Western Maryland Genealogy*, Vol. 16, No. 1, January 2000, p. 32)

Perry, William (1746-1799), was appointed a Commissioner of the Peace for Talbot County, 2 Feb 1774. (Ref: Maryland State Archives, Governor and Council Commissioner Records, 1726-1794, p. 280); Court Justice, Talbot County, 1774. (*Calendar of Maryland State Papers, No. 1 The Black Books*, p. 211)

Peter (Peters), Robert, of Frederick County, was appointed a Commissioner of the Peace, 1 Aug 1768 and 15 Aug 1774. (Ref: Maryland State Archives, Governor and Council Commissioner Records, 1726-1794, pp. 235, 284)

Philby, John, see John Hall.

Phillip, John, appointed Constable of Pipe Creek Hundred in Prince George's County, now Frederick County, 1747. (Ref: Prince George's County Court Records, 1736-1748, Extracts by Patricia Abelard Andersen, *Western Maryland Genealogy*, Vol. 18, No. 1, January 2002, p. 45)

Pierce, Andrew, appointed a Commissioner of the Peace for Cecil County, 22 Apr 1758. (Ref: Maryland State Archives, Governor and Council Commissioner Records, 1726-1794, p. 180)

Pierce, Thomas, see Negro York.

Pinkley, Peter, was appointed Constable of Conococheague Hundred in Frederick County in 1763. (Ref: *This Was The Life: Excerpts from the Judgment Records of Frederick County, Maryland, 1748-1765*, by Millard Milburn Rice, p. 249)

Pinkstone, John, of Kent County, convicted felon and burglar, was executed on 5 Mar 1740/41. (Ref: Maryland State Archives, Governor and Council Commissioner Records, 1726-1794, p. 69)

Piper, John, appointed a Commissioner of the Peace for Somerset County, 20 Mar 1775. (Ref: Maryland State Archives, Governor and Council Commissioner Records, 1726-1794, p. 288)

Pitney, William, appointed a Commissioner of the Peace for Charles County, 19 Oct 1770. (Ref: Maryland State Archives, Governor and Council Commissioner Records, 1726-1794, p. 252)

Planner, William, appointed a Commissioner of the Peace for Somerset County, 29 Oct 1730. (Ref: Maryland State Archives, Governor and Council Commissioner Records, 1726-1794, p. 17)

Plant, James, see Negro Mary.

Plater, George (1695-1755), Esq., commissioned a Provincial Justice by the Governor, 20 Oct 1729. (Ref: Maryland State Archives, Governor and Council Commissioner Records, 1726-1794, p. 12); commissioned Naval Officer for the Port of Patuxent on 25 Jul 1733. (Ref: Maryland Commission Book No. 82, p. 1; *Maryland Historical Magazine*, Vol. XXVI, p. 138); appointed a Commissioner of the Peace for Cecil County, Baltimore County, Kent County, Prince George's County, Anne Arundel County, Calvert County, Charles County, St. Mary's County, Queen Anne's County, and Talbot County, 4 Aug 1732 and 10 Aug 1732 and 20 Aug 1733. (Ref: Maryland State Archives, Governor and Council Commissioner Records, 1726-1794, pp. 32-37); commissioned Naval Officer of the Port of Annapolis, 29 Sep 1742. (Ref: Maryland Commission Book No. 82, p. 96; *Maryland Historical Magazine*, Vol. XXVI, p. 247); appointed a Privy Council on 10 May 1753. (Ref: *Archives of Maryland*, Vol. XXXI, "Proceedings of the Council of Maryland, 1753-1761," pp. 8, 14); appointed a Commissioner of the Peace for Cecil County, 10 May 1757. (Ref: Maryland State Archives, Governor and Council Commissioner Records, 1726-1794, p. 174); commissioned Naval Officer of Patuxent, 1 Aug 1767 and 28 Aug 1769. (Ref: Maryland Commission Book No. 82, pp. 203, 226; *Maryland Historical Magazine*, Vol. XXVI, pp. 356, 359); of St. Mary's County, commissioned Naval Officer of Patuxent, 29 Apr 1773. (Ref: Maryland Commission Book No. 82, p. 308; *Maryland Historical Magazine*, Vol. XXVII, p. 33); see Negro Judy and Negro Pompey.

Plowman, Jonathan, appointed a Commissioner of the Peace for Baltimore County, 31 Oct 1768 and 30 May 1774. (Ref: Maryland State Archives, Governor and Council Commissioner Records, 1726-1794, pp. 238, 283); appointed a Justice in Baltimore County, 22 Feb 1773. (Ref: *Inhabitants of Baltimore County, 1763-1774*, by Henry C. Peden, Jr., 1989, p. 49, citing *Calendar of Maryland State Papers, No. 1 The Black Books*, p. 208); see Edward Power.

Poe, George Jacob, see Michael Peck.

Polk, David, appointed a Commissioner of the Peace for Somerset County, 8 Jun 1763. (Ref: Maryland State Archives, Governor and Council Commissioner Records, 1726-1794, p. 210)

Polk, Robert, appointed a Commissioner of the Peace for Dorchester County, 1749 [exact date not given]. (Ref: Maryland State Archives, Governor and Council Commissioner Records, 1726-1794, p. 113)

Polk, William, appointed a Commissioner of the Peace for Caroline County, 15 Aug 1774. (Ref: Maryland State Archives, Governor and Council Commissioner Records, 1726-1794, p. 284)

Pollard, John, appointed a Press Master in Dorchester County in 1744. (Ref: Dorchester County Judgment Records, 1743-1745, p. 129; *Judgment Records of Dorchester, Queen Anne's and Talbot Counties, Maryland*, by F. Edward Wright, 2001, p. 46)

Pollard, Tobias (c1669-1749), was appointed a Commissioner of the Peace for Dorchester County, 1 Aug 1729 and 29 Oct 1730. (Ref: Maryland State Archives, Governor and Council Commissioner Records, 1726-1794, pp. 11, 17)

Pool, Moses, appointed Constable of Transquakin Hundred in Dorchester County, 1745. (Ref: Dorchester County Judgment Records, 1743-1745, p. 476; *Judgment Records of Dorchester, Queen Anne's and Talbot Counties, Maryland*, by F. Edward Wright, 2001, p. 60)

Porter, James, appointed a Commissioner of the Peace for Cecil County, 3 Mar 1772. (Ref: Maryland State Archives, Governor and Council Commissioner Records, 1726-1794, p. 260)

Porter, Richard, was commissioned Sheriff of Talbot County on 17 Sep 1742. (Ref: Maryland State Archives, Governor and Council Commissioner Records, 1726-1794, p. 74); doctor, commissioned Sheriff of Talbot County, 17 Sep 1744. (Ref: Maryland State Archives, Governor and Council Commissioner Records, 1726-1794, p. 86); sheriff of Talbot County in 1756. (Ref: *Archives of Maryland*, Vol. LII, "Proceedings and Acts of the General Assembly of Maryland, 1755-1756," p. 232)

Porter, Thomas, appointed a Commissioner of the Peace for Talbot County, 16 Jun 1741. (Ref: Maryland State Archives, Governor and Council Commissioner Records, 1726-1794, p. 70)

Postlethwait, Samuel, appointed a Commissioner of the Peace for Frederick County, 12 Mar 1763. (Ref: Maryland State Archives, Governor and Council Commissioner Records, 1726-1794, p. 209); Court Justice, 1763. (Ref: *This Was The Life: Excerpts from the Judgment Records of Frederick County, Maryland, 1748-1765*, by Millard Milburn Rice, p. 244)

Postley, John, appointed a Commissioner of the Peace for Worcester County, 26 Jul 1773. (Ref: Maryland State Archives, Governor and Council Commissioner Records, 1726-1794, p. 271)

Potter, Martin, see William Timbrill.

Potter, Nathaniel, appointed a Commissioner of the Peace for Dorchester County, 2 Nov 1773. (Ref: Maryland State Archives, Governor and Council Commissioner Records, 1726-1794, p. 278); appointed a Commissioner of the Peace for Caroline County, 8 Feb 1774. (Ref: Maryland State Archives, Governor and Council Commissioner Records, 1726-1794, p. 280)

Potter, Zebdial (Zabdiel) (d. 1761), appointed a Commissioner of the Peace for Dorchester County, 11 Jul 1757. (Ref: Maryland State Archives, Governor and Council Commissioner Records, 1726-1794, p. 175)

Potts, William, registration of sloop *Duke*, 50 tons, built in Somerset County, 1747. William Potts, master and co-owner. Jame Wardrop, co-owner. 5 May 1747. (Ref: Maryland Commission Book No. 82, p. 129; *Maryland Historical Magazine*, Vol. XXVI, p. 260)

Powell, John, appointed a Commissioner of the Peace for Prince George's County, 3 Mar 1726/7. (Ref: Maryland State Archives, Governor and Council Commissioner Records, 1726-1794, p. 3)

Powell, Mary, of Baltimore County, convicted for assisting Martha Bassett and John Berry in the murder of Sarah Clark, was executed on 10 Jan 1751/2. (Ref: Maryland State Archives, Governor and Council Commissioner Records, 1726-1794, p. 131)

Power, Edward, carpenter, of Baltimore County, convicted felon, pardoned for burglary of the store of Jonathan Plowman and banished on 15 Sep 1768 on condition of leaving the province within ten days from his release from jail and never return again. (Ref: Maryland Commission Book No. 82, p. 217; *Maryland Historical Magazine*, Vol. XXVI, p. 358; *Archives of Maryland*, Vol. XXXII, "Proceedings of the Council of Maryland, 1761-1770," pp. 24, 251)

Prather, Benjamin, appointed Constable of Lower Newfoundland Hundred in Frederick County, 1771. (Ref: "Frederick County Minute Book, March 1771, Extracts by Patricia Abelard Andersen," *Western Maryland Genealogy*, Vol. 18, No. 1, January 2002, p. 25)

Prather, John, appointed Constable of Liganore Hundred in Frederick County in 1753. (Ref: *This Was The Life: Excerpts from the Judgment Records of Frederick County, Maryland, 1748-1765*, by Millard Milburn Rice, p. 131); see Negro Thomas.

Prather, John Smith (1706-1763), was Constable of Collin Hundred in Prince George's County, now Frederick County, in 1733. (*Calendar of Maryland State Papers, No. 1 The Black Books*, p. 37); of Frederick County, Court Justice, 1754. (Ref: *This Was The Life: Excerpts from the Judgment Records of Frederick County, Maryland, 1748-1765*, by Millard Milburn Rice, p. 145); see Negro Tom.

Prather, Philip, was appointed Constable of Conococheague Hundred in Prince George's County, now Frederick County, 1744. (Ref: Prince George's County Court Records, 1736-1748, Extracts by Patricia Abelard Andersen, *Western Maryland Genealogy*, Vol. 18, No. 1, January 2002, p. 41)

Prather, Thomas, was appointed Constable from the mouth of the Monocacy to the Shannandore [Shenandoah] in Prince George's County, now Frederick County, 1738. (Ref: Prince George's County Court Records, 1736-1748, Extracts by Patricia Abelard Andersen, *Western Maryland Genealogy*, Vol. 18, No. 1, January 2002, p. 35); appointed a Commissioner of the Peace for Prince George's County, 6 Oct 1747. (Ref: Maryland State Archives, Governor and Council Commissioner Records, 1726-1794, p. 100); Court Justice, Frederick County, 1748. (Ref: *This Was The Life: Excerpts from the Judgment Records of Frederick County, Maryland, 1748-1765*, by Millard Milburn Rice, p. 1 Justice, p. 242 Sheriff); colonel, commissioned High Sheriff of Frederick County, 10 Nov 1762. (Ref: Maryland State Archives, Governor and Council Commissioner Records, 1726-1794, p. 197); appointed to a Special Commission to hear cases involving convicted felons on 31 Aug 1768. (Ref: *Archives of Maryland*, Vol. XXXII, "Proceedings of the Council of Maryland, 1761-1770," p. 247); Court Justice, 1769. (Ref: "Frederick County Court Minutes, March 1769," by Patricia Abelard Andersen, *Western Maryland Genealogy*, Vol. 15, No. 2, April 1999, p. 62); captain, appointed a Commissioner of the Peace, 15 Aug 1774. (Ref: Maryland State Archives, Governor and Council Commissioner Records, 1726-1794, p. 284)

Presbury, George Gouldsmith, was appointed a Commissioner of the Peace for Baltimore County, 30 May 1774. (Ref: Maryland State Archives, Governor and Council Commissioner Records, 1726-1794, p. 283); appointed Deputy Surveyor of Harford County, 1774. (*Calendar of Maryland State Papers, No. 1 The Black Books*, p. 211)

Preston, James, appointed a Commissioner of the Peace for Baltimore County, 23 May 1753. (Ref: Maryland State Archives, Governor and Council Commissioner Records, 1726-1794, p. 138)

Price, Andrew, appointed a Commissioner of the Peace for Queen Anne's County, 3 Mar 1726/7 and 30 Nov 1732. (Ref: Maryland State Archives, Governor and Council Commissioner Records, 1726-1794, pp. 2 and 36); see Richard Bennett and Samuel Chew, Jr.

Price, Richard, see Negro Joe.

Price, Thomas (1732-1795), appointed Constable of Frederick Town Hundred in Frederick County in 1753. (Ref: *This Was The Life: Excerpts from the Judgment Records of Frederick County, Maryland, 1748-1765*, by Millard Milburn Rice, p. 131); captain, appointed a Commissioner of the Peace, 12 Mar 1763. (Ref: Maryland State Archives, Governor and Council Commissioner Records, 1726-1794, p. 209); Court Justice, 1769. (Ref: "Frederick County Court Minutes, March 1769," by Patricia Abelard Andersen, *Western Maryland Genealogy*, Vol. 15, No. 2, April 1999, p. 62); appointed a Commissioner of the Peace, 2 Apr 1770 and 15 Aug 1774. (Ref: Maryland State Archives, Governor and Council Commissioner Records, 1726-1794, pp. 250, 284); Court Judge,

1774. (*Calendar of Maryland State Papers, No. 1 The Black Books*, p. 217); see William Hoskins.

Priggs, John Frederick Augustus, of Prince George's County, was commissioned Deputy Surveyor, 2 Dec 1771. (Ref: Maryland Commission Book No. 82, p. 273; *Maryland Historical Magazine*, Vol. XXVII, p. 31)

Prindowell, John, was commissioned a Coroner for Calvert County, 23 Aug 1734. (Ref: Maryland Commission Book No. 82, p. 20; *Maryland Historical Magazine*, Vol. XXVI, p. 141)

Pritchard (Pritchett), Edward (d. c1761), was appointed a Commissioner of the Peace for Dorchester County, 17 Oct 1734. (Ref: Maryland State Archives, Governor and Council Commissioner Records, 1726-1794, p. 44)

Pritchard, Edward, Jr., was appointed Constable of Streights Hundred in Dorchester County, 1742. (Ref: Dorchester County Judgment Records, 1742-1743, p. 84; *Judgment Records of Dorchester, Queen Anne's and Talbot Counties, Maryland*, by F. Edward Wright, 2001, p. 30, gave his name as Edward Pritchett, Jr.)

Probart, William, registration of brigantine *Revenge*, 20 tons, built in Virginia, 1739. Robert Stamper, master. William Probart, owner. 4 Feb 1739/40. (Ref: Maryland Commission Book No. 82, p. 78; *Maryland Historical Magazine*, Vol. XXVI, p. 155)

Purnell, John, commissioned Sheriff of Somerset County, 27 May 1728. (Ref: Maryland State Archives, Governor and Council Commissioner Records, 1726-1794, p. 7); of Sinapuxent, appointed a Commissioner of the Peace for Worcester County, 1 Jun 1743. (Ref: Maryland State Archives, Governor and Council Commissioner Records, 1726-1794, p. 78, spelled his name Purnall)

Purnell, Lemuel, appointed a Commissioner of the Peace for Worcester County, 16 Jan 1769. (Ref: Maryland State Archives, Governor and Council Commissioner Records, 1726-1794, p. 240)

Purnell, Richard, appointed a Commissioner of the Peace for Anne Arundel County, 28 Feb 1742/3. (Ref: Maryland State Archives, Governor and Council Commissioner Records, 1726-1794, p. 77)

Purnell, Samuel, appointed a Commissioner of the Peace for Worcester County, 8 Aug 1769. (Ref: Maryland State Archives, Governor and Council Commissioner Records, 1726-1794, p. 243)

Purnell, William (d. 1777), was appointed a Commissioner of the Peace for Worcester County, 26 Oct 1773. (Ref: Maryland State Archives, Governor and Council Commissioner Records, 1726-1794, p. 278)

Purnham, John, registration of sloop *Ganett*, 30 tons, built in Somerset County, 1735. John Purnham, master and owner. 17 Nov 1735. (Ref: Maryland Commission Book No. 82, p. 38; *Maryland Historical Magazine*, Vol. XXVI, p. 145)

Quinton, Dixon, appointed a Commissioner of the Peace for Worcester County, 30 Apr 1770 and 26 Oct 1773. (Ref: Maryland State Archives, Governor and Council Commissioner Records, 1726-1794, pp. 250, 278); Court Justice, Worcester County, 1774. (*Calendar of Maryland State Papers, No. 1 The Black Books*, p. 214)

Quinton, Philip, esquire, commissioned High Sheriff of Worcester County, 14 Jan 1776. (Ref: Maryland State Archives, Governor and Council Commissioner Records, 1726-1794, p. 280)

Quynn, Allen, was commissioned a Coroner of Anne Arundel County, 7 Nov 1765. (Ref: Maryland Commission Book No. 82, p. 175; *Maryland Historical Magazine*, Vol. XXVI, p. 354); commissioned a Coroner of Anne Arundel County, 30 Apr 1773. (Ref: Maryland Commission Book No. 82, p. 312; *Maryland Historical Magazine*, Vol. XXVII, p. 34)

Rainey, John, see Richard Floud.

Raitt, John, commissioned Sheriff of Anne Arundel County, 22 Nov 1756. (Ref: Maryland State Archives, Governor and Council Commissioner Records, 1726-1794, p. 163; *Archives of Maryland*, Vol. LII, "Proceedings and Acts of the General Assembly of Maryland, 1755-1756," p. 573)

Randall, Christopher, of Baltimore Counnty, was appointed a Commissioner of the Peace on 3 Mar 1726/7 and 15 Nov 1750. (Ref: Maryland State Archives, Governor and Council Commissioner Records, 1726-1794, pp. 2, 120)

Randall, Theophilus, see Samuel Massey.

Ranney, Robert, reverend, licensed to preach in St. Andrew's Parish, St. Mary's County, 25 Oct 1765. (Ref: Maryland Commission Book No. 82, p. 175;

Maryland Historical Magazine, Vol. XXVI, p. 353, mistakenly stated it was in Calvert County; *Directory of Ministers and the Maryland Churches They Served, 1634-1900*, by Edna Agatha Kanely, Vol. II, L-Z, p. 190, correctly stated it was in St. Mary's County and spelled his name Renny, but on p. 178 spelled his name Ranney); licensed to preach in St. Margaret's Westminster, Anne Arundel County, vacant by the removal of Rev. William West to St. Andrew's Parish, St. Mary's County, 18 Nov 1767. (Ref: Maryland Commission Book No. 82, p. 205; *Maryland Historical Magazine*, Vol. XXVI, p. 356); induction into St. Margaret's Westminster Parish, Anne Arundel County, 17 Jun 1769. (Ref: Maryland Commission Book No. 82, p. 225; *Maryland Historical Magazine*, Vol. XXVI, p. 359, spelled his name Ranny)

Ransburg, Stephen, was appointed Constable of Linganore Hundred in Prince George's County, now Frederick County, 1747. (Ref: Prince George's County Court Records, 1736-1748, Extracts by Patricia Abelard Andersen, *Western Maryland Genealogy*, Vol. 18, No. 1, January 2002, p. 45, misspelled his name as Runsburg); see Bridget Kelly and Patrick Sullivan.

Ransburgh, Jacob, was appointed Constable of the Middle Part of Monochosey [Monocacy] Hundred in Frederick County, 1771. (Ref: "Frederick County Minute Book, March 1771, Extracts by Patricia Abelard Andersen," *Western Maryland Genealogy*, Vol. 18, No. 1, January 2002, p. 26)

Rasin, William (1723-1762), registration of the schooner *Charming Polly*, 30 tons, built in Kent County, 1747. William Smith, master. William Rasin, owner. 27 Jan 1749/50. (Ref: Maryland Commission Book No. 82, p. 154; *Maryland Historical Magazine*, Vol. XXVI, p. 350); commissioned Sheriff of Kent County, 28 Nov 1753. (Ref: Maryland State Archives, Governor and Council Commissioner Records, 1726-1794, p. 142, spelled his name Rezin and p. 155 spelled it Rasin); appointed a Commissioner of the Peace for Kent County, 16 Nov 1757. (Ref: Maryland State Archives, Governor and Council Commissioner Records, 1726-1794, p. 179, spelled his name Resin)

Ratcliffe, Charles, appointed a Commissioner of the Peace for Somerset County, 25 Mar 1734. (Ref: Maryland State Archives, Governor and Council Commissioner Records, 1726-1794, p. 40)

Raven, Luke, appointed a Commissioner of the Peace for Baltimore County, 3 Mar 1726/7. (Ref: Maryland State Archives, Governor and Council Commissioner Records, 1726-1794, p. 2)

Rawle, Joseph, registration of schooner Hawke, 20 tons, built at Herring Bay, 1735. Joseph Rawle, master and owner. 27 Nov 1735. (Ref: Maryland Commission Book No. 82, p. 39; *Maryland Historical Magazine*, Vol. XXVI, p. 146)

Rawlings, Anthony, appointed a Commissioner of the Peace for Dorchester County, 1 Aug 1729 and 29 Oct 1730. (Ref: Maryland State Archives, Governor and Council Commissioner Records, 1726-1794, pp. 11, 17)

Rawlings, Daniel, commissioned Sheriff of Calvert County, 12 Aug 1747. (Ref: Maryland State Archives, Governor and Council Commissioner Records, 1726-1794, p. 99)

Rawlings, Daniel, Jr., appointed a Commissioner of the Peace for Calvert County, 12 Nov 1773. (Ref: Maryland State Archives, Governor and Council Commissioner Records, 1726-1794, p. 279)

Rawlings, David, see Jane Turner.

Rawlings, John, appointed a Commissioner of the Peace for Frederick County, 12 Nov 1748. (Ref: Maryland State Archives, Governor and Council Commissioner Records, 1726-1794, p. 109); Court Justice, Frederick County, 1748. (Ref: *This Was The Life: Excerpts from the Judgment Records of Frederick County, Maryland, 1748-1765*, by Millard Milburn Rice, p. 1, spelled his name Rawlins)

Rawlins, Isaac, commissioned Deputy Surveyor of Calvert County, 28 Nov 1743. (Ref: Maryland Commission Book No. 82, p. 106; *Maryland Historical Magazine*, Vol. XXVI, p. 250)

Razolini, Onorio, commissioned Master Gunner, Storekeeper, and Keeper of the Council Chamber in Annapolis, 4 Jun 1734. (Ref: Maryland Commission Book No. 82, p. 18; *Maryland Historical Magazine*, Vol. XXVI, p. 141)

Read, Alexander, appointed a Commissioner of the Peace for Kent County, 11 Nov 1763. (Ref: Maryland State Archives, Governor and Council Commissioner Records, 1726-1794, p. 212)

Read, John, appointed a Commissioner of the Peace for Cecil County, 2 Dec 1761. (Ref: Maryland State Archives, Governor and Council Commissioner

Read, John, appointed a Commissioner of the Peace for St. Mary's County, 2 Mar 1726/7. (Ref: Maryland State Archives, Governor and Council Commissioner Records, 1726-1794, p. 2)

Read, John Hatton, appointed a Commissioner of the Peace for Somerset County, 26 Jul 1773. (Ref: Maryland State Archives, Governor and Council Commissioner Records, 1726-1794, p. 272)

Read, Samuel, see George Watkins.

Reade, Robert, reverend, licensed to preach in Coventry Parish in Somerset and Worcester Counties, vacant by the death of Rev. Nathaniel Whitaker. 13 Jan 1767. (Ref: Maryland Commission Book No. 82, p. 198; *Maryland Historical Magazine*, Vol. XXVI, p. 355; *Calendar of Maryland State Papers, No. 1 The Black Books*, p. 200); induction into All Hallows Parish, Worcester County, 9 May 1767. (Ref: Maryland Commission Book No. 82, p. 204; *Maryland Historical Magazine*, Vol. XXVI, p. 356); induction into St. Paul's Parish, Kent County, 5 Dec 1767. (Ref: Maryland Commission Book No. 82, p. 205; *Maryland Historical Magazine*, Vol. XXVI, p. 356)

Reader, Henry, appointed a Commissioner of the Peace for Somerset County, 26 Jul 1773. (Ref: Maryland State Archives, Governor and Council Commissioner Records, 1726-1794, p. 2720

Reading, Phillip (d. 1778), reverend, licensed to preach in St. Augustine Parish, Cecil County, 15 Dec 1773. (Ref: Maryland Commission Book No. 82, p. 332; *Maryland Historical Magazine*, Vol. XXVII, p. 36)

Redgrave, Abraham, appointed a Commissioner of the Peace for Kent County, 3 Mar 1726/7. (Ref: Maryland State Archives, Governor and Council Commissioner Records, 1726-1794, p. 2)

Reeder, John, Jr. (c1732-1780), was appointed a Commissioner of the Peace for St. Mary's County on 26 Apr 1764 and again on 11 May 1769. (Ref: Maryland State Archives, Governor and Council Commissioner Records, 1726-1794, p. 215, and p. 241 spelled his name Reader)

Rees, William, of Baltimore County, was appointed a Ranger, 9 Aug 1775. (Ref: *Calendar of Maryland State Papers, The Red Books*, No. 4, Part 1, p. 5)

Reeves, Upgate, was commissioned a Coroner for St. Mary's County, 26 Oct 1737. (Ref: Maryland Commission Book No. 82, p. 51; *Maryland Historical Magazine*, Vol. XXVI, p. 150)

Reily, Bryan, Constable of the Lower Precinct of Mattapany Hundred in Prince George's County, now Frederick County, in 1733. (*Calendar of Maryland State Papers, No. 1 The Black Books*, p. 39)

Rench, Andrew, see John Harrison.

Rendell, John, see Charles Ridgeley and Christopher Grindall.

Rentz, Peter, native of Germany, naturalized 31 Aug 1739 and also his sons Joseph, John and Andrew. (Ref: Maryland Commission Book No. 82, p. 79; *Maryland Historical Magazine*, Vol. XXVI, p. 155)

Reynolds, Edward (d. by 1820), appointed a Commissioner of the Peace for Calvert County, 26 Jul 1773. (Ref: Maryland State Archives, Governor and Council Commissioner Records, 1726-1794, p. 272)

Reynolds, William, see William Roberts.

Richards, Daniel, appointed Constable of Manor Hundred in Frederick County, 1769. (Ref: "Frederick County Court Minutes November 1769 by Patricia Abelard Andersen," *Western Maryland Genealogy*, Vol. 16, No. 1, January 2000, p. 32)

Rice, William, servant of John Rutter, of Cecil County, convicted felon, was executed on 29 Dec 1752. (Ref: Maryland State Archives, Governor and Council Commissioner Records, 1726-1794, p. 136)

Richard, James, was commissioned Sheriff of Baltimore County, 23 Oct 1746. (Ref: Maryland State Archives, Governor and Council Commissioner Records, 1726-1794, p. 94)

Richard, James, of Baltimore County, convicted of burglary and larceny by breaking into a house and stealing papers, was whipped and stood in the pillory in 1769 and later pardoned and banished on 20 Mar 1770. (Ref: Maryland Commission Book No. 82, p. 221; *Maryland Historical Magazine*, Vol. XXVI, p. 359, spelled his name Richards; *Archives of Maryland*, Vol. XXXII, "Proceedings of the Council of Maryland, 1761-1770," pp. 260-261, 269-270, 349-351, spelled his surname Richard)

Richards, Richard, appointed a Commissioner of the Peace for Baltimore County, 1 Nov 1762. (Ref:

Maryland State Archives, Governor and Council Commissioner Records, 1726-1794, p. 206)

Richardson, Anthony, of Talbot County, was appointed a Commissioner of the Peace, 17 Oct 1734. (Ref: Maryland State Archives, Governor and Council Commissioner Records, 1726-1794, p. 44)

Richardson, John, see Henry Lowes.

Richardson, Joseph (1743-1786), was appointed a Commissioner of the Peace for Dorchester County, 2 Nov 1773. (Ref: Maryland State Archives, Governor and Council Commissioner Records, 1726-1794, p. 278)

Richardson, Joseph, of Anne Arundel County, appointed Constable in the Upper Part of Road [Rhode] River Hundred in 1774. (Ref: Anne Arundel County Court Minutes, 1725-1757, 1774)

Richardson, Richard, appointed a Commissioner of the Peace for Baltimore County, 30 May 1774. (Ref: Maryland State Archives, Governor and Council Commissioner Records, 1726-1794, p. 283)

Richardson, Thomas, appointed a Commissioner of the Peace for Talbot County, 29 Oct 1730. (Ref: Maryland State Archives, Governor and Council Commissioner Records, 1726-1794, p. 17)

Richardson, William (1735-1825), appointed a Commissioner of the Peace for Caroline County, 8 Feb 1774. (Ref: Maryland State Archives, Governor and Council Commissioner Records, 1726-1794, p. 280)

Riddell, George, see Negro James

Rider, John (1686-1739/40), of Dorchester County, captain, appointed a Deputy Commissary [government official who had certain duties to perform] on 11 Jul 1727. (Ref: *Abstracts of the Testamentary Proceedings and Prerogative Court of Maryland, Vol. XVII, 1724-1727*, by Vernon L. Skinner, Jr., p. 202, citing original Liber 28, f. 75); appointed a Commissioner of the Peace for Cecil County, Baltimore County, Kent County, Prince George's County, Anne Arundel County, Calvert County, Charles County, St. Mary's County, Queen Anne's County, and Talbot County, 4 Aug 1732 and 10 Aug 1732 and 20 Aug 1733. (Ref: Maryland State Archives, Governor and Council Commissioner Records, 1726-1794, pp. 32-37)

Ridgely, Charles (d. 1772), merchant, registered he sloop *Charles*, 20 tons, built in Baltimore County, 1740. Robert Goulding, master. Charles Ridgeley and John Rendell, owners. 28 Jan 1743/4. (Ref: Maryland Commission Book No. 82, p. 104; *Maryland Historical Magazine*, Vol. XXVI, p. 249; spelled his name Ridgeley); appointed a Commissioner of the Peace for Baltimore County, 22 Oct 1741. (Ref: Maryland State Archives, Governor and Council Commissioner Records, 1726-1794, p. 72)

Ridgely, Charles (1733-1790), was appointed to represent Baltimore County in the Provincial Convention, 1775. (Ref: *Calendar of Maryland State Papers, The Red Books*, No. 4, Part 1, p. 3)

Ridgely, Charles, of John (c1749-1786), was appointed to represent Baltimore County in the Provincial Convention, 1775. (Ref: *Calendar of Maryland State Papers, The Red Books*, No. 4, Part 1, p. 3)

Ridgely, Groomberry, of Anne Arundel County, was appointed a Commissioner of the Peace on 12 Aug 1752. (Ref: Maryland State Archives, Governor and Council Commissioner Records, 1726-1794, p. 133)

Ridgely, Henry, appointed a Commissioner of the Peace for Anne Arundel County, 1 Nov 1729. (Ref: Maryland State Archives, Governor and Council Commissioner Records, 1726-1794, p. 12); commissioned Deputy Surveyor of Anne Arundel County, 15 Mar 1733/4. (Ref: Maryland Commission Book No. 82, p. 9; *Maryland Historical Magazine*, Vol. XXVI, p. 140, spelled his name Ridgeley)

Ridgely, Henry (1728-1791), major, appointed a Commissioner of the Peace for Anne Arundel County, 18 Aug 1764. (Ref: Maryland State Archives, Governor and Council Commissioner Records, 1726-1794, p. 217)

Ridgely, John (c1723/24-1771), was appointed a Commissioner of the Peace for Baltimore County, 1 Jun 1750. (Ref: Maryland State Archives, Governor and Council Commissioner Records, 1726-1794, p. 117)

Ridout, John (1732-1797), commissioned Naval Officer of Annapolis, 28 Aug 1769 and 29 Apr 1773. (Ref: Maryland Commission Book No. 82, pp. 226, 306; *Maryland Historical Magazine*, Vol. XXVI, p. 359, and Vol. XXVII p. 33)

Rigbie, Skipwith, commissioned Deputy Surveyor of Baltimore County, 18 Mar 1748/9. (Ref: Maryland Commission Book No. 82, p. 139; *Maryland*

Historical Magazine, Vol. XXVI, p. 344); appointed a Commissioner of the Peace, 1 Jun 1750. (Ref: Maryland State Archives, Governor and Council Commissioner Records, 1726-1794, p. 117)

Rigby, John, see John Lumley.

Rigby, Nathan, appointed a Commissioner of the Peace for Baltimore County, 4 Aug 1735. (Ref: Maryland State Archives, Governor and Council Commissioner Records, 1726-1794, p. 49); commissioned Sheriff on 26 Oct 1737. (Ref: Maryland State Archives, Governor and Council Commissioner Records, 1726-1794, p. 58)

Riggen, Teague, of Morumsco, was appointed a Commissioner of the Peace for Somerset County, 20 May 1766. (Ref: Maryland State Archives, Governor and Council Commissioner Records, 1726-1794, p. 226)

Rightsman, John, appointed Constable of the Middle Part of Monocacy Hundred in Frederick County in 1753. (Ref: *This Was The Life: Excerpts from the Judgment Records of Frederick County, Maryland, 1748-1765*, by Millard Milburn Rice, p. 131)

Riley, Hugh, appointed Constable of the Lower Part of Potomac Hundred in Frederick County in 1751. (Ref: *This Was The Life: Excerpts from the Judgment Records of Frederick County, Maryland, 1748-1765*, by Millard Milburn Rice, p. 61)

Riley, John, appointed Constable of Sugar Loaf Hundred in Frederick County in 1753. (Ref: *This Was The Life: Excerpts from the Judgment Records of Frederick County, Maryland, 1748-1765*, by Millard Milburn Rice, p. 131)

Rimmar, Hugh, registration of brigantine *John and Peggy*, 55 tons, built in Dorchester County, 1741. Hugh Rimmar, master and owner. 20 Jun 1741. (Ref: Maryland Commission Book No. 82, p. 86; *Maryland Historical Magazine*, Vol. XXVI, p. 244)

Ringgold, Andrew, of Frederick County, was convicted of stealing an axe valued at fifteen pounds of tobacco from Henry Six in 1750, was sentenced to be set upon the pillory for fifteen minutes and then taken to the whipping post and receive twenty lashes on his bare back. (Ref: *This Was The Life: Excerpts from the Judgment Records of Frederick County, Maryland, 1748-1765*, by Millard Milburn Rice, p. 44, spelled his name Ringold)

Ringgold, James, Jr., commissioned one of the Coroners of Kent County, 3 Sep 1746. (Ref: Maryland Commission Book No. 82, p. 123; *Maryland Historical Magazine*, Vol. XXVI, p. 258, spelled his name Ringold); commissioned Sheriff of Kent County, 11 Aug 1747. (Ref: Maryland State Archives, Governor and Council Commissioner Records, 1726-1794, p. 99)

Ringgold, Thomas, appointed a Commissioner of the Peace for Kent County, 3 Mar 1726/7. (Ref: Maryland State Archives, Governor and Council Commissioner Records, 1726-1794, p. 2); registration of sloop *Speedwell*, 65 tons, built in Somerset County, 1749. George Bell, master. Thomas Ringold and James Tilghman, owners. 20 Apr 1750. (Ref: Maryland Commission Book No. 82, p. 157; *Maryland Historical Magazine*, Vol. XXVI, p. 352, spelled his name Ringold)

Ringgold, Thomas (1715-1772), of Kent Island, was appointed a Commissioner of the Peace for Queen Anne's County on 31 Oct 1768. (Ref: Maryland State Archives, Governor and Council Commissioner Records, 1726-1794, p. 239, spelled his name Ringold); Court Justice, 1774. (*Calendar of Maryland State Papers, No. 1 The Black Books*, p. 215)

Ringgold, William, commissioned a Coroner for Kent County, 16 Jul 1737. (Ref: Maryland Commission Book No. 82, p. 50; *Maryland Historical Magazine*, Vol. XXVI, p. 149, spelled his name Ringold); appointed a Commissioner of the Peace for Kent County, 26 Oct 1738, 18 Feb 1739/40, and 8 Mar 1754. (Ref: Maryland State Archives, Governor and Council Commissioner Records, 1726-1794, pp. 62, 66, 143); of Eastern Neck, appointed a Commissioner of the Peace for Kent County, 2 Nov 1762. (Ref: Maryland State Archives, Governor and Council Commissioner Records, 1726-1794, p. 207)

Risher, Peter, planter, of Baltimore County, native of High Germany, naturalized 4 Jun 1738 and also his children Daniel, Susannah and Elizabeth. (Ref: Maryland Commission Book No. 82, p. 58; *Maryland Historical Magazine*, Vol. XXVI, p. 151)

Risteau, John, appointed a Commissioner of the Peace for Baltimore County, 21 Feb 1735/6 and 4 Oct 1737. (Ref: Maryland State Archives, Governor and Council Commissioner Records, 1726-1794, pp. 51, 57); commissioned one of the Coroners of Baltimore

County, 23 Mar 1742/3. (Ref: Maryland Commission Book No. 82, p. 101; *Maryland Historical Magazine*, Vol. XXVI, p. 248); captain, commissioned Sheriff of Baltimore County, 21 Oct 1743. (Ref: Maryland State Archives, Governor and Council Commissioner Records, 1726-1794, p. 82, and p. 86 styled him as captain on 17 Sep 1744); late sheriff of Baltimore County, had ordinary license accounts still unpaid in 1756. (Ref: *Archives of Maryland*, Vol. LII, "Proceedings and Acts of the General Assembly of Maryland, 1755-1756," p. 568)

Risteau, Talbot, was commissioned one of the Coroners of Baltimore County, 26 Dec 1743. (Ref: Maryland Commission Book No. 82, p. 107; *Maryland Historical Magazine*, Vol. XXVI, p. 251)

Roberts, Benjamin, appointed a Commissioner of the Peace for Queen Anne's County, 18 May 1758. (Ref: Maryland State Archives, Governor and Council Commissioner Records, 1726-1794, p. 180)

Roberts, George, of Anne Arundel County, convicted of murder, was executed on 4 Aug 1742. (Ref: Maryland State Archives, Governor and Council Commissioner Records, 1726-1794, p. 73)

Roberts, Jonathan, appointed a Commissioner of the Peace for Queen Anne's County, 2 Oct 1762. (Ref: Maryland State Archives, Governor and Council Commissioner Records, 1726-1794, p. 205)

Roberts, Levin, see John Stinson.

Roberts, Timothy, appointed a Commissioner of the Peace for Cecil County, 1748 [exact date not given]. (Ref: Maryland State Archives, Governor and Council Commissioner Records, 1726-1794, p. 108)

Roberts, William, appointed Constable of Pipe Creek Hundred in Prince George's County, now Frederick County, 1745. (Ref: Prince George's County Court Records, 1736-1748, Extracts by Patricia Abelard Andersen, *Western Maryland Genealogy*, Vol. 18, No. 1, January 2002, p. 43); merchant, registration of ship *Rumney & Long*, 300 tons, built at Annapolis, 1746. William Strachan, master. William Roberts, owner. 2 Feb 1746/7. (Ref: Maryland Commission Book No. 82, p. 125; *Maryland Historical Magazine*, Vol. XXVI, p. 259); registration of snow *Russell*, 80 tons, built in Anne Arundel County, 1750. John Mackleraith, master. William Roberts, James Russell and James Dick, owners. 17 Apr 1750. (Ref: Maryland Commission Book No. 82, p. 156; *Maryland Historical Magazine*, Vol. XXVI, p. 351)

Roberts, William, sadler, registration of schooner *Carolina*, 20 tons, built in Annapolis, 1743. James Earl, master. William Roberts, owner. 1743/4 (Ref: Maryland Commission Book No. 82, p. 104; *Maryland Historical Magazine*, Vol. XXVI, p. 249); sadler, registration of ship *William and Ann*, 150 tons, built at Annapolis, 1744. William Strachan, master. William Roberts, owner. 19 Dec 1744. (Ref: Maryland Commission Book No. 82, p. 111; *Maryland Historical Magazine*, Vol. XXVI, p. 253); sadler, registration of sloop *Harp*, 15 tons, built at Braintree in New England, 1739, and called the *Hummingbird*. Richard Bentley, master. William Roberts, Aaron Lynn, William Reynolds and Richard Bentley, owners. 9 May 1745. (Ref: Maryland Commission Book No. 82, p. 113; *Maryland Historical Magazine*, Vol. XXVI, p. 254)

Robins, George, appointed a Commissioner of the Peace for Talbot County, 29 Oct 1730. (Ref: Maryland State Archives, Governor and Council Commissioner Records, 1726-1794, p. 17); registration of schooner *Nancy*, 20 tons, built in Talbot County, 1733. Thomas Marsh, master. George Robins, owner. 23 Oct 1733. (Ref: Maryland Commission Book No. 82, p. 7; *Maryland Historical Magazine*, Vol. XXVI, p. 139)

Robins, John, appointed a Commissioner of the Peace for Talbot County, 9 May 1732. (Ref: Maryland State Archives, Governor and Council Commissioner Records, 1726-1794, p. 23)

Robins, John Purnell (c1742-1780), appointed a Commissioner of the Peace for Worcester County, 26 Oct 1773. (Ref: Maryland State Archives, Governor and Council Commissioner Records, 1726-1794, p. 278, spelled his surname Robbins)

Robins, Thomas, see Duncan Murray, Jr.

Robins, William, appointed a Commissioner of the Peace for Talbot County, 2 Oct 1751. (Ref: Maryland State Archives, Governor and Council Commissioner Records, 1726-1794, p. 124)

Robinson, Alexander, appointed a Commissioner of the Peace for Somerset County, 4 Jul 1755. (Ref: Maryland State Archives, Governor and Council Commissioner Records, 1726-1794, p. 161)

Robinson, Daniel, see Jacob Giles.

Robinson, Elijah, appointed a Commissioner of the

Peace for Anne Arundel County, 15 Nov 1770 and 26 Jul 1773. (Ref: Maryland State Archives, Governor and Council Commissioner Records, 1726-1794, pp. 255, 272); Court Justice, 1774. (Ref: Anne Arundel County Court Minutes, 1725-1757, 1774)

Robinson, Thomas, labourer and chimney sweeper, of Baltimore County, convicted for burglary of the mansion house of Alexander McMechan, his master, from whom he stole one dollar out of his drawer by climbing down his master's chimney. Sentenced to be hanged, he was pardoned and banished on 15 Sep 1768 on condition of his leaving the province within ten days from his release from jail and never return again. He was a simple youth not exceeding sixteen years of age, easily persuaded by villainous people, and came into this country in 1765. (Ref: Maryland Commission Book No. 82, p. 217; *Maryland Historical Magazine*, Vol. XXVI, p. 358; *Archives of Maryland*, Vol. XXXII, "Proceedings of the Council of Maryland, 1761-1770," pp. 249-251)

Robison, Daniel, see Jacob Giles.

Rock, George, merchant, registration of sloop *Nancy*, 12 tons, built in Worcester County, 1744. Ralph Butler, master. George Rock, owner. 18 May 1748. (Ref: Maryland Commission Book No. 82, p. 134; *Maryland Historical Magazine*, Vol. XXVI, p. 263); merchant, registration of brigantine *Elk*, 60 tons, built in Cecil County, 1745. John Brett, master. George Rock and John Kankey, owners. 19 Apr 1745. (Ref: Maryland Commission Book No. 82, p. 113; *Maryland Historical Magazine*, Vol. XXVI, p. 254); appointed a Commissioner of the Peace for Cecil County, 27 Oct 1747. (Ref: Maryland State Archives, Governor and Council Commissioner Records, 1726-1794, p. 101); appointed a Commissioner of the Peace for Cecil County, 20 Feb 1774. (Ref: Maryland State Archives, Governor and Council Commissioner Records, 1726-1794, p. 281)

Rogers, Benjamin, appointed a Commissioner of the Peace for Baltimore County, 1 Nov 1762. (Ref: Maryland State Archives, Governor and Council Commissioner Records, 1726-1794, p. 206); appointed a Justice in Baltimore County, 22 Feb 1773. (Ref: *Inhabitants of Baltimore County, 1763-1774*, by Henry C. Peden, Jr., 1989, p. 49, citing *Calendar of Maryland State Papers, No. 1 The Black Books*, p. 208); appointed a Commissioner of the Peace for Baltimore County, 30 May 1774. (Ref: Maryland State Archives, Governor and Council Commissioner Records, 1726-1794, p. 283); see Negro Cesar.

Rogers, Richard, see Richard Mansfield.

Rogers, William, appointed a Commissioner of the Peace for Anne Arundel County, 15 Jun 1735. (Ref: Maryland State Archives, Governor and Council Commissioner Records, 1726-1794, p. 47)

Rogers, William, appointed a Commissioner of the Peace for Baltimore County, 24 Nov 1756. (Ref: Maryland State Archives, Governor and Council Commissioner Records, 1726-1794, p. 172)

Rogers, William, doctor, appointed a Commissioner of the Peace for Cecil County, 2 Jun 1774. (Ref: Maryland State Archives, Governor and Council Commissioner Records, 1726-1794, p. 283)

Rooke, Edward, see John Seegar.

Rose, William, see Patrick Creagh.

Ross, David, appointed a Commissioner of the Peace for Prince George's County, 8 Mar 1754. (Ref: Maryland State Archives, Governor and Council Commissioner Records, 1726-1794, p. 144); merchant, registration of sloop *Tryal*, 25 tons, built in Virginia, 1745. Robert Morrison, master. David Ross, owner. 1 Sep 1746. (Ref: Maryland Commission Book No. 82, p. 122; *Maryland Historical Magazine*, Vol. XXVI, p. 257); see Daniel Campbell.

Ross, James, see Richard Floud.

Rosse, John (d. 1775), reverend, induction into Coventry Parish in Somerset and Worcester Counties, 9 Nov 1767; induction into All Hallows Parish, Worcester County, 5 Dec 1767. (Ref: Maryland Commission Book No. 82, pp. 204, 205; *Maryland Historical Magazine*, Vol. XXVI, p. 356)

Round, Edward, appointed a Commissioner of the Peace for Somerset County, 25 Mar 1734. (Ref: Maryland State Archives, Governor and Council Commissioner Records, 1726-1794, p. 40)

Rousby, John (1685-1744), was appointed a Commissioner of the Peace for Cecil County, Baltimore County, Kent County, Prince George's County, Anne Arundel County, Calvert County, Charles County, St. Mary's County, Queen Anne's County, and Talbot County, 4 Aug 1732 and 10 Aug 1732 and 20 Aug 1733. (Ref: Maryland State

Routh, Christopher Cross, was appointed a Commissioner of the Peace for Queen Anne's County, 11 Nov 1763. (Ref: Maryland State Archives, Governor and Council Commissioner Records, 1726-1794, p. 212); Court Justice, 1774. (*Calendar of Maryland State Papers, No. 1 The Black Books*, p. 215)

Row, John, commissioned High Sheriff of Prince George's County, 4 Nov 1760. (Ref: Maryland State Archives, Governor and Council Commissioner Records, 1726-1794, p. 185)

Rudgkins, Edward, of ---- County, convicted felon, was executed on 4 Oct 1765. (Ref: *Archives of Maryland*, Vol. XXXII, "Proceedings of the Council of Maryland, 1761-1770," p. 108)

Rudolph, Tobias, appointed a Commissioner of the Peace for Cecil County, 21 Apr 1764 and 20 Feb 1774. (Ref: Maryland State Archives, Governor and Council Commissioner Records, 1726-1794, pp. 215, 281)

Rumney, Edward, of Annapolis, registration of schooner *Lark*, 20 tons, built in New England, 1722. George McClester. Master. 22 Jun 1742. (Ref: Maryland Commission Book No. 82, p. 92; *Maryland Historical Magazine*, Vol. XXVI, p. 246)

Rumsey, Charles, commissioned a Coroner of Cecil County, 6 Aug 1764. (Ref: Maryland Commission Book No. 82, p. 163; *Maryland Historical Magazine*, Vol. XXVI, p. 352); commissioned a Coroner of Cecil County, 23 Jun 1773. (Ref: Maryland Commission Book No. 82, p. 318; *Maryland Historical Magazine*, Vol. XXVII, p. 34)

Rumsey, John, appointed a Commissioner of the Peace for Harford County, 20 Feb 1774. (Ref: Maryland State Archives, Governor and Council Commissioner Records, 1726-1794, p. 281)

Rumsey, William (1698-1742/43), was appointed a Commissioner of the Peace for Cecil County on 29 Oct 1730. (Ref: Maryland State Archives, Governor and Council Commissioner Records, 1726-1794, p. 170); commissioned Naval Officer for the Cecil County District on 4 Aug 1733. (Ref: Maryland Commission Book No. 82, p. 2; *Maryland Historical Magazine*, Vol. XXVI, p. 139)

Rumsey, William (1729/30-c1777), captain, was appointed a Commissioner of the Peace for Cecil County, 17 Nov 1763 and 20 Feb 1774. (Ref: Maryland State Archives, Governor and Council Commissioner Records, 1726-1794, pp. 213, 281)

Russell, James, appointed a Commissioner of the Peace for Prince George's County, 12 Nov 1748. (Ref: Maryland State Archives, Governor and Council Commissioner Records, 1726-1794, p. 109)

Russell, James, registration of sloop *Charming Molly*, 15 tons, built at Herring Bay, 1733. Alexander Scougall, master. James Russel, owner. 18 May 1738. (Ref: Maryland Commission Book No. 82, p. 57; *Maryland Historical Magazine*, Vol. XXVI, p. 151); merchant, registration of ship *Nottingham*, 150 tons, built in Somerset County, 1740, and was then called *Britannia*. Robert Watson, master. James Wardrop, John Buchanan and James Russell, owners. 30 Aug 1742. (Ref: Maryland Commission Book No. 82, p. 95; *Maryland Historical Magazine*, Vol. XXVI, p. 246); merchant, registration of snow *Elizabeth*, 90 tons, built at Lymestone, Devon [England], 1730, and then called *Philleroy*, sold under decree of Admiralty to James Johnson, James Wardrop and James Russell. George Beal, master. 20 Mar 1743/4. (Ref: Maryland Commission Book No. 82, p. 108; *Maryland Historical Magazine*, Vol. XXVI, p. 251); registration of ship *Ogle*, 300 tons, built in Dorchester County, 1749. Walter Montgomery, master. James Russell, owner. 6 Jan 1749/50. (Ref: Maryland Commission Book No. 82, p. 154; *Maryland Historical Magazine*, Vol. XXVI, p. 350); see William Roberts and Negro Tony.

Russell, Richard, see Thomas Hodgkin.

Russell, William, appointed a Commissioner of the Peace for Baltimore County, 30 May 1774. (Ref: Maryland State Archives, Governor and Council Commissioner Records, 1726-1794, p. 283);of Baltimore County, Court Justice, 1774. (Ref: *Inhabitants of Baltimore County, 1763-1774*, by Henry C. Peden, Jr., 1989, p. 49, citing Baltimore County Court Proceedings, 1774); see Mary Godson.

Rustain, Robert, see Negro Robert Rustain,

Rustin, George, see Negro George.

Rutland, Edmund, see Daniel Wolstenholme.

Rutter, John, see William Rice.

Rutter, Moses, of Baltimore County, was appointed a

Ranger, 9 Aug 1775. (Ref: *Calendar of Maryland State Papers, The Red Books*, No. 4, Part 1, p. 5)

Ryan, Jacob, of Anne Arundel County, appointed Constable of Patuxent Hundred in 1774. (Ref: Anne Arundel County Court Minutes, 1725-1757, 1774)

Ryan, Lodowick, native of Germany, denization, 22 Jun 1771. (Ref: Maryland Commission Book No. 82, p. 259; *Maryland Historical Magazine*, Vol. XXVII, p. 30)

Sanderson, Francis, appointed a Commissioner of the Peace for Baltimore County, 6 Mar 1775. (Ref: Maryland State Archives, Governor and Council Commissioner Records, 1726-1794, p. 288)

Sandsbury, Thomas, see Negro Tony.

Sandwith, William (Quaker), registration of the schooner *Sarah*, formerly *Ann of Virginia*, 20 toms, built at Salisbury, Massachusetts, 1728. Adam Wallis, master. John Selby and William Sandwith, owners. 14 Mar 1733/4. (Ref: Maryland Commission Book No. 82, p. 9; *Maryland Historical Magazine*, Vol. XXVI, p. 140)

Satchell, Mary, see James Horner.

Saunders, James, see Darby Lux.

Saunders, William, commissioned a Coroner for Anne Arundel County, 18 Oct 1740. (Ref: Maryland Commission Book No. 82, p. 85; *Maryland Historical Magazine*, Vol. XXVI, p. 158)

Savin, Thomas, appointed a Commissioner of the Peace for Cecil County, 19 Dec 1751. (Ref: Maryland State Archives, Governor and Council Commissioner Records, 1726-1794, p. 131)

Savory, William, merchant, registration of the sloop *Penelope*, 30 tons, built in Ann Arundel County, 1745. Martin Johnson, master. William Savory, owner. 10 May 1746. (Ref: Maryland Commission Book No. 82, p. 120; *Maryland Historical Magazine*, Vol. XXVI, p. 256)

Sayers, James, registration of brigantine *Planter*, 70 tons, built in Somerset County, 1740. James Sayers, master. James Sayers and Richard Gildart, of Liverpool, owners. 8 Sep 1740. (Ref: Maryland Commission Book No. 82, p. 83; *Maryland Historical Magazine*, Vol. XXVI, p. 157)

Scarborough, John (c1694-1775), was appointed a Commissioner of the Peace for Worcester County, 11 Dec 1742. (Ref: Maryland State Archives, Governor and Council Commissioner Records, 1726-1794, p. 75); Court Justice, Worcester County, 1774. (*Calendar of Maryland State Papers, No. 1 The Black Books*, p. 214); appointed a Commissioner of the Peace for Somerset County, 5 Jan 1775. (Ref: Maryland State Archives, Governor and Council Commissioner Records, 1726-1794, p. 286)

Scarborough, John, Jr., commissioned Sheriff of Worcester County, 2 Oct 1751. (Ref: Maryland State Archives, Governor and Council Commissioner Records, 1726-1794, p. 127); commissioned a Coroner of Worcester County, 22 May 1765. (Ref: Maryland Commission Book No. 82, p. 168; *Maryland Historical Magazine*, Vol. XXVI, p. 353)

Schandrett, William, registration of sloop *Nancy*, 10 tens, built in New Jersey, 1736 and then called the *Fanny and Nancy*. William Schandrett and James Earle, owners. 16 Oct 1742. (Ref: Maryland Commission Book No. 82, p. 100; *Maryland Historical Magazine*, Vol. XXVI, p. 248); see Patrick Creagh.

Scheiff, William, appointed Constable of Piney Creek Hundred in Frederick County, 1771. (Ref: "Frederick County Minute Book, March 1771, Extracts by Patricia Abelard Andersen," *Western Maryland Genealogy*, Vol. 18, No. 1, January 2002, p. 25)

Scott, Absalom, labourer, of Queen Anne's County, convicted felon for breaking open and robbing the store of Joshua Clarke, was sentenced to death on 16 Apr 1770, but was pardoned and banished on 12 Apr 1770 on condition that he left the province within ten days. (Ref: Maryland Commission Book No. 82, p. 237; *Maryland Historical Magazine*, Vol. XXVI, p. 360; *Archives of Maryland*, Vol. XXXII, "Proceedings of the Council of Maryland, 1761-1770," pp. 335, 345)

Scott, Charles, appointed a Commissioner of the Peace for Kent County, 7 Mar 1746/7. (Ref: Maryland State Archives, Governor and Council Commissioner Records, 1726-1794, p. 98)

Scott, Daniel (c1680-1744/45), was appointed a Commissioner of the Peace for Baltimore County, 3 Mar 1726/7 and 22 Oct 1728. (Ref: Maryland State Archives, Governor and Council Commissioner Records, 1726-1794, p. 2; p. 8 spelled his name Scot)

Scott, Day, appointed a Commissioner of the Peace

for Somerset County, 28 Feb 1742/3. (Ref: Maryland State Archives, Governor and Council Commissioner Records, 1726-1794, p. 76); registration of sloop *Eleanor*, 10 tons, built in Somerset County, 1730. Day Scott, master and owner. Aug/Sep 1734. (Ref: Maryland Commission Book No. 82, p. 20; *Maryland Historical Magazine*, Vol. XXVI, p. 141); registration of sloop *Neptune*, 50 tons, built in Somerset County, 1750. Day Scott, master and owner. 13 Sep 1750. (Ref: Maryland Commission Book No. 82, p. 146; *Maryland Historical Magazine*, Vol. XXVI, p. 346); registration of snow *Neptune*, 50 tons, built in Somerset County, 1750. Day Scott, master and owner. 29 May 1751. (Ref: Maryland Commission Book No. 82, p. 149; *Maryland Historical Magazine*, Vol. XXVI, p. 348)

Scott, Edward, registration of sloop *Molly*, 50 tons, built in New England, 1749. William Smith, master. Edward Scott, James Smith and William Murray, owners. 21 Aug 1750. (Ref: Maryland Commission Book No. 82, p. 145; *Maryland Historical Magazine*, Vol. XXVI, p. 346)

Scott, George, appointed a Commissioner of the Peace for Prince George's County, 22 Mar 1742/3. (Ref: Maryland State Archives, Governor and Council Commissioner Records, 1726-1794, p. 77); appointed Crier of Frederick County Court in 1758. (Ref: *This Was The Life: Excerpts from the Judgment Records of Frederick County, Maryland, 1748-1765*, by Millard Milburn Rice, p. 179); commissioned High Sheriff of Prince George's County, 10 Nov 1762. (Ref: Maryland State Archives, Governor and Council Commissioner Records, 1726-1794, p. 197); appointed a Commissioner of the Peace for Frederick County, 2 Mar 1775. (Ref: Maryland State Archives, Governor and Council Commissioner Records, 1726-1794, p. 288)

Scott, George Day (1736/37-1800), appointed a Commissioner of the Peace for Somerset County, 19 May 1774. (Ref: Maryland State Archives, Governor and Council Commissioner Records, 1726-1794, p. 282)

Scott, James, appointed a Commissioner of the Peace for Baltimore County, 1 Jun 1750. (Ref: Maryland State Archives, Governor and Council Commissioner Records, 1726-1794, p. 117)

Scott, John, was appointed a Commissioner of the Peace for Somerset County, 29 Oct 1730. (Ref: Maryland State Archives, Governor and Council Commissioner Records, 1726-1794, p. 17); appointed a Commissioner of the Peace for Worcester County, 11 Dec 1742. (Ref: Maryland State Archives, Governor and Council Commissioner Records, 1726-1794, p. 75)

Scott, John, reverend, licensed to preach in Durham Parish, Charles County, 14 Sep 1769. (Ref: Maryland Commission Book No. 82, p. 228; *Maryland Historical Magazine*, Vol. XXVI, p. 359); licensed to preach in Stepney Parish in Somerset and Worcester Counties, vacant by the death of Rev. Alexander Adams. 22 Nov 1770. (Ref: Maryland Commission Book No. 82, p. 251; *Maryland Historical Magazine*, Vol. XXVII, p. 29); induction into Durham Parish, Charles County, 15 Sep 1770. (Ref: Maryland Commission Book No. 82, p. 249; *Maryland Historical Magazine*, Vol. XXVI, p. 361); induction into Stepney Parish in Somerset and Worcester Counties, 12 Apr 1771. (Ref: Maryland Commission Book No. 82, p. 257; *Maryland Historical Magazine*, Vol. XXVII, p. 30); see Ephraim Waggaman and Henry Fendall.

Scott, Joseph, see Ephraim Waggaman.

Scott, Mary, see Ephraim Waggaman.

Scott, Upton, commissioned High Sheriff of Ann Arundel County, 15 Nov 1757. (Ref: Maryland State Archives, Governor and Council Commissioner Records, 1726-1794, p. 171, and p. 181 styled him as doctor); commissioned Clerk of the Council of Maryland, 15 Dec 1764. (Ref: *Archives of Maryland*, Vol. XXXII, "Proceedings of the Council of Maryland, 1761-1770," p. 97); commissioned Clerk to the Governor and Council, 29 Apr 1773. On same day, commissioned Examiner General of All Plats, Surveys, and Resurveys. (Ref: Maryland Commission Book No. 82, pp. 304-305; *Maryland Historical Magazine*, Vol. XXVII, p. 33)

Scougall, Alexander, see Christopher Grindall, James Russell and James Walker.

Seager, John, appointed a Commissioner of the Peace for Queen Anne's County, 4 Nov 1749. (Ref: Maryland State Archives, Governor and Council Commissioner Records, 1726-1794, p. 114)

Seager, John, was Constable in Burnt House Woods Hundred in Frederick County in 1758. (Ref: *This Was

The Life: Excerpts from the Judgment Records of Frederick County, Maryland, 1748-1765, by Millard Milburn Rice, p. 185)

Seahon, John, registration of sloop *Mary*, 25 tons, built in Somerset Co., 1745. John Seahon, master and owner. 1 Mar 1745/6. (Ref: Maryland Commission Book No. 82, p. 119; *Maryland Historical Magazine*, Vol. XXVI, p. 256)

Seany, John, appointed a Commissioner of the Peace for Queen Anne's County, 13 Mar 1773. (Ref: Maryland State Archives, Governor and Council Commissioner Records, 1726-1794, p. 265)

Seavor, Nicholas, commissioned a Coroner for Codorus, Baltimore County, 6 May 1737. (Ref: Maryland Commission Book No. 82, p. 48; *Maryland Historical Magazine*, Vol. XXVI, p. 149)

Seegar, John, registration of schooner *Charles Town*, 40 tons, built in Cecil County, 1749. Edward Rooke, master. John Seegar, Henry Baker and Richard Patten, owners. 21 Jan 1749/50. (Ref: Maryland Commission Book No. 82, p. 154; *Maryland Historical Magazine*, Vol. XXVI, p. 350); registration of schooner *Charles Town*, 45 tons, built in Cecil County, 1749. Sweetnam Burn, master. Henry Baker, John Hamilton, Edward Mitchell, Herman Husbands and John Seegar, owners. 8 Jun 1750. (Ref: Maryland Commission Book No. 82, p. 143; *Maryland Historical Magazine*, Vol. XXVI, p. 345)

Segar, John, see William Govane.

Selby, Henry, see Negro Robin.

Selby, John (d. 1790), appointed a Commissioner of the Peace for Worcester County, 23 Mar 1756. (Ref: Maryland State Archives, Governor and Council Commissioner Records, 1726-1794, p. 166); Court Justice, Worcester County, 1774. (*Calendar of Maryland State Papers, No. 1 The Black Books*, p. 214); appointed a Commissioner of the Peace for Somerset County, 5 Jan 1775. (Ref: Maryland State Archives, Governor and Council Commissioner Records, 1726-1794, p. 286); see Negro Jack and William Sandwith.

Selby, Jonathan, of Anne Arundel County, appointed Constable of South River Hundred in 1774. (Ref: Anne Arundel County Court Minutes, 1725-1757, 1774)

Selby, Parker (d. 1773), commissioned High Sheriff of Worcester County, 20 Oct 1770. (Ref: Maryland State Archives, Governor and Council Commissioner Records, 1726-1794, p. 243)

Selby, Parker, of John, commissioned High Sheriff of Worcester County, 3 Mar 1773. (Ref: Maryland State Archives, Governor and Council Commissioner Records, 1726-1794, p. 254)

Selby, Samuel, appointed constable of ---- Hundred [probably Newfoundland] in Frederick County in 1752. (Ref: *This Was The Life: Excerpts from the Judgment Records of Frederick County, Maryland, 1748-1765*, by Millard Milburn Rice, p. 127)

Selby, Samuel, Jr., appointed Constable of the Lower Part of Newfoundland Hundred in Frederick County in 1763. (Ref: *This Was The Life: Excerpts from the Judgment Records of Frederick County, Maryland, 1748-1765*, by Millard Milburn Rice, p. 249)

Selby, William Magruder, appointed Constable of Eastern Branch Hundred in Prince George's County, now Frederick County, 1746, 1748. (Ref: Prince George's County Court Records, 1736-1748, Extracts by Patricia Abelard Andersen, *Western Maryland Genealogy*, Vol. 18, No. 1, January 2002, pp. 44, 46)

Semmes, Ignatius, see William Digges and Edward Neale.

Shanahan, Eve, see Negro Ben.

Shanks, John, Jr., appointed a Commissioner of the Peace for Somerset County, 26 Jul 1773. (Ref: Maryland State Archives, Governor and Council Commissioner Records, 1726-1794, p. 272)

Shelby, Evan, of Frederick County, Court Justice, 1763-1769. (Ref: *This Was The Life: Excerpts from the Judgment Records of Frederick County, Maryland, 1748-1765*, by Millard Milburn Rice, p. 242; "Frederick County Court Minutes, March 1769," by Patricia Abelard Andersen, *Western Maryland Genealogy*, Vol. 15, No. 2, April 1999, p. 62); captain, appointed a Commissioner of the Peace, 12 Mar 1763, 2 Apr 1770 and 15 Aug 1774. (Ref: Maryland State Archives, Governor and Council Commissioner Records, 1726-1794, pp. 209, 250, 284)

Sheredine, Francis, convicted felon, pardoned for the burglary of the storehouse of Col. John Ward, was banished from the Province on 15 Jan 1742/3. (Ref: Maryland Commission Book No. 82, p. 100; *Maryland Historical Magazine*, Vol. XXVI, p. 248)

Sheredine, Jeremiah, appointed a Commissioner of the Peace for Baltimore County, 20 Nov 1769 and 31 Oct 1772. (Ref: Maryland State Archives, Governor and Council Commissioner Records, 1726-1794, pp. 248, 264); appointed a Commissioner of the Peace for Harford County, 20 Feb 1774. (Ref: Maryland State Archives, Governor and Council Commissioner Records, 1726-1794, p. 281)

Sheredine, Thomas (1699-1752), was commissioned Sheriff of Baltimore County, 27 May 1728. (Ref: Maryland State Archives, Governor and Council Commissioner Records, 1726-1794, p. 7); appointed a Commissioner of the Peace for Baltimore County, 29 Oct 1730. (Ref: Maryland State Archives, Governor and Council Commissioner Records, 1726-1794, p. 16); commissioned Sheriff of Baltimore County, 10 Jul 1750. (Ref: Maryland State Archives, Governor and Council Commissioner Records, 1726-1794, p. 118); late sheriff of Baltimore County, had ordinary license accounts in 1750 still unpaid in 1756. (Ref: *Archives of Maryland*, Vol. LII, "Proceedings and Acts of the General Assembly of Maryland, 1755-1756," p. 568); late sheriff of Baltimore County, had ordinary license accounts in 1752 still unpaid in 1756. (Ref: *Archives of Maryland*, Vol. LII, "Proceedings and Acts of the General Assembly of Maryland, 1755-1756," p. 568, styled him as Jr.)

Sheredine, Upton (1740-1800), was appointed a Commissioner of the Peace for Frederick County, 20 Aug 1772 and 15 Aug 1774. (Ref: Maryland State Archives, Governor and Council Commissioner Records, 1726-1794, pp. 261, 284); Court Judge, 1774. (*Calendar of Maryland State Papers, No. 1 The Black Books*, p. 217)

Sherwood, Daniel (c1669-1738), appointed a Commissioner of the Peace for Talbot County, 29 Oct 1730. (Ref: Maryland State Archives, Governor and Council Commissioner Records, 1726-1794, p. 17); commissioned a Coroner of Talbot County, 8 Dec 1769. (Ref: Maryland Commission Book No. 82, p. 233; *Maryland Historical Magazine*, Vol. XXVI, p. 360);

Sherwood, Thomas (d. by 1790), commissioned High Sheriff of Talbot County, 5 Oct 1768. (Ref: Maryland State Archives, Governor and Council Commissioner Records, 1726-1794, p. 225); commissioned a Coroner of Talbot County, 16 Nov 1771. (Ref: Maryland Commission Book No. 82, p. 273; *Maryland Historical Magazine*, Vol. XXVII, p. 31)

Shipley, Richard, commissioned Deputy Surveyor of Anne Arundel County, 3 Sep 1746 and 17 Apr 1747. (Ref: Maryland Commission Book No. 82, pp. 123, 128; *Maryland Historical Magazine*, Vol. XXVI, pp. 258, 260)

Short, Stephen (Negro), of Anne Arundel County, convicted felon under sentence of death, was reprieved on 4 Jun 1729. (Ref: Maryland State Archives, Governor and Council Commissioner Records, 1726-1794, p. 10)

Shriock, Henry (c1736-1814), was appointed Constable of Salisbury Hundred in Frederick County, 1769, 1771. (Ref: "Frederick County Court Minutes November 1769 by Patricia Abelard Andersen," *Western Maryland Genealogy*, Vol. 16, No. 1, January 2000, p. 33; "Frederick County Minute Book, March 1771, Extracts by Patricia Abelard Andersen," *Western Maryland Genealogy*, Vol. 18, No. 1, January 2002, p. 26)

Shriock, Leonard, was appointed Constable of Salisbury Hundred in Frederick County, 1771. (Ref: "Frederick County Minute Book, March 1771, Extracts by Patricia Abelard Andersen," *Western Maryland Genealogy*, Vol. 18, No. 1, January 2002, p. 26)

Simmons, John, of Anne Arundel County, appointed Constable of Herring Creek Hundred in 1774. (Ref: Anne Arundel County Court Minutes, 1725-1757, 1774)

Simonett, George, of Baltimore County, convicted felon, was executed on 31 May 1749. (Ref: Maryland State Archives, Governor and Council Commissioner Records, 1726-1794, p. 111)

Simpson, Benjamin, of Anne Arundel County, was appointed Constable in Huntingdon Hundred in 1774. (Ref: Anne Arundel County Court Minutes, 1725-1757, 1774)

Simpson, Jeremiah, was appointed Constable of the Middle Part of Rock Creek Hundred in Frederick County, 1760-1763. (Ref: *This Was The Life: Excerpts from the Judgment Records of Frederick County, Maryland, 1748-1765*, by Millard Milburn Rice, pp. 216, 242)

Simson, Juliana, see Negro David.

Six, Henry, see Andrew Ringold.

Skidmore, Joseph, appointed Constable of Antietam Hundred in Prince George's County, now Frederick County, 1744. (Ref: Prince George's County Court Records, 1736-1748, Extracts by Patricia Abelard Andersen, *Western Maryland Genealogy*, Vol. 18, No. 1, January 2002, p. 41)

Skinner, Adderton (c1677-1756), of Calvert County, commissioned Deputy Surveyor of Calvert County, 25 Mar 1734. (Ref: Maryland Commission Book No. 82, p. 10; *Maryland Historical Magazine*, Vol. XXVI, p. 140); commissioned Deputy Surveyor of Calvert County, 1 Jun 1743, 23 Apr 1747 and 19 Oct 1749. (Ref: Maryland Commission Book No. 82, pp. 102, 128, 141; *Maryland Historical Magazine*, Vol. XXVI, pp. 249, 260, and p. 344 mistakenly listed him as Maryland Skinner; *A Biographical Dictionary of the Maryland Legislature, 1635-1789*, by Edward C. Papenfuse, et al., Vol. I-Z, p. 738)

Skinner, Henry, was commissioned one of the Coroners for Calvert County, 23 Apr 1747. (Ref: Maryland Commission Book No. 82, p. 129; *Maryland Historical Magazine*, Vol. XXVI, p. 260)

Skinner, John, commissioned Sheriff of Calvert County, 16 Sep 1749. (Ref: Maryland State Archives, Governor and Council Commissioner Records, 1726-1794, p. 111); appointed a Commissioner of the Peace for Calvert County, 22 Nov 1752 and 22 Oct 1756. (Ref: Maryland State Archives, Governor and Council Commissioner Records, 1726-1794, pp. 135, 171)

Skinner, Robert, appointed a Commissioner of the Peace for Prince George's County, 18 Feb 1731/2. (Ref: Maryland State Archives, Governor and Council Commissioner Records, 1726-1794, p. 21)

Skinner, Truman (Trueman), commissioned High Sheriff of Calvert County, 3 Dec 1763; appointed a Commissioner of the Peace for Prince George's County, 26 Jul 1773 (Ref: Maryland State Archives, Governor and Council Commissioner Records, 1726-1794, pp. 204, 272)

Skinner, William, commissioned one of the Coroners of Calvert County, 1 Jun 1743. (Ref: Maryland Commission Book No. 82, p. 102; *Maryland Historical Magazine*, Vol. XXVI, p. 249)

Skirven, George, appointed a Commissioner of the Peace for Kent County, 3 Mar 1726/7 and 12 Jun 1729. (Ref: Maryland State Archives, Governor and Council Commissioner Records, 1726-1794, pp. 2, 11)

Slater, Charles, of Liverpool, registration of ship *Nassua*, 220 tons, built in Talbot County, 1748. Charles Slater, master and co-owner. James Gildart, of Liverpool, co-owner. 14 Jul 1748. (Ref: Maryland Commission Book No. 82, p. 135; *Maryland Historical Magazine*, Vol. XXVI, p. 263)

Slater, Ellis, commissioned one of the Coroners of Somerset County, 10 Dec 1742. (Ref: Maryland Commission Book No. 82, p. 99; *Maryland Historical Magazine*, Vol. XXVI, p. 248); commissioned a Coroner of Calvert, 25 May 1749. (Ref: Maryland Commission Book No. 82, p. 141; *Maryland Historical Magazine*, Vol. XXVI, p. 344)

Slater, Jonathan, appointed a Commissioner of the Peace for Prince George's County, 3 Dec 1766. (Ref: Maryland State Archives, Governor and Council Commissioner Records, 1726-1794, p. 230)

Sloan (Sloane), Samuel (1740-1807), reverend, licensed to preach in St. Paul's Parish, Kent County, vacant by the death of Rev. James Sterling. 27 Jun 1766. (Ref: Maryland Commission Book No. 82, p. 178; *Maryland Historical Magazine*, Vol. XXVI, p. 354); induction into Worcester Parish, Worcester County, 5 Dec 1767. (Ref: Maryland Commission Book No. 82, p. 205; *Maryland Historical Magazine*, Vol. XXVI, p. 356, spelled his name Sloane); induction into Coventry Parish in Somerset and Worcester Counties, 20 Nov 1769. (Ref: Maryland Commission Book No. 82, p. 230; *Maryland Historical Magazine*, Vol. XXVI, p. 360); see Henry Fendall and John Montgomerie)

Smallwood, Bayne (c1711-1768), was appointed a Commissioner of the Peace for Charles County, 31 Mar 1736 and 1 May 1739. (Ref: Maryland State Archives, Governor and Council Commissioner Records, 1726-1794, pp. 51, 63)

Smallwood, Ledstone, see Negro James.

Smallwood, William, of Bayne (1732-1792), was appointed a Commissioner of the Peace for Charles County, 2 Oct 1762 and 19 Oct 1770. (Ref: Maryland State Archives, Governor and Council Commissioner Records, 1726-1794, pp. 205, 252)

Smart, John, see James Donaldson.

Smith, Alexander Hamilton (c1748-1784), appointed

a Commissioner of the Peace for Calvert County, 20 Nov 1769. (Ref: Maryland State Archives, Governor and Council Commissioner Records, 1726-1794, p. 248); appointed a Commissioner of the Peace for Calvert County, 26 Jul 1773. (Ref: Maryland State Archives, Governor and Council Commissioner Records, 1726-1794, p. 272)

Smith, Barbara, see Negro Joe, Negro Sambo and Negro Betty.

Smith, Basil, see Negro Jonathan.

Smith, Charles, of Talbot County, convicted felon, was executed on 19 May 1729. (Ref: Maryland State Archives, Governor and Council Commissioner Records, 1726-1794, p. 10)

Smith, Charles Somerset, appointed a Commissioner of the Peace for Charles County, 2 Mar 1726/7. (Ref: Maryland State Archives, Governor and Council Commissioner Records, 1726-1794, p. 2)

Smith, Charles Somerset, appointed a Commissioner of the Peace for Charles County, 26 Feb 1765. (Ref: Maryland State Archives, Governor and Council Commissioner Records, 1726-1794, p. 222)

Smith, Clement, commissioned High Sheriff of Calvert County, 16 Sep 1772. (Ref: Maryland State Archives, Governor and Council Commissioner Records, 1726-1794, p. 252)

Smith, David, appointed a Commissioner of the Peace for Cecil County, 3 Mar 1772. (Ref: Maryland State Archives, Governor and Council Commissioner Records, 1726-1794, p. 260)

Smith, Elias, see Negro Abraham.

Smith, Henry, of Liverpool, registration of the brigantine *Middleham*, 55 tons, built in Somerset County, 1737. Henry Smith, master. Henry Smith and John Gildart, owners, 15 Jul 1738. (Ref: Maryland Commission Book No. 82, p. 61; *Maryland Historical Magazine*, Vol. XXVI, p. 152)

Smith, James, appointed Constable of Antietam Hundred in Prince George's County, now Frederick County, 1747. (Ref: Prince George's County Court Records, 1736-1748, Extracts by Patricia Abelard Andersen, *Western Maryland Genealogy*, Vol. 18, No. 1, January 2002, p. 45); Frederick County Court Justice, 1753 and 1763. (Ref: *This Was The Life: Excerpts from the Judgment Records of Frederick County, Maryland, 1748-1765*, by Millard Milburn Rice, pp. 115, 242); of Antietam, appointed a Commissioner of the Peace for Frederick County, 12 Mar 1763. (Ref: Maryland State Archives, Governor and Council Commissioner Records, 1726-1794, p. 209); see Edward Scott.

Smith, James (1683-1760), of Kent County, Clerk of the Court, 1756 [actually served 1707 to 1760]. (Ref: *Archives of Maryland*, Vol. LII, "Proceedings and Acts of the General Assembly of Maryland, 1755-1756," p. 232)

Smith, James, of Baltimore County, was appointed a Ranger, 9 Aug 1775. (Ref: *Calendar of Maryland State Papers, The Red Books*, No. 4, Part 1, p. 5)

Smith, John, of Cecil County, sheriff, 1726. (Ref: *Abstracts of the Testamentary Proceedings and Prerogative Court of Maryland, Vol. XVII, 1724-1727*, by Vernon L. Skinner, Jr., p. 126, citing original Liber 27, f. 322)

Smith, John, appointed a Commissioner of the Peace for Calvert County, 14 Aug 1742. (Ref: Maryland State Archives, Governor and Council Commissioner Records, 1726-1794, p. 74)

Smith, John, captain, appointed a Commissioner of the Peace for Prince George's County, 18 Nov 1746. (Ref: Maryland State Archives, Governor and Council Commissioner Records, 1726-1794, p. 95)

Smith, John, colonel, commissioned High Sheriff of Calvert County, 19 Sep 1758. (Ref: Maryland State Archives, Governor and Council Commissioner Records, 1726-1794, p. 172)

Smith, John (d. 1738), commissioned a Provincial Justice by the Governor, 20 Oct 1729; colonel, Provincial Commission, 8 Jul 1735. (Ref: Maryland State Archives, Governor and Council Commissioner Records, 1726-1794, pp. 12, 49)

Smith, John, was commissioned Receiver of His Lordship's Quit Rents in Cecil County, 3 Sep 1746. (Ref: Maryland Commission Book No. 82, p. 123; *Maryland Historical Magazine*, Vol. XXVI, p. 258); commissioned Sheriff of Cecil County, 22 Oct 1746. (Ref: Maryland State Archives, Governor and Council Commissioner Records, 1726-1794, p. 94); late sheriff of Cecil County who had ordinary license accounts still unpaid in 1756. (Ref: *Archives of Maryland*, Vol. LII, "Proceedings and Acts of the General Assembly of Maryland, 1755-1756," p. 568)

Smith, John, was appointed Constable of Nanticoke Hundred in Dorchester County, 1744. (Ref: Dorchester County Judgment Records, 1743-1745, p. 185; *Judgment Records of Dorchester, Queen Anne's and Talbot Counties, Maryland*, by F. Edward Wright, 2001, p. 49)

Smith, John, doctor, appointed a Commissioner of the Peace for Queen Anne's County, 8 Mar 1754 and 18 May 1758. (Ref: Maryland State Archives, Governor and Council Commissioner Records, 1726-1794, pp. 144, 180)

Smith, John, of Anne Arundel County, commissioned Judge of Oyer, Terminer and Gaol [Jail] Delivery, 21 May 1736. (Ref: Maryland State Archives, Governor and Council Commissioner Records, 1726-1794, p. 52)

Smith, John, of Baltimore Hundred, Somerset Co., appointed a Commissioner of the Peace, 29 Oct 1730. (Ref: Maryland State Archives, Governor and Council Commissioner Records, 1726-1794, p. 17)

Smith, John, see Edward North, Richard Gresham and William Turner.

Smith, John Hamilton, of Calvert County,was appointed a Commissioner of the Peace, 3 Nov 1766. (Ref: Maryland State Archives, Governor and Council Commissioner Records, 1726-1794, p. 229)

Smith, Joseph, of Prince George's County, native of Germany, naturalized on 3 May 1740. (Ref: Maryland Commission Book No. 82, p. 80; *Maryland Historical Magazine*, Vol. XXVI, p. 156)

Smith, Joseph, appointed Constable of Marsh Hundred in Frederick County in 1751. (Ref: *This Was The Life: Excerpts from the Judgment Records of Frederick County, Maryland, 1748-1765*, by Millard Milburn Rice, p. 61); appointed a Commissioner of the Peace for Frederick County, 22 Nov 1752 and 8 Mar 1754. (Ref: Maryland State Archives, Governor and Council Commissioner Records, 1726-1794, pp. 135 and 144); appointed to a Special Commission to hear cases involving convicted felons on 31 Aug 1768. (Ref: *Archives of Maryland*, Vol. XXXII, "Proceedings of the Council of Maryland, 1761-1770," p. 247); appointed a Commissioner of the Peace for Frederick County, 15 Aug 1774. (Ref: Maryland State Archives, Governor and Council Commissioner Records, 1726-1794, p. 284)

Smith, Mrs., see Negro Abigail, Negro Rachel and Negro Samuel.

Smith, Nicholas (d. 1770), appointed a Commissioner of the Peace for Kent County, 8 Mar 1754. (Ref: Maryland State Archives, Governor and Council Commissioner Records, 1726-1794, p. 143)

Smith, Patrick, see Richard Floud.

Smith, Patrick Sim (1749-c1793), was appointed a Commissioner of the Peace for Calvert County, 24 Aug 1773. (Ref: Maryland State Archives, Governor and Council Commissioner Records, 1726-1794, p. 275)

Smith, Peter, of Prince George's County, native of Germany, naturalized on 3 May 1740. (Ref: Maryland Commission Book No. 82, p. 80; *Maryland Historical Magazine*, Vol. XXVI, p. 156)

Smith, Richard, appointed a Commissioner of the Peace for Charles County, 3 Sep 1757. (Ref: Maryland State Archives, Governor and Council Commissioner Records, 1726-1794, p. 176)

Smith, Richard, merchant, registration of the schooner *Molly*, 15 tons, built in Anne Arundel County, 1734. John Ford, master. Richard Smith and John Hall, owners. 9 Oct 1745. (Ref: Maryland Commission Book No. 82, p. 119; *Maryland Historical Magazine*, Vol. XXVI, p. 256)

Smith, Richard, of Calvert County, appointment as a Commissioner of the Peace renewed, 18 Feb 1726/7. (Ref: Maryland State Archives, Governor and Council Commissioner Records, 1726-1794, p. 4); was Sheriff by 1726 and commissioned again on 29 Jan 1728/9. (Ref: Maryland State Archives, Governor and Council Commissioner Records, 1726-1794, p. 9); *Abstracts of the Testamentary Proceedings and Prerogative Court of Maryland, Vol. XVII, 1724-1727*, by Vernon L. Skinner, Jr., p. 117, citing original Liber 27, f. 312)

Smith, Richard, of ---- County, convicted felon, was reprieved on 4 Oct 1765. (Ref: *Archives of Maryland*, Vol. XXXII, "Proceedings of the Council of Maryland, 1761-1770," p. 108)

Smith, Richard, see Negro Peter.

Smith, Robert, was appointed Constable of Marsh Hundred in Frederick County, 1769, 1771. (Ref: "Frederick County Court Minutes November 1769 by Patricia Abelard Andersen," *Western Maryland Genealogy*, Vol. 16, No. 1, January 2000, p. 33;

"Frederick County Minute Book, March 1771, Extracts by Patricia Abelard Andersen," *Western Maryland Genealogy*, Vol. 18, No. 1, January 2002, p. 26)

Smith, Samuel, commissioned High Sheriff of Anne Arundel County, 19 May 1742. (Ref: Maryland State Archives, Governor and Council Commissioner Records, 1726-1794, p. 73); commissioned a Coroner of Anne Arundel County. 27 Oct 1748. (Ref: Maryland Commission Book No. 82, p. 138; *Maryland Historical Magazine*, Vol. XXVI, p. 343)

Smith, Samuel, Jr., commissioned one of the Coroners of Anne Arundel County, 20 Jan 1743/4. (Ref: Maryland Commission Book No. 82, p. 107; *Maryland Historical Magazine*, Vol. XXVI, p. 251); commissioned Sheriff of Anne Arundel County on 4 Jul 1745. (Ref: Maryland State Archives, Governor and Council Commissioner Records, 1726-1794, p. 88)

Smith, Sarah, see Negro David.

Smith, Thomas, was appointed Constable of Marsh Hundred in Frederick County, 1769. (Ref: "Frederick County Court Minutes, March 1769," by Patricia Abelard Andersen, *Western Maryland Genealogy*, Vol. 15, No. 2, April 1999, p. 63)

Smith, Thomas, registration of sloop *Martha*, 60 tons, built in Massachusetts Bay, 1749. formerly the *Molly*. Elijah Stoddert, master. Thomas Smith and Richard Gresham, owners. 11 Aug 1750. (Ref: Maryland Commission Book No. 82, p. 145; *Maryland Historical Magazine*, Vol. XXVI, p. 346)

Smith, Walter (c1693-1748), of St. Leonard's, was appointed a Commissioner of the Peace for Calvert County, 22 Oct 1728. (Ref: Maryland State Archives, Governor and Council Commissioner Records, 1726-1794, p. 8)

Smith, Walter, of the Freshes, was appointed a Commissioner of the Peace for Calvert County, 3 Mar 1726/7. (Ref: Maryland State Archives, Governor and Council Commissioner Records, 1726-1794, p. 3)

Smith, Walter, appointed a Commissioner of the Peace for Calvert County, 26 Jul 1773. (Ref: Maryland State Archives, Governor and Council Commissioner Records, 1726-1794, p. 272)

Smith, Walter, see Robert Swan.

Smith, William, of Baltimore County, sheriff, 1726. (Ref: *Abstracts of the Testamentary Proceedings and Prerogative Court of Maryland, Vol. XVII, 1724-1727*, by Vernon L. Skinner, Jr., p. 115, citing original Liber 27, f. 310); appointed a Commissioner of the Peace for Baltimore County, 20 May 1746, 28 Oct 1747 and 10 No 1762. (Ref: Maryland State Archives, Governor and Council Commissioner Records, 1726-1794, pp. 92, 101, 207)

Smith, William, was Constable of Patuxent Hundred in Prince George's County, now Frederick County, in 1733. (*Calendar of Maryland State Papers, No. 1 The Black Books*, p. 38); appointed a Commissioner of the Peace for Prince George's County, 15 Jun 1739. (Ref: Maryland State Archives, Governor and Council Commissioner Records, 1726-1794, p. 64)

Smith, William, of Baltimore Town, appointed a Commissioner of the Peace for Baltimore County, 31 Oct 1768. (Ref: Maryland State Archives, Governor and Council Commissioner Records, 1726-1794, p. 238)

Smith, William, rope master, was appointed a Commissioner of the Peace for Baltimore County, 31 Oct 1772. (Ref: Maryland State Archives, Governor and Council Commissioner Records, 1726-1794, p. 264)

Smith, William, was appointed a Commissioner of the Peace for Harford County, 20 Feb 1774. (Ref: Maryland State Archives, Governor and Council Commissioner Records, 1726-1794, p. 281)

Smith, William, see Edward Scott, William Rasin and Outherbridge Horsey.

Smith, William, Jr., appointed a Commissioner of the Peace for Baltimore County, 6 Mar 1775. (Ref: Maryland State Archives, Governor and Council Commissioner Records, 1726-1794, p. 288)

Smith, William Hamilton, see Negro Sambo, Negro Joe and Negro Betty.

Smith, Winston, appointed a Commissioner of the Peace for Baltimore County, 29 Feb 1743/4. (Ref: Maryland State Archives, Governor and Council Commissioner Records, 1726-1794, p. 84)

Smithson, William (c1744-1809), was appointed a Commissioner of the Peace for Harford County, 2 Jun 1774. (Ref: Maryland State Archives, Governor and Council Commissioner Records, 1726-1794, p. 282)

Smoot, Edward (1724-1795), was appointed a

Commissioner of the Peace for Charles County, 17 Nov 1764. (Ref: Maryland State Archives, Governor and Council Commissioner Records, 1726-1794, p. 220)

Smoot, John, appointed Constable from the mouth of Seneca to the mouth of Monocacy in Prince George's County, now Frederick County, 1739 and 1740. (Ref: Prince George's County Court Records, 1736-1748, Extracts by Patricia Abelard Andersen, *Western Maryland Genealogy*, Vol. 18, No. 1, January 2002, pp. 36, 37)

Smoot, Thomas (1707-1777), was commissioned a Ranger of Charles County, 14 Apr 1738. (Ref: Maryland Commission Book No. 82, p. 57; *Maryland Historical Magazine*, Vol. XXVI, p. 151)

Smyth, Thomas, commissioned High Sheriff of Kent County, 2 Oct 1762. (Ref: Maryland State Archives, Governor and Council Commissioner Records, 1726-1794, p. 196, and p. 203 spelled his name Smith)

Smythers, Serjeant, registration of brigantine *Charming Betsy*, 40 tons, built in Somerset County, 1740. Serjeant Smithers, master. Simon Edgett and Serjeant Smythers, owners. 17 Apr 1741. (Ref: Maryland Commission Book No. 82, p. 85; *Maryland Historical Magazine*, Vol. XXVI, p. 158)

Snowden, Joshua, of Anne Arundel County, was appointed Constable of Patapsco Hundred in 1774. (Ref: Anne Arundel County Court Minutes, 1725-1757, 1774)

Snowden, Richard, see Negro Tom.

Soare, John, see Patrick Creagh.

Sollars, Sabrett, was appointed a Commissioner of the Peace for Calvert County, 3 Mar 1726/7. (Ref: Maryland State Archives, Governor and Council Commissioner Records, 1726-1794, p. 3)

Sollars, Thomas, of Patapsco Neck, Baltimore Co., was appointed a Commissioner of the Peace on 20 Nov 1769 and 3 May 1774. (Ref: Maryland State Archives, Governor and Council Commissioner Records, 1726-1794, pp. 248, 283); Court Justice in Baltimore County, 8 Oct 1773. (Ref: *Inhabitants of Baltimore County, 1763-1774*, by Henry C. Peden, Jr., 1989, p. 49, citing *Calendar of Maryland State Papers, No. 1 The Black Books*, p. 209)

Solomon, Henry, of Baltimore County, was appointed a Ranger, 9 Aug 1775. (Ref: *Calendar of Maryland State Papers, The Red Books*, No. 4, Part 1, p. 5)

Somervell, James, was appointed a Commissioner of the Peace for Calvert County, 22 Oct 1741; commissioned High Sheriff of Calvert County, 17 Sep 1744. (Ref: Maryland State Archives, Governor and Council Commissioner Records, 1726-1794, pp. 72, 85; and p. 89 styled him as doctor on 23 Sep 1745)

Somerville (Somervell), Alexander (1734-1783), commissioned High Sheriff of Calvert County on 19 Oct 1769. (Ref: Maryland State Archives, Governor and Council Commissioner Records, 1726-1794, p. 236); appointed a Commissioner of the Peace for Calvert County, 26 Jul 1773. (Ref: Maryland State Archives, Governor and Council Commissioner Records, 1726-1794, p. 272)

Somerville (Somervell), James (1731-1773), was appointed a Commissioner of the Peace for Calvert County, 15 Mar 1761. (Ref: Maryland State Archives, Governor and Council Commissioner Records, 1726-1794, p. 196)

Soope, George, appointed Constable of Pipe Creek Hundred in Frederick County in 1753. (Ref: *This Was The Life: Excerpts from the Judgment Records of Frederick County, Maryland, 1748-1765*, by Millard Milburn Rice, p. 131)

Soper, Thomas, see John Marr.

Sotheren, Samuel, was commissioned a Coroner of St. Mary's County, 18 Feb 1764. (Ref: Maryland Commission Book No. 82, p. 161; *Maryland Historical Magazine*, Vol. XXVI, p. 352)

Sothoron, Henry Greenfield (c1732-1793), was appointed a Commissioner of the Peace for St. Mary's County, 11 May 1769. (Ref: Maryland State Archives, Governor and Council Commissioner Records, 1726-1794, p. 241. spelled his name Southeron)

Spalding, Allot, registration of sloop *Molly*, 25 tons, built in Somerset County, 1734. Allot Spalding, master and owner. 26 May 1735. (Ref: Maryland Commission Book No. 82, p. 30; *Maryland Historical Magazine*, Vol. XXVI, p. 143)

Spear, William, appointed a Commissioner of the Peace for Baltimore County, 30 May 1774. (Ref: Maryland State Archives, Governor and Council Commissioner Records, 1726-1794, p. 283)

Spence, Adam, appointed a Commissioner of the Peace for Worcester County, 2 Mar 1754 and 17 Oct

1774. (Ref: Maryland State Archives, Governor and Council Commissioner Records, 1726-1794, pp. 142, 283)

Spencer, Isaac, appointed a Commissioner of the Peace for Cecil County, 2 Jun 1774. (Ref: Maryland State Archives, Governor and Council Commissioner Records, 1726-1794, p. 283)

Spencer, Isaac, of Jervis, appointed a Commissioner of the Peace for Kent County, 2 Nov 1762. (Ref: Maryland State Archives, Governor and Council Commissioner Records, 1726-1794, p. 207)

Spencer, Jarvis, appointed a Commissioner of the Peace for Kent County, 24 Nov 1735. (Ref: Maryland State Archives, Governor and Council Commissioner Records, 1726-1794, p. 50)

Spoore, Edward, of Virginia, registration of sloop *Ann*, 14 tons, built in Maryland, 1737. Edward Spoore, master and owner. 8 Jul 1738. (Ref: Maryland Commission Book No. 82, p. 64; *Maryland Historical Magazine*, Vol. XXVI, p. 152)

Sprigg, Edward (1697-1751) was appointed a Commissioner of the Peace for Prince George's County, 3 Mar 1726/7. (Ref: Maryland State Archives, Governor and Council Commissioner Records, 1726-1794, p. 3)

Sprigg, Edward (c1721-1790), son of Col. Sprigg, was appointed Constable of Rock Creek Hundred in Prince George's County, now Frederick County, 1746. (Ref: Prince George's County Court Records, 1736-1748, Extracts by Patricia Abelard Andersen, *Western Maryland Genealogy*, Vol. 18, No. 1, January 2002, p. 44)

Sprigg, Joseph (1736-1800), was appointed a Commissioner of the Peace for Prince George's County, 3 Dec 1766. (Ref: Maryland State Archives, Governor and Council Commissioner Records, 1726-1794, p. 230)

Sprigg, Osborn (c1707-1749/50), was a merchant who registered the ship *Marlborough*, 140 tons, built at Boston, 1743. James Cole, master. Osborn Sprigg, Thomas Clark and Joseph Belt, Jr., co-owners. 10 May 1744. (Ref: Maryland Commission Book No. 82, p. 110; *Maryland Historical Magazine*, Vol. XXVI, p. 252); commissioned Sheriff of Prince George's County, 18 Sep 1747. (Ref: Maryland State Archives, Governor and Council Commissioner Records, 1726-1794, p. 100); late sheriff of Prince George's County, had ordinary license accounts still unpaid in 1756. (Ref: *Archives of Maryland*, Vol. LII, "Proceedings and Acts of the General Assembly of Maryland, 1755-1756," p. 568)

Sprigg, Thomas (1715-1781), was appointed a Commissioner of the Peace for Anne Arundel County, 16 Mar 1748/9. (Ref: Maryland State Archives, Governor and Council Commissioner Records, 1726-1794, p. 110); appointed a Press Master in 1774. (Ref: Anne Arundel County Court Minutes, 1725-1757, 1774)

Stainton, Benton (d. 1781), was appointed a Commissioner of the Peace for Dorchester County on 8 Apr 1770, and was appointed a Commissioner of the Peace for Caroline County on 8 Feb 1774. (Ref: Maryland State Archives, Governor and Council Commissioner Records, 1726-1794, pp. 250, 280)

Stallands, Jacob, laborer, late of Frederick County, convicted felon, was pardoned for horse stealing on 3 Dec 1773. (Ref: Maryland Commission Book No. 82, p. 329; *Maryland Historical Magazine*, Vol. XXVII, p. 35)

Stamper, Robert, see William Probart.

Stanton, Thomas, pardon granted for theft of a bee hive from Thomas Vanderwert, of Queen Anne's County. 16 Jan 1741/2. (Ref: Maryland Commission Book No. 82, p. 89; *Maryland Historical Magazine*, Vol. XXVI, p. 245)

Steadman, John, of Anne Arundel County, convicted for murdering his wife, "and to be hung in chains about two hundred yards to the west of the gallows," executed 15 Dec 1749. (Ref: Maryland State Archives, Governor and Council Commissioner Records, 1726-1794, p. 121)

Steele, Henry (c1715-1782), was appointed a Commissioner of the Peace for Dorchester County, 11 Jul 1757. (Ref: Maryland State Archives, Governor and Council Commissioner Records, 1726-1794, p. 175)

Stephen, John (1741-1784), reverend, licensed to preach in All Faith's Parish, St. Mary's County, 15 Mar 1765; induction into All Faith's Parish, St. Mary's County, 27 Jul 1769. (Ref: Maryland Commission Book No. 82, p. 167; *Maryland Historical Magazine*, Vol. XXVI, pp. 353, 359)

Stephenson, Richard, appointed Constable of Pipe Creek Hundred in Frederick County, 1769, 1771. (Ref: "Frederick County Court Minutes November 1769 by Patricia Abelard Andersen," *Western Maryland Genealogy*, Vol. 16, No. 1, January 2000, p. 32; "Frederick County Minute Book, March 1771, Extracts by Patricia Abelard Andersen," *Western Maryland Genealogy*, Vol. 18, No. 1, January 2002, p. 25)

Sterling, James (d. 1763), reverend, induction into All Hallows Parish, Anne Arundel County, 16 Nov 1737. (Ref: Maryland Commission Book No. 82, p. 51; *Maryland Historical Magazine*, Vol. XXVI, p. 150); resignation from All Hallows Parish, Anne Arundel County, 18 Jul 1739. On same day, induction into St. Ann's Parish, Anne Arundel County; resignation from St. Anne's Parish, Anne Arundel County, 26 Aug 1740. On same day, induction into St. Paul's Parish, Kent County. (Ref: Maryland Commission Book No. 82, p. 83; *Maryland Historical Magazine*, Vol. XXVI, pp. 150, 154, 157); see Samuel Sloan.

Steuart, Adam, appointed a Commissioner of the Peace for Frederick County, 20 Aug 1772. (Ref: Maryland State Archives, Governor and Council Commissioner Records, 1726-1794, p. 261); Court Judge, 1774. (*Calendar of Maryland State Papers, No. 1 The Black Books*, p. 217)

Steuart, George (1700-1784), of Anne Arundel Co. [native of Scotland], doctor, was commissioned one of the Commissioners of the Paper Currency Office, 13 Dec 1746. (Ref: Maryland Commission Book No. 82, p. 124; *Maryland Historical Magazine*, Vol. XXVI, p. 258); appointed a Commissioner of the Peace for Anne Arundel County, 31 Oct 1747. (Ref: Maryland State Archives, Governor and Council Commissioner Records, 1726-1794, p. 103); merchant, registration of schooner *Bennett*, 75 tons, built in Cecil County, 1744. John Scott, master. George Steuart, Richard Bennett, James Calder, Bedingfield Hands and John Wallace, owners. 15 Sep 1744. (Ref: Maryland Commission Book No. 82, p. 110; *Maryland Historical Magazine*, Vol. XXVI, p. 252; merchant, registration of ship *Charming Nancy*, 140 tons, built at North East River [Cecil County], 1745. John Brown, master. George Steuart, Richard Bennett, John Wallace, James Calder and Bedingfield Hands, owners. 7 Dec1745. (Ref: Maryland Commission Book No. 82, p. 118; *Maryland Historical Magazine*, Vol. XXVI, p. 256; merchant, registration of ship *Ogle*, 200 tons, built in Cecil County, 1748. John Brown, master. George Steuart, Richard Bennett, John Wallace, James Calder and Bedingfield Hands, owners. 23 Apr 1748. (Ref: Maryland Commission Book No. 82, p. 134; *Maryland Historical Magazine*, Vol. XXVI, p. 262; merchant, registration of snow *Experiment*, 100 tons, built in Anne Arundel County, 1750. Alexander Cumming, master. George Steuart, owner. 20 Jun 1750. (Ref: Maryland Commission Book No. 82, p. 144; *Maryland Historical Magazine*, Vol. XXVI, p. 345; registration of snow *Wallace*, 100 tons, built in Cecil County, 1750. Thomas Kemp, master. George Steuart and John Wallace & County, owners, 20 Jun 1750. (Ref: Maryland Commission Book No. 82, p. 144; *Maryland Historical Magazine*, Vol. XXVI, p. 345); commissioned one of the Judges and Registers of the Land Office, 29 Apr 1773. (Ref: Maryland Commission Book No. 82, p. 301; *Maryland Historical Magazine*, Vol. XXVII, pp. 32-33); of Annapolis, commissioned Judge of Admiralty, 1 May 1773. (Ref: Maryland Commission Book No. 82, p. 312; *Maryland Historical Magazine*, Vol. XXVII, p. 34); see Thomas Dicke and Negro Sam.

Steuart, William, was a Court Justice, Anne Arundel County, 1774. (Ref: Anne Arundel County Court Minutes, 1725-1757, 1774)

Stevens, John, appointed a Commissioner of the Peace for Anne Arundel County, 1 Nov 1761. (Ref: Maryland State Archives, Governor and Council Commissioner Records, 1726-1794, p. 201)

Stevens, John (c1735-1794), was appointed a Commissioner of the Peace for Talbot County, 2 Feb 1774. (Ref: Maryland State Archives, Governor and Council Commissioner Records, 1726-1794, p. 280); commissioned High Sheriff, 31 Oct 1774. (Ref: Maryland State Archives, Governor and Council Commissioner Records, 1726-1794, p. 274); Court Justice, Talbot County, 1774. (*Calendar of Maryland State Papers, No. 1 The Black Books*, p. 211)

Stevens, Robertson (c1740 - d. after 1790), was commissioned High Sheriff of Dorchester County, 10 Sep 1773. (Ref: Maryland State Archives, Governor and Council Commissioner Records, 1726-1794, p. 265)

Stevens, Thomas, appointed a Commissioner of the

Peace for Queen Anne's County, 13 Mar 1773. (Ref: Maryland State Archives, Governor and Council Commissioner Records, 1726-1794, p. 265)

Stevens, William, see Ephraim Waggaman.

Stevenson, John, appointed a Commissioner of the Peace for Baltimore County, 2 Mar 1754. (Ref: Maryland State Archives, Governor and Council Commissioner Records, 1726-1794, p. 142)

Stevenson, Thomas, of Frederick Co., convicted felon in 1761 "for stealing one caster [beaver] hatt valued at 140 pounds of tobacco," was sentenced to be put on the pillory for five minutes and afterwards sent to the whipping post and receive ten lashes on his bare body. (Ref: *This Was The Life: Excerpts from the Judgment Records of Frederick County, Maryland, 1748-1765*, by Millard Milburn Rice, p. 227)

Stevenson, William, see Negro Shephon.

Steward, Charles, of Annapolis, Chyrurgeon or Apothecary, death sentence for burglary and felony, reprieved and banished from the State, 4 May 1734. (Ref: Maryland Commission Book No. 82, p. 12; *Maryland Historical Magazine*, Vol. XXVI, p. 140)

Stewart, Adam, appointed a Commissioner of the Peace for Frederick County, 15 Aug 1774. (Ref: Maryland State Archives, Governor and Council Commissioner Records, 1726-1794, p. 284)

Stewart, John, see John Harrison.

Stewart, John, Jr., appointed Constable of Little Choptank Hundred in Dorchester County, 1745. (Ref: Dorchester County Judgment Records, 1743-1745, p. 476; *Judgment Records of Dorchester, Queen Anne's and Talbot Counties, Maryland*, by F. Edward Wright, 2001, p. 60)

Stewart, William, commissioned High Sheriff of Anne Arundel County, 19 Nov 1766. (Ref: Maryland State Archives, Governor and Council Commissioner Records, 1726-1794, p. 219)

Stillwell, Elias, was appointed Constable of Linton Hundred in Frederick County in 1763. (Ref: *This Was The Life: Excerpts from the Judgment Records of Frederick County, Maryland, 1748-1765*, by Millard Milburn Rice, p. 249)

Stilly, Peter, appointed Constable of the Middle Part of Monocacy Hundred in Frederick County in 1751. (Ref: *This Was The Life: Excerpts from the Judgment Records of Frederick County, Maryland, 1748-1765*, by Millard Milburn Rice, p. 61)

Stinson, John, of Baltimore County, convicted felon for breaking open the house of Levin Roberts and stealing sundry goods and chattel, was granted a stay on 16 Sep 1769, but was executed on 22 Oct 1769. (Ref: Maryland Commission Book No. 82, p. 229; *Maryland Historical Magazine*, Vol. XXVI, p. 360; Maryland State Archives, Governor and Council Commissioner Records, 1726-1794, p. 234; *Archives of Maryland*, Vol. XXXII, "Proceedings of the Council of Maryland, 1761-1770," p. 314)

Stoddert, Benjamin, was appointed Constable of Potomac Hundred in Prince George's County, now Frederick County, 1742. (Ref: Prince George's County Court Records, 1736-1748, Extracts by Patricia Abelard Andersen, *Western Maryland Genealogy*, Vol. 18, No. 1, January 2002, p. 38)

Stoddert, Elijah, see Thomas Smith.

Stoddert, John (d. 1767), appointed a Commissioner of the Peace for Charles County, 24 Jul 1748. (Ref: Maryland State Archives, Governor and Council Commissioner Records, 1726-1794, p. 109); appointed to the Committee to Tax the Fees Due to the Several Officers of the Maryland House, 1755. (Ref: *Archives of Maryland*, Vol. LII, "Proceedings and Acts of the General Assembly of Maryland, 1755-1756," pp. 46, 66)

Stoddert, Thomas, appointed Constable of Potomac Hundred in Prince George's County, now Frederick County, 1744. (Ref: Prince George's County Court Records, 1736-1748, Extracts by Patricia Abelard Andersen, *Western Maryland Genealogy*, Vol. 18, No. 1, January 2002, p. 41)

Stoler, John, Constable of Baltimore Town West Hundred in Baltimore County, 1773. (Ref: *Inhabitants of Baltimore County, 1763-1774*, by Henry C. Peden, Jr., 1989, p. 56, citing a 1773 List of Taxables)

Stone, Thomas, appointed a Commissioner of the Peace for Charles County, 2 Mar 1726/7 and 29 Oct 1730. (Ref: Maryland State Archives, Governor and Council Commissioner Records, 1726-1794, pp. 2, 12); Court Justice, 1756. (*Calendar of Maryland State Papers, No. 1 The Black Books*, p. 132)

Stone, William (1666-1731), was appointed a Commissioner of the Peace for Charles County, 2 Mar

1726/7. (Ref: Maryland State Archives, Governor and Council Commissioner Records, 1726-1794, p. 2)

Stone, William, commissioned a Coroner of Charles County, 17 Sep 1773. (Ref: Maryland Commission Book No. 82, p. 323; *Maryland Historical Magazine*, Vol. XXVII, p. 35)

Stoner, Jacob, of Prince George's County, native of Germany, naturalized 3 May 1740, and also his sons John and Jacob. (Ref: Maryland Commission Book No. 82, p. 81; *Maryland Historical Magazine*, Vol. XXVI, p. 156)

Stonestreet, Thomas, was a Constable in Prince George's County, now Frederick County, 1733. (*Calendar of Maryland State Papers, No. 1 The Black Books*, p. 37)

Storey, Walter (1666-1726), was appointed a Commissioner of the Peace for Charles County, 2 Mar 17252/6. (Ref: Maryland State Archives, Governor and Council Commissioner Records, 1726-1794, p. 2)

Storm, John, native of Germany, denization, 22 Jun 1771. (Ref: Maryland Commission Book No. 82, p. 260; *Maryland Historical Magazine*, Vol. XXVII, p. 30)

Story, Robert, appointed a Commissioner of the Peace for Cecil County, 8 Mar 1735/6. (Ref: Maryland State Archives, Governor and Council Commissioner Records, 1726-1794, p. 51); registration of sloop *Squirrel*, 15 tons, built at North East River [Cecil County], 1734. James Turner, master. Robert Story, owner. 23 Jul 1735. (Ref: Maryland Commission Book No. 82, p. 32; *Maryland Historical Magazine*, Vol. XXVI, p. 144)

Stoughton, William, appointed a Commissioner of the Peace for Somerset County, 29 Oct 1730. (Ref: Maryland State Archives, Governor and Council Commissioner Records, 1726-1794, p. 17)

Strachan, William, see Samuel Lockwood and William Roberts.

Strange, George, see William Mill.

Strange, Jonathan, of Biddeford, registration of brigantine *Union*, 35 tons, built in Cecil County, 1737. Jonathan Strange, master and owner. 27 Jul 1737. (Ref: Maryland Commission Book No. 82, p. 49; *Maryland Historical Magazine*, Vol. XXVI, p. 149)

Strawbridge, Jane or Sarah, see Negro Tom.

Street, George, of Baltimore County, convicted felon, was executed on 19 Dec 1759. (Ref: Maryland State Archives, Governor and Council Commissioner Records, 1726-1794, p. 176)

Stretton, William, of Charles County, convicted felon, was executed on 11 Jul 1755 and "hung in chains as near the publick road as conveniently can be where the fact was committed." (Ref: *Archives of Maryland*, Vol. XXXI, "Proceedings of the Council of Maryland, 1753-1761," p. 69)

Strider, Gitton, appointed Constable of Sharps-burgh Hundred in Frederick County, 1771. (Ref: "Frederick County Minute Book, March 1771, Extracts by Patricia Abelard Andersen," *Western Maryland Genealogy*, Vol. 18, No. 1, January 2002, p. 26)

Stroble, Charity, see Enoch McDonald.

Stull, Christopher, appointed Constable of the Middle Part of Monocacy Hundred in Frederick County, 1769. (Ref: "Frederick County Court Minutes, March 1769," by Patricia Abelard Andersen, *Western Maryland Genealogy*, Vol. 15, No. 2, April 1999, p. 63, mistakenly spelled his name Shull; "Frederick County Court Minutes November 1769 by Patricia Abelard Andersen," *Western Maryland Genealogy*, Vol. 16, No. 1, January 2000, p. 32, spelled it correctly as Stull)

Stull, John (1733-1791), appointed a Commissioner of the Peace for Frederick County, 20 Aug 1772 and 15 Aug 1774. (Ref: Maryland State Archives, Governor and Council Commissioner Records, 1726-1794, pp. 261, 284); Court Judge, 1774. (*Calendar of Maryland State Papers, No. 1 The Black Books*, p. 217)

Stump, John, planter, of Cecil County, native of High Germany, naturalized 18 Oct 1738, and his children John and Henry Stump as well. (Ref: Maryland Commission Book No. 82, p. 63; *Maryland Historical Magazine*, Vol. XXVI, p. 152)

Sudler, Emory, appointed a Commissioner of the Peace for Cecil County, 1 Dec 1768 and 2 Jun 1774. (Ref: Maryland State Archives, Governor and Council Commissioner Records, 1726-1794, pp. 239, 283)

Sudler, Joseph, appointed a Commissioner of the Peace for Queen Anne's County, 6 Jun 1739. (Ref: Maryland State Archives, Governor and Council Commissioner Records, 1726-1794, p. 63)

Sulivane, Daniel (c1708-c1783), was appointed a Commissioner of the Peace for Dorchester County, 14 Dec 1751. (Ref: Maryland State Archives, Governor and Council Commissioner Records, 1726-1794, p. 130); commissioned Sheriff of Dorchester County, 22 Sep 1752. (Ref: Maryland State Archives, Governor and Council Commissioner Records, 1726-1794, p. 133); Court Justice, Dorchester County, 1774. (*Calendar of Maryland State Papers, No. 1 The Black Books*, p. 211)

Sulivane, David alias Daniel, of Anne Arundel County, was convicted of murdering Donald McKennie, "and his body to be hung in chains near the place where the murder was committed," executed on the Wednesday after 15 Apr 1751. (Ref: Maryland State Archives, Governor and Council Commissioner Records, 1726-1794, p. 122)

Sullivan, Patrick, of Frederick County, convicted felon, along with Bridget Kelly, alias Sullivan, for stealing the pocketbook of Stephen Ransberg in 1760, were sentenced to be set upon the pillory for one-half hour and then sent to the whipping post and receive twenty lashes on each of their bare bodies. (Ref: *This Was The Life: Excerpts from the Judgment Records of Frederick County, Maryland, 1748-1765*, by Millard Milburn Rice, p. 208)

Sumerfield, John, laborer, late of Baltimore County, pardoned for horse stealing, 3 Oct 1771. (Ref: Maryland Commission Book No. 82, p. 271; *Maryland Historical Magazine*, Vol. XXVII, p. 30)

Sutton, Ashbury, butcher, registration of the schooner *Samuel*, 8 tons, built at Annapolis, 1742. Horatio Samuel Middleton, master. Ashbury Sutton, owner; registration of the schooner *Samuel*, 8 tons, built in Annapolis, 1742. Ashbury Sutton, master and owner. 28 Sep 1748. (Ref: Maryland Commission Book No. 82, pp. 103, 136; *Maryland Historical Magazine*, Vol. XXVI, pp. 349, 342); registration of snow *Samuel*, of Maryland, 90 tons, built at Annapolis, 1733, George Foreman, master. Richard Bennett and Ashbury Sutton, owners. 27 Jul 1733. (Ref: Maryland Commission Book No. 82, p. 2; *Maryland Historical Magazine*, Vol. XXVI, p. 139)

Swan, John, appointed Constable of Marsh Hundred in Frederick County in 1753. (Ref: *This Was The Life: Excerpts from the Judgment Records of Frederick County, Maryland, 1748-1765*, by Millard Milburn Rice, p. 131)

Swan, Robert, merchant, registration of ship *Peggy*, 150 tons, built in Anne Arundel County, 1748. Robert Hamilton, master. Robert Swan and James Johnson. (Ref: Maryland Commission Book No. 82, p. 135; *Maryland Historical Magazine*, Vol. XXVI, p. 263); merchant, registration of ship *Newall*, 160 tons, built in Anne Arundel County, 1749. Walter Smith, master. Robert Swan and James Johnson, merchant of Glasgow, owners. 5 Jul 1749. (Ref: Maryland Commission Book No. 82, p. 141; *Maryland Historical Magazine*, Vol. XXVI, p. 344)

Swan (Swann), James (d. 1745/6), appointed a Commissioner of the Peace for St. Mary's County, 29 Oct 1730. (Ref: Maryland State Archives, Governor and Council Commissioner Records, 1726-1794, p. 12); commissioned a Coroner of St. Mary's County, 13 Apr 1744. (Ref: Maryland Commission Book No. 82, p. 109; *Maryland Historical Magazine*, Vol. XXVI, p. 252)

Swearingen, Joseph, was appointed Constable of Conococheague in Prince George's County, now Frederick County, 1746. (Ref: Prince George's County Court Records, 1736-1748, Extracts by Patricia Abelard Andersen, *Western Maryland Genealogy*, Vol. 18, No. 1, January 2002, p. 44)

Swearingen, Samuel, see Negro Tom.

Swift, Flower, was Constable of Monocosie [Monocacy] Hundred in Prince George's County, now Frederick County, 1733. (*Calendar of Maryland State Papers, No. 1 The Black Books*, p. 42)

Swift, Jeremiah, of Anne Arundel County, convicted for murdering Elizabeth Hatherly, "and his body to be hung in chains near the place where the murder was committed," executed on the Wednesday after 15 Apr 1751. (Ref: Maryland State Archives, Governor and Council Commissioner Records, 1726-1794, p. 122)

Swift, Theophilus (d. 1762), reverend, induction into Durham Parish, Charles County, 1 Mar 1741/2; induction into Port Tobacco Parish, Charles County, 18 Mar 1749/50. (Ref: Maryland Commission Book No. 82, pp. 91, 142; *Maryland Historical Magazine*, Vol. XXVI, p. 245, and p. 345 mistakenly listed his first name as Thomas)

Symmer, Alexander, appointed a Commissioner of the Peace for Prince George's County, 17 Nov 1764.

(Ref: Maryland State Archives, Governor and Council Commissioner Records, 1726-1794, p. 220)

Sympson, Patrick, see William Alexander.

Talbott, Thomas, of Gunpowder Forest in Baltimore County, appointed a Commissioner of the Peace, 20 Nov 1769. (Ref: Maryland State Archives, Governor and Council Commissioner Records, 1726-1794, p. 248)

Tannehill, Carlton, appointed Constable of the Lower Part of Monocacy Hundred in Frederick County in 1763. (Ref: *This Was The Life: Excerpts from the Judgment Records of Frederick County, Maryland, 1748-1765*, by Millard Milburn Rice, p. 249)

Tannyhill, Ninian, appointed Constable of Rock Creek Hundred in Prince George's County, now Frederick County, 1738 and 1739. (Ref: Prince George's County Court Records, 1736-1748, Extracts by Patricia Abelard Andersen, *Western Maryland Genealogy*, Vol. 18, No. 1, January 2002, pp. 35, 36)

Tannyhill, William, was appointed Constable of Monocacy Hundred in Prince George's County, now Frederick County, 1742. (Ref: Prince George's County Court Records, 1736-1748, Extracts by Patricia Abelard Andersen, *Western Maryland Genealogy*, Vol. 18, No. 1, January 2002, p. 38)

Tarvin, George, commissioned Sheriff of Charles County, 15 Dec 1742. (Ref: Maryland State Archives, Governor and Council Commissioner Records, 1726-1794, p. 75)

Tarvin, Richard, appointed a Commissioner of the Peace for Charles County, 29 Oct 1730. (Ref: Maryland State Archives, Governor and Council Commissioner Records, 1726-1794, p. 12)

Tasker, Benjamin (c1690-1768), was appointed a Commissioner of the Peace for Cecil County, Baltimore County, Kent County, Prince George's County, Anne Arundel County, Calvert County, Charles County, St. Mary's County, Queen Anne's County, and Talbot County, 4 Aug 1732 and 10 Aug 1732 and 20 Aug 1733. (Ref: Maryland State Archives, Governor and Council Commissioner Records, 1726-1794, pp. 32-37); commissioned a Provincial Justice by the Governor, 20 Oct 1729. (Ref: Maryland State Archives, Governor and Council Commissioner Records, 1726-1794, p. 12); commissioned Naval Officer, Port of Annapolis, 25 Jul 1733. (Ref: Maryland Commission Book No. 82, p. 1; *Maryland Historical Magazine*, Vol. XXVI, p. 138); commissioned one of the Commissary Generals and Judges for Probate of Wills, 5 Feb 1733/4. (Ref: Maryland Commission Book No. 82, p. 36; *Maryland Historical Magazine*, Vol. XXVI, p. 145); esquire, commissioned to be His Lordship's Agent within the Province of Maryland. 18 Nov 1742. (Ref: Maryland Commission Book No. 82, p. 98; *Maryland Historical Magazine*, Vol. XXVI, p. 248); appointed a Privy Council on 10 May 1753. (Ref: *Archives of Maryland*, Vol. XXXI, "Proceedings of the Council of Maryland, 1753-1761," pp. 8, 14); see Charles Carroll.

Tasker, Benjamin, Jr. (1720/21-1760), was commissioned Naval Officer of the Port of Annapolis. 29 Sep 1742. (Ref: Maryland Commission Book No. 82, p. 95; *Maryland Historical Magazine*, Vol. XXVI, p. 246); appointed a Privy Council on 10 May 1753. (Ref: *Archives of Maryland*, Vol. XXXI, "Proceedings of the Council of Maryland, 1753-1761," p. 8)

Taylor, Edward, see Mulatto Joe.

Taylor, Ignatius, appointed a Commissioner of the Peace for Somerset County, 26 Jul 1773. (Ref: Maryland State Archives, Governor and Council Commissioner Records, 1726-1794, p. 272)

Taylor, James, commissioned a Coroner in St. Mary's County, 13 Apr 1744. (Ref: Maryland Commission Book No. 82, p. 109; *Maryland Historical Magazine*, Vol. XXVI, p. 252)

Taylor, Jenifer, commissioned High Sheriff of St. Mary's County, 15 Oct 1770. (Ref: Maryland State Archives, Governor and Council Commissioner Records, 1726-1794, p. 242)

Taylor, Michael, convicted felon, was pardoned for assault on William Mauduit. 20 May 1738 (1739?). (Ref: Maryland Commission Book No. 82, p. 69; *Maryland Historical Magazine*, Vol. XXVI, p. 153)

Taylor, Peter (1680-c1747/48), was appointed a Commissioner of the Peace for Dorchester County, 1 Aug 1729 and 29 Oct 1730. (Ref: Maryland State Archives, Governor and Council Commissioner Records, 1726-1794, pp. 11, 17); commissioned Sheriff of Dorchester County, 23 May 1734. (Ref: Maryland State Archives, Governor and Council Commissioner Records, 1726-1794, p. 41); commission renewed for High Sheriff of Dorchester County, 12 Jul 1735. (Ref: Maryland Commission

Book No. 82, p. 32; *Maryland Historical Magazine*, Vol. XXVI, p. 144)

Tealby, John, laborer, of Anne Arundel County, pardoned and banished for burglary, 26 Jan 1771. (Ref: Maryland Commission Book No. 82, p. 252; *Maryland Historical Magazine*, Vol. XXVII, p. 29); of Anne Arundel County, convicted felon and burglar, was executed on 23 Jan 1771. (Ref: Maryland State Archives, Governor and Council Commissioner Records, 1726-1794, p. 244). Additional research will be necessary before drawing any conclusions.

Tenant, John, see Charles Palmer.

Tennelly, Thomas, was Constable in the Lower Part of Monocacy Hundred in Frederick County in 1758. (Ref: *This Was The Life: Excerpts from the Judgment Records of Frederick County, Maryland, 1748-1765*, by Millard Milburn Rice, p. 185)

Thatcher, John, of Frederick County, convicted felon, was executed on 21 Jun 1773. (Ref: Maryland State Archives, Governor and Council Commissioner Records, 1726-1794, p. 259)

Thomas, Christian, of Prince George's County, native of Germany, naturalized 3 May 1740, and also his son Henry. (Ref: Maryland Commission Book No. 82, p. 81; *Maryland Historical Magazine*, Vol. XXVI, p. 156)

Thomas, Hendrick, of Prince George's County, native of Germany, naturalized 3 May 1740. (Ref: Maryland Commission Book No. 82, p. 81; *Maryland Historical Magazine*, Vol. XXVI, p. 156)

Thomas, John, of Frederick Co., commissioned Sheriff of Frederick County, 12 Dec 1748. (Ref: Maryland State Archives, Governor and Council Commissioner Records, 1726-1794, p. 109)

Thomas, Notley, appointed Constable of the Lower Part of Monocacy Hundred in Frederick County in 1751. (Ref: *This Was The Life: Excerpts from the Judgment Records of Frederick County, Maryland, 1748-1765*, by Millard Milburn Rice, p. 61)

Thomas, Philip, commissioned Judge and Register of the Land Office. 13 Mar 1743/4. (Ref: Maryland Commission Book No. 82, p. 107; *Maryland Historical Magazine*, Vol. XXVI, p. 251); appointed a Privy Council on 10 May 1753. (Ref: *Archives of Maryland*, Vol. XXXI, "Proceedings of the Council of Maryland, 1753-1761," p. 8)

Thomas, Richard, commissioned High Sheriff of Cecil County, 15 Oct 1763 and 15 Oct 1771. (Ref: Maryland State Archives, Governor and Council Commissioner Records, 1726-1794, pp. 201, 248)

Thomas, Tristram, was commissioned one of the Coroners of Talbot County, 12 Dec 1746 and 1 Feb 1745/6. (Ref: Maryland Commission Book No. 82, pp. 118, 125; *Maryland Historical Magazine*, Vol. XXVI, pp. 256, 259); appointed a Commissioner of the Peace for Talbot County, 2 Oct 1751. (Ref: Maryland State Archives, Governor and Council Commissioner Records, 1726-1794, p. 124)

Thomas, William, commissioned Sheriff of Talbot County, 5 Oct 1734. (Ref: Maryland State Archives, Governor and Council Commissioner Records, 1726-1794, p. 43, styled him as Jr.); commission renewed for serving as High Sheriff of Talbot County, 15 Oct 1735. (Ref: Maryland Commission Book No. 82, p. 37; *Maryland Historical Magazine*, Vol. XXVI, p. 145); gentleman, of Talbot County, appointed to the Committee to Enquire into Indian Complaints, 1754. (Ref: *Archives of Maryland*, Vol. XXXI, "Proceedings of the Council of Maryland, 1753-1761," p. 30); appointed a Commissioner of the Peace for Talbot County, 2 Feb 1774. (Ref: Maryland State Archives, Governor and Council Commissioner Records, 1726-1794, p. 280); commissioned Rent Roll Keeper of the Eastern Shore, 29 Apr 1773. (Ref: Maryland Commission Book No. 82, p. 311; *Maryland Historical Magazine*, Vol. XXVII, p. 33); see Thomas Barkley.

Thomas, William, Sr., appointed Constable of the Lower Part of Monocacy Hundred in Frederick County, 1769. (Ref: "Frederick County Court Minutes, March 1769," by Patricia Abelard Andersen, *Western Maryland Genealogy*, Vol. 15, No. 2, April 1999, p. 63)

Thomas, Williamson, appointed a Commissioner of the Peace for Talbot County, 29 May 1737. (Ref: Maryland State Archives, Governor and Council Commissioner Records, 1726-1794, p. 56)

Thompson, Augustine (1691-1738/39), appointed a Commissioner of the Peace for Queen Anne's County, 3 Mar 1726/7. (Ref: Maryland State Archives, Governor and Council Commissioner Records, 1726-1794, p. 2)

Thompson, Augustine, of Queen Anne's County,

appointed a Commissioner of the Peace, 16 Jun 1773. (Ref: Maryland State Archives, Governor and Council Commissioner Records, 1726-1794, p. 266)

Thompson, Dowdall, appointed a Commissioner of the Peace for Queen Anne's County, 28 Feb 1742/3. (Ref: Maryland State Archives, Governor and Council Commissioner Records, 1726-1794, p. 76)

Thompson, James, Jr., registration of the sloop *Tryal*, 30 tons, built in Herring Bay, 1733. John Baptist Thompson, master. James Thompson, owner. (Ref: Maryland Commission Book No. 82, p. 79; *Maryland Historical Magazine*, Vol. XXVI, p. 155)

Thompson, John, appointed a Commissioner of the Peace for Queen Anne's County, 31 Oct 1768. (Ref: Maryland State Archives, Governor and Council Commissioner Records, 1726-1794, p. 239); Court Justice, 1774. (*Calendar of Maryland State Papers, No. 1 The Black Books*, p. 215)

Thompson, John, commissioned Sheriff of Cecil County, 14 Oct 1742. (Ref: Maryland State Archives, Governor and Council Commissioner Records, 1726-1794, p. 74)

Thompson, John Dockery (1743-1786), appointed a Commissioner of the Peace for Cecil County, 20 Feb 1774. (Ref: Maryland State Archives, Governor and Council Commissioner Records, 1726-1794, p. 281)

Thompson, Levi, alias Levi Game, alias Levi Fortune, of Somerset County, convicted of murdering Jacob Aires and Negro Scipio, was executed on 8 Jul 1767. (Ref: Maryland State Archives, Governor and Council Commissioner Records, 1726-1794, p. 216, spelled his name Thomson; *Archives of Maryland*, Vol. XXXII, "Proceedings of the Council of Maryland, 1761-1770," p. 200)

Thompson, Richard (c1680-1775), was appointed a Commissioner of the Peace for Cecil County, 3 Mar 1726/7. (Ref: Maryland State Archives, Governor and Council Commissioner Records, 1726-1794, p. 2); commissioned Ranger of the Woods in Cecil County, 25 Apr 1735. (Ref: Maryland Commission Book No. 82, p. 29; *Maryland Historical Magazine*, Vol. XXVI, p. 143); commissioned a Coroner for Cecil County, 9 Jun 1740. (Ref: Maryland Commission Book No. 82, p. 82; *Maryland Historical Magazine*, Vol. XXVI, p. 157

Thompson, Richard, appointed a Commissioner of the Peace for St. Mary's County, 29 Oct 1730. (Ref: Maryland State Archives, Governor and Council Commissioner Records, 1726-1794, p. 12)

Thompson, Richard, Jr. (1713-1789), of Cecil County, was commissioned a Ranger on 16 May 1750. (Ref: Maryland Commission Book No. 82, p. 143; *Maryland Historical Magazine*, Vol. XXVI, p. 345)

Thompson, Samuel, of Kent County, doctor ,was appointed a Commissioner of the Peace, 16 Jun 1764. (Ref: Maryland State Archives, Governor and Council Commissioner Records, 1726-1794, p. 217)

Thompson, Smallwood, see Negro Jonathan.

Thompson, William (1735-1785), reverend, was licensed to preach in St. Mary Anne Parish, Cecil County, vacant by death of Rev. John Hamilton. 1 May 1773; induction into St. Mary Anne's Parish, Cecil County, 23 Jun 1773. (Ref: Maryland Commission Book No. 82, pp. 316, 318; *Maryland Historical Magazine*, Vol. XXVII, p. 34)

Thornton, Edward, see William Thornton.

Thornton, John, reverend, was inducted into Christ Church Parish, Kent Island, 10 Oct 1748. (Ref: Maryland Commission Book No. 82, p. 137; *Maryland Historical Magazine*, Vol. XXVI, p. 342)

Thornton, Postumus, appointed a Commissioner of the Peace for Calvert County, 29 May 1734. (Ref: Maryland State Archives, Governor and Council Commissioner Records, 1726-1794, p. 42)

Thornton, William, appointed a Commissioner of the Peace for Cecil County, 4 Jan 1757 and 22 Apr 1758. (Ref: Maryland State Archives, Governor and Council Commissioner Records, 1726-1794, pp. 173, 180)

Thornton, William, registration of sloop *Betty*, 50 tons, built in Prince George's County, 1743. Edward Thornton, master. William Thornton, owner. 25 Aug 1749. (Ref: Maryland Commission Book No. 82, p. 153; *Maryland Historical Magazine*, Vol. XXVI, p. 350); commissioned Sheriff of Anne Arundel County, 13 Dec 1745 and 18 Dec 1747. (Ref: Maryland State Archives, Governor and Council Commissioner Records, 1726-1794, pp. 90, 105)

Tilden, John, appointed a Commissioner of the Peace for Kent County, 28 May 1756. (Ref: Maryland State Archives, Governor and Council Commissioner Records, 1726-1794, p. 168)

Tilden, Marmaduke (d. 1816), was appointed a Commissioner of the Peace for Kent County, 28 May 1756. (Ref: Maryland State Archives, Governor and Council Commissioner Records, 1726-1794, p. 168)

Tilghman, Edward (1713-1785), commissioned High Sheriff of Queen Anne's County, 20 Oct 1739. (Ref: Maryland State Archives, Governor and Council Commissioner Records, 1726-1794, p. 65); served on the Assembly's Committee of Laws, 1755. (Ref: *Archives of Maryland*, Vol. LII, "Proceedings and Acts of the General Assembly of Maryland, 1755-1756," pp. 46, 62); see Negro Sam Banning.

Tilghman, Isaiah, appointed a Commissioner of the Peace for Somerset County, 8 Jun 1763 and 20 Mar 1775. (Ref: Maryland State Archives, Governor and Council Commissioner Records, 1726-1794, p. 210 spelled his name Tilman, p. 288 spelled it Tilghman)

Tilghman, James, see Thomas Ringgold.

Tilghman, Matthew (1717/18-1790), of Talbot County, served on the Committee of Laws in 1755. (Ref: *Archives of Maryland*, Vol. LII, "Proceedings and Acts of the General Assembly of Maryland, 1755-1756," pp. 72, 81); appointed to the Committee to Apportion the Public Levies, 29 May 1756. (Ref: *Archives of Maryland*, Vol. LII, "Proceedings and Acts of the General Assembly of Maryland, 1755-1756," p. 291)

Tilghman, William (1711-1782), was appointed a Commissioner of the Peace for Queen Anne's County, 17 Oct 1734 and 16 Jun 1773. (Ref: Maryland State Archives, Governor and Council Commissioner Records, 1726-1794, pp. 44, 266)

Timbrill, William, registration of the brigantine *Charming Sally*, 50 tons, built 1733 [placed not indicated]. Martin Potter, master. William Timbrill, owner. 2 May 1737. (Ref: Maryland Commission Book No. 82, p. 48; *Maryland Historical Magazine*, Vol. XXVI, p. 148)

Todd, Lancelot, appointed a Commissioner of the Peace for Baltimore County, 3 Mar 1726/7. (Ref: Maryland State Archives, Governor and Council Commissioner Records, 1726-1794, p. 2, listed him as Lance Todd)

Todd, Lancelot, of Lancelot, was appointed a Commissioner of the Peace for Anne Arundel County, 11 Jul 1738. (Ref: Maryland State Archives, Governor and Council Commissioner Records, 1726-1794, p. 61)

Todd, Lancelott, appointed a Commissioner of the Peace for Anne Arundel County, 20 Apr 1773. (Ref: Maryland State Archives, Governor and Council Commissioner Records, 1726-1794, p. 266)

Todd, Thomas, appointed a Commissioner of the Peace for Anne Arundel County, 20 Apr 1773. (Ref: Maryland State Archives, Governor and Council Commissioner Records, 1726-1794, p. 266); appointed Constable iat Elk Landing in 1774. (Ref: Anne Arundel County Court Minutes, 1725-1757, 1774)

Todd, Thomas, appointed a Commissioner of the Peace for Baltimore County, 4 Aug 1735. (Ref: Maryland State Archives, Governor and Council Commissioner Records, 1726-1794, p. 49)

Tolley, Thomas (d. 1773), appointed a Commissioner of the Peace for Baltimore County, 3 Mar 1726/7 and 22 Oct 1728. (Ref: Maryland State Archives, Governor and Council Commissioner Records, 1726-1794, pp. 2, 49)

Tolley, Walter (d. 1783), appointed a Commissioner of the Peace for Baltimore County, 2 Mar 1754. (Ref: Maryland State Archives, Governor and Council Commissioner Records, 1726-1794, p. 142); appointed to represent Baltimore County in the Provincial Convention, 1775. (Ref: *Calendar of Maryland State Papers, The Red Books*, No. 4, Part 1, p. 3)

Tolley, Walter, Jr. (1744-1776), was appointed a Commissioner of the Peace for Baltimore County, 30 May 1774. (Ref: Maryland State Archives, Governor and Council Commissioner Records, 1726-1794, p. 283); appointed to represent Baltimore County in the Provincial Convention, 1775. (Ref: *Calendar of Maryland State Papers, The Red Books*, No. 4, Part 1, p. 3)

Tolson, John, of North Carolina, registration of the schooner *Hannah*, 8 tons, built in Virginia, 1740. John Tolson, master and owner. 20 Sep 1745. (Ref: Maryland Commission Book No. 82, p. 115; *Maryland Historical Magazine*, Vol. XXVI, p. 255)

Tomlinson, Joseph, appointed a Commissioner of the Peace for Frederick County, 1 Aug 1768. (Ref: Maryland State Archives, Governor and Council Commissioner Records, 1726-1794, p. 235)

Tootell, Richard, commissioned Master Gunner,

Storekeeper, and Keeper of the Council Chamber in Annapolis, 5 Sep 1741. (Ref: Maryland Commission Book No. 82, p. 88; *Maryland Historical Magazine*, Vol. XXVI, p. 245)

Tootle, James, appointed a Commissioner of the Peace for Dorchester County, 8 Apr 1770. (Ref: Maryland State Archives, Governor and Council Commissioner Records, 1726-1794, p. 250)

Tootle, John, appointed Constable of Fishing Creek Hundred in Dorchester County, 1744. (Ref: Dorchester County Judgment Records, 1743-1745, p. 185; *Judgment Records of Dorchester, Queen Anne's and Talbot Counties, Maryland*, by F. Edward Wright, 2001, p. 49)

Tovey, Samuel, appointed a Commissioner of the Peace for Kent County, 7 Mar 1746/7. (Ref: Maryland State Archives, Governor and Council Commissioner Records, 1726-1794, p. 98)

Towgood, Josias, appointed a Commissioner of the Peace for Anne Arundel County, 3 Mar 1726/7. (Ref: Maryland State Archives, Governor and Council Commissioner Records, 1726-1794, p. 3)

Townshend, William, see Outherbrdge Horsey and William Lane.

Townsin, Richard, of Baltimore County, convicted of murder, was executed on 23 Jun 1731. (Ref: Maryland State Archives, Governor and Council Commissioner Records, 1726-1794, p. 20)

Travers, Henry (d. 1765), registration of the schooner *Honest Trader*, 25 tons, built in Dorchester County, 1734. Henry Hickes, master. Henry Travers. Owner. 18 Nov 1743. (Ref: Maryland Commission Book No. 82, p. 105; *Maryland Historical Magazine*, Vol. XXVI, p. 250); appointed a Commissioner of the Peace for Dorchester County, 21 Apr 1735. (Ref: Maryland State Archives, Governor and Council Commissioner Records, 1726-1794, p. 46); commissioned a Coroner for Dorchester County, 28 Feb 1737/8. (Ref: Maryland Commission Book No. 82, p. 51; *Maryland Historical Magazine*, Vol. XXVI, p. 150); see Levin Travers)

Travers, Levin, registration of sloop *Endeavour*, 15 tons, built in Dorchester County, 1748. Levin Hodson, master. Levin Travers and Henry Travers, owners. 28 Aug 1749. (Ref: Maryland Commission Book No. 82, p. 153; *Maryland Historical Magazine*, Vol. XXVI, p. 350)

Travers, Levin, of Henry, was commissioned a Coroner of Dorchester County, 6 Oct 1766. (Ref: Maryland Commission Book No. 82, p. 181; *Maryland Historical Magazine*, Vol. XXVI, p. 354)

Triggs, Nathaniel, see Charles Carroll.

Trippe, Edward, was commissioned Sheriff of Dorchester County, 24 Jun 1740 and served to at least 1756. (Ref: Maryland State Archives, Governor and Council Commissioner Records, 1726-1794, p. 68, spelled his surname Tripp; *Archives of Maryland*, Vol. LII, "Proceedings and Acts of the General Assembly of Maryland, 1755-1756," p. 232)

Trippe, Elizabeth, see Negro Siladdy.

Trippe, Henry (d. 1744), of Dorchester County, was appointed a Commissioner of the Peace, 21 Apr 1735. (Ref: Maryland State Archives, Governor and Council Commissioner Records, 1726-1794, p. 46); see William Edmonson.

Trippe, Henry, commissioned Sheriff of Charles County, 12 Jul 1730. (Ref: Maryland State Archives, Governor and Council Commissioner Records, 1726-1794, p. 20)

Trippe, James, appointed a Commissioner of the Peace for Talbot County, 2 Feb 1774. (Ref: Maryland State Archives, Governor and Council Commissioner Records, 1726-1794, p. 280)

Trippe, John, Jr., appointed Constable of Little Choptank Hundred in Dorchester County, 1742. (Ref: Dorchester County Judgment Records, 1742-1743, p. 84; *Judgment Records of Dorchester, Queen Anne's and Talbot Counties, Maryland*, by F. Edward Wright, 2001, p. 30)

Trott, Samuel, see Edward North.

Trout, Hendrick, of Prince George's County, native of Germany, naturalized 3 May 1740, and also his son Jacob. (Ref: Maryland Commission Book No. 82, p. 80; *Maryland Historical Magazine*, Vol. XXVI, p. 156)

Truman, Henry, appointed a Commissioner of the Peace for Prince George's County, 21 Nov 1743. (Ref: Maryland State Archives, Governor and Council Commissioner Records, 1726-1794, p. 83)

Truman, Thomas, appointed a Commissioner of the Peace for Prince George's County, 3 Dec 1766. (Ref:

Maryland State Archives, Governor and Council Commissioner Records, 1726-1794, p. 230)

Tubman, Henry, was commissioned a Coroner in St. Mary's County, 9 May 1768. (Ref: Maryland Commission Book No. 82, p. 213; *Maryland Historical Magazine*, Vol. XXVI, p. 357); appointed a Commissioner of the Peace for Somerset County, 26 Jul 1773. (Ref: Maryland State Archives, Governor and Council Commissioner Records, 1726-1794, p. 272)

Tullap, John, see Gamaliel Butler.

Tumbleson, Nathaniel, appointed Constable of Marsh Hundred in Frederick County, 1749. (Ref: *This Was The Life: Excerpts from the Judgment Records of Frederick County, Maryland, 1748-1765*, by Millard Milburn Rice, p. 7)

Tunstall, John, registration of the schooner *Providence*, 20 tons, built in Somerset County, 1733. John Tunstall, master and owner. 17 Dec 1733. (Ref: Maryland Commission Book No. 82, p. 37; *Maryland Historical Magazine*, Vol. XXVI, p. 145); captain, of Somerset County, 1726. (Ref: *Abstracts of the Testamentary Proceedings and Prerogative Court of Maryland, Vol. XVII, 1724-1727*, by Vernon L. Skinner, Jr., p. 129, citing original Liber 27, f. 327)

Turbutt, William (1683/84-1729), appointed a Commissioner of the Peace for Queen Anne's County, 3 Mar 1726/7. (Ref: Maryland State Archives, Governor and Council Commissioner Records, 1726-1794, p. 2)

Turner, James, see Robert Story.

Turner, Jane, spinster, of Charles County, convicted felon for breaking and entering the house of David Rawlings and stealing sundry pieces of money, was sentenced to death; however, in the stay of execution, it was presented that she was a poor, silly woman who claimed to be pregnant, and also appeared to have been an accomplice in the offense. She was pardoned on 2 Jun 1769. (*Archives of Maryland*, Vol. XXXII, "Proceedings of the Council of Maryland, 1761-1770," pp. 273-274)

Turner, William, alias John Smith, of Anne Arundel County, convicted felon, was executed on 1 Jun 1738. (Ref: Maryland State Archives, Governor and Council Commissioner Records, 1726-1794, p. 63)

Turner, William, of Cecil County, convicted felon, reprieve of death sentence, 1 Jun 1739, banished from Province, 25 Jun 1739. (Ref: Maryland Commission Book No. 82, p. 74; *Maryland Historical Magazine*, Vol. XXVI, p. 154)

Twigg, John, the Elder, appointed Constable of Transquakin Hundred in Dorchester County, 1742. (Ref: Dorchester County Judgment Records, 1742-1743, p. 84; *Judgment Records of Dorchester, Queen Anne's and Talbot Counties, Maryland*, by F. Edward Wright, 2001, p. 30)

Twigg, Robert, appointed Constable of Andietum [Antietam] Hundred in Prince George's County, now Frederick County, 1748. (Ref: Prince George's County Court Records, 1736-1738, Extracts by Patricia Abelard Andersen, *Western Maryland Genealogy*, Vol. 18, No. 1, January 2002, p. 46)

Tyler, Robert (c1671-1738), of Prince George's County, sheriff, 1726. (Ref: *Abstracts of the Testamentary Proceedings and Prerogative Court of Maryland, Vol. XVII, 1724-1727*, by Vernon L. Skinner, Jr., p. 117, citing original Liber 27, f. 312); see Negro Charles and Negro James.

Tyler, Robert (1727-1777), was appointed a Commissioner of the Peace for Prince George's County, 25 Nov 1751. (Ref: Maryland State Archives, Governor and Council Commissioner Records, 1726-1794, p. 129)

Tyler, Thomas, registration of the shallop *Charming Molly*, 13 tons, built in Somerset County, 1746. Thomas Tyler, master and owner. 14 Mar 1746/7. (Ref: Maryland Commission Book No. 82, p. 126; *Maryland Historical Magazine*, Vol. XXVI, p. 259)

Ulderey, Stephen, planter, of Baltimore County, native of High Germany, naturalized 4 Jun 1738 and also his children Stephen, George, Daniel, John, Elizabeth and Susanna. (Ref: Maryland Commission Book No. 82, p. 57; *Maryland Historical Magazine*, Vol. XXVI, p. 151)

Uncles, Uncle, appointed Constable of Pipe Creek Hundred in Prince George's County, now Frederick County, 1746. (Ref: Prince George's County Court Records, 1736-1748, Extracts by Patricia Abelard Andersen, *Western Maryland Genealogy*, Vol. 18, No. 1, January 2002, p. 44)

Ungefare, John Martin, planter, of Baltimore County, native of High Germany, naturalized 4 Jun

1738 and also his children George, Francis and Catherine. (Ref: Maryland Commission Book No. 82, p. 57; *Maryland Historical Magazine*, Vol. XXVI, p. 151)

Ungle, Charles, sheriff, of Dorchester County, 1726. (Ref: *Abstracts of the Testamentary Proceedings and Prerogative Court of Maryland, Vol. XVII, 1724-1727*, by Vernon L. Skinner, Jr., p. 122, citing original Liber 27, f. 318)

Urquahart, John (d. 1764), reverend, induction into William and Mary Parish, Charles County, 25 Apr 1734; induction into All Faith's Parish, St. Mary's County, 25 Oct 1734. (Ref: Maryland Commission Book No. 82, pp. 10, 21; *Maryland Historical Magazine*, Vol. XXVI, pp. 40, 142)

VanBibber, Adam, appointed a Commissioner of the Peace for Cecil County, 9 Feb 1743/4. (Ref: Maryland State Archives, Governor and Council Commissioner Records, 1726-1794, p. 84)

VanBibber, Isaac, appointed a Commissioner of the Peace for Cecil County, 1 Oct 1768. (Ref: Maryland State Archives, Governor and Council Commissioner Records, 1726-1794, p. 240, spelled his name Vanbebber); appointed a Commissioner of the Peace for Baltimore County, 31 Oct 1772. (Ref: Maryland State Archives, Governor and Council Commissioner Records, 1726-1794, p. 264, spelled his name Vanbebber); Justice in Baltimore County, 8 Oct 1773. (Ref: *Inhabitants of Baltimore County, 1763-1774*, by Henry C. Peden, Jr., 1989, p. 49, citing *Calendar of Maryland State Papers, No. 1 The Black Books*, p. 209, spelled his name Van Bibber); appointed a Commissioner of the Peace for Baltimore County, 30 May 1774. (Ref: Maryland State Archives, Governor and Council Commissioner Records, 1726-1794, p. 283)

Vanderwert, Thomas, see Thomas Stanton.

Vandever, John, appointed Constable of Andietum [Antietam] Hundred in Prince George's County, now Frederick County, in 1739, and in Frederick County in 1749 and 1753. (Ref: *This Was The Life: Excerpts from the Judgment Records of Frederick County, Maryland, 1748-1765*, by Millard Milburn Rice, p. 131; Prince George's County Court Records, 1736-1748, Extracts by Patricia Abelard Andersen, *Western Maryland Genealogy*, Vol. 18, No. 1, January 2002, pp. 36, 37)

Vandicke, Thomas, doctor, was appointed a Commissioner of the Peace for Cecil County on 2 Jun 1774. (Ref: Maryland State Archives, Governor and Council Commissioner Records, 1726-1794, p. 283)

Vanmetre, John, appointed a Commissioner of the Peace for Prince George's County, 18 Feb 1731/2. (Ref: Maryland State Archives, Governor and Council Commissioner Records, 1726-1794, p. 21)

Vansant, Nicholas, was appointed Constable of Linganore Hundred in Prince George's County, now Frederick County, 1744 and 1745. (Ref: Prince George's County Court Records, 1736-1748, Extracts by Patricia Abelard Andersen, *Western Maryland Genealogy*, Vol. 18, No. 1, January 2002, pp. 41, 43)

Vaughan, John, reverend, induction into St. Margaret Westminster, Anne Arundel County, 7 Apr 1735. (Ref: Maryland Commission Book No. 82, p. 27; *Maryland Historical Magazine*, Vol. XXVI, p. 143); resignation from Parish of St. Margaret's Westminster in Anne Arundel County. 1 Mar 1741/2. On same day, induction into Christ Church Parish in Calvert County. (Ref: Maryland Commission Book No. 82, p. 91; *Maryland Historical Magazine*, Vol. XXVI, p. 245)

Vaughan, Jonathan, appointed a Commissioner of the Peace for Worcester County, 16 Jan 1769 and 30 Apr 1770. (Ref: Maryland State Archives, Governor and Council Commissioner Records, 1726-1794, pp. 240, 250)

Veatch, John, appointed Constable of Seneca Hundred to Monocacy in Prince George's County, now Frederick County, 1736. (Ref: Prince George's County Court Records, 1736-1748, Extracts by Patricia Abelard Andersen, *Western Maryland Genealogy*, Vol. 18, No. 1, January 2002, p. 35)

Veazey, Edward, was commissioned Sheriff of Cecil County, 2 Oct 1751. (Ref: Maryland State Archives, Governor and Council Commissioner Records, 1726-1794, p. 129, spelled his surname Vezey, and p. 134 spelled it Veazey)

Veazey, John (1701-1777), appointed a Commissioner of the Peace for Cecil County, 17 Oct 1734 and 8 Mar 1735/6. (Ref: Maryland State Archives, Governor and Council Commissioner Records, 1726-1794, pp. 43, 51, both spelled his surname Vesey); commissioned Deputy Surveyor of Cecil County, 18 Nov 1743. (Ref: Maryland Commission Book No. 82, p. 105; *Maryland Historical Magazine*, Vol. XXVI, p. 250, spelled his name Vezey); commissioned Naval Officer of the District in Cecil County, 8 Dec 1743. (Ref: Maryland Commission Book No. 82, p. 106; *Maryland Historical Magazine*, Vol. XXVI, p. 250, spelled his name Vezey); appointed a Commissioner of the Peace for Cecil County, 21 Apr 1764. (Ref: Maryland State Archives, Governor and Council Commissioner Records, 1726-1794, p. 215)

Veazey, John, Jr. (1722-c1780), was appointed a Commissioner of the Peace for Cecil County, 20 Feb 1774. (Ref: Maryland State Archives, Governor and Council Commissioner Records, 1726-1794, p. 281)

Venables, Benjamin, registration of the sloop *Betty*, 18 tons, built in Somerset County, 1750. William Venables, master and co-owner. Benjamin Venables, co-owner. 13 Sep 1750. (Ref: Maryland Commission Book No. 82, p. 145; *Maryland Historical Magazine*, Vol. XXVI, p. 346); see William Winder.

Venables, William, see Benjamin Venables and William Winder.

Vickers, Edward, see James Vickers.

Vickers, James, alias Edward Vickers, labourer, of Queen Anne's County, convicted felon for breaking open and robbing the store of Joshua Clarke, was sentenced to death on 19 Mar 1770 and later pardoned and banished from the province on 16 Apr 1770 on condition that he left the province within ten days. (Ref: Maryland Commission Book No. 82, p. 239; *Maryland Historical Magazine*, Vol. XXVI, pp. 360-361; *Archives of Maryland*, Vol. XXXII, "Proceedings of the Council of Maryland, 1761-1770," pp. 335, 345)

Virgin, James, see William Austin.

Volgamot, Joseph, was appointed Constable of Salisbury Hundred in Frederick County in 1753. (Ref: *This Was The Life: Excerpts from the Judgment Records of Frederick County, Maryland, 1748-1765*, by Millard Milburn Rice, p. 131)

Voss, James, Jr., was appointed Constable of Bridgetown Hundred in Dorchester County, 1744. (Ref: Dorchester County Judgment Records, 1743-1745, p. 185; *Judgment Records of Dorchester, Queen Anne's and Talbot Counties, Maryland*, by F. Edward Wright, 2001, p. 49)

Wabby, John, see Patrick Creagh.

Wade, William, laborer, of Anne Arundel County, pardoned for larceny, 26 Sep 1770. (Ref: Maryland Commission Book No. 82, p. 250; *Maryland Historical Magazine*, Vol. XXVII, p. 29)

Waggaman, Ephraim (d. 1758), was appointed a Commissioner of the Peace for Worcester County, 28 Oct 1747. (Ref: Maryland State Archives, Governor and Council Commissioner Records, 1726-1794, p. 102); registration of sloop *Betty & Molly*, 40 tons, built in Worcester County, 1749. William Handy, master, Ephraim Waggaman, John Scott, Joseph Scott, William Stevens and Mary Scott, owners. 29 Mar 1750. (Ref: Maryland Commission Book No. 82, p. 155; *Maryland Historical Magazine*, Vol. XXVI, p. 351); commissioned Sheriff of Worcester County, 2 Sep 1752. (Ref: Maryland State Archives, Governor and Council Commissioner Records, 1726-1794, p. 133; *Archives of Maryland*, Vol. LII, "Proceedings and Acts of the General Assembly of Maryland, 1755-1756," p. 577)

Waggaman, Henry (d. c1761), was appointed a Commissioner of the Peace for Somerset County, 20 Oct 1746. (Ref: Maryland State Archives, Governor and Council Commissioner Records, 1726-1794, p. 94); Court Justice, 1753. (*Calendar of Maryland State Papers, No. 1 The Black Books*, p. 112)

Wales, George, appointed a Commissioner of the Peace for Somerset County, 19 May 1774. (Ref: Maryland State Archives, Governor and Council Commissioner Records, 1726-1794, p. 282)

Walker, Abraham, Constable of Patapsco Upper Hundred in Baltimore County, 1773. (Ref: *Inhabitants of Baltimore County, 1763-1774*, by Henry C. Peden, Jr., 1989, p. 80, citing a 1773 List of Taxables)

Walker, James, registration of ship *Elizabeth*, 150 tons, built in Anne Arundel County, 1748. Alexander Scougall, master. James Walker and Thomas Harrison, owners. 1 Jun 1749. (Ref: Maryland Commission Book No. 82, p. 151; *Maryland Historical Magazine*, Vol. XXVI, p. 349)

Walker, Nathaniel, appointed Constable of the Lower Part of Kittocton [Catoctin] Hundred in Frederick County in 1763. (Ref: *This Was The Life: Excerpts from the Judgment Records of Frederick County, Maryland, 1748-1765*, by Millard Milburn Rice, p. 249)

Walker, Reneldeon (Renelden), was appointed Constable of the Lower Part of Kittocton [Catoctin]

Hundred in Frederick County, 1769, 1771. (Ref: "Frederick County Court Minutes November 1769 by Patricia Abelard Andersen," *Western Maryland Genealogy*, Vol. 16, No. 1, January 2000, p. 32; "Frederick County Minute Book, March 1771, Extracts by Patricia Abelard Andersen," *Western Maryland Genealogy*, Vol. 18, No. 1, January 2002, p. 26)

Wallace, Herbert, appointed Constable of the Lower Part of Potowmack [Potomac] Hundred in Frederick County, 1769. (Ref: "Frederick County Court Minutes, March 1769," by Patricia Abelard Andersen, *Western Maryland Genealogy*, Vol. 15, No. 2, April 1999, p. 62)

Wallace, James, registration of schooner *Sarah and Rebecca*, 12 tons, built at Elk River, 1733. James Wallace, master and owner. 7 Aug 1734. (Ref: Maryland Commission Book No. 82, p. 47; *Maryland Historical Magazine*, Vol. XXVI, p. 148)

Wallace, John, was commissioned a Coroner of Kent County, 7 Mar 1746/7. (Ref: Maryland Commission Book No. 82, p. 126; *Maryland Historical Magazine*, Vol. XXVI, p. 259)

Wallace, John, registration of schooner *Sarah*, 35 tons, built at Wiccocomoco River, 1731. William Gaitskell, master. James Heath, James Calder, Bedingfield Hands and John Wallace, owners. 13 Apr 1736. (Ref: Maryland Commission Book No. 82, p. 43; *Maryland Historical Magazine*, Vol. XXVI, p. 147); see George Steuart.

Wallace, Thomas, see John Pagan.

Wallace, William, was appointed Constable of Potomac Hundred in Prince George's County, now Frederick County, 1738. (Ref: Prince George's County Court Records, 1736-1748, Extracts by Patricia Abelard Andersen, *Western Maryland Genealogy*, Vol. 18, No. 1, January 2002, p. 35); see John Pagan.

Wallace, William, Jr., appointed Constable of the Lower Part of Potomac Hundred in Frederick County in 1753. (Ref: *This Was The Life: Excerpts from the Judgment Records of Frederick County, Maryland, 1748-1765*, by Millard Milburn Rice, p. 131)

Wallis, Adam, see William Sandwith.

Walls, Henry, of Annapolis, commissioned Master Gunner, 29 Sep 1748. (Ref: Maryland Commission Book No. 82, p. 136; *Maryland Historical Magazine*, Vol. XXVI, p. 342)

Wallis Hugh (1711-1766), was appointed a Commissioner of the Peace for Kent County, 9 Nov 1747. (Ref: Maryland State Archives, Governor and Council Commissioner Records, 1726-1794, p. 103, spelled his name Wallace)

Walter, John, of Charles County, appointed one of the inspectors of Piles' Warehouse, 1756. (Ref: *Archives of Maryland*, Vol. LII, "Proceedings and Acts of the General Assembly of Maryland, 1755-1756," p. 638)

Walters, Jacob, appointed a Commissioner of the Peace for Anne Arundel County, 16 Dec 1769. (Ref: Maryland State Archives, Governor and Council Commissioner Records, 1726-1794, p. 249)

Walters, John, appointed a Commissioner of the Peace for Somerset County, 1748 [exact date not given]. (Ref: Maryland State Archives, Governor and Council Commissioner Records, 1726-1794, p. 108)

Ward, Henry (d. 1734), appointed a Commissioner of the Peace for Cecil County, 3 Mar 1726/7. (Ref: Maryland State Archives, Governor and Council Commissioner Records, 1726-1794, p. 2); appointed a Commissioner of the Peace for Cecil County, Baltimore County, Kent County, Prince George's County, Anne Arundel County, Calvert County, Charles County, St. Mary's County, Queen Anne's County, and Talbot County, 4 Aug 1732 and 10 Aug 1732 and 20 Aug 1733. (Ref: Maryland State Archives, Governor and Council Commissioner Records, 1726-1794, pp. 32-37)

Ward, Henry (d. 1760), was commissioned a Coroner of Cecil County, 3 Sep 1746. (Ref: Maryland Commission Book No. 82, p. 122; *Maryland Historical Magazine*, Vol. XXVI, p. 258)

Ward, John (colonel), see Francis Sheredine.

Ward, John (c1671-1747/48), was appointed a Commissioner of the Peace for Cecil County, 3 Mar 1726/7. (Ref: Maryland State Archives, Governor and Council Commissioner Records, 1726-1794, p. 2)

Ward, John, commissioned a Coroner of Cecil County, April 1770. (Ref: Maryland Commission Book No. 82, p. 240; *Maryland Historical Magazine*, Vol. XXVI, p. 361)

Ward, John, Jr., commissioned a Coroner for Cecil County, 15 Aug 1737. (Ref: Maryland Commission Book No. 82, p. 50; *Maryland Historical Magazine*,

Vol. XXVI, p. 149)

Ward, John, of John, commissioned a Coroner of Cecil County, 23 Jun 1773. (Ref: Maryland Commission Book No. 82, p. 318; *Maryland Historical Magazine*, Vol. XXVII, p. 34)

Ward, Matthew Tilghman (c1676-1741), was commissioned Provincial Chief Justice by the Governor, 20 Oct 1729, and was appointed a Commissioner of the Peace for Cecil County, Baltimore County, Kent County, Prince George's County, Anne Arundel County, Calvert County, Charles County, St. Mary's County, Queen Anne's County, and Talbot County, 4 Aug 1732 and 10 Aug 1732 and 20 Aug 1733. (Ref: Maryland State Archives, Governor and Council Commissioner Records, 1726-1794, pp. 12, 32-37)

Ward, Peregrine, commissioned Sheriff of Cecil County, 3 Nov 1733; commissioned High Sheriff of Cecil County, 3 Nov 1735; appointed a Commissioner of the Peace for Cecil County, 15 Aug 1737. (Ref: Maryland State Archives, Governor and Council Commissioner Records, 1726-1794, pp. 39, 57, 145)

Ward, Richard Tilghman, was appointed a Commissioner of the Peace for Cecil County, Baltimore County, Kent County, Prince George's County, Anne Arundel County, Calvert County, Charles County, St. Mary's County, Queen Anne's County, and Talbot County, 4 Aug 1732 and 10 Aug 1732 and 20 Aug 1733. (Ref: Maryland State Archives, Governor and Council Commissioner Records, 1726-1794, pp. 32-37)

Ward, William (1727-1776), was appointed a Commissioner of the Peace for Cecil County, 1 Oct 1768 and 20 Feb 1774. (Ref: Maryland State Archives, Governor and Council Commissioner Records, 1726-1794, pp. 240, 281)

Wardrop, James, see James Russell, William Potts and Negro Peter.

Warfield, Alexander, of Richard (c1677-1755), appointed a Commissioner of the Peace for Anne Arundel County, 20 Nov 1739 and 14 Nov 1741. (Ref: Maryland State Archives, Governor and Council Commissioner Records, 1726-1794, pp. 66, 72); commissioned one of the Coroners of Anne Arundel County, 14 Mar 1743/4. (Ref: Maryland Commission Book No. 82, p. 108; *Maryland Historical Magazine*, Vol. XXVI, p. 251); Justice, Anne Arundel County Court, 1754. (Ref: Anne Arundel County Court Minutes, 1725-1757)

Warfield, Charles, of John, of Anne Arundel County, appointed Constable in Bare(?) Ground Hundred in 1774. (Ref: Anne Arundel County Court Minutes, 1725-1757, 1774)

Warford, Joseph, appointed a Commissioner of the Peace for Frederick County, 16 Nov 1763. (Ref: Maryland State Archives, Governor and Council Commissioner Records, 1726-1794, p. 213); Court Justice, 1764. (Ref: *This Was The Life: Excerpts from the Judgment Records of Frederick County, Maryland, 1748-1765*, by Millard Milburn Rice, pp. 259)

Waring, Basil 3rd, appointed a Commissioner of the Peace for Prince George's County, 26 Jul 1773. (Ref: Maryland State Archives, Governor and Council Commissioner Records, 1726-1794, p. 272)

Waring, Francis (1715-1769), was appointed a Commissioner of the Peace for Prince George's County, 22 Mar 1742/3. (Ref: Maryland State Archives, Governor and Council Commissioner Records, 1726-1794, p. 77)

Warner, Thomas, appointed a Commissioner of the Peace for Baltimore County, 24 Nov 1732. (Ref: Maryland State Archives, Governor and Council Commissioner Records, 1726-1794, p. 39)

Warren, Francis, appointed a Commissioner of the Peace for Prince George's County, 25 Jul 1759. (Ref: Maryland State Archives, Governor and Council Commissioner Records, 1726-1794, p. 185)

Warren, Thomas, appointed a Commissioner of the Peace for Baltimore County, 18 Feb 1731/2. (Ref: Maryland State Archives, Governor and Council Commissioner Records, 1726-1794, p. 21)

Warren, Thomas, appointed a Commissioner of the Peace for Frederick County, 2 Nov 1773 and 15 Aug 1774. (Ref: Maryland State Archives, Governor and Council Commissioner Records, 1726-1794, pp. 278, 284)

Warrin, Richard Marsh, see Negro Joe.

Warring, Thomas, of Frederick County, Court Judge, 1774. (*Calendar of Maryland State Papers, No. 1 The Black Books*, p. 217)

Waters, George, appointed a Commissioner of the Peace for Somerset County, 20 Mar 1775. (Ref:

Maryland State Archives, Governor and Council Commissioner Records, 1726-1794, p. 288)

Waters, Littleton, registration of sloop *Betty*, 25 tons, built at Patuxent, 1741. Joseph Crispin, master. Littleton Waters, owner. 8 May 1744. (Ref: Maryland Commission Book No. 82, p. 109; *Maryland Historical Magazine*, Vol. XXVI, p. 252)

Waters, John, appointed a Commissioner of the Peace for Somerset County, 29 May 1750. (Ref: Maryland State Archives, Governor and Council Commissioner Records, 1726-1794, p. 117, spelled his name Watters); Court Justice, 1753. (*Calendar of Maryland State Papers, No. 1 The Black Books*, p. 112, spelled his name Waters)

Waters, John, was appointed the Constable of Newfoundland Hundred in Frederick County, 1760. (Ref: *This Was The Life: Excerpts from the Judgment Records of Frederick County, Maryland, 1748-1765*, by Millard Milburn Rice, p. 216)

Waters, Peter (1744/45-1806), was appointed a Commissioner of the Peace for Somerset County, 20 Mar 1775. (Ref: Maryland State Archives, Governor and Council Commissioner Records, 1726-1794, p. 288)

Waters, William, registration of schooner *Rose*, 25 tons, built in Somerset County, 1744. William Waters, master and owner. 4 Oct 1744. (Ref: Maryland Commission Book No. 82, p. 111; *Maryland Historical Magazine*, Vol. XXVI, p. 253)

Waters, William, was appointed the Constable of Newfoundland Hundred in Frederick County in 1749. (Ref: *This Was The Life: Excerpts from the Judgment Records of Frederick County, Maryland, 1748-1765*, by Millard Milburn Rice, p. 6)

Waters, William, Jr., see Negro George.

Watkins, Evan, see Samuel Massey.

Watkins, George, registration of the schooner *Friendship*, formerly called *The Hawk*, 20 tons, built at Herring Bay, 1735. George Watkins, master. As appears by a former registration, Samuel Read and George Watkins, owners, 28 Aug 1741. (Ref: Maryland Commission Book No. 82, p. 87; *Maryland Historical Magazine*, Vol. XXVI, p. 244)

Watkins, John, of John, of Anne Arundel County, appointed Constable of West River Hundred in 1774. (Ref: Anne Arundel County Court Minutes, 1725-1757, 1774)

Watkins, Thomas, Jr., appointed a Commissioner of the Peace for Anne Arundel County, 24 Aug 1773. (Ref: Maryland State Archives, Governor and Council Commissioner Records, 1726-1794, p. 276); Court Justice, 1774. (Ref: Anne Arundel County Court Minutes, 1725-1757, 1774)

Watkins, Thomas, of Nicholas, head of South River, appointed a Commissioner of the Peace for Anne Arundel County, 17 Nov 1762. (Ref: Maryland State Archives, Governor and Council Commissioner Records, 1726-1794, p. 208)

Watkyns, Thomas, registration of sloop *Mary Anna*, 10 tons, built in Dorchester County, 1737. Thomas Watkyns, master and owner. 4 Aug 1737. (Ref: Maryland Commission Book No. 82, p. 50; *Maryland Historical Magazine*, Vol. XXVI, p. 149)

Watson, John, of St. Mary's County, convicted felon, ordered on 17 May 1739 to be executed. (Ref: Maryland State Archives, Governor and Council Commissioner Records, 1726-1794, p. 63)

Watson, John, appointed Constable of Northwest Hundred in Frederick County, 1771. (Ref: "Frederick County Minute Book, March 1771, Extracts by Patricia Abelard Andersen," *Western Maryland Genealogy*, Vol. 18, No. 1, January 2002, p. 25)

Watt, George, appointed a Commissioner of the Peace for Anne Arundel County, 5 Aug 1769. (Ref: Maryland State Archives, Governor and Council Commissioner Records, 1726-1794, p. 242

Watts, Daniel, of London, mariner, registration of schooner *Eleanor and Elizabeth*, 25 tons, built in Maryland, 1732. Daniel Watts and Samuel Hyde, merchant, of London, owners. June 1734. (Ref: Maryland Commission Book No. 82, p. 13; *Maryland Historical Magazine*, Vol. XXVI, p. 140); see Christopher Grindall.

Watts, George, appointed a Commissioner of the Peace for Anne Arundel County, 16 Dec 1769 and 26 Jul 1773. (Ref: Maryland State Archives, Governor and Council Commissioner Records, 1726-1794, pp. 249, 272); Court Justice, 1774. (Ref: Anne Arundel County Court Minutes, 1725-1757, 1774)

Watts, Robert, commissioned High Sheriff of St. Mary's County, 19 Oct 1769. (Ref: Maryland State Archives, Governor and Council Commissioner

Records, 1726-1794, p. 236)

Waughop, James, appointed a Commissioner of the Peace for St. Mary's County, 1 Apr 1736. (Ref: Maryland State Archives, Governor and Council Commissioner Records, 1726-1794, p. 51, spelled his surname Wauhop); commissioned a Coroner for St. Mary's County, 18 May 1737 and 26 Oct 1742. (Ref: Maryland Commission Book No. 82, p. 48; *Maryland Historical Magazine*, Vol. XXVI, pp. 149, 247)

Waughop, Thomas (d. 1735), was appointed a Commissioner of the Peace for St. Mary's County, 2 Mar 1726/7. (Ref: Maryland State Archives, Governor and Council Commissioner Records, 1726-1794, p. 2)

Weathered, Richard, appointed a Commissioner of the Peace for Kent County, 18 Feb 1739/40. (Ref: Maryland State Archives, Governor and Council Commissioner Records, 1726-1794, p. 66)

Weaver, Elizabeth, of Frederick County, indicted for stealing a sheet from Alexander Lamar in 1749. (Ref: *This Was The Life: Excerpts from the Judgment Records of Frederick County, Maryland, 1748-1765*, by Millard Milburn Rice, p. 15)

Webb, John, see Robert Jenckins Henry.

Webb, William, appointed a Commissioner of the Peace for Frederick County, 22 Nov 1752. (Ref: Maryland State Archives, Governor and Council Commissioner Records, 1726-1794, p. 135); Court Justice, Frederick County, 1753. (Ref: *This Was The Life: Excerpts from the Judgment Records of Frederick County, Maryland, 1748-1765*, by Millard Milburn Rice, p. 115)

Webb, William (d. 1778), appointed a Commissioner of the Peace for Harford County on 20 Feb 1774. (Ref: Maryland State Archives, Governor and Council Commissioner Records, 1726-1794, p. 281)

Wederstrandt, Conrad Theodore, native of France, denization, 3 May 1764. (Ref: Maryland Commission Book No. 82, p. 162; *Maryland Historical Magazine*, Vol. XXVI, p. 352)

Weeks, James, commissioned Sheriff of Calvert County, 20 Jun 1736. (Ref: Maryland State Archives, Governor and Council Commissioner Records, 1726-1794, p. 52)

Weeks, Joseph, appointed a Commissioner of the Peace for Queen Anne's County, 24 May 1737. (Ref: Maryland State Archives, Governor and Council Commissioner Records, 1726-1794, p. 56)

Weeks, Joseph, appointed a Commissioner of the Peace for Queen Anne's County, 16 Jun 1773. (Ref: Maryland State Archives, Governor and Council Commissioner Records, 1726-1794, p. 266)

Weems, David, appointed a Commissioner of the Peace for Anne Arundel County, 1 Nov 1729. (Ref: Maryland State Archives, Governor and Council Commissioner Records, 1726-1794, p. 12); see Negro London and Negro Ruben.

Weems, James (c1707-1781), was commissioned Sheriff of Calvert County, 23 May 1734. (Ref: Maryland State Archives, Governor and Council Commissioner Records, 1726-1794, p. 41); commission renewed for High Sheriff of Calvert County, 20 Jun 1735 and 20 Jun 1736. (Ref: Maryland Commission Book No. 82, p. 31; *Maryland Historical Magazine*, Vol. XXVI, p. 144; Maryland State Archives, Governor and Council Commissioner Records, 1726-1794, p. 52); see Negro Joe, Negro London and Negro Ruben.

Weems, James, Jr., see Mulatto Roger.

Weems, John, appointed a Commissioner of the Peace for Anne Arundel County, 9 Aug 1757. (Ref: Maryland State Archives, Governor and Council Commissioner Records, 1726-1794, p. 175)

Weems, John, Jr., was commissioned a Coroner of Calvert County, 29 Sep 1770. (Ref: Maryland Commission Book No. 82, p. 251; *Maryland Historical Magazine*, Vol. XXVII, p. 29)

Weems, William Lock, appointed a Commissioner of the Peace for Prince George's County, 17 Aug 1761. (Ref: Maryland State Archives, Governor and Council Commissioner Records, 1726-1794, p. 198)

Weimer, Bernard, planter, of Baltimore County, native of Germany, naturalized 20 May 1736. (Ref: Maryland Commission Book No. 82, p. 43; *Maryland Historical Magazine*, Vol. XXVI, p. 147)

Welder, John, Sr., commissioned a Coroner of Charles County, 17 May 1739. (Ref: Maryland Commission Book No. 82, p. 72; *Maryland Historical Magazine*, Vol. XXVI, p. 153)

Weldone, John, of Anne Arundel County, convicted felon, was executed on 8 May 1727. (Ref: Maryland State Archives, Governor and Council Commissioner Records, 1726-1794, p. 4)

Wells, George, appointed a Commissioner of the Peace for Queen Anne's County, 18 May 1758. (Ref: Maryland State Archives, Governor and Council Commissioner Records, 1726-1794, p. 180)

Wells, Humphrey, appointed a Commissioner of the Peace for Queen Anne's County, 3 Mar 1726/7. (Ref: Maryland State Archives, Governor and Council Commissioner Records, 1726-1794, p. 2)

Wells, Humphrey, appointed a Commissioner of the Peace for Queen Anne's County, 16 Jun 1773. (Ref: Maryland State Archives, Governor and Council Commissioner Records, 1726-1794, p. 266)

Wells, Humphrey, Jr., appointed a Commissioner of the Peace for Queen Anne's County, 28 Feb 1742/3. (Ref: Maryland State Archives, Governor and Council Commissioner Records, 1726-1794, p. 76)

Wells, John, appointed a Commissioner of the Peace for Queen Anne's County, 16 Jul 1735 and 24 May 1737. (Ref: Maryland State Archives, Governor and Council Commissioner Records, 1726-1794, pp. 49, 56)

Wells, Joseph, appointed a Commissioner of the Peace for Frederick County, 15 Aug 1774. (Ref: Maryland State Archives, Governor and Council Commissioner Records, 1726-1794, p. 284); Court Judge, 1774. (*Calendar of Maryland State Papers, No. 1 The Black Books*, p. 217)

Wells, Richard, appointed Constable of Pipe Creek Hundred in Frederick County, 1750. (Ref: *This Was The Life: Excerpts from the Judgment Records of Frederick County, Maryland, 1748-1765*, by Millard Milburn Rice, p. 37)

Wells, Thomas, appointed a Commissioner of the Peace for Anne Arundel County, 3 Mar 1726/7. (Ref: Maryland State Archives, Governor and Council Commissioner Records, 1726-1794, p. 3)

Wells, William, appointed a Commissioner of the Peace for Baltimore County, 31 Oct 1772. (Ref: Maryland State Archives, Governor and Council Commissioner Records, 1726-1794, p. 264)

Welsh, John, appointed a Commissioner of the Peace for Anne Arundel County, 3 Mar 1726/7. (Ref: Maryland State Archives, Governor and Council Commissioner Records, 1726-1794, p. 3)

Welsh, John, appointed a Commissioner of the Peace for Baltimore County, 30 May 1774. (Ref: Maryland State Archives, Governor and Council Commissioner Records, 1726-1794, p. 283)

West, John, appointed a Commissioner of the Peace for Anne Arundel County, 17 Nov 1749. (Ref: Maryland State Archives, Governor and Council Commissioner Records, 1726-1794, p. 114)

West, John, registration of sloop *Hummingbird*, 20 tons, built in Somerset County, 1743, and called the Eagle. John West, master an owner. 26 May 1747. (Ref: Maryland Commission Book No. 82, p. 130; *Maryland Historical Magazine*, Vol. XXVI, p. 260); see John Handy.

West, Samuel, appointed Constable of the Upper Part of Potomac Hundred in Frederick County, 1760, 1763, 1769 and 1771. (Ref: *This Was The Life: Excerpts from the Judgment Records of Frederick County, Maryland, 1748-1765*, by Millard Milburn Rice, pp. 216, 249; "Frederick County Court Minutes, March 1769," by Patricia Abelard Andersen, *Western Maryland Genealogy*, Vol. 15, No. 2, April 1999, p. 62; "Frederick County Minute Book, March 1771, Extracts by Patricia Abelard Andersen," *Western Maryland Genealogy*, Vol. 18, No. 1, Jan 2002, p. 25)

West, Stephen, see Negro Davey, Negro Scipio and Negro Jack Crane)

West, William, appointed a Commissioner of the Peace for Talbot County, 9 May 1732. (Ref: Maryland State Archives, Governor and Council Commissioner Records, 1726-1794, p. 23)

West, William (c1737-1791), reverend, licensed to preach in St. Margaret's Westminster, vacant by the death of Rev. Chalmers [no date]; induction into St. Margaret's Parish, Anne Arundel County, 5 Aug 1763. (Ref: Maryland Commission Book No. 82, pp. 159, 160; *Maryland Historical Magazine*, Vol. XXVI, p. 352; *Directory of Ministers and the Maryland Churches They Served, 1634-1900*, by Edna Agatha Kanely, Vol. II, L-Z, p. 355); induction into St. Andrew's Parish, St. Mary's County, 18 Nov 1767. (Ref: Maryland Commission Book No. 82, p. 205; *Maryland Historical Magazine*, Vol. XXVI, p. 356); induction into St. George's Parish, Baltimore County, 1 May 1772. (Ref: Maryland Commission Book No. 82, p. 278; *Maryland Historical Magazine*, Vol. XXVII, p. 31); see George Gowndrill.

Westinghaver, Christopher, native of Germany, denization, 22 Jun 1771. (Ref: Maryland Commission

Book No. 82, p. 260; *Maryland Historical Magazine*, Vol. XXVII, p. 30)

Wethered, John, appointed a Commissioner of the Peace for Cecil County, 2 Jun 1774. (Ref: Maryland State Archives, Governor and Council Commissioner Records, 1726-1794, p. 283)

Whalley, William, see Christopher Lowndes.

Wheat, Joseph, appointed Constable of the Middle Part of Rock Creek Hundred in Frederick County in 1753. (Ref: *This Was The Life: Excerpts from the Judgment Records of Frederick County, Maryland, 1748-1765*, by Millard Milburn Rice, p. 131)

Wheatly, Sampson, appointed a Commissioner of the Peace for Somerset County, 20 Oct 1746. (Ref: Maryland State Archives, Governor and Council Commissioner Records, 1726-1794, p. 94); Court Justice, 1753. (*Calendar of Maryland State Papers, No. 1 The Black Books*, p. 112)

Wheeler, John, was commissioned a Coroner of Dorchester County, 6 Oct 1766. (Ref: Maryland Commission Book No. 82, p. 181; *Maryland Historical Magazine*, Vol. XXVI, p. 354)

Wheeler, Prothesia, see Negro Peter.

Wheeler, Roger, appointed a Commissioner of the Peace for Calvert County, 8 Mar 1754. (Ref: Maryland State Archives, Governor and Council Commissioner Records, 1726-1794, p. 144)

Whichcoat (Whichcote), Paul, was appointed a Commissioner of the Peace for Kent County on 16 Oct 1750. (Ref: Maryland State Archives, Governor and Council Commissioner Records, 1726-1794, p. 119); see Buckler Partridge.

Whitacre, John, appointed a Commissioner of the Peace for Harford County, 2 Jun 1774. (Ref: Maryland State Archives, Governor and Council Commissioner Records, 1726-1794, p. 282)

Whitaker, Nathaniel, registration of sloop *Charming Jenny*, 40 tons, built in Worcester County, 1750. John Martin, master. Nathaniel Whitaker, owner. 12 Sep 1750. (Ref: Maryland Commission Book No. 82, p. 145; *Maryland Historical Magazine*, Vol. XXVI, p. 346)

Whitaker, Nathaniel, reverend, induction into St. Margaret's Westminster, Anne Arundel County, 7 May 1743. (Ref: Maryland Commission Book No. 82, p. 101; *Maryland Historical Magazine*, Vol. XXVI, p. 249; resignation from St. Margaret's Westminster, Anne Arundel County, 11 Jul 1748. On same day, induction into be Rector of Coventry Parish. (Ref: Maryland Commission Book No. 82, p. 134; *Maryland Historical Magazine*, Vol. XXVI, p. 263); see Robert Reade.

White, James, appointed Constable of Rock Creek Hundred in Prince George's County, now Frederick County, 1747. (Ref: Prince George's County Court Records, 1736-1748, Extracts by Patricia Abelard Andersen, *Western Maryland Genealogy*, Vol. 18, No. 1, January 2002, p. 45)

White, James, appointed Constable of Pipe Creek Hundred in Frederick County, 1760. (Ref: *This Was The Life: Excerpts from the Judgment Records of Frederick County, Maryland, 1748-1765*, by Millard Milburn Rice, p. 216)

White, John, appointed a Commissioner of the Peace for Dorchester County, 9 May 1732, 4 Aug 1732 and 29 May 1734. (Ref: Maryland State Archives, Governor and Council Commissioner Records, 1726-1794, pp. 25, 42, 115)

White, John, appointed a Commissioner of the Peace for Frederick County, 17 Nov 1749. (Ref: Maryland State Archives, Governor and Council Commissioner Records, 1726-1794, p. 115); of Antietam, appointed a Commissioner of the Peace for Frederick County, 3 Nov 1757. (Ref: Maryland State Archives, Governor and Council Commissioner Records, 1726-1794, p. 178)

White, Peter, appointed Constable of Marsh Hundred in Frederick County, 1771. (Ref: "Frederick County Minute Book, March 1771, Extracts by Patricia Abelard Andersen," *Western Maryland Genealogy*, Vol. 18, No. 1, January 2002, p. 26)

White, Samuel, appointed Constable of Patuxent Hundred in Prince George's County, now Frederick County, 1736. (Ref: Prince George's County Court Records, 1736-1748, Extracts by Patricia Abelard Andersen. *Western Maryland Genealogy*, Vol. 18, No. 1, January 2002, p. 34)

White, Thomas (d. 1795), appointed a Commissioner of the Peace for Dorchester County, 19 Mar 1764 and 8 Apr 177. (Ref: Maryland State Archives, Governor and Council Commissioner Records, 1726-1794, pp. 215, 250); appointed a Commissioner of the Peace for

Caroline County, 8 Feb 1774. (Ref: Maryland State Archives, Governor and Council Commissioner Records, 1726-1794, p. 280); Court Justice, Dorchester County, 1774. (*Calendar of Maryland State Papers, No. 1 The Black Books*, p. 211)

White, Thomas, appointed a Commissioner of the Peace for Baltimore County, 13 Oct 1732. (Ref: Maryland State Archives, Governor and Council Commissioner Records, 1726-1794, p. 26); commissioned Deputy Surveyor of Baltimore County, 4 Mar 1733/4, 13 Jun 1743 and 29 Apr 1747. (Ref: Maryland Commission Book No. 82, pp. 8, 102, 129; *Maryland Historical Magazine*, Vol. XXVI, pp. 140, 249, 260)

White, William, commissioned a Coroner of Talbot County, 21 Oct 1743. (Ref: Maryland Commission Book No. 82, p. 104; *Maryland Historical Magazine*, Vol. XXVI, p. 250)

White, William, servant of Edward Owens, of Frederick County, stabbed Benedict Wood, of Prince George's County, on 7 Oct 1766 and was committed to jail. Wood died on 7 Nov 1766 and White was still in jail. (Ref: *Archives of Maryland*, Vol. XXXII, "Proceedings of the Council of Maryland, 1761-1770," p. 168)

Whittill, William, see Jonathan Hodgson.

Whittington, William, of Somerset County, registration of the sloop *Success*, 20 tons, built at Hunting Creek in Accomack County, Virginia, 1727. John Donaldson, master, and William Whittington and John Donaldson, owners. 27 Jul 1734. (Ref: Maryland Commission Book No. 82, p. 19; *Maryland Historical Magazine*, Vol. XXVI, p. 141)

Wickham, Nathaniel, Jr., was appointed a Commissioner of the Peace for Prince George's County, 1 Mar 1734/5, 21 Feb 1735/6 and 29 Mar 1738. (Ref: Maryland State Archives, Governor and Council Commissioner Records, 1726-1794, pp. 46, 56, 59); Court Justice, Frederick County, 1748. (Ref: *This Was The Life: Excerpts from the Judgment Records of Frederick County, Maryland, 1748-1765*, by Millard Milburn Rice, p. 1); Constable of Manor Hundred in Frederick County, 1771. (Ref: "Frederick County Minute Book, March 1771, Extracts by Patricia Abelard Andersen," *Western Maryland Genealogy*, Vol. 18, No. 1, January 2002, p. 25)

Wickham, Samuel, Constable in the Upper Part of Monocacy Hundred in Frederick County in 1758. (Ref: *This Was The Life: Excerpts from the Judgment Records of Frederick County, Maryland, 1748-1765*, by Millard Milburn Rice, p. 185)

Wightt, John, appointed Constable of Rock Creek Hundred in Prince George's County, now Frederick County, 1745. (Ref: Prince George's County Court Records, 1736-1748, Extracts by Patricia Abelard Andersen, *Western Maryland Genealogy*, Vol. 18, No. 1, January 2002, p. 43)

Wilcoxen, Jesse, appointed Constable of the Lower Part of Potomack [Potomac] Hundred in Frederick County, 1769, 1771. (Ref: "Frederick County Court Minutes November 1769 by Patricia Abelard Andersen," *Western Maryland Genealogy*, Vol. 16, No. 1, January 2000, p. 32, and "Frederick County Minute Book, March 1771, Extracts by Patricia Abelard Andersen," *Western Maryland Genealogy*, Vol. 18, No. 1, January 2002, p. 25)

Wilde, John, native of Germany, denization, 22 Jun 1771. (Ref: Maryland Commission Book No. 82, p. 259; *Maryland Historical Magazine*, Vol. XXVII, p. 30)

Wilkinson, Betty, see Negro Jenny.

Wilkinson, Joseph, appointed a Commissioner of the Peace for Calvert County, 30 Oct 1732. (Ref: Maryland State Archives, Governor and Council Commissioner Records, 1726-1794, p. 27)

Wilkinson, Thomas, appointed a Commissioner of the Peace for Queen Anne's County, 24 May 1737. (Ref: Maryland State Archives, Governor and Council Commissioner Records, 1726-1794, p. 56)

Wilkinson, Thomas, appointed a Commissioner of the Peace for Queen Anne's County, 16 Jun 1773. (Ref: Maryland State Archives, Governor and Council Commissioner Records, 1726-1794, p. 266)

Wilkinson, William (d. 1755), was appointed a Commissioner of the Peace for Charles County, 30 Oct 1732. (Ref: Maryland State Archives, Governor and Council Commissioner Record, 1726-1794, p. 27)

Willett. Thomas, was appointed Constable of Potomac Hundred in Prince George's County, now Frederick County, 1746. (Ref: Prince George's County Court Records, 1736-1748, Extracts by Patricia Abelard Andersen, *Western Maryland Genealogy*, Vol. 18, No. 1, January 2002, p. 44)

Williams, Aaron, Jr., commissioned a Coroner of Calvert County, 27 Feb 1767. (Ref: Maryland Commission Book No. 82, p. 199; *Maryland Historical Magazine*, Vol. XXVI, p. 355)

Williams, Baruch, commissioned a Coroner of Prince George's County, 9 Sep 1749. (Ref: Maryland Commission Book No. 82, p. 141; *Maryland Historical Magazine*, Vol. XXVI, p. 344)

Williams, Cornelius, see Robert Harvey.

Williams, John, appointed a Commissioner of the Peace for Prince George's County, 29 Oct 1730. (Ref: Maryland State Archives, Governor and Council Commissioner Records, 1726-1794, p. 12)

Williams, John, appointed Constable of Tonol-loway Hundred in Prince George's County, now Frederick County, 1745. (Ref: Prince George's County Court Records, 1736-1748, Extracts by Patricia Abelard Andersen, *Western Maryland Genealogy*, Vol. 18, No. 1, January 2002, p. 43)

Williams, John, of Frederick County, convicted felon, was executed on 22 Nov 1754. (Ref: Maryland State Archives, Governor and Council Commissioner Records, 1726-1794, p. 146)

Williams, John, of Pocomoke, was appointed a Commissioner of the Peace for Somerset County, 19 Jul 1738. (Ref: Maryland State Archives, Governor and Council Commissioner Records, 1726-1794, p. 61); registration of ship *Integrity*, 150 tons, built in Somerset County, 1750. John Coward, master. John Williams and Anthony Bacon, owners. 19 May 1750. (Ref: Maryland Commission Book No. 82, p. 156; *Maryland Historical Magazine*, Vol. XXVI, p. 351); Court Justice, 1753. (*Calendar of Maryland State Papers, No. 1 The Black Books*, p. 112); see Henry Lowes, Levin Gale and Negro Tom.

Williams, Nathan, of Anne Arundel County, appointed Constable of Magotty [Magothy] Hundred in 1774. (Ref: Anne Arundel County Court Minutes, 1725-1757, 1774)

Williams, Planner, appointed a Commissioner of the Peace for Somerset County, 1 Oct 1762. (Ref: Maryland State Archives, Governor and Council Commissioner Records, 1726-1794, p. 204)

Williams, Reese, labourer, of Queen Anne's County, under sentence of death for the highway robbery of John Foreman, was reprieved on 20 Mar 1770, later pardoned and banished on 16 Apr 1770. (Ref: Maryland Commission Book No. 82, pp. 236-237; *Maryland Historical Magazine*, Vol. XXVI, p. 360(*Archives of Maryland*, Vol. XXXII, "Proceedings of the Council of Maryland, 1761-1770," p. 334)

Williams, Thomas, appointed a Commissioner of the Peace for Kent County, 18 Feb 1739/40. (Ref: Maryland State Archives, Governor and Council Commissioner Records, 1726-1794, p. 66)

Williams, Thomas, appointed a Commissioner of the Peace for Somerset County, 9 May 1732. (Ref: Maryland State Archives, Governor and Council Commissioner Records, 1726-1794, p. 23)

Williams, Thomas, Jr., of Kent County, was appointed a Commissioner of the Peace, 26 Oct 1738. (Ref: Maryland State Archives, Governor and Council Commissioner Records, 1726-1794, p. 62)

Williams, Thomas, Sr., appointed a Press Master in Prince George's County, now Frederick County, 1748. (Ref: Prince George's County Court Records, 1736-1738, Extracts by Patricia Abelard Andersen, *Western Maryland Genealogy*, Vol. 18, No. 1, January 2002, p. 46)

Williams, Thomas M., of St. Mary's County, was appointed a Commissioner of the Peace, 1 Apr 1736. (Ref: Maryland State Archives, Governor and Council Commissioner Records, 1726-1794, p. 51)

Williams, William, see Samuel Galloway.

Williamson, Alexander (c1727-1787), of Kent County, appointed to Committee for Enquiring into the Accounts and Vouchers Relating to the Disposal of the Sum of £6000 Granted by Act of Assembly for His Majesty's Service, 14 Mar 1755. (Ref: *Archives of Maryland*, Vol. LII, "Proceedings and Acts of the General Assembly of Maryland, 1755-1756," pp. 46, 85); appointed to a Committee for Enquiring into Ways and Means to Raise a Sum Sufficient for Payment of Eighty Rangers to Defend and Protect the Frontiers, 28 Jun 1755. (Ref: Maryland State Archives, Governor and Council Commissioner Records, 1726-1794, p. 151); reverend, licensed Curate, vice Reverend George Murdock, lately deceased, Prince George's Parish, 23 Feb 1761. (Ref: Maryland Commission Book No. 82, p. 158; *Maryland Historical Magazine*, Vol. XXVI, p. 352)

Williamson, John, appointed a Commissioner of the

Peace for Kent County, 18 Oct 1744. (Ref: Maryland State Archives, Governor and Council Commissioner Records, 1726-1794, p. 86); commissioned Sheriff of Kent, 21 Jul 1750. (Ref: Maryland State Archives, Governor and Council Commissioner Records, 1726-1794, p. 118)

Williamson, Samuel (1658-1729), appointed a Commissioner of the Peace for St. Mary's County, 2 Mar 1726/7. (Ref: Maryland State Archives, Governor and Council Commissioner Records, 1726-1794, p. 2)

Williamson, Thomas, registration of the sloop *Samuel*, – tons, built in Worcester County, 1749. Thomas Clifton, master. Thomas Williamson, owner. 13 Apr 1749. (Ref: Maryland Commission Book No. 82, p. 151; *Maryland Historical Magazine*, Vol. XXVI, pp. 348-349)

Willis, Richard, was commissioned a Coroner for Dorchester County, 20 Feb 1737/8. (Ref: Maryland Commission Book No. 82, p. 51; *Maryland Historical Magazine*, Vol. XXVI, p. 150)

Wilmer, Lambert (1682-1732), was appointed a Commissioner of the Peace for Kent County, 3 Mar 1726/7 and 12 Jun 1729. (Ref: Maryland State Archives, Governor and Council Commissioner Records, 1726-1794, pp. 2, 11)

Wilmer, Simon (1686-1737), was commissioned Sheriff of Kent County, 16 May 1738; appointed a Commissioner of the Peace for Kent County, 18 Oct 1744. (Ref: Maryland State Archives, Governor and Council Commissioner Record, 1726-1794, pp. 60, 86)

Wilson, David (1704-1750), of Somerset County, appointed a Deputy Commissary [government official who had certain duties to perform] on 11 Jul 1727. (Ref: *Abstracts of the Testamentary Proceedings and Prerogative Court of Maryland, Vol. XVII, 1724-1727*, by Vernon L. Skinner, Jr., p. 208, citing original Liber 28, f. 88); appointed a Commissioner of the Peace for Somerset County, 9 May 1732. (Ref: Maryland State Archives, Governor and Council Commissioner Records, 1726-1794, p. 23); commissioned Deputy Surveyor of Somerset County, 14 Mar 1743/4. (Ref: Maryland Commission Book No. 82, p. 108; *Maryland Historical Magazine*, Vol. XXVI, p. 251); see Roger Kellet.

Wilson, Ephraim, appointed a Commissioner of the Peace for Somerset County, 30 Jul 1754. (Ref: Maryland State Archives, Governor and Council Commissioner Records, 1726-1794, p. 156); commissioned High Sheriff of Somerset County, 8 Oct 1761. (Ref: Maryland State Archives, Governor and Council Commissioner Records, 1726-1794, p. 190)

Wilson, George, appointed a Commissioner of the Peace for Cecil County, 2 Jun 1774. (Ref: Maryland State Archives, Governor and Council Commissioner Records, 1726-1794, p. 283)

Wilson, George, appointed a Commissioner of the Peace for Kent County, 12 Jun 1729 and 2 Jun 1732. (Ref: Maryland State Archives, Governor and Council Commissioner Records, 1726-1794, pp. 11, 23)

Wilson, George, of St. Mary's County, convicted of murder, was executed on 5 Jun 1752 and "after he is dead his body to be hung in chains as near as can be to the place where the murder was committed." (Ref: Maryland State Archives, Governor and Council Commissioner Records, 1726-1794, p. 132)

Wilson, James, appointed a Commissioner of the Peace for Prince George's County, 15 Jun 1739. (Ref: Maryland State Archives, Governor and Council Commissioner Records, 1726-1794, p. 64)

Wilson, James, appointed a Commissioner of the Peace for Prince George's County, 31 Mar 1773. (Ref: Maryland State Archives, Governor and Council Commissioner Records, 1726-1794, p. 266)

Wilson, James, Jr., appointed a Commissioner of the Peace for Kent County, 3 Mar 1726/7. (Ref: Maryland State Archives, Governor and Council Commissioner Records, 1726-1794, p. 2)

Wilson, John, labourer, of Anne Arundel County, convicted felon confined in Annapolis under hard irons and chains under sentence of death, pardoned and banished on 30 Apr 1767 on condition of his leaving the city in six hours and the province in four days. (Ref: Maryland Commission Book No. 82, p. 201; *Maryland Historical Magazine*, Vol. XXVI, p. 355; *Archives of Maryland*, Vol. XXXII, "Proceedings of the Council of Maryland, 1761-1770," pp. 198-199)

Wilson, Jonathan, appointed a Commissioner of the Peace for Frederick County, 12 Mar 1763. (Ref: Maryland State Archives, Governor and Council Commissioner Records, 1726-1794, p. 209)

Wilson, Joseph, was appointed Constable of the Lower Part of Monocacy Hundred in Frederick

County in 1749. (Ref: *This Was The Life: Excerpts from the Judgment Records of Frederick County, Maryland, 1748-1765*, by Millard Milburn Rice, p. 7)

Wilson, Lingan, was commissioned a Coroner of Prince George's County, 2 Mar 1749/50. (Ref: Maryland Commission Book No. 82, p. 142; *Maryland Historical Magazine*, Vol. XXVI, p. 345)

Wilson, Samuel, registration of sloop *Martha*, 30 tons, built in Somerset County, 1734. John Allen, master. Samuel Wilson, owner. 1736. (Ref: Maryland Commission Book No. 82, p. 45; *Maryland Historical Magazine*, Vol. XXVI, p. 148); Commissioner of the Peace for Somerset County, 28 Feb 1742/3. (Ref: Maryland State Archives, Governor and Council Commissioner Records, 1726-1794, p. 76)

Wilson, Thomas, Constable of New Scotland Hundred in Prince George's County, now Frederick County, in 1733. (*Calendar of Maryland State Papers, No. 1 The Black Books*, p. 43)

Wilson, Thomas, appointed Constable of Seneca Hundred in Prince George's County, now Frederick County, 1745. (Ref: Prince George's County Court Records, 1736-1748, Extracts by Patricia Abelard Andersen, *Western Maryland Genealogy*, Vol. 18, No. 1, January 2002, p. 43); appointed Constable of the Upper Part of Monocacy Hundred in Frederick County in 1753. (Ref: *This Was The Life: Excerpts from the Judgment Records of Frederick County, Maryland, 1748-1765*, by Millard Milburn Rice, p. 131)

Wilson, William, appointed a Commissioner of the Peace for Somerset County, 8 Mar 1754. (Ref: Maryland State Archives, Governor and Council Commissioner Records, 1726-1794, p. 143)

Winder, William (1714/15-1792), registration of schooner *Betty*, 18 tons, built in Somerset County, 1750. William Venables, master and co-owner, and William Winder and Benjamin Venables were also co-owners. 18 Oct 1750. (Ref: Maryland Commission Book No. 82, p. 147; *Maryland Historical Magazine*, Vol. XXVI, p. 347); appointed a Commissioner of the Peace for Somerset County, 23 Mar 1756. (Ref: Maryland State Archives, Governor and Council Commissioner Records, 1726-1794, p. 166)

Winders, James, was appointed Constable of the Upper Part of Andieatum [Antietam] Hundred in Frederick County in 1763. (Ref: *This Was The Life: Excerpts from the Judgment Records of Frederick County, Maryland, 1748-1765*, by Millard Milburn Rice, p. 249)

Windfield, Andrew, labourer, of Baltimore County, convicted for murdering Negro Davy, was pardoned on 22 Oct 1768. (Ref: Maryland Commission Book No. 82, p. 219; *Maryland Historical Magazine*, Vol. XXVI, p. 358; *Archives of Maryland*, Vol. XXXII, "Proceedings of the Council of Maryland, 1761-1770," pp. 255)

Windsor, John, see Aaron Lynn.

Wing, Robert, see Thomas Nevett.

Wing, Thomas, appointed Constable of Fishing Creek Hundred in Dorchester County, 1745. (Ref: Dorchester County Judgment Records, 1743-1745, p. 476; *Judgment Records of Dorchester, Queen Anne's and Talbot Counties, Maryland*, by F. Edward Wright, 2001, p. 60)

Winter, John, appointed a Commissioner of the Peace for Charles County, 28 Feb 1742/3. (Ref: Maryland State Archives, Governor and Council Commissioner Records, 1726-1794, p. 77); appointed one of the Inspectors of Piles' Warehouse, 1756. (Ref: *Archives of Maryland*, Vol. LII, "Proceedings and Acts of the General Assembly of Maryland, 1755-1756," p. 638); Court Justice, 1756. (*Calendar of Maryland State Papers, No. 1 The Black Books*, p. 132)

Wise, Francis, of Prince George's County, native of Germany, naturalized 3 May 1740, and also his children Mary, Jacob and Elizabeth. (Ref: Maryland Commission Book No. 82, p. 80; *Maryland Historical Magazine*, Vol. XXVI, p. 156)

Wise, Samuel, see Alexander Buncle, John Henry and Robert Jenckins Henry.

Withcoat, Paul, appointed a Commissioner of the Peace for Kent County, 9 Nov 1747. (Ref: Maryland State Archives, Governor and Council Commissioner Records, 1726-1794, p. 103)

Witticomb, Thomas, see Anthont Gott.

Wolfe, John, commissioned Sheriff of Anne Arundel, 11 Nov 1732. (Ref: Maryland State Archives, Governor and Council Commissioner Records, 1726-1794, p. 30)

Wolstenholme, Daniel (d. 1795), of Annapolis, Anne Arundel County, merchant, procured the sloop *Elizabeth* (Edmund Rutland, master) at the request of

Christopher Kilby, Esq., one of the contractors for his Majesty's troops in North America, in March 1757 and purchased a quantity of provisions for the use of the forces to be employed in the defense of South Carolina. (Ref: *Archives of Maryland*, Vol. XXXI, "Proceedings of the Council of Maryland, 1753-1761," p. 204)

Wood, Jack, see Negro Jack Wood.

Wood, James, of Charles County, convicted felon, was executed on 15 Nov 1738. (Ref: Maryland State Archives, Governor and Council Commissioner Records, 1726-1794, p. 62)

Wood, Joseph, appointed Constable of Pipe Creek Hundred in Frederick County in 1749. (Ref: *This Was The Life: Excerpts from the Judgment Records of Frederick County, Maryland, 1748-1765*, by Millard Milburn Rice, p. 6-7); of Israels Creek, appointed a Commissioner of the Peace for Frederick County, 22 Nov 1752. (Ref: Maryland State Archives, Governor and Council Commissioner Records, 1726-1794, p. 135)

Wood, Joseph, Court Justice, Frederick County, 1769. (Ref: "Frederick County Court Minutes, March 1769," by Patricia Abelard Andersen, *Western Maryland Genealogy*, Vol. 15, No. 2, April 1999, p. 62); appointed a Commissioner of the Peace, 15 Aug 1774. (Ref: Maryland State Archives, Governor and Council Commissioner Records, 1726-1794, p. 284); Court Judge, 1774. (*Calendar of Maryland State Papers, No. 1 The Black Books*, p. 217)

Wood, Robert, of Frederick County, magistrate, 1766. (Ref: *Archives of Maryland*, Vol. XXXII, "Proceedings of the Council of Maryland, 1761-1770," p. 166)

Woodgate, John, appointed Constable of Fork Hundred in Dorchester County, 1742. (Ref: Dorchester County Judgment Records, 1742-1743, p. 84; *Judgment Records of Dorchester, Queen Anne's and Talbot Counties, Maryland*, by F. Edward Wright, 2001, p. 30)

Woodward, Amos, appointed a Commissioner of the Peace for Anne Arundel County, 9 Jun 1732. (Ref: Maryland State Archives, Governor and Council Commissioner Records, 1726-1794, p. 24)

Woolden, Michael, of Baltimore Co., convicted burglar, was executed on 16 Oct 1771. (Ref: Maryland State Archives, Governor and Council Commissioner Records, 1726-1794, p. 247)

Woolford, James (c1680-1758), commissioned Sheriff of Dorchester County, 30 Jun 1727. (Ref: Maryland State Archives, Governor and Council Commissioner Records, 1726-1794, p. 6)

Woolford, Roger (1670-1730), commissioned a Provincial Justice by the Governor, 20 Oct 1729. (Ref: Maryland State Archives, Governor and Council Commissioner Records, 1726-1794, p. 12)

Woolford, Thomas (c1699-c1750), appointed a Commissioner of the Peace for Dorchester County, 1 Aug 1729 and 29 Oct 1730. (Ref: Maryland State Archives, Governor and Council Commissioner Records, 1726-1794, pp. 11, 17)

Wootton, Thomas Sprigg (d. 1789), appointed a Commissioner of the Peace for Frederick County on 1 Aug 1768 and 15 Aug 1774. (Ref: Maryland State Archives, Governor and Council Commissioner Records, 1726-1794, p. 235); Court Justice, 1769. (Ref: "Frederick County Court Minutes, March 1769," by Patricia Abelard Andersen, *Western Maryland Genealogy*, Vol. 15, No. 2, April 1999, p. 62); appointed a Commissioner of the Peace for Frederick County, 2 Apr 1770. (Ref: Maryland State Archives, Governor and Council Commissioner Records, 1726-1794, p. 250); Court Judge, 1774. (*Calendar of Maryland State Papers, No. 1 The Black Books*, p. 217)

Wootten, Turner (c1695-1760), was appointed a Commissioner of the Peace for Prince George's County, 18 Feb 1731/2. (Ref: Maryland State Archives, Governor and Council Commissioner Records, 1726-1794, p. 21); commissioned High Sheriff of Prince George's County, 10 Jan 1753. (Ref: Maryland State Archives, Governor and Council Commissioner Records, 1726-1794, p. 137(Ref: *Archives of Maryland*, Vol. LII, "Proceedings and Acts of the General Assembly of Maryland, 1755-1756," p. 573)

Wootten, William Turner (d. 1777), commissioned High Sheriff of Prince George's County on 30 Oct 1767. (Ref: Maryland State Archives, Governor and Council Commissioner Records, 1726-1794, p. 223)

Worthington, Charles, of Baltimore County, was appointed a Commissioner of the Peace, 16 Dec 1751. (Ref: Maryland State Archives, Governor and Council Commissioner Records, 1726-1794, p. 131)

Worthington, Nicholas (1733-1793), was a Court Justice, Anne Arundel County, 1774. (Ref: Anne Arundel County Court Minutes, 1725-1757, 1774); appointed a Commissioner of the Peace, 1 Aug 1768, 16 Dec 1769 and 20 Nov 1769. (Ref: Maryland State Archives, Governor and Council Commissioner Records, 1726-1794, pp. 234, 249, 272)

Worthington, Samuel (1734-1815), appointed a Commissioner of the Peace for Baltimore County, 20 Nov 1769. (Ref: Maryland State Archives, Governor and Council Commissioner Records, 1726-1794, p. 248)

Worthington, William, of Anne Arundel County, appointed a Commissioner of the Peace, 13 Mar 1737/8. (Ref: Maryland State Archives, Governor and Council Commissioner Records, 1726-1794, p. 59)

Worthington, William, of John, was appointed a Commissioner of the Peace for Anne Arundel County, 4 Oct 1737. (Ref: Maryland State Archives, Governor and Council Commissioner Records, 1726-1794, p. 57)

Wright, Abraham, of Frederick County, convicted of murder and executed on 22 Oct 1773. (Ref: Maryland State Archives, Governor and Council Commissioner Records, 1726-1794, p. 265)

Wright, John, of Anne Arundel County, convicted along with Mulatto Toney of murdering Capt. William Curtis, ordered to be executed 13 Jul 1754 "at the common gallows and afterwards hung in chains at King's Point." (Ref: Maryland State Archives, Governor and Council Commissioner Records, 1726-1794, p. 143; *Archives of Maryland*, Vol. XXXI, "Proceedings of the Council of Maryland, 1753-1761," p. 46)

Wright, Nathan Samuel Turbutt (c1725-1792), appointed a Commissioner of the Peace for Queen Anne's County, 18 May 1758. (Ref: Maryland State Archives, Governor and Council Commissioner Records, 1726-1794, p. 180)

Wright, Nathan, of Edward (c1690-1758), was appointed a Commissioner of the Peace for Queen Anne's County, 1 Dec 1746. (Ref: Maryland State Archives, Governor and Council Commissioner Records, 1726-1794, p. 95)

Wright, Nathan, the Elder, was appointed a Commissioner of the Peace for Queen Anne's County, 1 Dec 1746. (Ref: Maryland State Archives, Governor and Council Commissioner Records, 1726-1794, p. 95)

Wright, Nathaniel (d. 1770), was appointed a Commissioner of the Peace for Queen Anne's County, 4 Nov 1749. (Ref: Maryland State Archives, Governor and Council Commissioner Records, 1726-1794, p. 114)

Wright, Richard, of Anne Arundel County, convicted felon, was executed on 27 May 1737. (Ref: Maryland State Archives, Governor and Council Commissioner Records, 1726-1794, p. 55)

Wright, Robert Norrest (d. 1746/7), appointed a Commissioner of the Peace for Queen Anne's County on 17 Oct 1734. (Ref: Maryland State Archives, Governor and Council Commissioner Records, 1726-1794, p. 44)

Wright, Thomas, see Negro George.

Wright, Thomas Hynson (1687/8-1747), was appointed a Commissioner of the Peace for Queen Anne's County, 3 Mar 1726/7. (Ref: Maryland State Archives, Governor and Council Commissioner Records, 1726-1794, p. 2); commissioned Sheriff of Queen Anne's County, 24 Nov 1733. (Ref: Maryland State Archives, Governor and Council Commissioner Records, 1726-1794, p. 39); commission renewed for High Sheriff of Queen Anne's County, 17 Nov 1735. (Ref: Maryland Commission Book No. 82, p. 38; *Maryland Historical Magazine*, Vol. XXVI, p. 145); commissioned a Ranger of Queen Anne's County, 21 Mar 1738/9. (Ref: Maryland Commission Book No. 82, p. 71; *Maryland Historical Magazine*, Vol. XXVI, p. 153)

Wright, Thomas Hynson, appointed a Commissioner of the Peace for Queen Anne's County, 16 Jun 1773. (Ref: Maryland State Archives, Governor and Council Commissioner Records, 1726-1794, p. 266); Court Justice, 1774. (*Calendar of Maryland State Papers, No. 1 The Black Books*, p. 215, listed him as Thomas Wright)

Wright, Turbutt (c1741-1794), Court Justice, Queen Anne's County, 1774. (*Calendar of Maryland State Papers, No. 1 The Black Books*, p. 215)

Wright, William, commissioned High Sheriff of Anne Arundel County, 7 Dec 1775. (Ref: Maryland State Archives, Governor and Council Commissioner

Records, 1726-1794, p. 279)

Wye, William (1684-1744), reverend, resignation from Somerset Parish, Somerset County, 16 Oct 1736. On same day, induction into Mary Anne Parish, Cecil County. (Ref: Maryland Commission Book No. 82, p. 45; *Maryland Historical Magazine*, Vol. XXVI, pp. 147-148)

Wye, William, Jr., registration of sloop *Seahorse*, 6 tons, built in Somerset County, 1733. William Wye, master and owner. 6 Jun 1738. (Ref: Maryland Commission Book No. 82, p. 60; *Maryland Historical Magazine*, Vol. XXVI, pp. 151-152)

Wyvell, William, appointed Constable of Eastern Branch Hundred in Prince George's County, now Frederick County, 1738. (Ref: Prince George's County Court Records, 1736-1748, Extracts by Patricia Abelard Andersen, *Western Maryland Genealogy*, Vol. 18, No. 1, January 2002, p. 35)

Yates, Robert (c1692-1743), was appointed a Commissioner of the Peace for Charles County, 29 Oct 1730, 25 Apr 1735 and 19 May 1743. (Ref: Maryland State Archives, Governor and Council Commissioner Records, 1726-1794, pp. 12, 47, 78); Court Justice, 1756. (*Calendar of Maryland State Papers, No. 1 The Black Books*, p. 132)

Yates, Theophilus, commissioned a Coroner of Charles County, 26 Oct 1767 and 17 Sep 1773. (Ref: Maryland Commission Book No. 82, pp. 205, 323; *Maryland Historical Magazine*, Vol. XXVI, p. 356, and Vol. XXVII, p. 350

Young, Benjamin, of Anne Arundel County, commissioned Judge of Oyer, Terminer and Gaol [Jail] Delivery, 21 May 1736. (Ref: Maryland State Archives, Governor and Council Commissioner Records, 1726-1794, p. 52); of Annapolis, commissioned Examiner General of all plats and surveys, 29 Sep 1738. On same day, commissioned one of three Commissioners for Emitting Bills of Credit. (Ref: Maryland Commission Book No. 82, p. 63; *Maryland Historical Magazine*, Vol. XXVI, p. 152); commissioned Judge of the Admiralty Court in Maryland. 30 Dec 1742. (Ref: Maryland Commission Book No. 82, p. 100). *Maryland Historical Magazine*, Vol. XXVI, p. 248); esquire, of Anne Arundel County, commissioned Surveyor General of the Eastern Shore, 18 Sep 1745. (Ref: Maryland Commission Book No. 82, p. 117; *Maryland Historical Magazine*, Vol. XXVI, p. 255); appointed a Privy Council on 10 May 1753. (Ref: *Archives of Maryland*, Vol. XXXI, "Proceedings of the Council of Maryland, 1753-1761," pp. 8, 14)

Young, Benjamin, of Cecil Co., was commissioned Surveyor General, 29 Apr 1773. (Ref: Maryland Commission Book No. 82, p. 310; *Maryland Historical Magazine*, Vol. XXVII, p. 33)

Young, George, appointed a Commissioner of the Peace for Calvert County, 2 Mar 1731/2. (Ref: Maryland State Archives, Governor and Council Commissioner Records, 1726-1794, p. 22)

Young, Henry, mariner, of Biddeford, registration of the brigantine *Peace*, 80 tons, built in Kent County, 1749. Henry Young, master and co-owner. John Luxon and Thomas Kenney, co-owners. 31 Jul 1749. (Ref: Maryland Commission Book No. 82, p. 152; *Maryland Historical Magazine*, Vol. XXVI, p. 349)

Young, Jacob (d. 1805), appointed a Commissioner of the Peace for Frederick County, 2 Mar 1775. (Ref: Maryland State Archives, Governor and Council Commissioner Records, 1726-1794, p. 288)

Young, Joseph, commissioned Sheriff of Kent County on 4 Jun 1729. (Ref: Maryland State Archives, Governor and Council Commissioner Records, 1726-1794, p. 10)

Young, Joseph, Provincial Commission [Mister, rank and/or position not stated], 8 Jul 1735. (Ref: Maryland State Archives, Governor and Council Commissioner Records, 1726-1794, p. 49); of Anne Arundel County, commissioned Judge of Oyer, Terminer and Gaol [Jail] Delivery, 21 May 1736. (Ref: Maryland State Archives, Governor and Council Commissioner Records, 1726-1794, p. 52)

Young, Parker, appointed a Commissioner of the Peace for Calvert County, 2 Oct 1751. (Ref: Maryland State Archives, Governor and Council Commissioner Records, 1726-1794, p. 126)

Young, Robert, appointed a Commissioner of the Peace for Charles County, 2 Nov 1773. (Ref: Maryland State Archives, Governor and Council Commissioner Records, 1726-1794, p. 279)

Young, Samuel, commissioned Sheriff of Calvert County, 20 Feb 1731/2. (Ref: Maryland State Archives, Governor and Council Commissioner Records, 1726-1794, p. 22)

Young, William, was appointed a Commissioner of the Peace for Baltimore County, 22 Oct 1741. (Ref: Maryland State Archives, Governor and Council Commissioner Records, 1726-1794, p. 72); was commissioned Sheriff of Baltimore County, 28 Apr 1753. (Ref: Maryland State Archives, Governor and Council Commissioner Records, 1726-1794, p. 140; *Archives of Maryland*, Vol. LII, "Proceedings and Acts of the General Assembly of Maryland, 1755-1756," p. 63)

Young, William (d. 1732/33), was appointed a Commissioner of the Peace for Calvert County, 3 Mar 1726/7. (Ref: Maryland State Archives, Governor and Council Commissioner Records, 1726-1794, p. 3); commissioned Sheriff of Calvert County, 29 Jan 1728/9. (Ref: Maryland State Archives, Governor and Council Commissioner Records, 1726-1794, p. 9)

Young, William, appointed Constable of Rock Creek Hundred in Prince George's County, now Frederick County, 1736 and 1748. (Ref: Prince George's County Court Records, 1736-1748, Extracts by Patricia Abelard Andersen, *Western Maryland Genealogy*, Vol. 18, No. 1, January 2002, pp. 34, 46)

Young, William, appointed a Justice in Baltimore County, 22 Feb 1773. (Ref: *Inhabitants of Baltimore County, 1763-1774*, by Henry C. Peden, Jr., 1989, p. 49, citing *Calendar of Maryland State Papers, No. 1 The Black Books*, p. 208)

Youngblood, Peter, of Prince George's County, native of Germany, naturalized 6 Mar 1739/40, and also his sons William and Peter, and his daughters Sarah and Mary. (Ref: Maryland Commission Book No. 82, p. 79; *Maryland Historical Magazine*, Vol. XXVI, p. 155)

Heritage Books by Henry C. Peden, Jr.:

1890 Reconstructed Census of Harford County, Maryland, Volume 1: A-J

1890 Reconstructed Census of Harford County, Maryland, Volume 2: K-Z

A Closer Look at St. John's Parish Registers [Baltimore County, Maryland], 1701–1801

A Collection of Maryland Church Records

A Guide to Genealogical Research in Maryland: 5th Edition, Revised and Enlarged

Abstracts of Marriages and Deaths in Harford County, Maryland, Newspapers, 1837–1871

Abstracts of the Ledgers and Accounts of the Bush Store and Rock Run Store, 1759–1771

Abstracts of the Orphans Court Proceedings of Harford County, 1778–1800

Abstracts of Wills, Harford County, Maryland, 1800–1805

African American Cemeteries in Harford County, Maryland

Anne Arundel County, Maryland, Marriage References 1658–1800
Henry C. Peden, Jr. and Veronica Clarke Peden

Baltimore City [Maryland] Deaths and Burials, 1834–1840

Baltimore County, Maryland, Overseers of Roads, 1693–1793

Bastardy Cases in Baltimore County, Maryland, 1673–1783

Bastardy Cases in Harford County, Maryland, 1774–1844

More Bastardy Cases in Harford County, Maryland, 1773–1893

Bible and Family Records of Harford County, Maryland, Families: Volume V

*Biographical Dictionary of Harford County, Maryland, 1774–1974:
Over 1,200 Sketches of Prominent Citizens during the First 200 years of the County's
History with Seventeen Appendices Listing Public Officials from 1774 to 2020*
Henry C. Peden, Jr. and William O. Carr

Cecil County, Maryland Marriage References, 1674–1824
Henry C. Peden, Jr. and Veronica Clarke Peden

Children of Harford County: Indentures and Guardianships, 1801–1830

Colonial Delaware Soldiers and Sailors, 1638–1776

*Colonial Families of the Eastern Shore of Maryland
Volumes 5, 6, 7, 8, 9, 11, 12, 13, 14, 16, and 19*
Henry C. Peden, Jr. and F. Edward Wright

Colonial Families of the Eastern Shore of Maryland: Volume 21 and Volume 23

Colonial Maryland Commissions, Appointments and Other Proceedings, 1726–1776

Colonial Maryland Soldiers and Sailors, 1634–1734

Colonial Tavern Keepers of Maryland and Delaware, 1634–1776

Dorchester County, Maryland, Marriage References, 1669–1800
Henry C. Peden, Jr. and Veronica Clarke Peden

Dr. John Archer's First Medical Ledger, 1767–1769, Annotated Abstracts

Early Anglican Records of Cecil County

*Early Harford Countians, Individuals Living in Harford County, Maryland in Its Formative Years
Volume 1: A to K, Volume 2: L to Z, and Volume 3: Supplement*

Family Cemeteries and Grave Sites in Harford County, Maryland, (Revised Edition)

Farm Directory, 1774–2024, Harford County, Maryland

First Presbyterian Church Records, Baltimore, Maryland, 1840–1879

Frederick County, Maryland, Marriage References and Family Relationships, 1748–1800
Henry C. Peden, Jr. and Veronica Clarke Peden

Genealogical Gleanings from Harford County, Maryland, Medical Records, 1772–1852
Winner of the Norris Harris Prize from MHS for the best genealogical reference book in 2016!

Harford County Taxpayers in 1870, 1872 and 1883

Harford County, Maryland Death Records, 1849–1899

Harford County, Maryland Deponents, 1775–1835

Harford County, Maryland Divorces and Separations, 1823–1923

Harford County, Maryland, Death Certificates, 1898–1918: An Annotated Index

Harford County, Maryland, Divorce Cases, 1827–1912: An Annotated Index

Harford County, Maryland, Inventories, 1774–1804

Harford County, Maryland, Marriage References and Family Relationships, 1774–1824
Henry C. Peden, Jr. and Veronica Clarke Peden

Harford County, Maryland, Marriage References and Family Relationships, 1825–1850

Harford County, Maryland, Marriage References and Family Relationships, 1851–1860
Henry C. Peden, Jr. and Veronica Clarke Peden

Harford County, Maryland, Marriage References and Family Relationships, 1861–1870
Henry C. Peden, Jr. and Veronica Clarke Peden

Harford County, Maryland, Marriage References and Family Relationships, 1871–1875

Harford County, Maryland, Marriage References and Family Relationships, 1876–1880

Harford County, Maryland, Marriage References and Family Relationships, 1881–1885

Harford County, Maryland, Marriage References and Family Relationships, 1886–1889

*Harford (Maryland) Homicides: Cases of Murder and Attempted Murder:
Committed by Men and Women Who Were "Seduced by the Instigation of the Devil"
in Harford County, Maryland During the 18th and 19th Centuries*

*Harford (Maryland) Suicides: Cases of Self-killings and Attempted Suicides Committed by Men and
Women Who Suffered from an "Aberration of the Mind" in Harford County, Maryland, 1817–1947*

*Harford (Old Brick Baptist) Church, Harford County, Maryland, Records and Members (1742–1974),
Tombstones, Burials (1775–2009) and Family Relationships*

Heirs and Legatees of Harford County, Maryland, 1774–1802

Heirs and Legatees of Harford County, Maryland, 1802–1846

Inhabitants of Baltimore County, Maryland, 1763–1774

Inhabitants of Cecil County, Maryland 1774–1800

Inhabitants of Cecil County, Maryland, 1649–1774

Inhabitants of Harford County, Maryland, 1791–1800

Inhabitants of Kent County, Maryland, 1637–1787

Insolvent Debtors in 19th Century Harford County, Maryland: A Legal and Genealogical Digest

*Joseph A. Pennington & Co., Havre De Grace, Maryland, Funeral Home Records:
Volume II, 1877–1882, 1893–1900*

Kent County, Maryland Marriage References, 1642–1800
Henry C. Peden, Jr. and Veronica Clarke Peden

Marriages and Deaths from Baltimore Newspapers, 1817–1824

Maryland Bible Records, Volume 1: Baltimore and Harford Counties

Maryland Bible Records, Volume 2: Baltimore and Harford Counties

Maryland Bible Records, Volume 3: Carroll County

Maryland Bible Records, Volume 4: Eastern Shore

Maryland Bible Records, Volume 5: Harford, Baltimore and Carroll Counties

Maryland Bible Records, Volume 7: Baltimore, Harford and Frederick Counties

Maryland Deponents, 1634–1799

Maryland Deponents: Volume 3, 1634–1776

Maryland Prisoners Languishing in Goal, Volume 1: 1635–1765

Maryland Prisoners Languishing in Goal, Volume 2: 1766–1800

*Maryland Public Service Records, 1775–1783: A Compendium of Men and Women of Maryland
Who Rendered Aid in Support of the American Cause against Great Britain during the Revolutionary War*

Marylanders and Delawareans in the French and Indian War, 1756–1763

Marylanders to Carolina: Migration of Marylanders to North Carolina and South Carolina prior to 1800

Marylanders to Kentucky, 1775–1825

Marylanders to Ohio and Indiana, Migration Prior to 1835

Marylanders to Tennessee

McComas Funeral Home Interments, 1901–1941, Harford County, Maryland

Methodist Records of Baltimore City, Maryland: Volume 1, 1799–1829

Methodist Records of Baltimore City, Maryland: Volume 2, 1830–1839

*Methodist Records of Baltimore City, Maryland: Volume 3, 1840–1850
(East City Station)*

Ministers Directory, 1774-1924, Harford County, Maryland

More Maryland Deponents, 1716–1799

More Marylanders to Carolina: Migration of Marylanders to North Carolina and South Carolina prior to 1800

More Marylanders to Kentucky, 1778–1828

More Marylanders to Ohio and Indiana: Migrations Prior to 1835

Orphans and Indentured Children of Baltimore County, Maryland, 1777–1797

Outpensioners of Harford County, Maryland, 1856–1896

Presbyterian Records of Baltimore City, Maryland, 1765–1840

Quaker Records of Baltimore and Harford Counties, Maryland, 1801–1825

Quaker Records of Northern Maryland, 1716–1800

Quaker Records of Southern Maryland, 1658–1800

Revolutionary Patriots of Anne Arundel County, Maryland, 1775–1783

Revolutionary Patriots of Baltimore Town and Baltimore County, 1775–1783

Revolutionary Patriots of Calvert and St. Mary's Counties, Maryland, 1775–1783

Revolutionary Patriots of Caroline County, Maryland, 1775–1783

Revolutionary Patriots of Cecil County, Maryland, 1775–1783

Revolutionary Patriots of Charles County, Maryland, 1775–1783

Revolutionary Patriots of Delaware, 1775–1783

Revolutionary Patriots of Dorchester County, Maryland, 1775–1783

Revolutionary Patriots of Frederick County, Maryland, 1775–1783

Revolutionary Patriots of Harford County, Maryland, 1775–1783

Revolutionary Patriots of Kent and Queen Anne's Counties, 1775–1783

Revolutionary Patriots of Lancaster County, Pennsylvania, 1775–1783

Revolutionary Patriots of Maryland, 1775–1783: A Supplement

Revolutionary Patriots of Maryland, 1775–1783: Second Supplement

Revolutionary Patriots of Montgomery County, Maryland, 1776–1783

Revolutionary Patriots of Prince George's County, Maryland, 1775–1783

Revolutionary Patriots of Talbot County, Maryland, 1775–1783

Revolutionary Patriots of Washington County, Maryland, 1776–1783

Revolutionary Patriots of Worcester and Somerset Counties, Maryland, 1775–1783

St. George's (Old Spesutia) Parish Harford County, Maryland Church and Cemetery Records, 1820–1920

St. John's and St. George's Parish Registers, 1696–1851

Slaves and Slave Owners, Harford County, Maryland, 1814: Information Gleaned from 1814 Property Tax Assessments and Supplemented with Data from Subsequent Manumissions, Slave Sales and Runaway Notices

Survey Field Book of David and William Clark in Harford County, Maryland, 1770–1812

Talbot County, Maryland Marriage References, 1662–1800
Henry C. Peden, Jr. and Veronica Clarke Peden

The Crenshaws of Kentucky, 1800–1995

The Delaware Militia in the War of 1812

Union Chapel United Methodist Church Cemetery Tombstone Inscriptions, Wilna, Harford County, Maryland

www.ingramcontent.com/pod-product-compliance
Lightning Source LLC
Chambersburg PA
CBHW080551230426

43663CB00015B/2796